The Revolt Against Dualism

The Revolt Against Dualism

An Inquiry Concerning the Existence of Ideas

Arthur O. Lovejoy

With a new introduction by
Jonathan B. Imber

Transaction Publishers
New Brunswick (U.S.A.) and London (U.K.)

New material this edition copyright © 1996 by Transaction Publishers, New Brunswick, New Jersey 08903.
Originally published in 1930 by The Open Court Publishing Company; second edition 1960.

Library of Congress Catalog Number: 95-20118
ISBN: 1-56000-847-4
Printed in the United States of America

Library of Congress Cataloging-in-Publication Data

Lovejoy, Arthur O. (Arthur Oncken), 1873–1962.
    The revolt against dualism : an inquiry concerning the existence of ideas / Arthor O. Lovejoy ; with a new introduction by Jonathan B. Imber.
        p. cm.
    Originally published: Chicago : Open Court Pub. Co., c1930.
    Includes bibliographical references and index.
    ISBN 1-56000-847-4 (pbk. : alk. paper)
    1. Dualism. 2. Knowledge, Theory of. 3. Mind and body. 4. Idea (Philosophy) I. Title.
B945.L583R48 1995
121'.4—dc20   95-20118
                                                                              CIP

CONTENTS

INTRODUCTION TO THE TRANSACTION EDITION

THE VOCATION OF ACADEMIC FREEDOM

Arthur O. Lovejoy is best known for *The Great Chain of Being: A Study of the History of an Idea,* published in 1936. Although fixed permanently in the pantheon of outstanding works in the history of ideas, it represents only one aspect of Lovejoy's scholarly vocation. *The Revolt Against Dualism,* first published in 1930 and republished in a second edition in 1960, belongs to a tradition in philosophical theorizing that Lovejoy called "descriptive epistemology." In the United States, this tradition owes much of its force to the writings of William James, Lovejoy's teacher, whose clarifications of such ideas as perception are distinguished by their resourceful and sophisticated common sense.

Lovejoy's principal aim in *The Revolt Against Dualism* is to clarify the distinction between the quite separate phenomena of the knower and the known, something regularly obvious to common sense, if not always to intellectual understanding. This work is as much an argument about the ineluctable differences between subject and object and between mentality and reality, as it is a subtle polemic against those who would stray far from acknowledging these differences. With a resolve that lasts four hundred pages, Lovejoy offers candid evaluations of a generation's worth of philosophical discussions that address the problem of epistemological dualism.

In what follows, I offer a reassessment of Lovejoy's career as a thinker and as an active participant in the worldly affairs of academic life. I do not review systematically the large corpus of Lovejoy's writings or the extensive commentary on them.[1] Instead, I hope to introduce to a new generation of readers some enduring principles of the vocation of the scholar to which Lovejoy not only subscribed but also gave substance through his activities as an academic man.

I.

Arthur Oncken Lovejoy was born in Berlin on October 10, 1873.[2] Before he was two years old, his family settled in Boston where his father pursued a career in medicine. Lovejoy's mother died of an accidental drug overdose shortly after the move to Boston. His father abandoned the practice of medicine to become an Episcopal minister and remarried in 1881. The elder Lovejoy's evangelical enthusiasms never especially impressed his son, who saw them only as resistances to his plans to study philosophy rather than to become a minister as his father wished. Arthur Lovejoy's early life was typical of many especially bright but religiously uninspired young men who sought intellectual challenges and refreshment in the newly forming graduate programs in the humanities and social sciences.

Lovejoy was by no means hostile to religious conviction; he was simply not interested in being its personal advocate. His struggles with his father were undoubtedly significant to his intellectual development, but psychoanalytic explanation became sociological reality: he applied his intellectual energies to scholarly and professional tasks that collectively would help to disestablish the central role and intellectual prestige of Protestant clergymen in the administration of higher education in America.[3] Throughout the nineteenth century, these clergymen were gradually replaced by a leadership dominated by university degrees other than those in theology. Daniel Coit Gilman, first president of the Johns Hopkins University, had considered the ministry but decided against it because he sought rather to impose a duty on society in general rather than on individuals in particular. He understood better than most that the future of the university was passing to a new kind of leadership called scientific. This required organizational change that no church-man or church movement could singlehandedly effect.

At the same time, the rapid expansion of universities to-ward the end of the nineteenth century led to the formaliza-tion of academic credentials, in part, for the sake of some out-ward consistency in curricula. When he enrolled in Harvard University in 1895 to do graduate work in philosophy, Lovejoy was immediately caught up in the larger debate about the pur-suit of the Ph.D. William James, in his famous repudiation of this pursuit, "The Ph.D. Octopus," regarded formal require-ments with suspicion because they diverted "the attention of aspiring youth from direct dealing with truth to the passing of examinations."[4] Lovejoy completed his M.A. but never earned a Ph.D.

From James's point of view, the true test of a student's com-petence was measured by criteria that were at once more per-sonal and hence more arbitrary. Recommendations, rather than degrees, would be the most stable source of currency in an academic market vulnerable to Gresham's law. The value of a recommendation could never be worthless, even though the person recommended might be. The recommender had the choice (or, as is said today, held the power), fateful as it was (and always will be insofar as intelligence and character are inseparable in each person). James deplored academic snob-bery, but why he objected so much to the meritocratic impulse implicit in examinations is related to his vision of higher educa-tion generally. Both he and Lovejoy shared an enthusiasm for ideas and for a clarity of purpose in the pursuit and analysis of them. Cookie-cutter Ph.D programs were inimical to the free-dom required to permit ideas to go wherever they might go. The first key to understanding Lovejoy's lifelong defense of aca-demic freedom is represented in his remark to David Starr Jor-dan, president of Stanford University, who hired Lovejoy in his first academic position: "I am personally very indifferent about it [the Ph.D. degree] and regard it as unwise for a man to go at all out of the way of his own philosophical interests in order to conform to the requirements of this exercise."[5]

The snobbery of James and Lovejoy was inner- rather than other-directed. Each man exemplified the privilege to determine the intellectual status of ideas; each formed canons as much as taught them. But this was a privilege of aristocratic rather than meritocratic talent. The greatest tragedy of the abundance of high intelligence today is the absence of a *noblesse oblige* that historically has attended to an aristocracy of talent. Meritocracies of talent, including those constructed under the dubious proposition of affirmative action, have been destructive to the expectation that professionals have a moral obligation to work together toward common goals. "Career goals" are simply not the same goals.

Sociological explanations of occupational status have never satisfactorily addressed the social psychology of social class.[6] Lovejoy was the quintessential successor to Boston Brahmin self-confidence. But such self-confidence cannot be reduced to class or culture or to any number of other forms of determinism that draw the life out of explanation and make of those explained only a "type." The second key to understanding Lovejoy's defense of academic freedom is found in the self-confidence of his actions in relation to his vocation. After two years at Stanford, in 1901, he resigned in protest to the firing of Edward Alsworth Ross (1866–1951) by the university.

Ross, who would later become one of the most well-known sociologists of his time, was dismissed toward the end of 1900 by Jane Lanthrop Stanford, the widow of Leland Stanford, former governor of California and U.S. senator.[7] Under terms establishing the founding of the university, both Stanfords had assumed complete authority over its operation, and when Leland Stanford died, the same authority passed to his wife. Mrs. Stanford had expressed disapproval of Ross over a number of years. David Starr Jordan had mediated on Ross's behalf in an earlier episode, but Mrs. Stanford could no longer be appeased when, in the spring of 1900, Ross spoke disparagingly of those who had profited from the construction of railroads with the use of cheap ("coolie") labor. The Stanford family fortune had been made in railroads.

The details of Ross's dismissal are recounted in a number of places.[8] An imposing man with, in the words of Mary O. Furner, "well over six feet of brawn," Ross had regularly expressed his opinions on many controversial subjects, and so he was not entirely surprised by his firing.[9] James Mohr has documented that Ross was not an innocent player in the entire affair. By setting out consciously to make his dismissal a public event, Ross staged an early version of a drama that is now regularly played out in the academy. The public and the press came thundering to his defense when his dismissal was reported across the nation. He even hired news clipping services to keep track of public opinion, which was overwhelmingly in his favor. Mrs. Stanford was characterized as standing in the way of scientific progress, though Stanford students and alumni were largely supportive of her actions.[10]

Although the Ross case is now part of the hagiography of early developments in the defense of academic freedom, both his actions and the reasons for his dismissal are not entirely pure or impure. Largely lost in the historical mists is an account of the events following Ross's termination, which led Arthur Lovejoy to resign from the Stanford faculty. Not long after Ross was fired, one of the original members of the faculty, a historian named George E. Howard, who was twenty years older than Ross, is reported to have interrupted himself as he was about to lecture on the French Revolution to say that new forms of repression and bigotry were asserting themselves and that he deplored the firing of Ross and his denial of academic freedom. For his remarks in class as well as a similar statement to the press, Howard was also fired.[11]

As Richard Hofstadter and Howard Metzger describe, the dismissal of Howard, which President Jordan unsuccessfully sought to avert, produced a chain reaction.[12] Lovejoy's only account in writing about what happened at Stanford (in distinction to what principles of academic freedom were at stake, about which he did write) is contained in the utterly flamboyant book *The Goose-step: A Study of American Education,* by Upton Sinclair, published in 1923.[13] I quote from a letter which Lovejoy sent to Sinclair and which Sinclair reprints almost in its entirety:

Late in the academic year, near the beginning of which Professor Ross was dismissed, a statement addressed to the public and designed for signature by members of the Stanford faculty was drawn—by whom I do not know—and an attempt was made to secure the signatures of all members (I believe) above the rank of instructor. Each teacher was invited to come separately to the office of one of the senior professors, a close personal friend of President Jordan; was there shown certain correspondence between Mrs. Stanford and President Jordan, which had not been made public; and was thereupon invited to sign the statement—which was to the effect that the signers, having seen certain unpublished documents, had arrived at the conclusion that President Jordan was justified in the dismissal of Professor Ross and that there was no question of academic freedom involved in the case. It was perfectly well understood by me, and I think by all who were shown the letters, that we were desired by the university authorities to sign the "round-robin"; and it was intimated that if any, after seeing the correspondence, should reach a conclusion contrary to that in the "round-robin," they were at least expected to keep silence.

Because of this last intimation I myself for some time refused to have the letters shown me; and consented finally to examine them only after stipulating that I should retain complete freedom to take such action afterwards as the circumstances might seem to me to require. When I read the letters they appeared to me to prove precisely the opposite to the two propositions contained in the statement to the public. They showed clearly (a) that President Jordan—who under the existing constitution of the university was the official responsible in such matters—had been originally altogether unwilling to dismiss Ross, and had consented to do so only under pressure from Mrs. Stanford; (b) that the express grounds of Mrs. Stanford's objection to Ross were certain public utterances of his, and that, therefore the question of academic freedom was distinctly involved. I drew up a short statement to this effect, and after the "round-robin" was published, communicated it to the newspapers, at the same time declining the reappointment of which I had previously been notified. I was thereupon directed to discontinue my courses immediately. About the same time another man—one of the best scholars and the most effective teachers in his department—who had refused to sign, and was known to disapprove strongly of the administration's conduct, but who had given no public expression of his opinion was notified that he would not be reappointed; and it was currently reported in the faculty that the vice-president, then acting president, of the university, Dr. Branner, had announced a policy of (in his own phrase) "shaking off the loose plaster."[14]

Sinclair quotes Lovejoy as remembering that "one of the signers of the collective statement to the public told me that he had
signed with great reluctance and with a sense of humiliation,
but, since he had a family of young children, he had not felt
that he could afford to risk the loss of his position." Lovejoy,
who never married, acknowledged that "practically all the men
who resigned were either unmarried or were married men without children."

No conformity goes completely unrewarded, including the
opportunity to retain a livelihood. The Ross case may now
be remembered in the purer cause of academic freedom, but
in the mess that life is several other insights about the assertion of personal principles are worth noting. First, Lovejoy's
reactions were the unintended consequence of Ross's desire for public notice. Mrs. Stanford argued, however inef-
fectually, that she was defending an institution by purging it
of someone seen to be hostile to it. By their actions, both
Ross and Mrs. Stanford forced others to stand up and be
counted or to remain silent. Loyalty, in contrast to dissent, is
not one of the highly cultivated virtues among the professoriate. Personal principle and self-interest are obviously not
mutually exclusive categories. We mistake one for the other,
in ourselves and in others, regularly. The less that is known
about E. A. Ross's ambitions, the less self-interest appears to
have guided his actions; the more known about them, the
more it does.

Second, everything that Lovejoy has to say about the circumstances of his own decisions speaks to a defense not simply of
Ross's academic freedom but of the freedom of other faculty
members to determine without threat to their livelihoods what
their relationship would be to Ross's actions. I believe that
Lovejoy objected most of all to the persecution of those who
were in no way responsible for what Ross had done but who
were nevertheless implicated in his disloyalty by simply defending his right to speak out. The worm in the wood was too obvious to ignore.

And third, with a sympathy that was characteristic of his feeling intellect, Lovejoy further recognized that anyone intimidated into signing for fear of losing his job was not to be singled out and humiliated as some condemnable species of coward.[15] On the contrary, Ross's own egocentricity amounted to a form of cowardice insofar as he used public intimidation to further his case. Today, anyone aggrieved in any way hires a lawyer who serves as a publicist in a war waged for a public opinion that is evermore fragmented and fickle. This desire to be heard above all others is one of the most peculiar disorders of intellectual egocentricity. Its remedy is first achieved in the silent struggle of writing at length rather than speaking in sound bites. Even Lovejoy's explanation to Upton Sinclair seems peculiarly out of place in a book that is otherwise strident in its depiction of higher education in America, however entertaining that depiction may be.[16]

Lovejoy was not a polemicist in his public role as an academic man. On the contrary, he would later in his life make a fateful choice about the meaning of membership in the academy, during the 1940s and 1950s, when higher education was rocked once again by accusations of subversion and conformity, a motif that stands for much of American intellectual life over the past two centuries.

II.

Lovejoy's voluntary departure from Stanford University in 1901 shaped his commitment to the ideal of academic freedom. He accepted positions at Washington University and the University of Missouri, and in 1910 moved to The Johns Hopkins University where he remained until his retirement in 1938. Instances of violations of academic freedom, in the form of dismissals, continued to occur in the first decade of the twentieth century, most of them reflecting the tensions between overbearing administrators and outspoken professors.

Hofstadter and Metzger rightly argue that no consistent typology can be applied to all the cases of dismissal; nor is each one unique.[17] To understand the complexity of Lovejoy's own commitment, it is useful to distinguish between the precipitating factors that may or may not have motivated him to personal action and the principles that inspired him to press for a greater formalization of due process in the many different types of cases. The absence of this due process is a perennial problem, as is evidenced in recent years in the fumbling of cases involving accusations of sexual harassment.

A third key to understanding Lovejoy's defense of academic freedom is evident in his strong belief in evolution and evolutionary ideas. The study of the history of ideas is built upon the proposition that language and ideas evolve over time into new contexts and new meanings, even as they retain a distinctive identity that enables the scholar to recognize in the past, elements of the present, and *vice versa*. The development of academic freedom in the United States incorporates the idea of evolution as a secular ideal that progresses toward an ever increasing openness about everything, though ideal and reality have been and remain often at serious odds with one another.

The conflict between competing theological doctrines as well as between theology and science, dominated intellectual debate during the nineteenth century. Arthur Lovejoy's academic career began just as the vindication of evolution in higher education had been fully achieved in the natural sciences. No longer principally a dispute about the relationship between science and religion, academic freedom was now said to be threatened by the conflict between science and wealth, that is, between the vested interests of the wealthy on the one hand and the scientific, and thus progressive, inquiries of the professoriate on the other.[18] The necessity of academic freedom—at least in the less sectarian colleges and public universities—had also evolved, rendering religious disagreements less significant than political ones. Political commitment remains the reigning emblem of authenticity in the university. At the same time, the sectarian impulse so deeply ingrained in the American experience has not dissipated in the evolving controversies over academic freedom, it has simply found new forms of expression.

The central piety of criticism in higher education belongs to the tradition best exemplified in the life and writings of Thorstein Veblen. Yet that piety has also evolved to the extent that the rhetorical celebration of science in Veblen's work has been largely abandoned in the postmodern critique of every social activity. Veblen gave vivid shape to the concern about the accumulating wealth of *all* institutions. Lovejoy's apparent indifference to this concern was due in part to the fact that he distinguished between the responsibilities of institutions and the obligations of individuals. The relevance of Veblen to sociology, beyond the elective affinity between his ideas and the sentiments of the vast majority of sociologists, is found in the tension, as well as the confusion, between such responsibilities and obligations. In this regard, Veblen was an exemplary monist, just as Lovejoy was an unflappable dualist.

Hofstadter and Metzger conclude that "Critics of the period [such as Veblen] looked to the *culture of capitalism* [my emphasis], rather than to the machinations of capitalists, as the source of academic evils."[19] The "culture of capitalism" was the deep well into which was poured many inconsistent criticisms of American life. Lovejoy was not captivated by the authenticity of one type of critique over another because his evolutionism and abiding attention to history compelled him to rise above the full spectrum of opinions in order to place them all in a context that reaffirmed the goals of higher learning. In one era, before the Gilded Age, heresy was religious. At the dawn and demise of the Progressive Era, heresy was political.

In 1910, Lovejoy helped to protest, without success, the withdrawal of support by the Carnegie Foundation for service pensions for college teachers. He maintained a consistent approach to speaking for the collective interests of faculty members in all ranks of colleges and universities. This approach, free of hyperbole and rigorously argued, was to be the aim of an association to oversee the special interests and concerns of faculty.

Lovejoy's capacity to assess carefully such matters led him to preside over a case that is regarded as a principal reason for the formation in 1915 of the American Association of University Professors (AAUP) whose first president would be John Dewey and first secretary, Arthur Lovejoy.[20]

In 1913, three years after joining Johns Hopkins, Lovejoy chaired an investigation of the forced resignation of John Moffatt Mecklin (1871–1956), professor of philosophy and psychology, from Lafayette College. Because no national association of professors existed to evaluate the circumstances of Mecklin's departure, a Committee of Inquiry was formed by the American Philosophical Association and the American Psychological Association. Lovejoy was joined by six others, including William Ernest Hocking of Yale and George Herbert Mead of the University of Chicago. Together, they issued a report, "The Case of Professor Mecklin," published in *The Journal of Philosophy, Psychology, and Scientific Methods* in 1914.[21]

John Mecklin had been called to the Lafayette faculty in late 1904. Like others of his generation, he studied in Germany and wrote his inaugural dissertation in 1899 on early Church history. He was an ordained minister of the Presbyterian church. His thorough knowledge of Christianity, combined with strong progressive convictions, resulted in a fascinating range of publications, including *Democracy and Race Friction: A Study of Social Ethics* (1914); *The Ku Klux Klan: A Study of the American Mind* (1924); *The Survival Value of Christianity* (1926); *The Story of American Dissent* (1934); and *The Passing of the Saint: A Study of a Cultural Type* (1941), all published after his departure from Lafayette.[22]

The subject of "social ethics" (in the title of Mecklin's 1914 book) symbolized the growing influence of evolutionary ideas in disciplines beyond the natural sciences. Lafayette, during the time of Mecklin's tenure, has been described by Hofstadter and Metzger as "facing in two directions: toward its early nonsectarian idealism and toward the orthodox high Calvinism of Princeton Seminary and its autocratic president. The desire to have the best of both worlds created great confusion as to what could be taught at the college."[23] In this interpretation, Mecklin was seen to endorse, by way of evolutionary ideas, a relativistic view of morals. This probably summarizes accurately what was at stake in the college's argument with him about teaching the newer ethical writings by philosophers such as John Dewey.[24]

Lovejoy's Committee of Inquiry examined as much circumstantial evidence as it could obtain and concluded that Mecklin had been denied his academic freedom. The ostensible reasons for Mecklin's forced departure were of the deepest concern to the committee, but it objected just as much to the unwillingness of E. D. Warfield, president of the college (and of Princeton Theological Seminary), to specify the "precise restrictions imposed upon freedom of inquiry and teaching in philosophy and psychology at Lafayette College."[25] Warfield made it plainly clear that he did not recognize the authority of either professional association to raise questions about how his institution administered to its faculty.[26] He did report that Professor Mecklin in resigning was "granted a year's salary."

In a footnote, Lovejoy seemed intent on demonstrating that Warfield was not only undermining his own position as chief executive officer by refusing to cooperate but was also being undermined by others around him, in particular, a member of the Lafayette Board of Trustees who informed Lovejoy that the Board had not asked for Mecklin's resignation.[27] Much of the intrigue in this case seems to have occurred at the level of Lafayette's curriculum committee, which had assumed responsibility for reviewing the specific contents of Mecklin's courses. Considerably more intrigue and argument must have followed, for two weeks after the committee released its report, "Warfield was dismissed by the Lafayette trustees."[28]

In contrast to the E. A. Ross case at Stanford, which was as much about his rights under the First Amendment as it was about the more restricted idea of academic freedom, the Mecklin case was about what could and could not be taught in the classroom. Lovejoy must have understood this very well when the committee noted:

> American colleges and universities fall into two classes: those in which freedom of inquiry, of belief, and of teaching is, if not absolutely unrestricted, at least subject to limitations so few and so remote as to give practically no occasion for differences of opinion; and those which are frankly instruments of denominational or political propaganda. The committee does not consider itself authorized to discuss the question whether the existence of both sorts of institution is desirable. If, therefore, the present case were one in which a teacher in a professedly denominational college had in his teaching expressly repudiated some clearly defined and generally accepted doctrine of that denomination, the committee would not feel justified in proceeding further with the matter.[29]

This passage is remarkable for its extraordinary concession to the second class of institutions it describes. Lafayette College was in the process of classifying itself—that is precisely what the internal struggle over Mecklin's case represented. Mecklin lost the battle, but the doctrinal war was to be decisively settled against the Warfields of this world. As mediator of this battle, Lovejoy looked for a way at least to acknowledge the claims of those second class of institutions that did not afford clear protection of academic freedom. The concept of "church school," for example, is fraught with ambiguities over what kind of authority prevails. This explains, in part, why the lower down one goes in the status system of higher education, the more likely the pieties will seem regressive in evolutionary terms.[30]

But what is to be made of the pieties at the top of our present status system? What evolutionary principles account for ideological assertions under the present dispensations of multiculturalism and its shibboleths of race, class, and gender? The principles of progress and regress are in an entirely confused state today in the bureaucratic and intellectual offices of higher education. The lately heralded "culture wars," when brought into the university are the same wars that separated the likes of Ross and Mecklin from the likes of Stanford and Warfield. The most peculiar people are presently protected in the shaky cease-fire that is contemporary academic freedom, and this may be one reason, among a number of reasons, why the concept remains as contentious at the end of the twentieth century as it was at the beginning.

III.

When he retired in 1938 at the age of 64, Arthur Lovejoy was at the height of his intellectual powers. Only eight years before he published *The Revolt Against Dualism*, the work that demonstrated his philosophical acumen. And in 1936 he published *The Great Chain of Being*, the work that chiefly inspired the academic discipline of the history of ideas. Yet his intellectual realism was not infectious among the vast majority of graduate students who at the time were attracted to the philosophical camps of either logical positivism or Marxism, neither of which Lovejoy admired. A visiting year at Harvard in 1937–38 convinced him that his formal days of teaching were behind him.[31] He was of two distinct minds, combining the strongest defense of academic freedom with an equally strong impatience for fads in philosophical thinking. Students overwhelmed by their own searches for personal meaning and social salvation must have found his approach to such fads arrogant, if not disillusioning.

The Revolt Against Dualism is a work of relentless criticism of epistemological monism in all of its variations. Those variations include approaches to knowledge that claim an apprehension of an Absolute Being (e.g., one form of idealism) as well as those that claim an unmediated apprehension of objects by the subject (e.g., monistic realism). Lovejoy sorts through a quarter-of-a-century's worth of philosophical discussions, among realists, idealists, and pragmatists, about consciousness, its intentions and objects, and he concludes that many philosophers of his generation have contributed to a persistent confusion over the fundamental nature of human knowing. "Man," he says,

is by nature an epistemological animal; for his irrepressible knowledge-claim is itself a thesis *about* knowledge, and therefore about himself and his relation to nature and to the life of his fellows; and it is a thesis which cries out for clarification, and for correlation with the conclusions about other natural phenomena to which this natural phenomenon of knowing has brought him. (p. 14)[32]

From this naturalistic description of epistemology, Lovejoy concludes that the "human animal, in short, does not for the most part live where its body is—if an organism's life is made up of what it really experiences; it lives where the things are of which it is aware, upon which its attention and feeling are directed" (p. 15). In an observation not directly related to the purposes of his argument but nevertheless stated in momentous terms, Lovejoy anticipates contemporary debates in philosophy about artificial intelligence and sociobiology:

One of the most curious developments in the entire history of thought is the invention in our day of what may best be named the Hypodermic Philosophy—the doctrine, resulting from the application to a cognitive animal of the biological concepts found sufficient in the study of animals assumed to be non-cognitive, that the organic phenomenon of knowing may be exhaustively described in terms of molecular displacements taking place under the skin. (pp. 15–16)

Following Lovejoy's botanical analogy, our present age is characterized by the warfare between epidermal and hypodermic philosophies, both of which lend intellectual legitimacy to the claim that ideas cannot be distinguished from those who defend or criticize them. Both philosophies are monistic insofar as they assert the exclusiveness of either organic or inorganic determinants in the cognitive processes of thinking and knowing. Lovejoy's "cognitive animal" is, by nature, a dualistic creature.

Epistemological dualism is the defense of the difference between datum and *cognoscendum*, between the thing perceived at a given moment (sense-datum) and the thing itself existing in time and space. This first dualism is a reflection of what Lovejoy insists is common sense, part of a "natural realistic creed" (p. 31). Related to it is psychophysical dualism, in which we are able to distinguish between the force of our thoughts and the reality of the world in which they occur: "The arrow with which you so pleasingly shot your enemy in your dream left him disappointingly intact the next morning" (p. 35). Life is not a dream, nor is a dream anything more than a part of life. The gradual ability to distinguish between mental and physical worlds (the basis to psychophysical dualism) constitutes the intellectual progress of *homo sapiens*:

> The discovery—or the invention—of a second world to which could be allocated all experienced objects which did not appear to satisfy the rules of membership in the physical system was an indispensable and all-important step in the early development of science; for without it the progressive theoretical reduction of the physical world to a relatively simple and uniform order, a reign of law, and of laws of a high degree of generality, would probably have been impossible. (p. 36)

The bifurcation of nature has proven to be a double-edged sword, and although Lovejoy's task in *The Revolt Against Dualism* is not devoted to defending some uses of science over and against others, his analysis gives clear expression to the moral dilemma of dualism, to which the monist feels always compelled to respond and dissolve:

> The world of "mental" entities served as an isolation-camp for all the "wild data," the refractory and anomalous facts, which would have disturbed the tidiness and good order of the physical universe; and it left the theorist, primitive or modern, free to remold the scheme of things nearer, not to his heart's desire, but to the demands of his intellect. (pp. 36–37)

The theologian postulating an argument from design occupies the same "second world" as the astronomer calculating the number of moons around Jupiter. Psychophysical dualism, far from being a residue of "medieval prejudices in the minds of seventeenth-century philosophers," protected the astronomer from the theologian when the theologian proposed to define what could and could not be included in that second world, that is, when dualistic-inspired theology became monistic-inflicted persecution. But how do "wild data" tame themselves into an evermore orderly theory of physical reality? Lovejoy insisted that psychophysical dualism created intelligible data once epistemological dualism was admitted and fused with it. In other words, theory was confirmed by the order it imposed on the world and by the world thus re-created in its vision.

Yet the theorist who, in Lovejoy's brilliant insight, turns pre-conceptions on their heads also assumes a responsibility that is not fully captured in the phrase "demands of his intellect." Sounding remarkably like Max Weber in "Science as a Vocation," Lovejoy reiterated an idealism about science in theory that still must be distinguished from science in its institutional practices.[33] The "wild" and tame data are by no means assigned exclusively to separate realms in the social realities of scientific work. Weber believed in the idea of character shaping institutions as well institutions shaping character. But the critique of Lysenkoism, or of alchemy for that matter, has had little to do with a sustained examination of the character of individual persons. The scientific imagination, once subject to control by abstract theories of social or cosmic order is equally, if not more, vulnerable to damage by the absence of characterological expectations about honesty, persistence, and trust.

Max Weber's defense of science as a vocation conceals the exhaustion of millennia of Jewish and Christian elaborations of individual responsibility. In formulating a second world in which "wild" and tame data co-exist, Lovejoy takes for granted that scientific work shows the way to new truths about order in physical reality. But theories of order in that second world come from below as well as above, at least in the traditions out of Jerusalem and Athens. Those "wild data" could produce a vast disorder, the likes of which Lovejoy understood to be coming in Adolf Hitler's rise to power.[34] Lovejoy's dualisms serve as grounds for a natural hierarchy in the theories of physical order and moral order. He stops short of acknowledging what is at stake in such necessity, the physical order being subordinate to moral order, as earth is to heaven.[35]

I have endeavored in these few pages to describe the two dualisms that Lovejoy sets out to defend in his book. In light of sixty-five years of philosophical discussions about epistemology that have taken place since the first publication of *The Revolt Against Dualism*, Lovejoy's descriptive and analytical powers are of more than passing, historical interest. Debates of more

immediate philosophical urgency, such as those on epistemological and cultural relativism, owe more than a citational debt
to the standard of argumentation to which Lovejoy aspires. This
work prefigures the epistemological investigation of theories
and data from many disciplines, thus questioning (and possibly
undermining) what those disciplines at any moment count as
knowledge.[36]

From this vantage point, *The Revolt Against Dualism* is as
much a work of philosophical criticism as it is a methodological
tour de force in the tradition of the sociology of knowledge.[37] I
admit in what follows to taking the reader a fair distance from
the substantive arguments contained in Lovejoy's book. Yet the
exposition of fault lines in monistic thinking does suggest a comparable exercise in the sociology of knowledge.[38] Lovejoy would
have rejected the simplistic correlation between knowledge and
class interest, for example, but he might have appreciated the
dualistic assumptions underlying the critique itself, that is, the
recognition of forces beyond the individual, forces that can affect what the individual becomes (e.g., extrinsic interpretation)
but that are nevertheless distinct from the power of the individual to reckon with them (e.g., intrinsic interpretation). An
individual is not the sum of those forces anymore than those
forces are simply the hallucinations of individuals.[39]

Psycho-genetic explanations—including the role of the unconscious—along with socio-determinist explanations—including the
role of the class system, or more recently, racial and gender
identity—are said to account not only for the fundamental nature of the individual (i.e., ontology) but also to define the limitations of an individual's knowledge and understanding of the
world (i.e., epistemology). When focus is put on such limitations, there then appears the "discovery" of false consciousness, (or, on the other side of the same coin, feminist epistemology (e.g., "women's ways of knowing") and Afrocentrism).[40]
Although it may weaken the distinctive claim of W. E. B. Du
Bois to argue that the double consciousness inscribed in the
souls of black folk is not unique to them, the social dualism of

belonging and not belonging is experienced to some degree by all God's children. The revolt against that dualism has come expressly in the form of claims to racial and gender exclusivity, both examples of social monism in which the ineluctable differences between self and society are mistakenly and tragically rendered as ineluctable differences among aggregates of people.[41] Anyone who reads Du Bois as emphasizing the *fact* of not belonging over the *wish* to belong misses entirely the genius of his idea. Yet, how is it that among the most secure black middle class to have ever existed in American history, the wish not to belong overwhelms the fact of belonging?

The analogy I offer here to Lovejoy's critical posture toward epistemological monism is a critical posture toward monistic forms of social consciousness. These forms are expressed in ideological contents, the stock of which is painfully familiar, including the nearly incessant attack against Jews as the cosmic cause of alienation. Hatred of Jews is the most persistent monism in covenantal history, the deepest of all the wells from which any counter-identity can be drawn. Dualistic forms of social consciousness unite human beings in common struggles for freedom and against tyranny. Monistic forms subserve the revolts against any faith that demands the renewal and re-creation for each generation of its religious, moral, and civic obligations and responsibilities. Just as the logical positivists were impotent in relating their own endeavors to the rise of Hitler's brutalities, so the postmodernists deny the *reality* of the double consciousness that makes individual freedom and social reality both possible and subject to exploration.

Lewis Feuer has argued that "It was probably the strange phenomenon of anti-intellectualism among intellectuals, exhibited in such writers as Henri Bergson and Georges Sorel, that led Lovejoy and his collaborator George Boas to probe the varieties of 'primitivism' in their book *Primitivism and Related Ideas of Antiquity* (1935)."[42]

In this collaboration, Lovejoy examined "the discontent of the civilized with civilization," and in the process exposed the ideologies endorsing a return to the state of nature, "whether for the propertyless, stateless, spouseless, sinless, machineless states of nature, and, in a case like Bernard Shaw's, for a vegetarian overcoming an estrangement from animals."[43] Contemporary multiculturalism—a conflation of civilization with its discontents, and a form of intellectual dishonesty about the achievements of Western civilization in particular—is a type of primitivism.

Yet the administrators of multiculturalism make no pretense about returning themselves or their students to the state of nature, preferring instead to remain comfortable in endowed chairs. Their allegiance is not to pluralism but to the monistic denial of any claim to superiority of what is deemed Western, white, or male. The dead-white-European male alone is returned to the state of nature. Along with the monism that is multiculturalism (a lottery of victimhood in which the winners are all self-appointed) comes Holocaust denial. Jews are quietly criticized by those who should know better for making a claim to special victim status, while being denied the authenticity of their experience which is interpreted as a lie. Calls for close examination of Jews as slaveholders as well as for equal representation of "the Nazi point of view" in the instruction of the young are primitivist recyclings of a future world in which Jews will either pay for their special crimes or cease to exist. It is the sense of utter disproportion contained in such calls that reveals their true, monistic, and primitivistic animus.

IV.

"In our own time the tradition of 'humble, arduous, tenacious scholarship,' together with the broader values it embodies, may be on the verge of disappearing once and for all."

Christopher Lasch[44]

Counter-revolutions are always deemed conservative in their intellectual and social implications. Arthur Lovejoy's *The Revolt Against Dualism* is a great work in the tradition of counter-revolutions, and it remains instructive not least of all for its efforts to expose fault lines in monistic arguments. His rejection of the monistic habits of thought of his contemporaries in philosophy was matched by his exposure of primitivistic urges in the history of ideas generally. Revolution encourages primitivism along with the murdering of thought and persons required to achieve it. Counter-revolution is the constructive response toward what appear to be inevitable monistic and primitivistic tendencies in masses as well as elites. As Lewis Feuer concludes, "In philosophy, history, and social theory, Lovejoy was probably the least ideological of American thinkers. That is why his work, though never acquiring a vogue like that enjoyed by some contemporaries, may prove to be more enduring. It embodied, as did Lovejoy, in his personality, the principle of integrity in American scholarship."[45]

Lovejoy's strong national loyalty led him to support with a full and uninhibited voice American participation in two world wars. This deeply patriotic, yet remarkably thoughtful, man who helped to make academic freedom a piety among academics, never lost sight of the larger purpose of his intellectual responsibilities as they related to his institutional commitments. That purpose is perhaps best conveyed in what appears to be an inconsistent stand he took against the employment of members of the Communist party in universities after the Second World War.[46]

The same man who gave up his job rather than submit to the demands of university authorities to tell him how to think about another colleague never wavered in his belief that the university was a precinct whose standards were set apart from those of the larger society. It is terribly misleading to see in Lovejoy's vocation as a scholar and academic man any argument that equates academic freedom with the freedom of association, even though the cold war disputes about communism have long been represented in universities in terms of freedom of speech.

In 1941, Lovejoy wrote: "No teacher should be dismissed for holding and expressing publicly the opinion that Communism is an economic system preferable to the existing one."[47] He defended the right of the teacher to express that opinion "so long as he did not proselytize and gave a fair hearing to alternative views."[48] His objection was not to the articulation of the theory of communism but to those whose actions in relation to that theory would undermine the purposes and goals of teaching and scholarship. Membership in the Communist party represented an action injurious to the university. What is perhaps less known in regard to Lovejoy's position is that he applied the same principle to members of "the Nazi or Italian Fascist parties."[49]

Lovejoy concluded that faculty abrogated their academic freedom by submitting their thoughts and actions to the dictates of party authority. They were no longer independent scholars in pursuit of the truth wherever it might lead them. Perhaps willing to accept the inevitability of the Ph.D., he drew the line on the Communist party. In so doing, he found himself arguing for limits to academic freedom—the same man who had once been president of the association devoted to furthering its cause.

Academic freedom was not an abstraction. Its defense and abuse had real, human consequences for universities, research, and students. The university had evolved, in Lovejoy's mind, well beyond the conflicts that John Mecklin's case at Lafayette had symbolized. Communist party members were considered agents who were charged with overthrowing the very principles that academic freedom was intended to uphold. In contrast to President Warfield who believed that Professor Mecklin's "social ethics" undermined the institutional authority of the college to educate students in the faith tradition in which it was founded, the communist did not appeal to the past or to faith traditions but instead accepted the political principle that all knowledge, including knowledge of the physical world, is subject to political approval. President Warfield was no Stalinist before Stalinism. He also lost his job, but for resisting rather than affirming the separation of faith and education, a separation that until the end of the nineteenth century did not cross the minds of the vast majority of defenders of the separation of church and state.

What is most striking about Lovejoy's stand on communists, which he expressed and argued for in both philosophical and public journals, is the absence of any call for help from the outside, from government for example. The American Association of University Professors, like the American Medical Association, was supposed to police its membership.

Because the AAUP has been historically portrayed as the defender of academic freedom, just as the AMA is portrayed as the defender of professional autonomy, the expectation that either organization would ever be capable of policing deviant members is sociologically naive. On the contrary, the growing role of courts of law in matters of professional association points to the failure of professions to define and defend little more than the minimum standards for gaining entrance to them. Lovejoy must have realized at some point that the AAUP could only realistically defend individuals against their unprofessional institutions rather than institutions against unprofessional individuals.

When he died on December 30, 1962, Arthur O. Lovejoy had been in academic retirement for almost twenty-five years. His death came before the next significant chapter in the history of academic freedom: the student revolts of the 1960s. Others carried on in Lovejoy's spirit, such as Sidney Hook with whom he had worked on the question of communism and academic freedom.[50] The belief that universities could be transformative agents in society at large was heralded from above in the writings of such figures as Herbert Marcuse and from below in the criminal activities of student liberationists of many different stripes. The disruptions to teaching and learning, in the cause of some ill-defined hope of social transformation, have yet to subside.

The vast majority of students in universities at the height of the student unrest went on to lead perfectly bourgeois lives, in all walks of life, including government. Like the organization men before them, they have sought their liberations in private pleasures rather than public causes. Drug experimentation has become drug dependency. Entrepreneurial virtues are traded for limited left-wing causes through the sale of artery-clogging ice cream to legions of the worried-well by healthier people living the good life in Vermont. Whatever remain of leftist convictions about empowering the poor have long since passed over to the ranks of anti-governmental theorists and practitioners. Nostalgia on the left now evokes the virtues of "pre-market" societies, as if the present world's population could sustain itself under such conditions.

Lovejoy's university is nevertheless recognizable in most of its academic organization and administration. Tenure survives, though it seems destined for a reconsideration sooner rather than later. The pleas for the professoriate to heal itself—the deepest meaning of Lovejoy's belief in and defense of academic freedom—are dismissed by many inside academia as attacks by politically motivated forces in the larger society. Elite academic institutions have been especially vulnerable to criticisms that they have become laboratories for indoctrination, from the dormitory to the classroom. These criticisms may be exaggerated as is evidenced by the disingenuous, and characteristically anti-intellectual, attempts to cite one instance as representative of many. But the criticisms speak to a singular failure on the part of all but a few academic leaders to recognize how much academic freedom has become a shield behind which nearly anything can be taught by anyone.

The fear of contemporary faculty is that the revocation of tenure will lead down a slippery slope toward the threatened silencing of all faculty. Such silencing occurred long before the present wave of criticisms received widespread reporting in the national media. The ante has been raised considerably by the protection that academic freedom allegedly affords to those who teach out-and-out lies, who distort the historical record to serve their own ideological agendas, and who defend their right to do so because they believe what they are saying is true. But if a teacher tells lies about history or about any subject in which there is a well-established body of professional knowledge and professional argument, what other recourse is there for a profession to heal itself? The fact is that Lovejoy was far too tough for most academic men and women's tastes. Combine those tastes with a therapeutic regard for the self-appointed oppressed, and a faculty may end up unable to agree upon any common goals for the education of its students. The legitimation crisis of higher education is about the few who do not belong there but who cannot be removed for fear of exposing something suspect about a much larger number of others.

Many of those others are now part of the more publicly visible academic and administrative elites who cultivate celebrity and publicity for their own sakes. The present crisis of Western universities is not all that surprising; for that crisis is, at its heart, about the vocation of teachers and scholars. Lovejoy maintained a consummate disinterest in the kind of ambition that C. S. Lewis once described as "the desire to get ahead of other people" and "the wish to be more conspicuous or more successful than someone else." But today celebrity is everywhere in the ethos of higher learning.

The problem with celebrity and publicity is that they set the terms for how debate and discussion about intellectual matters are conducted. Intellectuals who resist these terms are routinely designated as obscure and unknown, but not necessarily uninfluential. Lovejoy was undeniably a public intellectual in his own right, especially when it came to matters of professional responsibility and institutional obligation. But he also recognized the limits to his vocation as much as its responsibilities. Those limits must be reiterated by each generation of academic leaders (who are not too busy pursuing their own celebrity or careers, or both) in the academy, because they help to define to the softer-spoken the true objects of their vocation. The classroom ought to be a sanctuary, a defense against the clamor that reaches from the outside to disturb the hearts and minds of students.

Lovejoy did not enjoy a large student following, if it is to be enjoyed at all. In the age of celebrity, the popular teacher may often be confused for the teacher from whom a student has something to learn. But how will students understand this? Perhaps by luck or fate, if nothing else.

The lesson to be learned from Lovejoy's experience with academic politics is that the monists and primitivists are always with us; some of them may be our friends. I see no way out of the dilemma that Lovejoy faced squarely in his life of scholarship and service. That dilemma simply put was that the academy consists of many different temperaments, no matter how careful it may be in selecting some types over others. Feminism is a case in point. Imagine Lovejoy's reaction to political correctness. He would no doubt have called himself an equity feminist but not a gender feminist. Yet his disinterest toward the phenomena of equity and gender feminism would have served him well (and may serve us well) in viewing the conflict as between dualists and monists.[51]

Political correctness is also a problem for its detractors, regardless of the enthusiasm of their alleged disinterest. The National Association of Scholars, born of the reluctance of established organizations—including the AAUP—to take on the climate of censorship in elite colleges and universities, is too much beholden to the same dynamics that created the early career of E. A. Ross. The victims of political correctness make an odd collection of sorts. I am not for a moment doubting the vast majority of their claims. But there must be some revitalization of pressures from within the university to slow the dynamic in which violations of academic freedom are equated with the First Amendment and then taken to the courts and the press. That equation debases both the vocation of the scholar and the distinction between the privilege to teach and the right to speak. The wiles of the academically minded ought to be in part devoted to how to avoid public controversy. For every such controversy is finally about winning and losing in the court of public opinion, about being heard and being supported. After the rallies have ended, what fate awaits the classroom far from the adrenal spotlights of the media?

Arthur Lovejoy remarks in *The Revolt Against Dualism* that "The great trouble with philosophy has been that so many philosophers have been the sort of men who fall in love with an idea at first sight" (p. 321). The attraction of ideas has its risks. Lovejoy never fell in love at first sight. Perhaps he missed something. Perhaps it is not for us to decide whether dualistic intellect can ever live fully apart from monistic feeling. In any case, if he is to endure, he must be read. The reprinting of this great work makes his being forgotten less likely.

JONATHAN B. IMBER

Wellesley, Massachusetts
May, 1995

NOTES

1. See Daniel J. Wilson, ed., *Arthur O. Lovejoy, an Annotated Bibliography* (New York: Garland Publishing, 1982).
2. I rely on the excellent intellectual biography by Daniel J. Wilson, *Arthur O. Lovejoy and the Quest for Intelligibility* (Chapel Hill: University of North Carolina Press, 1980). I am indebted to the analytical approach taken by Lewis Feuer toward Lovejoy's intellectual career in Lewis S. Feuer, "Arthur O. Lovejoy," *The American Scholar* 46 (1977): 358–66; and "Lovejoy, Arthur O.," *International Encyclopedia of the Social Sciences, Biographical Supplement*, vol. 18 (New York: Macmillan, 1979), 464–69.
3. See Lewis S. Feuer, "The Philosophical Method of Arthur O. Lovejoy: Critical Realism and Psychoanalytical Realism," *Philosophy and Phenomenological Research* 23, no. 4 (June 1963): 493–510. Feuer writes, "I have wondered whether this sturdy realist's devotion to the history of theology and romantic metaphysics is not a kind of re-enactment of trauma of his own intense upbringing by his father, a Reformed Episcopal clergyman, who drilled his young son to read the Bible in Greek and Hebrew" (p. 496).
4. As quoted in Wilson, *Quest for Intelligibility*, 26. See William James, "The Ph.D. Octopus," in *The Works of William James, Essays, Comments, and Reviews*, edited by Frederick Burkhardt and Fredson Bowers (Cambridge, MA: Harvard University Press, 1987), 67–74. The essay first appeared in 1903, four years after Lovejoy left Harvard. It might be viewed as the culminating expression of convictions that James must have routinely articulated to students under his influence and direction.
5. Quoted in Wilson, *Quest for Intelligibility*, 26. Lovejoy's most-often referred to definition of academic freedom is contained in the entry he wrote for the *Encyclopaedia of the Social Sciences* in 1930: "Academic freedom is the freedom of the teacher or research worker in higher institutions of learning to investigate and discuss the problems of his science and to express his conclusions, whether through publication or in the instruction of students, without interference from political or ecclesiastical authority, or from the administrative officials of the institution in which he is employed, unless his methods are found by qualified bodies of his own profession to be clearly incompetent or contrary to professional ethics." Arthur O. Lovejoy, "Academic Freedom," in *Encyclopaedia of the Social Sciences*, vol. 1, edited by Edwin R. A. Seligman (New York: Macmillan, 1930), 384–87.

6. The anxious wealthy and the proud poor (especially as these represent ends of the continuum of the American middle class) are but two anomalies in the sociology of self-satisfaction, which any theory of vocation must address. Marx and Engels sought to explain such anomalies in terms of false consciousness, although, they also proposed an historical argument more akin to Max Weber's Protestant ethic than to Marxist and sociological explanations of occupational status: "The Bourgeoisie has stripped of its halo every occupation hitherto honored and looked up to with reverent awe. It has converted the physician, the lawyer, the priest, the poet, the man of science, into its paid wage-laborers," *The Communist Manifesto* [1848] (New York: International Publishers, 1948), 11. See Bruce Kimball, *The "True Professional Ideal" in America: A History* (Oxford: Blackwell, 1992), who argues that the rhetorical claims of eighteenth- and nineteenth-century ministers and lawyers about the meaning of their vocations as professions must not be measured against contemporary social scientific arguments about professional powers.
7. See James C. Mohr, "Academic Turmoil and Public Opinion: The Ross Case at Stanford," *Pacific Historical Review* 39, no. 1 (1970): 39–61.
8. *Ibid.;* see also Richard Hofstadter and Walter P. Metzger, *The Development of Academic Freedom in the United States* (New York: Columbia University Press, 1955), 436–45; Mary O. Furner, *Advocacy and Objectivity: A Crisis in the Professionalization of American Social Science, 1865–1905* (Lexington: University of Kentucky Press, 1975), 234–59.
9. Furner, *Advocacy and Objectivity,* 230–31.
10. Mohr, "Academic Turmoil and Public Opinion," notes that the strong identification of alumni and students with Stanford may have been inspired by the fact that the preservation of its reputation was consequential for its financial survival at the time.
11. Burton J. Bledstein writes that "The competitiveness of professional historians revealed itself when within a week of the Howard vacancy, the president at Stanford hired a young Ph.D. from Harvard, who accepted the position on the recommendation of Harvard's senior historians." Bledstein notes that "The historical profession's inaction in Howard's defense has generally been ignored in the successful outcome of both Ross's own professional career and his case against Stanford." Burton J. Bledstein, *The Culture of Professionalism: The Middle Class and the Development of Higher Education in America* (New York: Norton, 1976), 305 and 305n27.
12. Hofstadter and Metzger, *The Development of Academic Freedom,* 442. I rely also on the extended accounts in Mohr, "Academic Turmoil and Public Opinion," and Furner, *Advocacy and Objectivity.*
13. Sinclair's 1923 book was reprinted in 1970 by AMS Press, Inc.
14. Quoted in Sinclair, *The Goose-step,* 156–57. See also Wilson, *Quest for Intelligibility,* 36f.
15. Mary O. Furner characterizes Lovejoy's resignation much differently than I do, and she makes no reference to his letter quoted in Sinclair's book. Furner writes, "From the related field of philosophy, Arthur O. Lovejoy was so appalled by the docility of most of his colleagues that he felt compelled to express his disapproval by resigning too" (*Advocacy and Objectivity,* 242). Given his own characterization of events, Lovejoy's personal motivation to resign was unlikely the result of his contempt for those colleagues who signed Stanford's loyalty oath.
16. If anyone doubts the existence of a long tradition of holding colleges and universities culpable for the failure to educate youth, Sinclair's long-forgotten work may help to put the current tirades into perspective. Of course, a much less flamboyant tradition of institutional self-criticism exists along side the more racy. For an example that stands up much better against Sinclair as a responsible criticism of teaching and that was published nine years later, see Willard Waller, *The Sociology of Teaching* (New York: John Wiley, 1932). For two contemporary examples of similar responsible criticism that stand behind and above much of the more recent exposés, see Robert Nisbet, *The

Degradation of the Academic Dogma: The University in America, 1945–1970 (New York: Basic Books, 1971); and Philip Rieff, *Fellow Teachers: Of Culture and Its Second Death,* 2d ed. (Chicago: University of Chicago Press, [1973] 1985).

17. Hofstadter and Metzger, *The Development of Academic Freedom.*
18. *Ibid.,* 421.
19. *Ibid.,* 452.
20. See Hofstadter and Metzger, *The Development of Academic Freedom,* 475.
21. "The Case of Professor Mecklin, Report of the Committee of Inquiry of the American Philosophical Association and the American Psychological Association," in *The Journal of Philosophy, Psychology, and Scientific Methods* 11 (1914): 67–81.
22. Mecklin's autobiography was published under the title, *My Quest for Freedom* (New York: C. Scribner, 1945). From 1920, he spent the remainder of his academic career at Dartmouth College in the Department of Sociology.
23. Hofstadter and Metzger, *The Development of Academic Freedom,* 475n.
24. See Mecklin's own brief account in *The Journal of Philosophy, Psychology, and Scientific Methods* 10, no. 20 (25 September 1913): 559–60.
25. "The Case of Professor Mecklin," 72.
26. *Ibid.,* 71.
27. *Ibid.,* 70n.
28. Hofstadter and Metzger, *The Development of Academic Freedom,* 475n.
29. "The Case of Professor Mecklin," 73.
30. Catholic institutions of higher education have been subject to precisely the criticisms that Lovejoy would probably have not considered legitimate, given his willingness to acknowledge doctrinal authority in private institutions as superior to any countervailing definition of academic freedom in public and nonsectarian schools. Lafayette's struggle with itself in 1913 was about how to become post-Protestant without abandoning Protestantism entirely. For discussions of the Catholic case on academic freedom, see Edward Manier and John Houck, eds., *Academic Freedom and the Catholic University* (Notre Dame: University of Notre Dame Press, 1967); Philip Gleason, "American Catholic Higher Education, 1940–1990: The Ideological Context," in George M. Marsden and Bradley J. Longfield, eds., *The Secularization of the Academy* (New York: Oxford University Press, 1992), 234–58; and George S. Worgul, Jr., ed., *Issues in Academic Freedom* (Pittsburgh: Duquesne University Press, 1992).
31. Wilson, *Quest for Intelligibility,* 191–92.
32. All page numbers in parentheses that follow refer to this edition.
33. Weber's famous address is contained in H. H. Gerth and C. Wright Mills, *From Max Weber: Essays in Sociology* (New York: Oxford University Press, 1946), 129–56.
34. See Wilson, *Quest for Intelligibility,* 195–96. On November 14, 1933, Lovejoy delivered an address entitled "Hitler as Pacifist," to the Baltimore Branch of the American Jewish Congress (which subsequently published it). He concluded: "Hitler *is* a menace to the peace of the world; but I hasten to add that he need be a serious menace only if the rest of the world believes his present protestations that he isn't" (p. 18). To have recognized this so early in the coming darkness speaks to Lovejoy's profound knowledge of the history of ideas, in particular, the idea of race and its special place in *Mein Kampf.*
35. See Feuer, "The Philosophical Method of Arthur O. Lovejoy: Critical Realism and Psychoanalytical Realism," 509. As to the radical separating of "the knowing of finite beings" and "Absolute Mind," a meaningless dualism in Lovejoy's view, Lovejoy writes: "Any other kind of knowing is an affair of the Absolute alone, which throws no light upon the situation in the temporal world" (p. 385). See note 36 for a further development of this problem.
36. For a work that carries Lovejoy's agnosticism to our present moment of hostility toward the sacred, see Susan Haack, *Evidence and Inquiry: Towards Reconstruction in Epistemology* (Oxford: Blackwell, 1993). Haack proposes

not to address the implications of religious experience for epistemological investigations of empirical beliefs. This philosophical agnosticism is then contrasted to the worldview of the evangelical Christian (not what Lovejoy would have called Absolute Mind):

> This manoeuvre, no doubt, will be regarded as profoundly unsatisfactory by Calvinist proponents of "Reformed epistemology," whose attitude, I dare say, will be as expressed in this quotation: "Sin creates a widespread abnormality. Trust in God which ought to be a spontaneous act providing us with intuitive first principles of knowledge is lacking in most people. Christians should not be embarrassed to say frankly that this is the issue. If one trusts in God, one will view some evidence differently than a person who basically denies God."

> G. Marsden, "The Collapse of American Evangelical Academia," in A. Plantinga and N. Wolterstorff, eds., *Faith and Rationality* (Notre Dame, IN: University of Notre Dame Press, 1983), 257, 234, note 16.

37. See Gerard Radnitzky and W. W. Bartley III, eds., *Evolutionary Epistemology, Rationality, and the Sociology of Knowledge* (La Salle, IL: Open Court, 1987). The one school of thought that seems to have had a consistent relationship to many of the arguments developed by Lovejoy in *The Revolt Against Dualism* is phenomenology. Herbert Spiegelberg recognized this relationship and developed approaches for exploring it in "The Phenomenon of Reality and Reality," in *Doing Phenomenology: Essays on and in Phenomenology* (The Hague: Martinus Nijhoff, 1975), 130–72.

38. See Werner Stark's useful discussion of the problems of intrinsic and extrinsic interpretations in the sociology of knowledge in *The Sociology of Knowledge: An Essay in Aid of a Deeper Understanding of the History of Ideas* (London: Routledge and Kegan Paul, 1958), 214f. Stark acknowledges his debt to Lovejoy's work in the history of ideas.

39. I am, of course, reconstructing, in part, an argument made by Emile Durkheim; in part, because Durkheim conflated many dualisms. I am interested here only in that form of double consciousness that apprehends the world outside oneself (for example, how I am treated by others) and my own understanding and response to that world. Durkheim might have stopped there, thus avoiding his rejection of a sacred order that is not otherwise social in origin. See Emile Durkheim, "The Dualism of Human Nature and Its Social Conditions," in Kurt H. Wolff, ed., *Emile Durkheim, 1858–1917* (Columbus: Ohio State University Press, 1960), 325–40.

40. The demands for black, women's, and gay and lesbian studies—from which is derived the monistic fusion of the "personal is political"—are not about pluralism but rather about social transformation, in which everyone is encouraged, however politely, to explore the dimensions of race and gender across the curriculum. Of course, deeper explorations of class relations seem peculiarly unwelcome in this transformative effort. What if the personal is economic? The insults E. A. Ross hurled at his version of economic oppressors seem quaint compared to the totalitarian charges of racism and homophobia hurled willy nilly today. Ross's concept of oppression was deeply rooted in Protestant guilt about the responsibilities of wealth. Would that such guilt were still a powerful form of self-criticism among intellectuals. Instead, self-criticism has become an excuse for intimidating others rather than a justification for acting as an example to others. For an illustration of this intimidation and the response to it, see Gilbert Meilaender, "On Bringing One's Life to a Point," in *First Things* (November 1994, no. 47): 31–35.

41. Explanations that attribute biological differences to different groups are criticized when those explanations are said to apply to individuals within different groups. But who criticizes the arguments made about racial differences when they suit political agendas at the level of the hiring of individuals?

42. Feuer, "Lovejoy, Arthur O.," 467 (see note 2). See Arthur O. Lovejoy and George Boas, *A Documentary History of Primitivism and Related Ideas*, vol. 1 (Baltimore: Johns Hopkins Press, 1935).

43. Feuer, "Lovejoy, Arthur O.," 467.
44. Christopher Lasch, *The Agony of the American Left* (New York: Knopf, 1969), 186.
45. Feuer, "Lovejoy, Arthur O.," 468.
46. See Wilson, *Quest for Intelligibility*, 200-206.
47. Wilson, *Quest for Intelligibility*, 201. These are Lovejoy's words.
48. *Ibid.* These are Wilson's words.
49. *Ibid.*, 231, note 28. The words are Lovejoy's.
50. Sidney Hook's approach to academic freedom deserves fuller treatment than can be given here. In 1953, the American Philosophical Association sponsored a symposium on "The Ethics of Academic Freedom," in which Hook and George Boas delivered papers. Boas was a longtime colleague of and collaborator with Lovejoy at Hopkins. Hook's paper was largely a response to Boas's paper. Hook wrote,

    Sometimes our language about academic and other freedoms betrays us into an absolutism we do not intend and which suggests that a right is unconditionally valid, i.e., irrespective of its consequences upon the complex of other rights involved. I know of no such absolute right not even the right to search for and speak the truth in all circumstances. Some of the Nazi scientists sought to discover the truth about the survival thresholds of torture by immersion. One of them in a court proceeding defended himself on the ground that important truths were thereby attained. Yet all of us would regard such a quest for truth as a moral abomination even if the results obtained might some day be useful in saving lives—which in fact was part of the plea in extenuation. A scientist who practices upon human beings as if they were experimental animals is a stock example of insanity in popular literature. But suppose a community felt about vivisection of animals somewhat as we do about vivisection of human beings, would it be a violation of academic freedom to forbid such experiment? In a world of limited resources and opportunities would it be a limitation of academic freedom to prevent, to stretch our fancy, say publication of a discovery that would abolish death, until some provision was made for the limitation of births? On Mr. Lovejoy's definition the answer would be clearly yes, but most of us would agree that the limitations were justifiable just as we would agree that limitations on freedom of worship if such worship involves child marriage or infanticide are justifiable. This indicates that moral questions are relevant not *in* knowledge but *to* knowledge.

    In Morton White, ed., *Academic Freedom, Logic, and Religion* (Philadelphia: University of Pennsylvania Press, 1953), 36. See also Sidney Hook, *Academic Freedom and Academic Anarchy* (New York: Cowles Book Co., 1969); Nathan Glazer, *Remembering the Answers: Essays on the American Student Revolt* (New York: Basic Books, 1970); Sidney Hook, ed., *In Defense of Academic Freedom* (New York: Pegasus, 1971); and Sidney Hook, *Out of Step: An Unquiet Life in the 20th Century* (New York: Harper & Row, 1987).
51. Race, class, and gender are among the allegedly progressive, but fictive, pieties in higher education today. Lovejoy, I believe, would have been appalled at such an evolutionary outcome, not because he was a white male, but because he knew the difference between an argument and a fiction. Across the ocean, another man of extraordinary patience and learning, but of utterly different sentiments about matters of faith, echoed Lovejoy's convictions that we live and die by our distinctions and by our ability and inability to make them:

    What we need to be particularly on our guard against are precisely the vogue-words, the incantatory words, of our own circle.... These are, of all expressions, the least likely to be intelligible to anyone divided from you by a school of thought, by a decade, by a social class.... And our private language may delude ourselves as well as mystifying outsiders. Enchanted words seem so full of meaning, so illuminating. But we may be deceived. What we derive from them may sometimes be not so much a clear conception as a heart-warming sense of being at home and among our own sort. "We understand one another" often means "We are in sympathy." Sympathy is a good thing. It may even be in some ways a better thing than intellectual understanding. But not the same thing.

    C. S. Lewis, "Before We Can Communicate," in *God in the Dock: Essays on Theology and Ethics* (Grand Rapids, MI: William B. Eerdmans, 1970), 254-57.

PREFACE TO THE SECOND EDITION

The present edition of *The Revolt Against Dualism* is, except for the correction of some typographical errors,* identical in content with the first (clothbound) edition of 1930. The reasonings presented in the first edition are not qualified or materially supplemented here. The debate concerning epistemological and psychophysical dualism, which the book seeks to record, analyze, and evaluate, has in some respects become less active than it was in 1930; but it cannot be said that the subsequent thirty years of debate have produced any close approach to unanimity among philosophers on the issues discussed. Nevertheless, I think that the issues are genuine and that philosophers should continue to examine them in the manner indicated in the original preface.

Arthur O. Lovejoy

Baltimore, Maryland

October, 1960

---

*EDITOR'S NOTE: We are deeply indebted to Professor Lovejoy and to his editorial assistant, Mr. Bernard R. Mathews, for their very painstaking reading of the text, and for their aid in pointing out errors and suggesting corrections, clarifications, and revisions. As a result this edition has been materially improved by the correction of all errors in the first edition which altered or obscured the meaning of Professor Lovejoy's words.

PREFACE

The principal purpose of this volume is not to present a private and original speculation, but to show, through a critical survey of the reflection of the greater part of a generation of philosophers in America and Great Britain upon two important philosophical issues, that certain conclusions with respect to those issues have thereby been definitely established. The practice of philosophizing *in vacuo* I have always regarded with distaste and suspicion. Philosophy seems to me essentially a collective and coöperative business. Effective coöperation among philosophers consists, it is true, primarily in disagreement. For, given a sufficiently well defined problem, philosophy can really get forward with it only by bringing together in their logical interconnection all the considerations which have occurred, or are likely to occur, to acute and philosophically initiated minds as significantly pertinent to that problem. These considerations will always be numerous, they will always, during the progress of any philosophical inquiry, be conflicting, and they must be contributed by many minds of diverse types and different training and preconceptions. But no typical and, so to say, normal consideration can with safety be left unconsidered, if the philosopher's distinctive but difficult duty of logical circumspection is to be observed, and if the joint inquiry is to be brought to a critically reasoned and convincing result—a result which may fairly objectively be said to be more probable than any alternative, at least in the light of the existing state of empirical knowledge, and of the relevant reflections which have thus far presented themselves to the human mind. The true procedure of

philosophy as a science—as distinct from the philosophic idiosyncrasies of individuals—is thus that of a Platonic dialogue on a
grand scale, in which the theses, proposed proofs, objections,
rejoinders, of numerous interlocutors are focused upon a given
question, and the argument gradually shapes itself, through its
own immanent dialectic, to a conclusion.

It is this conception of the method in which fruitful philosophical inquiry is to be conducted that has determined the procedure
followed in the greater part of the following lectures. I have tried
to review what seem the main "points" that have been brought
forward in the debate upon the two questions here chiefly dealt
with; and, in so far as is consistent with brevity, I have for the
most part put those points which to me seem unconvincing in the
terms of those writers who have (so far as I recall) best presented
them. I am very far from meaning by this that I conceive such a
method to be adequately exemplified in this volume. It is not to
be assumed that all the arguments which have been advanced in
twenty-five years of many-sided discussion with respect to these
questions are here expounded, analyzed and weighed. Some omis-
sions are, no doubt, due to forgetfulness, ignorance, or congenital
logical blind-spots, in the author; and there are others which have
been imposed by limitations of space and time. This last is especially true in the case of the second lecture. Nevertheless, the
discussion seems to me to have been carried on for a sufficiently
long time, in a sufficiently connected manner, by a sufficiently
large number of dissimilar, independent, ingenious and subtle
philosophic minds, to make the essential outlines of the resultant
logical situation plain, or at the least, to make it possible, by
means of a certain amount of analysis and of discrimination between what philosophers' reasonings prove and what their authors
say they prove, to show that the long and often involved argument
has come, on some crucial matters, to a decisive issue.

I should, however, be guilty of misleading the non-philosophic
reader if, in saying this, I should cause him to suppose that there
now reigns among philosophers—or even among English-speak-

ing philosophers—a tedious unanimity on the principal topics here considered. The lectures themselves will, perhaps, seem all too plainly to show the contrary. There has, indeed, I think, long been a striking convergence of opinion towards certain conclusions at which the present study also arrives—a convergence further illustrated by some important books which have appeared since the lectures were completed. And there is also a far greater extent of unconscious or unavowed unanimity than the less observant readers of a number of recent doctrines are likely to perceive. For the contemporary philosophical world is full of the kindred of M. Jourdain—philosophers who utter, and, indeed, prove, certain truths apparently *sans le savoir.* This, no doubt, seems an odd and improbable thing to assert; it is, nevertheless, one of the significant facts which I have sought to exhibit in the following pages. There remains a considerable residuum of real disagreement; and it is not chiefly in an actual *consensus philosophorum,* but in an examination into the logical course of the debate over the two kinds of dualism, that the justification is to be found for the summing-up of its results which I have attempted.

A good deal of this book is concerned with epistemology. This subject is one which many men of science and certain philosophers seem to consider not merely unprofitable but repulsive. Since those who profess this antipathy manifestly have epistemologies, tacit or explicit, of their own, it must be assumed that what they are really expressing is a dislike for inquiries into the subject which do not begin by accepting their conclusions. It appears to be sometimes conceived that the problem is sufficiently disposed of by the remark that knowing is, after all, "a natural event," one among the organic functions exercised by certain animals. The observation is undisputable, since anything which happens is a natural event, and knowings of some sort are commonly supposed to happen. But the proposition usually conceals the assumption that knowing is a kind of natural event which can be adequately described in terms of other organic functions, or of the ulterior utilities which it serves, or at all events of a general philosophy of nature which has been formulated without much special attention to the question as to the precise kind of phenomenon that knowing is.

These appear to me to be among the most curious aberrations to be found in contemporary thought, though they are, no doubt, natural enough manifestations of that impatience to simplify and synthetize which is the sin that doth most easily beset both philosophy and theoretical science. I should have thought it fairly evident that knowing is, on the face of it, a rather peculiar and by no means unimportant or uninteresting organic function, that it is as fitting a subject for patient scientific investigation as any other, that it is probably an especially difficult one, and that any inquiry into it should begin by regarding it as what it appears to be, namely, a phenomenon by means of which some other things— get known.   Certain theorems which appear to me fundamental in what may be called descriptive epistemology I have tried to make clear and to justify in the concluding lecture. They are not, for the most part, new; but they appear to be far from generally familiar or generally accepted among specialists in what are too invidiously and exclusively called the natural sciences; and I am afraid that they are not so current among philosophers as I could wish.   I am, however, very sensible of the fragmentariness of the treatment of the subject in that lecture.   The topic in many of its aspects lay beyond the bounds of the special questions chosen as the theme of this course; and it could not be adequately treated without unduly distending the volume.   I have, therefore, merely set down what I believe to be some necessary brief prolegomena to any future account of the nature of the knowing of particular existences.

I shall not attempt to name here the philosophers, living and dead, to whom I am probably indebted for most of the "considerations" which this volume contains; the number necessarily includes nearly all of those who have taken part in the long collective inquiry with which the lectures deal, and of which I have set forth what I conceive to be the not unimportant outcome. But I should like to say that I am not least mindful of an indebtedness to those honored contemporaries from whose reasonings I have felt constrained to dissent. For in philosophy, even more than in other matters, a man often learns most from those with whom in the end he disagrees.

ARTHUR O. LOVEJOY

The Johns Hopkins University
    Baltimore, March 1930.

I

CARTESIAN DUALISM AND
NATURAL DUALISM

I propose in these lectures to review the course and to attempt
to estimate the results of a movement of thought which has been,
on the whole, the most characteristic and most ambitious philosophic effort of our generation in the English-speaking part of the
world. The last quarter-century, it may fairly confidently be predicted, will have for future historians of philosophy a distinctive
interest and instructiveness as the Age of the Great Revolt against
Dualism; though it is possible that they may prefer to describe
this uprising as a phase of a wider Revolt of the Twentieth Century against the Seventeenth. We approach the tercentenary of
the earliest writings of Galileo and Descartes; and the occasion is
being joyously celebrated in several quarters by the issuance of
declarations of independence directed against those thinkers. For
they and a few of their contemporaries forged a scheme of ideas
which—as it is now the fashion to say, not altogether untruly—
has bound the minds of reflective men, and especially of men of
science, ever since. The great physicist-philosophers of that *grand
siècle* have been described by M. Meyerson as "the legislators of
modern science"; more precisely, they were the framers of, at
least, its constitutional law; and although there have been many
amendments to the instrument they drafted, and occasional local
insurrections against its authority, it is only in our own generation
—or so, at all events, some of our own generation enthusiastically
assure us—that there has developed a really thorough-going philo-

sophical radicalism which proposes to discard that constitution altogether, and is at the same time provided with the draft of a new one constructed on wholly different principles—or, as it would perhaps be more accurate to say, with several new ones, constructed on principles differing from one another hardly less than from those which they are to supersede. From many sides may now be heard the rallying-cries of groups inspired by highly diverse motives to attack the common enemy—and there are not wanting resounding proclamations that the enemy has in fact been already overthrown. "The history of modern philosophy," observes a recent writer, "is a history of the development of Cartesianism in its dual aspect of idealism and mechanism. Only within recent years has that triumphant progress been checked. The manifold errors of the system have always been obvious and freely criticized. But only now have we begun to realize how totally wrong are its very first assumptions; only now have we begun to see in this simple and direct philosophy the source of all the great intellectual sophisms of our age."[1] Thus we who have watched the fall of so many long-established political dynasties have also, it would appear, been witnesses of what may in the end be recognized as a far more important event—"the dethronement of Descartes." So Professor Whitehead has found in the characteristic theses or rather preconceptions of the seventeenth century the *fons et origo malorum*—the artificial and "quite unbelievable" set of "scientific abstractions" by which "modern philosophy has been ruined."[2] Professor Burtt likewise, through another course of reflection, has been brought to the belief that the worst confusions and perplexities of modern thought have arisen from the failure of all the great thinkers of the past two and a half centuries to "subject to a critical examination the whole system of categories which had come to its clearest expression in Newton's *Principia*"; and he sees in such a drastic reëxamination, leading to

---

[1] "The Dethronement of Descartes," leading article in the London *Times Literary Supplement*, Sept. 9, 1926.
[2] *Science and the Modern World*, p. 79.

a reconstruction upon new foundations, the imperative task of the philosopher of to-day. Much greater, however, is the number of contemporary thinkers who, less concerned to define their views in terms of their historical relations, are nevertheless in fact zealously engaged in attempts to emancipate philosophy from one or another of those fundamental assumptions which—as is supposed —a few men of genius between 1630 and 1690 were able to impose upon a great part of the thought of all the generations between them and ourselves.

The motives inspiring these efforts are, as I have intimated, various and in part somewhat incongruous; and the "seventeenth-century ideas" which are the subjects of attack are correspondingly diverse. But the phase of the insurrection which has been the most conspicuous, which, in the issues it raises, is the most important, which has had the widest support and has enlisted the greatest and most various philosophical talents, has been the attempt to escape from that double dualism which the seventeenth-century philosophers did not, indeed, originate, but to which they gave reasoned and methodical expression—the epistemological dualism of the theory of representative perception, and the psychophysical dualism which conceives empirical reality to fall asunder into a world of mind and a world of matter mutually exclusive and utterly antithetic. The supposition, so long accepted as unchallengeable, that all apprehension of objective reality is mediated through subjective existents, that "ideas" forever interpose themselves between the knower and the objects which he would know, has become repellent and incredible to many of our contemporaries; and the cleavage of the universe into two realms having almost no attributes in common, the divorce between experience and nature, the isolation of the mental from the physical order, has seemed to not a few representative and influential thinkers to be unendurable in itself and the source of numerous artificial problems and gratuitous difficulties which can be solved only by denying their presupposition. Thus the thing above all others needful for philosophy in our time has appeared to many acute intelligences to be to get rid of this "bifurcation of nature" —without falling into the idealism or phenomenalism which had hitherto seemed the only alternatives, and which, in fact, were, in their historic genesis, mainly consequences of the same fundamental preconceptions. Against both dualisms, then, our age has witnessed an assault—in neither case wholly unprecedented—but bolder, more sustained, more resourceful, and upon a wider front, than can be found anywhere in the previous history of philosophy.

There may, it is true, be heard from other quarters equally confident and apparently not less numerous voices declaring that our own day has been made forever memorable by the final triumph of the ideas which the seventeenth century first systematically elaborated. The promulgation of the Einsteinian doctrine of relativity can hardly be considered an unimportant incident of the past quarter-century; and that doctrine as a whole—*i. e.,* the special and the general theory taken together—has appeared to some of its most eminent expositors to be simply the consummation and justification of the program initiated by Galileo and Descartes. The bifurcation of nature into a subjective and an objective order and the exclusion of all non-geometrical properties and non-mechanical processes from the latter—these principles, which the founders of the modern philosophy of science discerned but were unable to formulate altogether correctly or to carry through consistently and convincingly, have now, we are told, through the work of Einstein, been established and given their ultimate, generalized, and exact interpretation and application. Thus Bergson speaks of *la démonstration complète du mécanisme cartésien qu'aura peutêtre réalisée Einstein*[3]—complete, that is to say, for the external, spatial or quasi-spatial order with which physical science is concerned. Similarly M. Abel Rey writes that

> The theory of relativity is the present culmination of the system of science that is based upon the mathematization of the knowledge of material reality—and consequently upon the conceptions of arrangement and

[3] *Durée et simultanéité,* p. 42. But for Bergson, it is perhaps needless to add, the spatial order has only a derivative and, for pure metaphysics, a specious reality.

movement in space as the universal and necessary—if not the sufficient—characteristics of such reality.[4]

And the same writer sees also in Einstein's theory the final extension of the Cartesian dualism—or of a dualism even older than Descartes': the doctrine of relativity is, he declares, "precisely the continuation of that evolution which, at earlier stages, consisted in the establishment of the distinction between dream and waking life, and between the illusions of the senses and the objective data of experience."[5] Numerous other philosophers and physicists have regarded the theory of relativity as proving, not that Galileo and Descartes were moving in the wrong direction, but only that neither moved far enough in the right direction—that, namely, of excluding the characters of our perceptual experience from the non-relative, independent, objective realm of being which is the physical world. In Einstein's generalized theory, Weyl has remarked, "Descartes' dream of a purely geometrical physics seems about to be fulfilled in a wonderful way which could not have been foreseen by him."[6] Einstein's achievement, says Eddington, "consists essentially in this: he has succeeded in separating far more completely than hitherto the share of the observer and the share of external nature in the things we see happen."[7] M. Meyerson likewise recognizes in the general theory of relativity a new version of that identification of matter with space which is, he observes, "the postulate upon which the whole (Cartesian) system rests"; but he is unwilling to grant that the credit for the clearer expression and bolder application of this postulate is to be given to its twentieth-century representatives: *les relativistes y mettent infiniment moins de hardiesse et de clarté, mais le résultat final*

[4] *Revue philosophique,* 1922, p. 215.
[5] *Ibid.,* p. 214.
[6] *Raum, Zeit, Materie, 3te Aufl.,* p. 244.
[7] *Space, Time and Gravitation,* pref., p. v. In spite of the remark cited, it should be added, Eddington elsewhere in the same volume declares that "the object of the relativity theory is not to attempt the hopeless task of apportioning responsibility between the observer and the external world" (p. 33); but then proceeds once more to show in detail how just this "hopeless task" has been accomplished by Einstein (pp. 33-6).

est bien le même.[8] And he too finds that what the relativistic physicist seeks to attain is "a representation of the physical phenomenon purged of all the peculiarities actually found in the perceptions of each particular observer," which "he can only do by detaching the phenomenon more completely from the observer than science has ever done before."[9] Finally, to conclude these illustrations, an American physicist in an important recent work on the philosophy of science has declared that "it is precisely in an improved understanding of our mental relations to nature that the permanent contribution of relativity is to be found."[10]

Such is the conflict of opinion among presumably competent judges concerning the true outcome of the philosophy and theoretical physics of these last twenty-five years, and therefore concerning the standing of sevententh-century ideas at the bar of twentieth-century thought—which in any event, it is perhaps seemly to recall, is not necessarily identical with the bar of Eternal Justice. Descartes has been dethroned; his sovereignty in the philosophy of science has been at last decisively vindicated. The dualism of subjective appearance and objective reality is "a passed mode, an outworn theme"; the same dualism is the corner-stone of the new physics. It is now demonstrable that there are no "psychic additions to nature"; it has now been demonstrated that a far greater part of the content of experience than had ever before been imagined consists of "psychic additions." Not even the secondary qualities of perceived things are subjective; not even the primary qualities of perceived things are objective. The scheme of ideas devised "by mathematicians for mathematicians" in the seventeenth century has at length been seen to be inherently incredible; a revision and extension of the same scheme of ideas, devised "by mathematicians for mathematicians" in the twentieth century, is the culminating triumph of modern thought. The abstractions and rigidity of the mechanical conception of the physi-

---

[8] *La Déduction relativiste*, p. 135.
[9] *Revue de métaphysique et de morale*, 1924, p. 33.
[10] Bridgman, *The Logic of Modern Physics*, p. 2.

cal world have been finally overcome; a purely geometrical conception of the physical world, yet more abstract and rigid, has been definitively established.

I have thought it pertinent to begin with these reminders of the curious and piquant opposition of tendencies in contemporary opinion with respect to the issues mentioned; for it partly defines the topic of this book, in its historical as distinct from its purely logical aspect. Whether the main assumptions of the principal and most representative seventeenth-century philosophies of nature and theories of knowledge have been justified or overthrown by the reflection of our time, is a question to which in the end we shall seek an answer. Our immediate concern, however, is with the manner in which the revolt against the two forms of "Cartesian dualism" broke out, and with certain confusions of issues and objectives which characterized its outset—confusions which it is important to eliminate from our own consideration of the matter from the start.

Whatever be the truth or falsity of the essential doctrine, the specific forms which were given both to epistemological and to psychophysical dualism by Descartes and most of the older realistic philosophers were undeniably and, indeed, notoriously, confused and incompletely excogitated. The traditional phrase, for example, for describing the status or locus of sense-data and other "ideas" was "in the mind"—an expression devoid of any clear meaning, which is happily disappearing, though it has not yet quite wholly disappeared, from the vocabulary of philosophy and psychology. And since the Cartesian dichotomy of the universe assigned "ideas" to the mental part of reality and declared this to be distinguished from the physical part by lacking the attribute of extension, sense-data seemed to be denied that attribute—though there is nothing that more certainly has position and extension in space—that is to say, in *some* space—than the visual and tactual content of perception, from which all our notions of extension and position are derived. This confusion was at once facilitated and complicated by the curious neglect of many generations of philosophers and psychologists, following Descartes' example, to distinguish sharply in their terminology between the—*ings* and the —*eds* (to adopt an expression of Professor S. Alexander's)—between the terms "sensation," "perception" or "thought" as signifying the event, function or act of sensing, perceiving, thinking, *etc.*, and the same terms as signifying the items sensed, perceived or thought. Even "consciousness" tended to be confused with content, that which we are conscious of. The result of this was that characteristics which could at least plausibly be ascribed to the —*ings* were often, without any feeling of incongruity transferred to the —*eds,* to which they appear (when the distinction is made) manifestly inapplicable.

These unnecessary aberrations of the early and long-accepted forms of dualism in modern philosophy and psychology had some part, I think, in provoking the twentieth-century insurrection against those doctrines; they, and in particular the confusion last mentioned, at all events determined the initial objectives of the attack. It was the bold raising of the standard of revolt by William James in his famous essay "Does Consciousness Exist?" twenty-six years ago, and by G. E. Moore in his "Refutation of Idealism," a year earlier, that gave the revolutionary movement its first great impetus in America and Great Britain respectively—though neither writer was the earliest to denounce the supposed Cartesian usurpation.[11] And both of these essays were primarily attacks upon the confusion of "consciousness" and "content"; in the discovery that this *was* a confusion, the polemic against the older sort of realism won its first skirmish—which, as is usual in the early days of all wars, was by many mistaken for something more than a skirmish. And—what is a curious feature of the recent history of philosophy—from the same discovery were simultaneously drawn precisely opposite conclusions by these two pioneers of the anti-dualistic campaign. Once clearly realize the

[11] Among other early manifestations of the tendency should especially be mentioned Professor Kemp Smith's *Studies in the Cartesian Philosophy,* 1902, and Professor R. B. Perry's "Conceptions and Misconceptions of Consciousness," *Psychological Review,* XI, 1904, pp. 284–296.

logical distinction between "thought" as a supposed psychic state or process and "thoughts" as concrete data, between —*ing* and —*ed*—said James in substance—and you will see that the former is a fiction. "Consciousness as a kind of impalpable inner flowing," a "bare *Bewusstheit* or *Bewusstsein überhaupt*," evaporates to the "estate of pure diaphaneity"; it is, in short, not introspectively discoverable, and therefore does not exist. "Experience has no such inner duplicity." Once clearly realize the same logical distinction—said Mr. Moore in substance—and you will necessarily perceive that experience *has* an inner duplicity, that there is introspectively discoverable an element which "is as if it were diaphanous," a simple, unanalyzable activity or state of "consciousness" or "awareness," present in a uniform way in all perception and cognition, and entirely separate from any content upon which it may be directed—in short, a *Bewusstheit überhaupt*.

Yet both these opposed conclusions, based upon the same initial distinction, were promptly turned to pretty much the same use; they seemed almost, if not quite, equally serviceable as weapons against the usual dualistic kind of realism. Since there is no "consciousness," argued James, all the data of perception must consist of the self-same independent physical things of which the real world is composed; when "experienced," these have merely entered into certain transitory and unessential relations to other things of the same kind, and there is no mental image, as the "representative" theories of perception suppose, intervening between the percipient organism and its objects; we "see the room and the book immediately just as they physically exist." Since there *is* a consciousness, argued Mr. Moore, but a consciousness which is purely diaphanous, a mere psychical function of being-aware, then also the data of perception consist of the independent realities of which the external world is composed. There is thus "no question of how we are to get outside the circle of our ideas and sensations. Merely to have a sensation is already to *be* outside of that circle. It is to know something which is as truly and really *not* a part of *my* experience, as anything which I can ever know." [12] We have therefore "no reason for supposing that there are such things as mental images at all."

As is known to all who have any acquaintance with recent philosophy, the division of counsels thus apparent at the outset of the new movement has persisted. From those early days of the century to the present, the attack upon dualism has been carried on by two distinct philosophical groups, operating from different positions—one of these groups, the less radical one, being active chiefly though not exclusively in Great Britain, the other chiefly though not exclusively in the United States. The former, following the original doctrine of Mr. Moore, has continued to admit the reality of "consciousness" or "awareness" as a unique, non-physical type of phenomenon, and thus retains a residuum of psychophysical dualism; while the other party, following James in rejecting "consciousness" altogether, has, in so far as its program has become clear-cut and consistent (as it was not in the case of James himself), tended towards behaviorism or materialism. (I disregard, for the present, the fact that both movements have been further divided through the growth of powerful heretical sects who would elevate the objects of sense-perception itself

In die schönen Regionen
Wo die reinen Formen wohnen,

making of the patch of color I see at a definite place in my visual field, or the musical tone I fleetingly hear, eternal Platonic essences.) Into the internal dissension between the right and left wings of monistic realism I do not, in this lecture, intend to enter. It is only the contention common to both that we are here to consider. This contention, pending further analysis, can be expressed only in an ambiguous phrase, as the theory of the objectivity of all content; but in the first phase, at least, of the revolt this has usually meant two propositions of a somewhat less equivocal character: *viz.* (a) that all that is known is apprehended directly and not through intermediaries, either mental or physical,

[12] *Philosophical Studies,* p. 27.

and (b) that all perceptual content consists of parts of the physical world. The latter view may be called, for short, content-materialism. While the point of difference between the two schools is assuredly important, it is less important than the point in which they agree. If all the contents of perception are independent physical reals, the result, for a large part of the theory of science and the philosophy of nature, is the same, whether we say that these reals, when experienced, have entered without modification into a transient external relation to a bodily organism, or that they have, equally without modification, been transiently contemplated in an otiose "psychic act" of awareness.

The more significant issue, and the one specifically before us, being thus distinguished, it is worth noting that the arguments with which the anti-dualistic movement began were really irrelevant to that issue, that the opening assault was misdirected. Neither James's denial of the existence of consciousness as psychic process nor G. E. Moore's assertion of the existence of a consciousness which is pure psychic process had, in strictness, any implications whatever as to the "independence" of immediate data or their identity with parts of the "physical world." It is perfectly possible to conceive of the existence of psychic content dependent on the physiological act of perception without admitting any "impalpable inner flowing" that never has the status of content. Indeed, even a phenomenalist might without inconsistency agree with James's rejection of a *Bewusstsein überhaupt*—might, in other words, adopt the theory that experience, and therefore what is knowable of reality, consists of "thoughts" in their concreteness, and includes no such insensible stuff as pure thinking. This, in fact, would have been the more natural outcome of the argument; a subjectivist or a dualist, for whom all content is "mental" *ab initio,* surely has less need to supplement it by a bare awareness than has one by whom the supposition that extra-experiential material things directly "get reported" (in James's phrase) must be rendered intelligible. It is equally possible to admit that experience discloses or presupposes a "diaphanous"

activity of awareness without inferring from this that the objects
directly apprehended must or can exist outside the total situation
of which this awareness is an element. Nothing that is introspectively discoverable (assuming that something *is* so discoverable) about the nature of consciousness as such, can prove anything about the causal dependence or independence of data upon
the percipient event as a whole or about the propriety of classifying them as "physical" qualities or things. To judge whether an
entity empirically given is a "part of the physical world," it is
necessary first of all to have, so to say, some criterion of eligibility
for admission to the physical world; and it is by comparing the
known or assumed characteristics of, *e. g.,* perceptual content with
this criterion—not by considering the characteristics of something
which by definition is not content—that the question must be
answered. Nevertheless these initial confusions have persisted
through a good deal of the subsequent history of the movement;
they seem to me to be partly responsible for the curiously unques-
tioning acceptance by many "new" realists of the pseudo-axiom
that nothing can be caused or conditioned by the occurrence of a
psychical or even of a physical percipient event.[13] It may well be,
so far as anything yet said would show, that nothing is so conditioned; but that is a proposition requiring proof, and it is not to
be proved by mere inspection of the notion of "consciousness"
taken by itself.

It is evident, then, that the movement under consideration was at
first aimed, at least in part, against a rather vague, confused and
aberrant form of dualism, and was itself, partly in consequence of
this, involved in certain irrelevancies and misdirected efforts. It
will, therefore, be well for us, before proceeding further, to define
the dualistic position more discriminatingly, reducing it to its
simple essentials, without the accidental redundancies of its seventeenth-century and traditional expression. We are now, in other
words, to call to mind the natural genesis of both epistemological

---

[13] *Cf.* the writer's paper "La théorie de la stérilité de la conscience," *etc., Bulle-
tin de la Société française de philosophie,* XXV, 1925, Nos. 4–5, p. 98.

and psychophysical dualism, the situations in experience out of which those ways of thinking (whether ultimately tenable or not) intelligibly and normally and, indeed, inevitably arise as "moments" in the progress of man's reflection. In this simplified and normalized statement of dualism and its sources we shall, of course, be recalling what in the main is—or at all events should be—a familiar story; what now follows in this introductory lecture must be largely a recital of commonplaces. But they are commonplaces which it is essential to have in mind as the background of the movement which we are to review and examine; and there is, I think, special need to recall them to some philosophers of our time. The past quarter-century's discussion has shown that it is not easy for the critics of dualism to keep clearly in view its essential outlines in their entirety and in their simplicity, free from extraneous complications and confusions, and to recognize that it, rather than what is called "naïve" or "direct" realism, is the way of thinking natural to man so soon as he becomes even a little reflective about certain facts, of which most are matters of ordinary experience, and all have long been generally accepted. It appears to be especially difficult for some philosophers and men of science to keep the issues concerning the two dualisms distinct and to apprehend clearly their logical relations. We shall, then, follow the good counsel of Professor Dewey, the first Carus Lecturer, and attempt "as philosophers to go back to the primitive situations of life that antecede and generate these reflective interpretations, so that we re-live former processes of interpretation in a wary manner, with eyes constantly upon the thing to which they refer."

(1) Let us take epistemological dualism first. Men are normally led to accept it simply because they have formed certain preconceptions as to what an object of knowledge ought to be, and then, comparing the characteristics of the thing directly presented in their experience with these preconceptions, have found that the two do not match. In knowing, or attempting to know, man makes certain claims or pretensions, the remarkable nature of

which he usually fails to see because he makes them so confidently
and habitually. He assumes that, in so far as he ever succeeds in
one or another form of the cognitive enterprise, some very curious
things must be true about the known fact's or object's relation to
himself and his act of knowing. These assumptions are no far-
fetched inventions of the philosopher; they are all manifestations
of the primary and most universal faith of man, his inexpugnable
realism, his two-fold belief that he is on the one hand in the midst
of realities which are not himself nor mere obsequious shadows
of himself, a world which transcends the narrow confines of his
own transient being; and, on the other hand, that he can himself
somehow reach beyond those confines and bring these external
existences within the compass of his own life, yet without annul-
ment of their transcendence. It is precisely this achievement that
men naturally mean by "knowing"; I have but put in general and
explicit terms what everyone (except, possibly, a few philosophers) supposes himself to be doing when he is engaged in true
perception, retrospection, forecast, or social communication. In
the persistent human demand that this singular achievement shall
be possible, and the consequent necessity of making intelligible
how it can be possible, of describing precisely what happens when
it is accomplished, lie the perennial sources of that most human
of all the activities of reflective thought which is called epistemology. Man, in short, is by nature an epistemological animal; for
his irrepressible knowledge-claim is itself a thesis *about* knowledge, and therefore about himself and his relation to nature and
to the life of his fellows; and it is a thesis which cries out for
clarification, and for correlation with the conclusions about other
natural phenomena to which this natural phenomenon of knowing has brought him. So long as he continues to feel any normal
curiosity about himself and his rôle amid the rest of things, he
will necessarily wish to know himself *as* knower, and therefore to
understand the seeming mystery and challenging paradox of
knowledge—the possibility which it implies of going abroad while
keeping at home, the knower's apparent transcendence of the ex-

istential limits within which he must yet, at every moment of his knowing, confess himself to be contained.

Specifically, men naturally make at least five assumptions (we need not yet ask whether they are valid assumptions) about the character or status of what may, for short, be called *cognoscenda* —the things-to-be-known-if-possible. (1) Many *cognoscenda*, including most of those to be known, if at all, visually, are assumed to be at places in space external to the body of the percipient. Man may be described biologically as an animal whose habitual and paradoxical employment is the endeavor to reach outside his skin. As a physical organism *homo sapiens*, like other creatures, has a definite spatial boundary of rather irregular outline, formed chiefly of a single material substance. All that, physically or spatially speaking, constitutes the organic functioning of an individual of the species takes place within the narrow room defined by this epidermal surface. What the man as a biological unit is, and what the events that make up his life are, are sought by the biologist wholly within those confines. Yet man is forever attempting, and, as he is wont to believe, with success, to apprehend, to "get at," things which lie beyond this surface. The individual's actual existence, as it appears *to him,* can in only very small part be described as a succession of subcuticular events. The stuff of which it *seems* to be mainly composed consists of entities and happenings on the far side of the boundary, some of them so slightly removed from the epidermal surface that they are said to be in contact with it, others incalculably remote. The human animal, in short, does not for the most part live where its body is—if an organism's life is made up of what it really experiences; it lives where the things are of which it is aware, upon which its attention and feeling are directed. (How far this may be true of other creatures we cannot judge.) One of the most curious developments in the entire history of thought is the invention in our day of what may best be named the Hypodermic Philosophy—the doctrine, resulting from the application to a cognitive animal of the biological concepts found sufficient in the study of animals assumed to be non-cognitive, that the organic phenomenon of knowing may be exhaustively described in terms of molecular displacements taking place under the skin.

(2) Equally insistent in man, and yet more paradoxical—had most men but the capacity for philosophic wonder which would enable them to see it so—is the demand that he shall have a real traffic with things that are not, because they are by-gone or have not yet come into being. What time and nature have extinguished he makes the matter of his present contemplation, and gains thereby his power to foresee what is still unborn. In memory and in forecast and anticipation he expressly conceives himself to be apprehending entities or events (even though they may be only other experiences of his own) which are not co-existent with the acts or states through which they are apprehended—to be reaching what is nevertheless at that moment in some sense beyond his temporal reach.

(3) An even more exigent desire for knowledge normally arises in man—though some philosophers who profess to have rid themselves of it would have us believe that it is equally wanting in others. Besides his craving to reach that which is spatially and temporally external to himself at the moment of cognition, there is, plainly, in the natural man a wish to attain an acquaintance with entities as they *would be if unknown,* existences not relative to the cognitive situation—in short, with things as they literally are in themselves. He has a persistent, if not easily gratified, curiosity about what M. Meyerson calls the *être intime,* the private life, of things. Tell him that at every moment of his existence he is contemplating nothing but the ghostly offspring of that moment's contemplation itself—even though they be projected into other places—and you contradict one of the most tenacious of his convictions—and, as he will point out to you, if he should be something of a dialectician, you also contradict yourself. He may, under pressure from philosophers, surrender this conviction with regard to one and another limited class of the contents of

his experience; surrender it wholly, neither he nor the most subjectivistic philosopher has ever really done.

And (4) this tenacity in believing that through what goes on within the individual's experience he can know what is other than that experience and as real as it is, is greatest with respect to his knowledge of the experiences of others of his kind.. There are a few philosophers among us who profess not only to be satisfied with automatic sweethearts and mindless friends, but also to be unable to attach meaning to the proposition that these automata have any being beyond that which they have in the philosopher's own private and (as some would add) corporeal existence. (It is, of course, evident that if this philosophy is true—supposing the word "true" still to have meaning—there are not several such philosophers, but only one.) But this queer affectation, a hypertrophy of the logic of scientific empiricism, is manifestly belied at every moment by the behavior and speech of the philosophers who assume it; it denies the meaningfulness of a belief which every creature of our kind seems inevitably to hold and from which all the distinctive quality of man's moral consciousness and all the tang and poignancy of his social experience derive—the belief that he is surrounded by beings like himself but not himself, having inner lives of their own which are never in the same sense *his* own, but of which, nevertheless, he can attain some knowledge, and to whom, reciprocally, he can convey some understanding of that which is going on within himself. This social realism also, which is manifestly a piece of pure epistemology, seems to be one of the specific characters of *homo sapiens,* as properly a part of his zoölogical definition as his upright posture or his lack of a tail. It is implicit in all his most distinctive modes of feeling and behavior—his elaboration of language and art as means of expression, his craving for affection, the curious and immense potency over the individual's conduct which is possessed by his beliefs about the thoughts and feelings of others about himself, and his occasional ability to recognize the interests of other sentient creatures as ends in themselves. Apply the principle of relativity to men's apprehensions of one another, and you destroy the very idea of a society of the characteristically human type.

(5) Finally, the *cognoscenda* which the individual knower ascribes to places and times in the external world where his body is not, and in which his cognitive act is not occurring, he also conceives to be potentially, if not actually, apprehensible by these other knowers; they must be things capable of verification in experiences other than the one experience in which, at a given moment, they are in some sense before him. Out of his belief in a multiplicity of knowers other than himself, or a multiplicity of knowings which, though now knowable by him, are not *his present* knowing, he has framed the category of publicity, the notion of a world of objects for common knowledge; and he tends to treat this attribute of common verifiability as the criterion of that independence of the percipient event or the cognitive act which he naturally attributes to the *cognoscendum*. In other words, his character as a social animal has profoundly and permanently infected his very notion of knowing, so that the experience of objects which he has when, in dream or madness, he steps aside into a world of his own—be it never so vivid and never so coherent— is not, when seen to be thus private, taken as equivalent to that access to reality which he seeks.

These, then, are the five articles of the natural and spontaneous epistemological creed of mankind—a creed which, as I have said, contains its own apparent mysteries, or diverse aspects of the one mystery of the presence of the absent, the true apprehension, by a being remaining within certain fixed bounds, of things beyond those bounds. Epistemological dualism arises when reflection, initially accepting these articles, inquires about their implications and brings them into connection with certain familiar facts of experience. There is, indeed, as should be evident from what has already been said, a sense in which all realism is intrinsically dualistic; in all its forms, namely, it asserts that the thing known may be other in time and place and nature than the *event or act by means of which* the thing is known.[14] Thus the event of seeing, as we have remarked, if conceived physiologically as a neuro-cerebral change, does not appear to occur either where the visual object is seen or where the real object is assumed to be. A happening inside of a given body somehow achieves the presentation, in the individual stream of experience connected with that particular body, of an entity outside the body. And even if the cognitive event be conceived as a purely psychic and non-spatial act of awareness, that act has at least a date which need not (*e. g.*, in memory) be the date, and a *quale* which is by hypothesis not the *quale,* of the object known. But it is not this fundamental sort of dualism necessarily inherent in any realistic theory of knowledge which we shall here mean by "epistemological dualism"; the term stands for the assertion of quite another (though not unrelated) duality, that of the content or datum at a given moment immediately and indubitably presented, and the reality said to be known thereby. Even the datum, of course, *seems,* in the case of sight and touch, to be situated outside the body, though whether it truly is or not must be a matter for subsequent consideration. I do not actually see the desk inside the head of which I at the same time can see a small bit—namely, the tip of my nose—and to the rest of which I give in thought a spatial position definitely related to that bit. But epistemological dualism (as here understood) declares that not even the visible desk which is thus directly perceived as spatially external to the perceived body is the same existent as the "real" desk, *i. e.,* the *cognoscendum.* And the existential distinctness of datum and *cognoscendum* which is thus held by the dualist to be exemplified in the case of visual perception is also asserted by him, *mutatis mutandis,* in the case of other modes of perception and other forms of cognitive experience; so that, in his view, all knowing is mediated through the presence "before the mind"—as the traditional phrase goes—of entities

14 Some recent forms of realism, such as Mr. Bertrand Russell's, may at first seem to constitute exceptions to this generalization; it will be shown in a later lecture that they do not really do so.

which must be distinguished from an ulterior reality which is the true objective of knowledge.

Now you obviously cannot discuss whether two particulars—two in the sense that they have been provisionally distinguished in discourse—are identical unless you already know or assume something about both. If you are in a state of blank ignorance about either one, no question concerning the nature of their relations can be raised. It is therefore necessary to know, or postulate, certain propositions about the class *cognoscenda* before we can compare it with the class "data" to ascertain whether the two satisfy our criteria of identity. To assert their non-identity is to ascribe to the one a spatial or a temporal or a spatio-temporal position, or a set of qualities, which is inconsistent with those empirically exhibited by the other. Philosophers, it is true, have often attempted to go about the matter in what seems a different way. They have begun by provisionally assuming that they know nothing whatever except the passing immediate datum, and have then sought to determine, by reflecting upon the nature or implications of this, how much knowledge of existents which are not immediate data they must, or may, suppose themselves to possess. This was, of course, essentially the method of Descartes, though he applied it confusedly and inconsistently. But it is not the natural road to epistemological dualism. That road starts from the position of natural realism—from the assumption that we already have certain information about realities which are not *merely* our immediate, private, and momentary data; and it leads to the discovery, or supposed discovery, that this very assumption forbids us to believe that our acquaintance with these realities is at first hand. The time, place, context, or qualities which we have ascribed to them prove inconsistent with those which belong to the data. Not only is this the natural approach to the dualism of datum and *cognoscendum,* but it is also the only approach which is at all likely to be persuasive to those averse to that theory. The argument starts from the premises of those who would, if possible, avoid its conclusion. We shall, then, in this and the next lecture, not attempt an affectation of universal doubt, but shall tentatively accept—with nearly all of the early and many even of the later insurgents—the broad outlines of the picture of nature familiar to common sense and sanctioned by the older physics. We shall, in particular, not initially question the supposition that there are extended external objects, such as pennies, tables, planets, and distant stars, having at least the primary and possibly also the secondary qualities; having determinable positions in a space like that of visual and tactual perception, whether or not it is identical with it; capable of motion and causal interaction; acting, by means of processes in space, upon our sense-organs; and thereby conditioning the presence in our experience of the data which, whether or not identical with the objects, are our sources of information about them. When these natural assumptions are provisionally adopted, there nevertheless prove to be at least five familiar aspects of experience in which it seems plain that the object of our knowing must be different in the time or place or mode of its existence, or in its character, from the perceptual or other content which is present to us at the moment when we are commonly said to be apprehending that object, and without which we should never apprehend it at all.

(1) Of these, the first is implicit in the second of the above-mentioned articles of man's natural realistic creed. Intertemporal cognition, the knowing at one time of things which exist or events which occur at another time, seems a patent example of a mode of knowledge which we are under the necessity of regarding as potentially genuine and yet as mediate. When I remember, for example, not only is there a present awareness distinct from the past memory-object (that alone would imply only the duality of act and content), but the present awareness manifestly has, and must have, a compresent content. But the past event which we say the memory is *of* cannot be this compresent content. In saying this I am, it is true, including among the natural grounds of epistemological dualism an assumption which some dualistic philoso-

phers—and even some who repudiate the naïvely dualistic theory of memory—regard as unsound. Mr. Broad, for example, has said that there "is no general metaphysical objection to such a theory" on the ground that when an event is past it ceases to exist. "Once an event has happened it exists eternally"; past events, therefore, "are always 'there' waiting to be remembered; and there is no *a priori* reason why they should not from time to time enter unto such a relation with certain present events that they become objects of direct acquaintance." [15] This view, however, implies an inconceivable divorce of the identity of an event from its date. The things which may be said to subsist eternally are essences; and the reason why they can so subsist is that, by definition, they have no dates. They do not "exist" at all, in the sense in which dated and located things do so; and if "events" eternally existed after they had "once happened" (and when they were no longer "happening"), they would likewise exist before they happened; eternalness can hardly be an acquired character. The present image and the past event may be separate embodiments of the same essence; they are not identical particulars, because the particularity of each is undefinable apart from its temporal situation and relations. The duality of the memory-image and the bygone existence to which it refers seems to be inherent in what we *mean* by remembrance; if the two were one our intertemporal knowing would defeat its own aim of apprehending the beyond, by annulling its beyondness. The very wistfulness of memory implies such duality; the past, in being known, still inexorably keeps its distance. Plainest of all is it that a man's own experienc*ing* of yesterday, the event of his then *having* an experience, does not seem to him, in being remembered, to become today's experiencing. Common sense, however much inclined in its more self-confident moments to believe in direct perception, has never, I suppose, believed in direct memory; it has been well aware that what is present in retrospection is a duplicate which somehow and

[15] *The Mind and its Place in Nature*, p. 252.

in some degree discloses to us the character, without constituting the existence, of its original.

(2) It is not alone in the case of memory that there is a temporal sundering, and therefore an existential duality, of the content given and the reality made known to us through that content. This second reason for dualism has not, it is true, like some of the others, always been discoverable by the simplest reflection upon every-day experience. But the fact upon which it rests has long been one of the elementary commonplaces of physical science; and the probability of it had suggested itself to acute minds long before its verification. There had at times occurred to him, wrote Bacon in the *Novum Organum,* "a very strange doubt," a *dubitatio plane monstrosa,* "namely, whether the face of a clear and starlight sky be seen at the instant at which it really exists, and not rather a little later; and whether there be not, as regards our sight of heavenly bodies, a real time and an apparent time (*tempus visum*), just as there is a real place and an apparent place taken account of by astronomers." For it had appeared to him "incredible that the images or rays of the heavenly bodies could be conveyed at once to the sight through such an immense space and did not rather take some appreciable time in travelling to us."[16] Unfortunately for his reputation Lord Bacon was able to overcome this doubt by invoking against it several bad reasons, which need not be here recalled; but his subtler medieval namesake had not only propounded but embraced and defended the same conjecture three centuries earlier.[17] Roemer's observation in 1675, through which it became established as one of the fundamental theorems of empirical science, is not usually mentioned in the histories of philosophy; but the omission merely shows how badly the history of philosophy is commonly written, for the discovery was as significant for epistemology as it was for physics and astronomy. It appeared definitely to forbid that naïvely realistic way of taking the content of visual perception to which

[16] *Novum Organum,* II, 46.
[17] Roger Bacon, *Opus Majus,* ed. Bridges, II., pp. 68–74.

all men at first naturally incline. The doctrine of the finite velocity of light meant that the sense from which most of our information about the world beyond our epidermal surfaces is derived never discloses anything which (in Francis Bacon's phrase) "really exists" in that world, at the instant at which it indubitably exists in perception.[18] It is with a certain phase in the history of a distant star that the astronomer, gazing through his telescope at a given moment, is supposed to become acquainted; but that phase, and perhaps the star itself, have, ages since, ceased to be; and the astronomer's present sense-data—it has therefore seemed inevitable to say—whatever else they may be, are not identical with the realities they are believed to reveal. They might perhaps be supposed to be identical with the peripheral effect produced by the light-ray on its belated arrival at the eye—in other words, with the retinal images; but two present and inverted retinal images *here* are obviously not the same as one extinct star formerly existing elsewhere, and the duality of datum and object would therefore remain. This particular hypothesis, moreover, is excluded by the now familiar fact established by the physiological psychologists, that there is a further lag—slight, but not theoretically negligible—in the transmission of the neural impulse to the cortical center, and therefore—since the percept does not appear until the impulse reaches the brain—a difference in time between the existence of a given pair of retinal images, or any other excitation of peripheral nerve-endings, and the existence of the corresponding percept. Never, in short, if both the physiologists and the physicists are right, can the datum or character-complex presented in the perception of a given moment be regarded as anything but the report of a messenger, more or less tardy and more or less

[18] The retardation of auditory sensation must so soon and so constantly have forced itself upon the notice of primitive man that an implicit epistemological dualism with respect to sound may be supposed to have prevailed from an early period in the history of the race. It was, however, a vague dualism because a sound does not so clearly present itself as occupying a definite place, or as an adjective of an object or event in such a place.

open to suspicion, from the original object which we are said to know by virtue of that perception.

(3) Another class of empirical facts which are familiar, in their simpler forms, to all men have seemed by the plainest implication to show that perceptual content, even though it appears as external to the physical organs of perception, is not identical with the particular objects about which it is supposed to convey information. It is commonly assumed that the object, or objective, of a given perception can, first of all, be identified, at least roughly, by its position in space and time. What I am "perceiving" at a certain moment is the ink-bottle two feet away from my hand, or the star a hundred light-years distant. Even if the position is defined only vaguely, the thing is at least supposed to be (or have been) "out there" somewhere. This identification of the object referred to is, obviously, possible only by means of the same perception; yet, assuming such identification, experience shows that what I perceive is determined by events or conditions intervening in space and time between that object and my so-called perception of it. The qualities sensibly presented vary with changes which appear to occur, not in the place where *the* object is supposed to exist, but in regions between it and the body itself, and, in particular, in the very organs of perception. The examples are trite: a man puts a lens before his eyes, and the size or shape or number or perceived distance of the objects presented is altered; he puts certain drugs into his stomach, and the colors of all the perceived objects external to his body change; he swallows other drugs in sufficient quantity, and sees outside his body objects which no one else can see, and which his own other senses fail to disclose. The discovery of this primary sort of physical relativity, which is really one of the most pregnant of philosophical discoveries, begins in infancy with the earliest experience of the illusions of perspective, or the observation that the objects in the visual field change their spatial relations when looked at with first one eye and then the other. If *homo sapiens* had at the outset been blind, the first seeing man, a paleolithic Einstein,

when he reported this astonishing fact—the relativity of position to the motions of eyelids—to his fellow cave-men, would presumably have seemed to them a deviser of intolerable paradoxes, and have been made acquainted with those more effective methods for repressing strange doctrines which cave-men, no doubt, knew how to employ. The evidence of this dependence of the nature of what is perceived upon happenings which, as themselves experienced, do not happen in the right place to permit them to be regarded as changes in the *cognoscendum* itself, has constantly increased with the progress of the sciences of optics, neuro-cerebral physiology, and psychology; the eventual determination of the character of the percept has been removed farther and farther, not only from the external object, but even from the external organ of sense. As Professor Dewey remarked, in the preceding series of these lectures, "it is pure fiction that a 'sensation' or peripheral excitation, or stimulus, travels undisturbed in solitary state in its own coach-and-four to either the brain or consciousness in its purity. A particular excitation is but one of an avalanche of contemporaneously occurring excitations, peripheral and from proprioceptors; each has to compete with others, to make terms with them; what happens is an integration of complex forces." [19]   And even in the earliest and easiest phases of this discovery, the variability of the percept with conditions extrinsic to the object to be perceived manifestly affects those attributes by which the very identity of the individual object should be defined: it is not colors only but shapes, not shapes only but perceived positions, that prove to be functions of the processes spatially and temporally intervenient between the object and the perception, and therefore not attributable to the former. Thus what is actually perceived could be regarded only as the terminal effect of a more or less long and complex causal series of events happening at different places and times, only at the perceptually inaccessible other end of which series the *cognoscendum* was supposed to have—or rather, to have had—its being. Aside from

[19] *Experience and Nature,* first ed., p. 333.

any empirical evidences of the sort mentioned, it has apparently seemed to many minds virtually axiomatic that, if the *cognoscendum* in perception is conceived (as it is in ordinary thought and in most physical theory) as a "causal object" acting upon the bodily organs of perception in the determination of the character of the content experienced, that which is acted *upon* must also have a part—must, indeed, have the last and decisive word—in determining the character of that content. How under these circumstances the exterior causal object could be known at all is an obviously difficult question; this argument for epistemological dualism, and especially the rôle assigned in it to the organs of perception, gives rise to that "crux of realistic theories" which Mr. C. A. Strong has very precisely expressed: "to explain how a sensation which varies directly only with one physical object, the nervous system, can yet vary with another physical object sufficiently to give knowledge of it." [20] But with these ulterior difficulties we are not for the moment concerned; whatever *their* solution, they obviously do not annul the difficulty, for any realistic philosophy, of identifying the end-term with the initial term of the physico-physiological causal series.

(4) This physical and physiological conditionedness of the data manifestly implies that the contents of the experience of percipients having different spatial and physical relations to a postulated external object cannot be wholly identical. But this implication is independently confirmed and extended through that communication and comparison of experiences which is supposed to be possible through language. While the many knowers are, by the fifth article of the natural epistemological creed, dealing with what is said to be one and the same object—and if they are not doing so are not achieving what is meant by knowledge—they notoriously are not experiencing the same sensible appearances. There is an assumed identity of the region of space at which the observers are all gazing, and this serves for the requisite antecedent identification of the common *cognoscendum;* but what they

[20] *Mind*, N. S., 1922, p. 308.

severally find occupying this supposedly single locus consists of character-complexes which are not merely diverse but (according to the logic almost universally accepted until recently) contradictory. So long as it is assumed either that there are certain sets of sensible qualities—e. g., two or more colors—which are incompatible, i.e., cannot both occupy the same place or the same surface of a material object at the same time, or that there are in nature "things" which at a given moment have a single and harmonious outfit of geometrical and other properties, the conclusion has seemed inevitable that the many discrepant appearances cannot "really" inhabit the one place or be the one thing at that place. So soon as the dimmest notion that there is such a phenomenon as perspective distortion dawned upon men, they began *eo ipso* to be epistemological dualists. It is of course conceivable, so far as the present consideration goes, that *one* of the discordant appearances might be identical with the object-to-be-known or with some part of it; but even so, since all the other observers are also supposed to be apprehending the object, *their* apprehension, at least, must be mediated through data which are *not* identical with it. Nor does it seem a probable hypothesis that, while *almost* all perception is mediate, a few privileged observers now and then attain direct access to the object.

(5) Finally, the experience of error and illusion, however difficult it may be to render philosophically intelligible, seems to have at least one direct and obvious implication: namely, that the thing which at any moment we err about—otherwise than by mere omission—cannot be a thing which is immediately present to us at that moment, since about the latter there can be no error. It, at least, *is* what it is experienced as. In so far as *cognoscendum* and content are identified, error is excluded; in so far as the possibility of error is admitted, *cognoscendum* and content are set apart from one another. It may perhaps seem that this reasoning applies only to the cases in which there *is* error, and that in true judgments (or in veridical perception) the content may still be the same as the *cognoscendum*. And if the term "true judgments"

includes the mere awareness of an immediate datum, then in such judgments there is in fact no duality. But these constitute, at best, only a tiny part of the subject-matter of our claims to potential knowledge, the range of our possible judgments at any given time; and it is, indeed, an obviously inconvenient use of language to call them judgments at all. For the most part we are occupied, when judging, with matters conceived to be so related to us that we are not, from the very nature of that relation, necessarily immune against error; doubt as to the validity of our judgments about them is assumed to be not meaningless. But where error is *conceivable,* the relation between content and *cognoscendum* must be the same as in the case of actual error. The generic nature of judgments-potentially-erroneous must be conceived in such a way as to permit the genus to have both judgments actually true and judgments actually false as its species—and to make it intelligible that the latter are aiming at the same mark as the former without hitting it. But a judgment is about something in particular; it has to do with a specific portion of reality. Since in actually erroneous judgments it is impossible that that portion can be the immediate datum, error must consist in attributing some character now present in perception or imagery, or represented by a verbal symbol, to *another* locus in reality, where it in fact is not present; and the species of actually true judgments will correspondingly be defined as the attribution of some such character to another locus in reality where it in fact *is* present. In all this, once more, I have only been putting explicitly the way of thinking about truth and error which seems to be common to all mankind, barring a few philosophers of more or less recent times. That bit of baldly dualistic epistemology known as the correspondence-theory of truth is one of the most deeply ingrained and persistent of human habits; there is much reason to doubt whether any of the philosophers who repudiate it actually dispense with it; yet *it* is not merely an instinctive faith, but has behind it certain simple and definite logical considerations which it appears absurd to deny. This also, among the five points of natural epistemological dual-

ism, may plausibly be supposed to have been a part of the un-
formulated working epistemology of our race from an early stage
in the progress of intelligence; for there can hardly have been
many featherless bipeds so naïve as not to have learned that man
is liable to error, and so dull as to be unable to see, at least dimly,
that in direct contemplation there is no room for error.

These, then, are the roots of epistemological dualism in human
nature, common experience, and natural reflection. Even this
summary reminder of them is sufficient to show that the way of
thinking so named by philosophers is no accidental or artificial
product of seventeenth-century metaphysics, no sophistication of
speculative minds; it is simply the account which man, grown capable of holding a number of facts together in a single view and
drawing what seem plain inferences from them, will normally
give of the situation in which he finds himself when he is engaged
in what he calls "knowing." From these roots the same conclusions would, in all probability, perennially grow again, though
Descartes were not only dethroned but forgotten, and his works
and those of all his contemporaries and successors up to the present, were destroyed—unless the philosophers of our own or some
subsequent day are really able to provide an alternative interpretation of the same facts of experience—not merely of some, but of
all of them—so clear and cogent that all men of intelligence shall
see that it supersedes and abrogates this natural dualism. Whether
this alternative interpretation has yet been given it will be our
eventual business to determine.

It is, however, undeniable that the dualistic outcome thus
reached by bringing certain familiar empirical facts into connection with the ideal of the *cognoscendum* embodied in man's
natural realistic creed has a certain air of incongruity with that
creed. Not only is the apprehension of the object found to be
vicarious, but, because vicarious, it may naturally seem to be un-
certain. This is especially apparent in the case of the third, or
physico-physiological, argument; it has the look of one of those

arguments which destroy their own premises as they proceed. It begins, we saw, by assuming that at least the position, relative to certain other objects, of the particular object-to-be-known is given through visual perception; but it ends by concluding that not even the relative position of anything given in visual (or, indeed, tactual) perception can be a direct disclosure of the position of anything not so given. This conclusion, moreover, is arrived at on the ground that events between the intended object and the percipient determine the character of what is given; but these intervenient events could, by the same reasoning, be shown to be themselves similarly conditioned, and therefore to be not directly or infallibly disclosed in perception—and so on, until the physiologically immediate is finally pursued to its lair in some cortical event which unfortunately is not disclosed by perception at all. But the question whether the argument is in fact finally self-destructive belongs to a later stage of our inquiry. It is sufficient for the present definition of the nature and primary grounds of epistemological dualism to sum it up as a hypothetical proposition: *if* you postulate the externality of the entities to be known, in *any one* of the five ways in which it is asserted in the natural realistic creed—*i.e.*, spatial externality to the knower's body, temporal externality to the date of the event of perceiving or remembering, causal independence of that event, the identity of the objects known by many observers, and the actual "otherness" of your neighbor's experience—then in that specific case your knowledge cannot be direct; the presented content upon which the knowledge depends must be numerically other than the thing which the knowledge is about, for one or more of the reasons given. And if you postulate externality in all five cases, then all your knowledge is indirect; the existents which convey it are not the existents which it means. This may be a puzzling result, demanding—as it assuredly does—much further analysis before it becomes clear *how* knowledge is obtainable in this manner; but that is not, to the dualist, reason for denying that it *must* be obtained in this manner, if at all. Any attempts to construe realism in a non-dualistic fashion would, as it seems to him, be equivalent to asserting that particulars which at a defined time are in one place are at the same time in another place; that the same particular spatial entity has—or consists of—many shapes, many sets of color-patterns, *etc.*, simultaneously; that an identical event which has one date, in a determinate time-order, also has another date in the same order; that the final term in certain long series of causes and effects is always qualitatively and numerically identical with the first term; and—if the thesis of the identity of content with *cognoscendum* is generalized—that error is impossible. The task of the insurgent against epistemological dualism who would still adhere to a realistic theory of knowledge must be to show, with respect to each of these propositions, either that it does not follow from his premises, or else that it is not the absurdity which the dualist has supposed it to be.

In our statement of the natural grounds of epistemological dualism, you will observe, no sort of psychophysical dualism has been assumed. We have not defined sense-data or other content as "mental," and nothing in the reasoning outlined has presupposed their exclusion from the physical order. It is important to bear in mind that the argument for the one sort of dualism is thus independent of the other; for much confusion upon this point is prevalent—sometimes even among philosophers, but still more among specialists in the natural sciences, when they deal with these matters. The historical fact that both dualisms converged in seventeenth-century philosophy in the hypothesis of "ideas" (in the Cartesian and Lockian sense) has blurred the distinction between the two issues, and has caused attacks upon both doctrines to be often made with weapons effective (if effective at all) only against one or the other of them. An "idea" was representative, *i.e.*, it was an *indirect* means of knowledge of external objects, and it was immaterial or "psychical." There are intelligible motives for wishing to escape from either view, if possible; but the reasons for antipathy to the one are not reasons for antipathy to the other—except in so far as both antipathies arise from a sort of general dyophobia common in our time. Even if you are disposed to assume by an act of faith that the world is not composed of two radically disparate kinds of stuff, you are not thereby justified in affirming that in perception, memory, or other cognitive experiences, what is given as content is the same particular existent as what is known; for the proof offered by those who hold that it is not the same does not require an initial admission that the world is composed of two kinds of stuff. If, on the other hand, you find an insuperable difficulty in understanding how indirect knowing can constitute knowledge at all, you are not thereby justified in denying that the world is composed of two radically disparate kinds of stuff; for the proof offered by those who hold that it is so composed does not rest wholly or mainly upon the supposition that knowing is indirect. It may, it is true, be the case that epistemological dualism in the end implies psychophysical dualism; *i.e.*, it may prove impossible to find a place among "physical objects" (when a definition of that term has been agreed upon) for percepts, memories, *etc.*, if those entities are not identical with their *cognoscenda*. In other words, the historic fusion of the two dualisms may turn out to have been justified. Whether or not it was we must later try to determine. But we must not assume this in advance; the case for or against each of the defendants must not, because of that possible outcome, be entangled with the case against or for the other.

Let us now turn to psychophysical dualism, and attempt a similar sketch of its natural grounds and normal genesis. Though distinct, the process is in general analogous to that which gave rise to the epistemological kind of dualism. A notion is first formed, implicitly or explicitly, of the properties which an existent ought to possess if it is to be conceived to be a true part of the "physical" world; experience and reflection presently show, or seem to show, that a part of the actual content of perception does not satisfy the specifications thus set up; and that content is thereupon relegated to another realm of being. The initial preconception, a development of man's natural realism, is that of an order having five essential characteristics. (1) It is spatial as well as temporal; (2) some or all parts of it continue to exist during the interperceptual intervals of any and all percipients, and no part belongs to it solely by virtue of the occurrence of a perception; (3) the extended things, or groups of characters, existing in it go through that sort of uniformly correlated change usually called causal interaction, the laws of these interactions being in some degree determinable; (4) these causal processes continue their regular sequences when not attended to by any percipient; (5) this order is a common factor in or behind the experience of all percipients. The physical world is thus conceived as filling for thought the temporal gaps between actual perceptions, as keeping the business of nature going while you or all men are heedless or asleep; and it links the experiences of individuals into a system of interacting events through the common relation—however that be further defined—which they have to it. This belief in a continuity in nature which is not in fact exemplified in anybody's experience is, of course, as Mr. Bertrand Russell has remarked, "a piece of audacious metaphysical theorizing," but it is one for which "our savage ancestors in some very remote prehistoric epoch" were probably responsible. The conception, in short, may well have been entirely familiar to the cave-man, however incapable he was of expressing it in abstract terms; and it apparently is still (with somewhat extensive refinements) implicit in the cosmology of an Einstein.

The cave-man, however, may also have supposed, or rather, may never have thought of questioning, that all the content of his experience, all the things he perceived and heard and felt and dreamed and imagined, fell within such a world. But at some undetermined phase in the early history of reflection it began to be noted that there are some contents of experience which do not seem to meet all the requirements for admission to this world. This was most plainly the case with the objects of dream and hallucination. There was ground for suspecting that they lack the third, fourth and fifth qualifications; and it could be inferred, though in all probability it was not immediately inferred, that they lack the second. In other words, they do not appear to act causally upon other objects in space, in the same way in which these objects seem to act upon one another; they give no indirect evidence, as other things do, of going through uniform sequences of change during the intervals when they are not attended to; their existence is sensibly verifiable only by one percipient; and thus there is no good reason for crediting them with existence during the interperceptual intervals. The arrow with which you so pleasingly shot your enemy in your dream left him disappointingly intact the next morning; you could light an imaginary fire with no fear that it would burn up your goods when you were not watching it; and the strange monsters you saw after prolonged fasts or deep potations were invisible to the clansmen who were sitting beside you at the time. Here, then, was a plain, empirical cleavage of arrows, fires, animals, and other things, into two great classes, the distinction between them being of the utmost practical importance to savage as to civilized man. There was discovered a variety of actually perceived and therefore indubitable existences which yet were not physical or "real" existences; clearly, then, there was, besides the physical world, a second world encountered in experience.

This, like so many of the decisive philosophical discoveries of mankind, does not usually appear in the histories of philosophy; but it was a crucial point in the progress of reflection, because it was the first rift in the lute, the beginning of the bifurcation of nature. The cave-man was perhaps the only thorough-going non-bifurcationist until our own generation—if, indeed, there are any such in our own generation. The discovery was not, of course, made all at once, or through quite such direct and simple reasoning as I have been indicating. Several familiar features of what are called primitive religion and magic represent, in part, some of the earlier phases of man's struggle to make intelligible to himself this mysterious duality in the content of his experience. He apparently did not readily admit that the objects of dream exist only during the dream and for the dreamer; he was prone to credit them with a more or less persistent being of their own, and thus to attribute to them a peculiar semi-physical status. It was doubtless only through some slow progress of scepticism, some gradual, obscure realization of the uselessness and inconvenience of supposing such entities to perdure, without any efficacy in the ordinary, public, physical world, when unperceived, that the category of "mere appearance," of "existence in the mind only," was developed and extended to all the content of dream, hallucination, illusion, error, and imagination. But the details of this process are problems for the anthropologist; for our purpose it is sufficient to recognize that it was out of this class of experiences, and through some such reflection upon them as has been suggested, that the primary form of psychophysical dualism naturally arose, and must, sooner or later, inevitably have arisen.

The discovery—or the invention—of a second world to which could be allocated all experienced objects which did not appear to satisfy the rules of membership in the physical system was an indispensable and all-important step in the early development of science; for without it the progressive theoretical reduction of the physical world to a relatively simple and uniform order, a reign of law, and of laws of a high degree of generality, would probably have been impossible. If the arrows that inflict no wounds, the fires that never cause conflagrations and leave no ashes, the animals that require no food and are perceptible only in dreams or delirium, had not been definitely set apart in a limbo of their own, subject to different laws, if to any, nature would have appeared hopelessly various, complicated, confused, irregular, and discontinuous; its bifurcation was the first thing needful, if it was to be made intelligible. The world of "mental" entities served as an isolation-camp for all the "wild data," the refractory and anomalous facts, which would have disturbed the tidiness and good order of the physical universe; and it left the theorist, primitive or modern, free to remold the scheme of things nearer, not to his heart's desire, but to the demands of his intellect. One of the earliest phases of this process must have been the tacit adoption of certain postulates about the rules of space-occupancy and of motion in the physical world. What Professor Montague calls "the axiom of spatial exclusiveness," *i. e.,* the principle that there are certain qualities, or sets of qualities, two of which cannot be in the same place at the same time (which some recent doctrines reject), and the assumption that touch gives more trustworthy testimony than sight concerning the presence of a physical object in a place, may plausibly be supposed to have been accepted by men from a comparatively primitive stage in the development of intelligence; but so modern and scientifically sophisticated a thinker of our time as Mr. Bertrand Russell—and one so desirous of escaping from psycho-physical dualism—has, not long since, argued in substance that we must exclude images from the physical world, in order to hold fast to these two postulates. We find, he observes,

that some data are not localized at all, or are localized at a place already physically occupied by something which would be inconsistent with them if they were regarded as part of the physical world. If you have a visual image of your friend sitting in a chair which in fact [this presumably means tactually] is empty, you cannot locate the image in your body because it is visual, nor as a phenomenon in the chair because the chair, as a physical object, is empty. Thus it seems to follow that the physical world does not include all that we are aware of.[21]

Other assumptions which it was possible to apply to the physical world only if certain data that actually appear in space were barred out from that world, were that there are in it more or less perduring individual objects which cannot be in two places at once, and can move from one place to another only by passing through the intervening space; and this pair of assumptions also Mr. Russell, in the same work, saved by extruding images from physical nature. The visual image, seen with shut eyes, of the friend sitting in the arm-chair, "if thrust into the world of phys-

---

[21] *The Analysis of Mind,* p. 120. This is not precisely Mr. Russell's present view (1929); that is summarized and examined in Lecture VII.

ics, contradicts all the usual physical laws. My friend reached the chair without coming in at the door in the usual way; subsequent inquiry will show that he was somewhere else at that moment. If regarded as a sensation, my image has all the marks of the super-natural. My image, therefore, is regarded as an event in me, not as having that position in the orderly happenings of the public world that belongs to sensations." [22]

Arising, then, out of a fact of universal human experience—the actual disparateness of the properties and behavior of two great classes of objects—psychophysical dualism, to which it is the fash-ion among some philosophical writers to refer as a "mysticism" generated by religious yearnings, has in fact served throughout history as the safeguard of developing physical science, as the means whereby men have been enabled increasingly to conceive that "the public world" *is* one of "orderly happenings." I am not here contending that this form of dualism is permanently indis-pensable for that purpose; that, again, is a question lying beyond the province of the present lecture. I am only suggesting that a conception which has had this secular rôle cannot be regarded as a species of historical accident, an aberration attributable to the persistence of certain medieval prejudices in the minds of seven-teenth-century philosophers; and that, if it is now to be aban-doned, some substitute capable of performing the same necessary office must at the same time be provided.

But this account of the natural genesis and motivation of this sort of dualism may perhaps make it seem paradoxical that the content of normal and veridical perception and memory should ever have been assigned to the class of non-physical entities. If the "mental" includes primarily the illusory, and if the stronghold of the belief in its existence lies in our experiences of "wild data," how can the data which are supposed to give us whatever true knowledge of the physical world we possess be placed in that category? In fact, however, such an extension of the realm of "mental" or "subjective" existence appears intelligible and nat-

[22] *Ibid.*, p. 153.

ural—whether or not it is inevitable—when the epistemological dualism previously outlined is admitted. For, upon that theory, the datum in, *e. g.,* what is called veridical visual perception, is not identical, either in its characters or its time of existence, with the one physical object with which naïve realism would identify it, namely, the *cognoscendum;* and with all other entities recognized as physical objects either by common sense or science— even by a rather naïvely realistic sort of science—it seems equally incapable of identification. It is, as the slightest reflection shows, not the same thing as one of the retinal images; you cannot, it would seem, locate it in your body, because, as Mr. Russell remarked of the imaginary figure in the empty chair, it is "visual," *i. e.,* is seen "out there" in front of your eyes, not behind them; but if you assume the presence in the space before you of a physical object with the character which the percept is experienced as possessing, *at the time when it is experienced,* you disturb the order of the physicist's world, and even of the world of common sense, not less than if you thrust into it the creatures of your imagination or your dream. If the datum is in that space at all, it is not there in the way in which physical objects, in the ordinary sense, are there; for to suppose that it figures in the dynamic order of nature, as such objects do, would, seemingly, overthrow the whole fabric of science. The astronomer, for example, takes account in his computations of the distant star which *was* in a certain region of the heavens some thousands of years ago; but he does not assume, in addition to this, that there is *now* in that region a second star with precisely the same spectrum and luminosity, and therefore the same chemical constitution, as the first. Nor can the star-percepts be any more plausibly located, as physical objects, anywhere between the former locus of the astronomical star and the eyes of the observers. In the physical world, then, even the "veridical" percept appears to have no place to go. And of the memory-image this seems still more evidently the case.

The fusion of epistemological with psychophysical dualism is thus as comprehensible, natural, and rationally motivated an outcome of reflection upon the facts of experience as is the separate and logically independent development of each. The datum, once distinguished from the *cognoscendum,* and finding no other local habitation in the physical world, fell into that "inner" world of "appearances" which had long since been discovered by man through his experiences of illusion and phantasy and dream and error; but by virtue of the cognitive function ascribed to it, it assumed in the latter world a place of special dignity, as a (more or less) "true" appearance, a "representative idea." Of this outcome no more than of those previously mentioned, am I at present asserting the finality; but I am indicating the nature of the tasks which must be undertaken and the difficulties which must be faced by those who would transcend either dualism, while still holding that a real physical world exists. The two dualisms, though distinct in their origins and capable of defense on separate grounds, now appear interrelated. If (a) the argument for epistemological dualism is cogent, and if (b) no place among physical objects can be found for perceptual and other data as epistemological dualism conceives of them, then, on these grounds alone, psychophysical dualism (with respect to content) would be established. The insurgent against the latter dualism must therefore show that either (a) or (b) is false: *i. e.,* he must either prove that the percept or the memory-content is identical with the object perceived or remembered, or, if not that, he must definitely show how and where *another* place in the physical world is to be found for both percepts and memories. But even if he accomplishes this, his task will not be completed; it will still be necessary for him to deal with the several types of wild data, and with affective content, and show us how to locate these also among the objects of the physicist's world. If he is able to demonstrate the physicality— in an unequivocal sense—of *both* veridical and wild data, he will have escaped from psychophysical dualism, so far as content (in contrast with "awareness") is concerned, but he will not, simply by this means, impair the argument for epistemological dualism; he will, on the contrary, render it in one respect easier of acceptance, by ridding it of the odium attaching to it, for some minds, because of its apparent implication of psychophysical dualism. To escape from it also, then, the five reasons, earlier outlined, for holding the datum and the object-known not to be identical must one by one be met and shown to be invalid. Such—if I may revert to the military metaphor—were the outlines of the real strategic problem confronting the leaders of the revolt of which we are to examine the logical fortunes—though these outlines were not, I think, fully and clearly apprehended from the outset by all, or perhaps by any, of the participants in the enterprise.

II

THE FIRST PHASE OF THE REVOLT AND
ITS OUTCOME

While dualism of both sorts was—to sum up again in a word the general result of the first lecture—a normal and inevitable outcome of men's effort rationally to adjust their native realistic faith to familiar facts of experience and elementary postulates of reflection, it was, no doubt, equally inevitable and natural that there should sooner or later arise, among reflective minds who still held to that faith, a revulsion against the dualistic form of it. The general and fundamental motives of the revolt which we are to consider are intelligible enough; and it is impossible not to sympathize with them. It might or might not prove in the end logically possible to escape from dualism—without giving up realism; but there were at least strong reasons for wishing to escape from it. For it undeniably was, in the first place, to the realistically minded, a *pis aller*. Its theory of knowledge granted you no actual access to the reality in which you believed and about which you desired to know. The craving to *possess* your object, to meet it face to face, instead of being limited to reports from it given by deputies whose credentials were perhaps dubious, had not been effectually extirpated from the human mind by the course of reflection which had led to dualism; and this repressed desire (along with many others) began in our own century to reassert itself openly. "Ever not-quite" was (at best) the discouraging prospect with which a dualistic epistemology confronted the spontaneous disposition of a constitutionally cognitive animal to believe that his organ of knowledge, like his other organs, is capable of the function for which it seems to be designed. Even among some of the most subtle and sophisticated of contemporary minds one may discern a clearly emotional repugnance to conceiving that the conditions and process of knowing may add ingredients of their own making to the content of experience, that perception does not, so far as it goes, afford an unadulterated and unmediated disclosure of what is present in "nature." The dualistic account of what occurs in sense-perception, moreover, appeared to belie the actual character of that mode of experience. Objects are not sensibly presented in duplicate; and in the warmth and facility of perceiving, it is somewhat difficult even for the convinced dualist to bear in mind that the table he sees or the pen that he feels between his fingers is merely a private "idea" (in the Lockian sense), distinct from the independent existent which is once for all "out there" (as he at least supposes) for his and other men's knowing. To think dualistically all the time puts, at the least, a considerable strain upon the human mind; and it was natural to seek relief from that strain.

But it is not only such biological promptings—if I may so describe them—such propensities of the "animal faith" of man, that make intelligible the appearance in our time of a vigorous reaction against dualism. Certain of the most fundamental preconceptions and methodological postulates of natural science also seemed to demand that an alternative should, if possible, be found. The primary, and almost conclusive, objection to dualism of either sort, I gather, for many men of science, is simply that it is dualistic. It is, on its face, a negation of that assumption of the eventual unifiability of our understanding of things, the continuity and fundamental homogeneity of nature, through the acceptance of which science has in the past achieved some of its greatest triumphs—but also (it must be added) been led into some of its most notorious errors. A generation of scientifically trained persons (I am referring rather to a quarter-century ago than to the present) which had witnessed certain of the most notable of these reductions of seemingly disparate and unique phenomena to unity, and had usually an earnest faith—upon which the subsequent development of science has cast some shadows—in the possibility of simple quasi-mechanical explanations of all manner of things, could hardly fail to find something antipathetic in a philosophy which proclaimed, not only that the system of nature is composed of two completely irreducible kinds of stuff, but that one of these consists of (or includes) such "ghostly" things as "ideas" or "mental contents"—entities plainly alien to the categories and laws of the reputable and successful sciences and inaccessible to a rigorously experimental method of investigation. Knowing, again, as dualism described it, seemed an extraordinarily complicated, clumsy and improbable sort of phenomenon; surely (it was natural to feel) some simpler hypothesis as to the *modus operandi* of the cognitive function ought to be given a trial. And it, too, seemed to constitute a breach in the continuity of nature; no parallel or analogue to it could be found among the processes investigated by either physics or biology; and if types of natural events are not to be multiplied beyond necessity, it was well to inquire searchingly into the necessity of admitting the reality of so singular an event as the production, by certain organisms, of a species of evanescent, imponderable, and physically inefficacious secretions, and the attainment, by this curious means, of information concerning quite other entities—material, often extraneous to the body, and sometimes immeasurably distant from it.

Such general preconceptions as these constituted not only intelligible but reasonable grounds for desiring and hoping for the overthrow of the hypothesis of ideas, and the establishment in its stead of a form of realism monistic in its theory of perceptual and other knowledge, and affirming the non-mental status of sensory and other data. But the apparent reasonableness of a hope is not a guarantee of its fulfilment; and the considerations mentioned were not sufficient to justify a philosopher in rejecting dualism forthwith. For that theory was based upon arguments—and upon arguments which, whether finally valid or not, could hardly be denied to have some plausibility. The revolt as a serious philosophical movement, therefore, though it was certainly largely inspired by these *a priori* assumptions and natural prejudices, could not legitimately be, and in fact was not, based wholly or chiefly upon them. It was based upon the belief that certain specific fallacies were to be found in the dualist's reasoning—non-sequiturs, inconsistencies, and assumptions irreconcilable with empirical fact; and upon the further belief that a definite alternative type of realism could be formulated which would be internally coherent and secure against any possible dualistic counter-revolution. It is with an examination of these two aspects of the first phase of the movement—its attack upon definite points (real or supposed) in the dualistic position, and its constructive program —that we shall be occupied for the rest of this lecture.

If future historians of the philosophy of our time are to make their narrative as profitable for instruction as it ought to be, they will not fail to point out, first of all, the large part played in the causation—or at all events in the polemic—of the revolt by misconceptions of the meaning and grounds of dualism—misconceptions which the seventeenth-century formulations of the notion of "ideas" no doubt helped to produce. What many of the insurgents rebelled against was an imaginary monster, a weird caricature of the "natural" dualism of which we have reconstituted the simple outlines in the preceding lecture; but it was a caricature for which the dualistic philosophers were in some degree to blame.

(1) The most extreme example of such confusion is to be found in an early work of one of the leaders of the uprising in America:

> For primary and secondary qualities alike, the representative theory of knowledge asks us to believe that these are "known" by means of entities which have neither extension, shape, size, motion, color, sound, odor, taste nor touch. These marvellous representatives constitute the "subjective" realm, or "consciousness." . . . Shapes and qualities are . . . according to (this) theory "represented" by shapeless representations of shape, motionless representations of motion, colorless representations of color, and odorless representations of odor. Whereas the fact is that my knowledge is neither shapeless, motionless, colorless, nor odorless. Of course, the experience of every waking moment shows that this pallid herd of

sensations and perceptions thus conjured up by the representative theory constitutes the life experience of no man.[1]

If the "representative theory" really implied this sort of thing, it was obvious nonsense, which might well be rejected without more ado. But in fact no one, I suppose, had ever held such a theory as this; certainly Descartes, Galileo, Hobbes, Locke, and the other formulators of modern dualism, epistemological or psychophysical, had not done so, since one of their most characteristic contentions was that it is *only* in the "subjective realm" that colors, odors, and the like, are to be found. Descartes, for example, surely repeats with sufficient frequency that "ideas" have in them all the sensible qualities which external objects can be supposed to have, besides others of their own: *tout ce que nous concevons comme étant dans les objets des idées, tout cela est objectivement ou par représentation dans les idées mêmes.*[2] As that stout defender of epistemological (though not of psychophysical) dualism, Hobbes, put it, "the image in vision *consists* of color and shape," and "the subject of the inherence" of these qualities is "not the object but the sentient."[3] For the supposition that epistemological dualism somehow implies that our sense-data have no sensory qualities there was, therefore, not much reason; but there was some, arising from the common confusion of the attributes of sensing with those of sense-data, and from the Cartesian and traditional assumption that "mental" means "non-spatial"—which might seem to imply (though for the classic dualists it did not really imply) that, e. g., visual percepts are without extension, shape, or size. That these assumptions are no necessary or proper part of either epistemological or psychophysical dualism is, I trust, sufficiently clear from the first lecture; and the irrelevance of the sort of attack illustrated by the passage cited is therefore evident.

(2) A much more comprehensible misapprehension of the

[1] E. B. Holt, *The Concept of Consciousness*, p. 142.
[2] *Méditations: Réponse aux secondes objections.* It is probably unnecessary to remind any who may read these lectures that in seventeenth-century usage *objectivement* means what we now mean by "subjectively."
[3] *Human Nature*, chap. II; italics mine.

dualistic theory was manifested in a criticism precisely opposite to the last. If the sensible qualities were held by the dualist really to be "in us," or "in our minds," or "in consciousness," to inhere "not in the object but the sentient," this seemed to imply that they are the stuff of which the mind, or consciousness, is made; and, to those who believed in a mind, or admitted the reality of consciousness as mental process or operation, this supposed implication of dualism appeared an absurdity. The very term "mental content" should presumably signify "content having the attributes of mind." But if sense-data are "mental content," then "blue" and "green" and "ill-smelling," and the like, must designate attributes of mind. Now, as Professor Woodbridge observed in one of the early American expressions of dissatisfaction with the dualism then current in psychology:

One does not ordinarily or readily believe that his consciousness or his mind is made up of colors, sounds, tastes, smells, and the like. Indeed, most well-trained and scientifically minded persons experience a shock if they are told that consciousness is so constituted. They may be willing to admit that they are conscious only when they see or hear or perform similar operations, but they find consciousness unrecognizable when told that it is made up of what they see or hear, or that such things are the elements of mind, the first things in the way of consciousness. The psychologist may be justified in using the word sensation to denote the objects of sense as well as the operation, but he is under the serious obligation of showing by what right he regards the distinctively qualitative characters of these objects as sensations, mental elements, mental factors, mental functions, or mental processes; by what right he regards as conscious or mental anything whatsoever which is characteristic of the object.[4]

Partly, then, on these grounds, Professor Woodbridge suggested that we ought to abandon "the belief in sensations," *i. e.,* the belief "in a kind of thing which is neither the stimulus nor the effect which it produces through the sense-organs on the nervous system, but which is believed to be a mental equivalent of that effect."

No doubt the infelicity of the terminology of not a few dualistic philosophers and psychologists had been such as to explain

[4] "The Belief in Sensations," *Journal of Philosophy,* 1913, p. 604. The essay was first delivered in 1910.

the imputation to them of the view that colors, sounds, *etc.,* are "consciousness," or constitute the "elements of mind"; but no such notion is essential to the doctrine, nor has it, I think, been really held even by the writers whose language tends to suggest it. When the dualist describes sensory content as "mental," he need not be understood to say that it has the same properties as are (for some philosophers) connoted by the noun "mind," nor yet that the "mind" has the properties which sensory data are experienced as having. And even when he speaks—as, unhappily, he has sometimes been known to do—of "conscious content," his too elliptical phrase should not be supposed to imply that he asserts that "content," such as color or a smell, is "conscious." All that he means, in either case, is that the particular which is the content in question exists only as a function of the event of sensing or perceiving, or the like; that it is not existentially identical with the particulars constituting the experienced content of other percipients, nor with the postulated common *cognoscendum* of them all; and that it is not a true part of the physical world.

(3) Another old confusion which perhaps helped to cause the revolt lay in the ambiguity of the word "subjective." By the "subject" of consciousness has often been meant some central, unifying entity, or point of reference, which it has been thought necessary to assume as the explanation of the individuatedness of complexes of content, as the focus through their common relation to which the elements of a perceptual field get their "unique sort of togetherness." In this sense, the "subject," or Ego, is antithetic to the object possessing definite sensible and other qualities, which is "over against" it, is "for" it, or "belongs to it." But if the contrast of "subjective" and "objective" be taken as parallel in meaning to this subject-object polarity, it is obvious that no content, whether of perception or thought, is subjective. It is of the essence of the antithesis that all determinate objects of consciousness shall not be (to use a phrase of Wilhelm Schuppe) *in den Ichpunkt hineingesetzt.* Even the things beheld in dreams or hallucinations are, in this sense, wholly objective; they, not less than

true physical objects, stand in the "over-against" relation to the Ego—whatever else may be meant by that term. The dualist, therefore, when he says that the immediate data of perception or memory are subjective existents manifestly cannot mean that they are "in the subject."

(4) The importance of keeping distinct the grounds of epistemological and those of psychophysical dualism has been emphasized in the first lecture. It is not surprising that when arguments advanced in support of one of these hypotheses were taken to be intended as direct arguments in support of the other, the reasoning was found unconvincing. A potent cause or reënforcement of the revolt against both dualisms, but especially against the psychophysical sort, originated in precisely such a misunderstanding. Certain of the evidences of the existential duality of content and *cognoscendum* were supposed to be offered as sufficient evidences of the non-physical nature of content; and since they plainly did not prove this conclusion, the conclusion itself became suspect. This objection to the dualist's argumentation, manifest in numerous writers, has been effectively put by Professor Dewey: "That the time of the visibility of light does not coincide with the time at which a distant body emitted the light is used to support an idealistic [*sc.,* dualistic] conclusion," and "the dislocation in space of the light seen and the astronomical star is used as evidence of the mental nature of the former." But how can the fact that two similar things exist at two times or places prove that one of them is "mental"—especially when the differences in date or position follow from purely physical laws?

The doubling of images of, say, the finger when the eyeball is pressed, is frequently proffered as a clincher. Yet it is a simple matter to take any body that reflects light, and by a suitable arrangement of lenses to produce not only two but many images, projected into space. If the fact that under definite physical conditions (misplacement of lenses) a finger yields two images proves the psychical character of the latter, then the fact that under certain conditions a sounding body yields one or more echoes is, by parity of reasoning, proof that the echo is made of mental stuff.[5]

[5] *Essays in Experimental Logic*, p. 250.

Of the reasoning thus imputed to the dualist this comment is destructive. But if any dualist ever reasoned in this manner, he had a poor understanding of the proper grounds of his creed. The facts mentioned—perspective distortions, diplopia, the multiplicity of visual images of a supposed single object, the finite velocity of light and sound—prove, *by themselves,* merely that perceptual content is no more identical with the object with which it is supposed to acquaint us than the image on a camera plate is numerically identical with the subject of the photograph, or the echo of a steamer's siren with the blowing of the siren; and it is only as evidence of such non-identity that the dualist cites these facts. Whether the content is physical or mental is a different question, to be examined in the light of further considerations.

It is not, however, an unrelated question. When it is once admitted that a given visual datum is not the self-same entity as the object of which it informs us, it follows that, if the datum is to be regarded as non-mental, *i. e.,* as a part of the physical world, it must be shown to behave as physical objects are assumed to behave, and to be assignable, without conflict with physical laws, to some position in space. And it is to the difficulty, not to say the impossibility, of showing this that the dualist points as "evidence that what is seen is mental content." That there may be in one place physical effects of the presence of an object in another place, and that some of these effects may resemble the object—*i. e.,* that there may be, as common sense assumes, physical images, more or less distorted—he does not, of course, deny. But he asks whether the particular images (supposing them to be such) which are experienced in perception have the specific sort of properties and relations that—at the level of common sense and traditional physics, which is the level on which the polemic of the first phase was chiefly conducted—the images on camera plates and on the retina are assumed to have, properties in virtue of which the latter images are, at that level of analysis, commonly called physical. And he finds the answer to be in the negative. The percept, unlike the image in the camera, fails, in definite ways, to manifest the usually accepted criteria of membership in the material world. Put the percept, *in addition* to the objects which it is taken to reveal, into that world at the actual moment of perception, and you seem to play havoc with the laws of physics—as has been sufficiently pointed out in the first lecture.[6] The shape and relative size of a given visual percept are, no doubt, partially dependent upon the shape and size of the images cast upon the retinas, and are thus conditioned by the optical laws which determine the characters of such images. But the percept is obviously not a retinal image; nor are there any optical laws which account for the appearance of the percept at the place at which it sensibly appears, namely, before, not behind, the eyes. There are, undeniably, optical instruments for projecting light; but they do not at all resemble the cerebral cortex and the anatomical structures surrounding it; nor, if there is in perception a projection of something into the space before the eyes, does that which is projected have the properties of light. The suggested analogy between the double images produced by pressure on the eyeball and stereopticon projections would hold only if the latter were (a) projected without the production of light-waves, (b) without a reflecting surface, (c) without producing any physical effects in the places to which they were projected, and, (d) in such a way that each image was present in the region of projection only "for" the particular stereopticon which projected it—assuming that such an expression could have any meaning as applied to stereopticons. These not only are not simple matters for the physicist, but are wholly foreign to the nature of physical processes as he conceives them.

(5) The criticism last cited rested upon two considerations; it was not solely based upon the observation that the duality of object and datum is not of itself evidence of the "mental" nature of the datum, but also upon the fact that the peculiarities of the data

---

[6] Attempts to meet the difficulty will be considered later; the point here is that at the outset of the revolt it was often simply overlooked—as by some critics of dualism it apparently still is.

which we call illusory can be physically explained. The dualist was conceived to reason in the following simple manner: "The characters I perceive are often not the character of things as they really are. The stick thrust partly under water is (as I must assume) really straight; the stick I see is bent. The latter, therefore, is not a reality but an appearance. Appearances, however, must be due to the mind and can have only a subjective existence; *ergo,* the occurrence of illusions shows that some subjective and non-physical entities exist." But—the critic observes—such illusions are consequences of processes occurring in the material world in accordance with the laws of physics. The stick seen could not be other than bent, the laws of the transmission of light and the respective densities of air and water being what they are. The same effects occur—at least a philosophical realist may consistently hold that they do—where no mind is concerned. "The visible convergence of the railway tracks," Professor Dewey wrote, "is cited as evidence that what is seen is a mental 'content,' but this convergence follows from the physical properties of light and a lens, and is physically demonstrated in a camera."[7] There is, then, no occasion to invoke a "mind" to account for illusions, nor any need to conjure up a world of "subjective appearances" or "mental content" for them to exist in.

Now if there were any dualists who really made use of the simple argument outlined—and I suppose that there were—this criticism also was sound, so far as it related to the ordinary illusions of perspective, refraction, *etc.* The illusoriness of this particular class of data, if by their illusoriness was meant simply their difference, in the ways specified, from the assumed object which they represent, was undeniably explicable on purely physical principles; and it was not necessary for a realist to assume that similar "illusions," in that sense of the term, do not exist in the material world. But, on the other hand, it did not follow from this, as the critic of dualism implied, that illusory data can be regarded as·

[7] *Op. cit.*

parts of the material world—as the physical world was then usually conceived. For they have certain additional peculiarities which physical images do not appear, and cannot be assumed, to possess; and it was from these additional peculiarities that the dualist argued—or should have argued—to the non-physical status of the data. The physicist's explanation of an illusion of perspective is complete—up to the point at which images are cast upon the two retinas; beyond that point, as has been shown, it breaks down. And—if the old story must be once more repeated—the visual sense-datum, since it can be identified neither with the two retinal images nor with the brain-state nor with the object from which the light was emitted, and since it entirely fails to manifest the properties of material bodies or to conform to the laws of physics, remains alien to the physical world even of common sense —to say nothing of recent physics. The additional peculiarities which forbid its inclusion therein are not, however, all limited to illusory data; in general they belong also to the percepts commonly regarded as veridical. But a veridical datum *corresponds* to an extra-retinal physical object; an illusory datum corresponds neither to such an object nor to the two retinal images.

There are, moreover, illusions of other kinds; and from these, the so-called "psychological illusions," another piece of evidence in favor of psychophysical dualism may be drawn. To dwell upon the physical explicability of certain purely optical illusions is therefore again to misconceive the true grounds of the dualist's opinion. For the psychological illusions are not physically explicable. Many of them are, indeed, commonly said to be effects of former experiences of the percipient; and it is possible to form a plausible picture of the physiological conditions under which such effects are produced. The stimulation of certain receptors, along with which certain other receptors have previously, and perhaps habitually, been stimulated, may be supposed to result in a reproduction of the whole of the original cortical excitation, whereupon certain quasi-sensory characters are experienced which correspond to nothing in either the present external object or the stimulus. But this conjecture as to the neuro-cerebral antecedents of the emergence of these illusions does not bring them under the laws of physics, nor does it justify their inclusion among the components of the physical world. No such "mnemic phenomena" as these are known to the physicist. Camera-plates do not make "unconscious arguments from analogy," as Helmholtz sometimes called them.[8] In the familiar illusion known as Zöllner's lines, the visual percepts consist of figures in which the long lines are—apparently for everyone—convergent. But these lines as drawn upon the printed page can be shown by measurement to be parallel; and there is, I believe, no principle known to either the old or the new physics by which two parallel lines, or their images or projections, become physically convergent when short lines are drawn across them at certain angles.

The thing chiefly significant, however, about the experience of illusions is that we are capable of recognizing them *as* illusions. This means, among other things, that the stimuli which give rise to them also give rise to images which do not correspond to those supposed to be produced in accordance with physical laws. I see the tracks as convergent, but I know that the "real tracks" are not convergent; in making this judgment I am conceiving of parallel tracks as present at the distant point—beside such and such a landmark—at which the apparent complete convergence occurs. This second effect does *not* "follow from the physical properties of light and a lens," and it cannot be "physically demonstrated in a camera."

8 "These unconscious conclusions derived from sensations are equivalent in their consequences to the so-called conclusions from analogy. Inasmuch as in an overwhelming majority of cases, whenever the parts of the retina in the outer corner of the eye are stimulated, it has been found to be due to external light coming into the eye from the direction of the bridge of the nose, the inference we make is that it is so in every case when this part of the retina is stimulated." Helmholtz, of course, adds that "just because they are not free acts of conscious thought, these unconscious conclusions from analogy are irresistible, and the effect of them cannot be overcome by a better understanding of the real relations. It may be ever so clear how we get an idea of a luminous phenomenon in the field of vision when pressure is exerted on the eye; and yet we cannot get rid of the conviction that this appearance of light is actually there at a given place in the visual field." (*Physiological Optics*, Southhall tr., 1925, III, pp. 4–5.)

(6) While misconceptions of the dualist's arguments thus had no small part in causing the revolt, the new movement perhaps owed not less to sheer lapses of memory on the part of philosophers. Certain of the natural grounds of one or the other dualism were simply forgotten, with the result that it had the look of an arbitrary and gratuitous theory offering no appreciable advantages of its own. This is illustrated in one of the important early documents of the movement, Professor Norman Kemp Smith's *Studies in the Cartesian Philosophy*. The passage is the more interesting because it too rests upon an interpretation of the representative theory of knowledge opposite to that exemplified in the first criticism cited. Professor Kemp Smith rightly recognized that, so far from excluding from "ideas" the qualities of the sensible objects of common sense, a consistent epistemological dualism transfers to its "ideas" most (at least) of those qualities; and just for this reason it seemed to him that nothing of consequence could be gained by adding a world of mental objects to the world of physical things.

> The problem how the mind can know anything, be it only a mental image, is surely as great and as real a problem as how the mind should know a material body, for all the characteristics of the external object are to be found in the image that copies it, not excluding, as Augustine insists, its extendedness. Saving the local difference between the mind and external object, there is not one difficulty that is removed by naming the image "mental."[9]

Occurring in the work of so learned and fair-minded a writer, this seems to me to exemplify especially well the part played in philosophy by a mere forgetting of considerations. One, and one only, conceivable advantage appears to be here recognized as belonging to the hypothesis of perceptual images—*viz.*, that it removes, or attempts to remove, the difficulty of conceiving how an object distant in space can be known, if we suppose the mind to be somehow localized where the brain is. But to deny that any other

[9] *Op. cit.*, (1902) p. 14*n*. It should, of course, not be assumed that this necessarily expresses its author's present view. The same caution should be observed in reading other passages here cited in illustration of early phases of the movement under discussion.

difficulties are removed by the assumption of "mental images" is to forget at least four of the principal arguments for that hypothesis. "Mental images," have at least the merits (which the "external object" does not have) of existing, by hypothesis, at the same time as the percipient event, of being directly conditioned by it, of being many and therefore of not requiring the attribution of seemingly contradictory qualities to a single entity; and the admission of their reality keeps the physical order free from the intrusion of what would be a very disturbing lot of members. These may or may not be sufficient reasons for accepting epistemological and (with respect to percepts) psychophysical dualism; but it will hardly be denied that, so far as they go, they are definite and important considerations in favor of that view. Inevitably, when they were forgotten, dualism seemed a doctrine which it was desirable, and apparently easy, to overthrow.

(7) When William James, in the essay which had so important a part in the genesis of the new realistic movement in America, turned from the question of the existence of "consciousness" to that of the status of perceptual content, he propounded a certain obvious but, as he believed, a neglected logical consideration as the solvent of the difficulty which had given rise to both epistemological and psychophysical dualism. That there is a sort of duality implied by the phenomenon of perception could not, he saw, be denied by any realist. The perceived object is by hypothesis "out there," yet it is also in some fashion "in" the mind; and the problem thereupon arose how an identical thing could occupy both positions. Thus "the whole philosophy of perception from Democritus's time downwards has been just one long wrangle over the paradox that what is evidently one reality should be in two places at once, both in outer space and in a person's mind." Representative theories of perception declared that two realities must be admitted, one in the external world, the other in the mind, but related to the former in a peculiar manner. While this seemed to James to "avoid the logical paradox," it violated "the reader's sense of life, which knows no intervening mental image,

but seems to see the room and the book just as they physically exist." The solution, overlooked by the dualist, which does justice to both aspects of our perceptual experience, lies in the simple fact that one thing may without contradiction be a member of two or more classes. "The puzzle of how the one identical room can be in two places is at bottom just the puzzle of how one identical point can be on two lines. It can, if it be situated at their intersection." [10] The physical object and the datum may thus be regarded as one and the same entity; but *quâ* object, this entity is related to one context or group of associates that constitutes the "impersonal" or "objective world," and *quâ* datum it is related to another context, constituting "the inner history of a person." Thus the real duplicity which characterizes the perceptual situation can be admitted, and yet both the numerical duality of ideas and their objects, and the metaphysical disparateness of physical things and mental contents, can be denied. "The one self-identical thing" in one context is "your 'field of consciousness'; in another it is 'the room in which you sit'; and it enters both contexts in its wholeness, giving no pretext for being said to attach itself to consciousness by one of its parts or aspects, and to outer reality by another."

Nothing could illustrate better than James's belief in the pertinency and efficacy of this short and easy method for disposing of dualism how little the true grounds of that hypothesis were kept in view twenty-five years ago, even by the ablest of those who then set about the establishment of an alternative form of realistic philosophy. It has, I trust, been made sufficiently evident in the preceding lecture that neither the thesis of the non-identity of perceptual content and *cognoscendum*, nor that of the non-physicality of content, rests upon arguments so simple and slight that they can be dissipated merely by bringing to mind the logical truism that a thing may without contradiction belong to two classes. Few philosophers can have been unaware of this possibility. But from the general possibility you cannot infer the particular fact. We

---

[10] "Does Consciousness Exist?" in *Essays in Radical Empiricism,* pp. 11ff.

may always entertain, in advance of inquiry, the hypothesis that a thing known to have certain properties or relations, *abc,* may be numerically identical with a thing which is otherwise known to have certain other properties, *xyz.* But identity is not even possible unless the attributes *abc* are compatible with *xyz.* And the whole point of the argument for the two sorts of dualism lies in the contention that the experienced properties and relations of the datum are, *in certain specific respects,* incompatible with those assumed to belong to the particular *cognoscendum,* and are also incompatible with the defining properties of the class "physical objects." I shall not again repeat these arguments; but it is evident that the dualist's premises could be relevantly and effectually attacked only by examining, point by point, the specific differences asserted by him to subsist between perceptual content and physical object, and proving each of them separately to be a difference which does not exclude existential identity.

It is true that in one passage of the same essay James seems to have recognized this as the real issue. "If"—he supposes the dualist to ask—"it be the self-same piece of pure experience, taken twice over, that serves now as the thought and now as the thing, how comes it that its attributes should differ so fundamentally in the two takings?" James accordingly considers certain—by no means all—of these incongruities between the supposed attributes of "thoughts" and those of "things." Some of them he is able to eliminate; these are attributes mistakenly imputed to "thoughts" in consequence of the old confusion between "thinking" and "thought-content," or of the assumption that when sense-data are said to be "mental" they are thereby said to be unextended. But in the end the sharpest possible contrast is set up by James himself between "mental" and "real" entities:

Mental fire is what won't burn real sticks; mental water is what won't necessarily (though of course it may) put out even a mental fire. Mental knives may be sharp, but they won't cut real wood. . . . With "real" objects, on the contrary, consequences always accrue; and thus the real experiences get sifted out from the mental ones, the things from our thoughts of them, fanciful or true, and precipitated together as the stable part of the whole experience-chaos, under the name of physical world.

This, it will be observed, applies even to our "true thoughts" of things; but, in particular, there is in our experience "a world of laxly connected fancies and mere rhapsodical objects" floating "like a bank of clouds. In the clouds all sorts of rules are violated. . . . Extensions there can be indefinitely located; motion there obeys no Newton's laws."

Now the attributes here assigned to "mental" and "real" objects respectively are plainly irreconcilable with the identity of the two classes. If the knife which is, either in fancy or in "true" perception, my immediate datum is incapable of cutting "real" wood, it has not the characteristics which, by the definition given, are essential to "real" knives. While we may "take" an individual thing or event in two relations or contexts, we do not thereby make it possible for it at once to have and not have the *same* relation to a given other term, or to cause and not cause the same effect. The final outcome of James's reasoning on the matter is thus a complete relapse into the dualism from which he set out to escape. But of this he does not seem to have been clearly aware; he apparently continued to believe that by means of the simple analogy of the point at the intersection of two lines he had justified the belief in the numerical identity of percepts and concepts with the physical objects they disclose.

Facilitated and strengthened though the revolt was by these misunderstandings and forgettings, it was prompted also by several objections which were at least pertinent to the actual dualistic position. Whether or not they were sufficient we shall consider as we now review them.

(8) One of the principal historic grounds of epistemological dualism—the argument from the physical and physiological conditionedness of our sensations—seemed to some philosophers to owe its plausibility to the neglect of a very simple logical distinction. A necessary condition for the apprehension of an event is not necessarily a determinant of the character or even of the oc-

currence of that event; its rôle may be simply permissive or instrumental rather than causal. That certain processes in outer space and in our bodies are prerequisite to the presence of sensible objects in our experience is no doubt true; but is it not a non sequitur to infer from this that the entity we directly perceive is begotten by those processes and probably owes its qualities to them? In the words of Professor Laird, we are, no doubt, "in a position to infer by exceedingly probable reasoning, that the nervous system must be stimulated whenever perception occurs," but "the most that can be extracted from this circumstance is that the nervous system is an indispensable instrument for perceiving; and this harmless truism is consistent with any theory" [11]—and therefore with the theory of the direct perception of independent physical realities.

In this criticism of the physico-physiological argument a measure of validity must be recognized. That argument has undeniably been overstrained in some classic expressions of it—for example, by Helmholtz, some of whose utterances on the subject I shall have occasion to quote in a later lecture. The mere fact that we have no visual perception of an object unless (*pace* some recent writers on theoretical physics) light has travelled from it to us, images have been cast upon the retinas, neural impulses been transmitted to the visual centers in the cortex, *etc.*, does not *of itself* enable us to decide whether the eventual percipient event is generative or merely instrumental. Yet even so, the theory of the purely instrumental rôle of the processes would be the less probable; it would appear unlikely, though not impossible, that what is found at the end of so long and complicated a series of events in nature, namely, the perceptual content, is absolutely the same— qualitatively and existentially—as the state of the remote object from which the whole transaction started. And if we begin by assuming that we have, through perception, *some* true knowledge about light, retinas, nerves, and so on, we find definite empirical evidence that certain variations in these media are followed by

[11] *A Study of Realism*, p. 30.

certain variations in the characters of our visual data. We must, then, admit either that we do *not* know the media, or else that they do not play a wholly neutral part in the transaction. And the conclusion that they do not is corroborated by the other arguments already mentioned. If the total process prerequisite to a perception is a process that takes time, its final term cannot be existentially identical with the initial one; if it admittedly produces dissimilar final terms in the experience of percipients having diverse physiological characteristics or differing spatial and temporal relations to the original position and state of the common external object, and if it does not exclude the possibility of erroneous judgments about that object—the process manifestly is not merely instrumental. Each of the arguments mentioned, in short, reënforces the others; each points to a fact which the others would naturally lead you to expect, and the whole forms a harmonious hypothesis. The logical discovery of the abstract possibility of an "instrumental theory" of perception, therefore, did not appreciably weaken the case for epistemological dualism.[12]

(9) An inherent vice in the epistemological dualist's reasoning, dubbed by some of his critics "the fallacy of transcendent implication," has been said to lie in "the supposition that one can by means of inference or implication somehow get outside content; it being self-evident, on the contrary, that if the inference or implication is followed through it cannot but terminate in an object which, like the initial object, is exhibited to the mind."[13] Such a criticism, avowedly a borrowing from Berkeley, was evidently, it need hardly be said, a curious one for a realist, even though of another sect, to urge; for it seemed to imply that the very notion of "transcendent implication" is meaningless, that only actual content can conceivably be an object of either perception or thought. This, if admitted, would seem to be as fatal to one sort of realism as to another. The epistemological monist, if he is to be a realist

---

[12] The reasons for rejecting the instrumental theory, in its generalized form, have been more fully, and very lucidly, stated by C. D. Broad in the fourth chapter of his *Perception, Physics and Reality*, especially pp. 187–204.

[13] R. B. Perry, *Journ. of Philosophy*, VII, (1910), p. 342.

at all, must assert that he knows that things which are not "exhibited to the mind" exist, and that things which happen to be at the moment objects of his perception may continue to exist at times when they are objects of nobody's perception. This assertion appears meaningless unless it means either that existences which are *not* now content can now be known as existing, or else that existences which *are* content can be *conceived as* existing "outside content"—can be "present as absent." You cannot meaningfully say that things exist unperceived and unthought-of without implying that you are somehow thinking of things as unperceived and unthought-of. The realistic thesis, in short, cannot be so much as stated except in terms of "transcendent implication." To profess a knowledge of anything whatever beyond the present content of your private consciousness is to concede, once for all, the possibility that that which is known *may* be existentially other than that which is present in consciousness at the time when it is known; and if the monistic realist claims for himself such a power of conceiving of the transcendent, he can hardly deny his dualistic brother the privilege of doing likewise. If, on the other hand, he does not claim it (and there are obvious reasons why it is illogical for him to do so), his realism is of the sort that overleaps itself and falls into a more than Berkeleian subjectivism.

(10) More happily conceived for the service of direct realism than this injudicious borrowing from the arsenal of Bishop Berkeley, is an argument which turns upon precisely the opposite consideration. Since the epistemological dualist must in the end, *i. e.,* when he attains his knowledge, such as it is, of the *cognoscendum,* claim an apprehension of the transcendent, of that which is not merely his content, why should he not assume that he is apprehending the same transcendent reality in the first place? The point has been summarily but clearly put by Professor Dunlap:

Of what use is the image? What is its function in the process of ideation? Since, in addition to being conscious of the image, I must also be conscious of the object to which it refers, should I not get on just as well if I were conscious of the object alone? Or rather, should I not get along better, since I should then have but one thing to deal with instead of two? . . . Thus the "mental image" theory is logically a failure, because it does not accomplish the specific purpose for which it apparently has been needed. As a thought-mechanism, the "mental image" is super-fluous, because consciousness must, even if it apprehends a "mental image" apprehend nevertheless, the object to which the "mental image" refers.[14]

This criticism implies more, however, than the mere redundancy of the supposititious image; it amounts to a charge of inevitable inconsistency against any generalized theory of mediate knowledge. The dualist, it is suggested, holds that we can, e. g., be aware of a thing which no longer exists; and from the fact that it no longer exists he infers that the thing must be represented by a present image of it. But—the critic now replies—the dualist himself pro-fesses to be able to contrast the present image with its original, the not-present real object. His very assertion that he knows the per-cept to be other than the object implies that he has the latter as well as the former "before his mind." But to imply this is to con-cede the falsity of his objection to the monistic view and the needlessness of the supposition that external objects cannot be apprehended directly. To prove—or even to formulate—the proposition that thoughts which are not identical with things can alone be in consciousness, he is compelled to begin by admitting that both things and thoughts can be in consciousness, and can there be distinguished and compared—the premise thus contra-dicting the conclusion which is drawn from it.

The criticism has, no doubt, an appearance of force; but it is likely to leave unshaken the dualist who keeps steadily in mind the grounds of his opinion. For it does nothing to remove those grounds. In the case of memory, for example, he will still find it impossible to conceive that a present remembrance can have no

14 "Images and Ideas" in *Johns Hopkins University Circular,* 1914, No. 3, pp. 27, 38. Substantially the same argument is employed in Professor Kemp Smith's *Prolegomena to an Idealist Theory of Knowledge,* p. 61: "Why, if the self cannot realize what lies outside itself, should we expect to find our apprehension of these objects made any more understandable when they are thus brought before the 'mind' in the form of images? Are we not simply restating in a subjectivist form that fundamental fact of self-transcendence, which, in its initial, actually experienced form, we treated as paradox, and as such refused to recognize?"

present content—that he can now remember without now having something "before the mind"; and he will still find it equally impossible to conceive that his present content is identical with a physical object which, by hypothesis, has physically ceased to exist. If that object is to be known at all through memory, then it will appear to him that it must be known through a present substitute. No objection which does not directly meet these two considerations, by showing definitely how at least one of these things which appears to him impossible *is* possible, will seem to him convincing.

It was, nevertheless, quite true that, as Dunlap complained, "the doctrine of mental images," as usually set forth, did "not in the least explain *how* consciousness can be of an absent object." The dualist, in other words, had failed to fulfil one of the obligations entailed by his theory. Convinced that there was—that if knowledge is possible at all there must be—such a phenomenon as the "consciousness of an absent object," he had omitted to describe in detail, in intelligible psychological terms consistent with his hypothesis, precisely in what this phenomenon consisted. The paradox which appeared to be implicit in the theory thus remained unalleviated; and the term "transcendent reference," lacking such definition and psychological elucidation, had about it an air of mystery which was naturally repellent to critical minds —though, doubtless, naturally alluring to minds that craved a dash of incomprehensibility in their metaphysics. Until this failure of the dualist was repaired, his position was undeniably insecure. At best the opposition of the two types of epistemology seemed to end in an antinomy. The dualist apparently could, on his side, show the theory of the epistemological monist to be impossible; but he had not clearly disposed of a consideration which his adversary regarded, and could plausibly regard, as rendering the dualistic theory unintelligible, or even self-contradictory.

The dualist, to be sure, was in this respect in no worse case than any other realist—even the sort of realist who, though calling himself an idealist, believes that he knows today events of yesterday which, whatever be true of the Absolute, are not now truly present in his own finite experience. "Transcendent implication," the assumption of the possibility of a consciousness of absent objects, is, as we have seen, inherent in any philosophy except "the solipsism of the specious present"—if that be a philosophy. But the fact was not explicitly recognized by other and less self-observant philosophers, whereas the dualist expressly insisted upon it; and the failure to clarify this concept was therefore more injurious to his doctrine than to any other. In this instance, then, the critic of dualism attacked a point of real weakness—though, as he remained happily unaware, his own position was equally weak at the same point.

(11) To some resolute realists at all times since the middle of the eighteenth century, epistemological dualism has seemed a doctrine sufficiently condemned by its history. It is, they have been accustomed to point out, a synthesis of conceptions with which the philosophic mind has already experimented; and the result of the experiment is patent. The Cartesian and Lockian attempt to combine the belief in a (more or less) knowable physical world with the hypothesis of representative ideas speedily broke down into the subjective idealism of Berkeley and the scepticism of Hume; and any new endeavor to compound a philosophy out of the same ingredients may be expected to pass through the same phases to the same outcome. This moral had been drawn from the history of modern philosophy by Reid almost a century and a half before the outbreak of the contemporary revolt against the theory of ideas. Descartes, observed Reid,

no sooner began to dig in this mine than scepticism was ready to break in upon him. He did what he could to shut it out. Malebranche and Locke, who dug deeper, found the difficulty of keeping out this enemy still to increase; but they labored honestly in the design. Then Berkeley bethought himself of an expedient. . . . By giving up the material world, which he thought might be spared without loss and even with advantage, he hoped, by an impregnable partition, to secure the world of spirits. But, alas! the "Treatise on Human Nature" wantonly sapped the foundations of this partition, and drowned all in one universal deluge. These

facts . . . give reason to apprehend that Descartes' system of human understanding . . . hath some original defect; that this scepticism is inlaid
in it, and reared along with it.[15]

Now the initiators of the new movement in British and American philosophy at the beginning of the present century were not
of a sceptical humor. The native realistic faith of man was vigorously resurgent in them. Their revolt being primarily against
idealism in all its forms, their aversion from the theory of representative ideas, it is usually pretty clear, was not a little inspired
by the feeling, to which history thus seemed to give abundant
sanction, that a dualistic realism is a hopelessly insecure kind of
realism. Let the dualist protest never so stoutly that he too believes in the possibility of a knowledge of objective truths and in
the reality of a physical world; in declaring the immediate data
of perception, or the contents of our reflective judgments, to be
subjective things distinct from the objects known, he has left an
opening through which, precisely as Reid described, the tide of
subjectivism will sweep and eventually submerge the whole position. For the historically actual result of the Cartesian dualism
has appeared to such latter-day revivers of realistic philosophy to
be also a logically inescapable consequence. To say that we never
apprehend material things directly is to imply that we never really
apprehend them at all; a dualistic theory of perception simply
makes a knowledge of the external world inconceivable.

As a reply to the reasonings of the epistemological dualist this
criticism, by itself, was not merely inconclusive; it tended to a conclusion opposite to that expressed. For the dualist's contention,
in part, was that certain propositions about the physical world
which the realistic authors of the criticism necessarily admit to be
true, clearly imply that we cannot know the objects in that world
directly. For example, the critic does not deny that light and
sound have a finite velocity; nor that we have brains and nervous
systems and that our sensations can be empirically shown to be

[15] *Inquiry into the Human Mind*, chap. I, Sect. 6. For the same argument as
elaborated by more recent critics of dualism, *cf. The New Realism*, pp. 5–10.

conditioned by these; nor that our acquaintance with objects out-side the body is mediated through long sequences of physical processes in external space; nor that the observers of what the critic (at least usually) holds to be one physical object get from it dissimilar percepts. The dualist—wherever he may end—starts in his reasoning from precisely the picture of the world which the realist who would reject dualism accepts as a true picture; and it is primarily in this picture that the evidence for the non-identity of perceptual content and known object is found. What the epistemological dualist is most certain about, in short, is that physical realism is incompatible with the hypothesis of the immediacy of knowledge—and also with that of the physical status of all content. You do not meet *this* argument by retorting that the conclusion of it places realism itself in a perilous position. Unless the specific reasons for regarding realism and the theory of direct perception as a logically impossible combination are dealt with and shown to be invalid, that conclusion stands; if it can in turn be demonstrated that a dualistic realism must inevitably lapse into subjectivism, then, obviously, it is Bishop Berkeley who, at the end of this family quarrel between the two sorts of realists, remains upon the scene as the *tertius gaudens.* But the family quarrel ought to be settled first. It is to an attempt to settle it that these lectures are in the main to be devoted. It is, at any rate, clear that the logically primary questions, when the new movement began, were not whether the dualist's conclusion leads to consequences unwelcome to realistically-minded philosophers, nor even whether it has consequences which destroy its own prem-ises; but whether the premises can by any realist, and especially by an adherent of direct realism, be denied, and whether from such premises the conclusion in fact follows. Nevertheless, the fact that this conclusion had historically tended—and might plausibly be thought to tend of necessity—to a consequence which itself seemed to such philosophers impossible, was a good reason for at least making a fresh attempt to combine the two doctrines which both the dualist and the idealist had declared to be incapable of logical synthesis.

The constructive program of the first main phase of the revolt was of the sort that the necessities of the situation seemed to require. Since it appeared that to grant that any content is "mental," *i. e.*, is produced by or relative to the cognitive event, leads to the conclusion that all of it is, and since this in turn was supposed to lead, and in one great historic instance had led, to subjectivism, the only sure way to save realism, it seemed, was to maintain that no content is psychically generated or dependent upon the percipient function. This implied the adoption—though for different reasons—of the one or the other of the views about "consciousness" suggested by the articles of James and G. E. Moore to which I have referred; *i. e.*, the fact, hitherto designated by that term, that things are experienced, or "get reported," must be regarded either as the entrance of independent objective entities into an "external relation" to the percipient bodily organism, or else as a bare and sterile awareness of such entities. And since indirect or representative knowledge was assumed to be inconceivable, it must be held that the immediate content of an experience is always identical with the reality cognized in that experience. No shadowy "ideas" could be permitted to obtrude themselves between us and the real world. Percepts, therefore, must always be not only physical objects (or parts thereof), but *the* physical objects with which knowing is concerned. Thus everything which is ever "before the mind" at all must be regarded as "objective." We must, it was proclaimed by the authors of a celebrated revolutionary manifesto, return to a metaphysical state of nature, to that "naïve or natural realism" which "makes no distinction between seeming and being," but believes that "things *are* just what they seem." [16]

These pronunciamentos, however, did not always mean all that they at first seemed to mean; and the program of some of the

[16] *The New Realism*, pp. 10 and 2.

revolutionists was less simple and also much less thorough than it looked. For an important group among them, while nominally preaching a return to naïve realism, in fact adhered to a highly sophisticated metaphysical theory which in certain respects had much in common with the dualism which it was designed to supplant—if, indeed, it presented any alternative to it. In the doctrine of some American neo-realists, in particular, a distinction, unknown to common sense, between "being" and "reality," or "real being," was fundamental. And it was primarily with the world of being and not with the world of reality that their philosophy had to do. Their realism, in short, was first of all a logical realism; if it denied that there are such things as ideas, it emphatically affirmed that there are such things as Ideas. The world of "being" was defined as including all actual or possible objects of thought—not only all that it has entered into the mind of man to conceive, but all that an infinitely more comprehensive and imaginative mind might conceive. It is, in short, equivalent to the realm of "possibles" of the orthodox metaphysical tradition. It contains fairies, hobgoblins, false gods, golden mountains, the square root of minus one, as well as trees and tables and organic bodies and atoms and electrons. While some of these are not "real," i. e., do not "exist," all alike "subsist"; they *are*, whether any mind chances at any moment to be aware of them or not. The essential thesis of this form of the new realistic doctrine was then, in sum, "that every content, whether term or proposition, real or unreal, subsists in its own right in the all-inclusive universe of being; that it has being as any mathematical or physical term has being; and that this being is not 'subjective' in its nature." [17]

That such a realism is far from "naïve" is evident from its definition. It is much less congenial to the plain man than is the dualism outlined in the preceding lecture. For the plain man certainly does not conceive that the table that he sees and touches is an eternal and immutable subsistent; nor that the monsters he sees in a nightmare have a "being" of their own when undreamed of;

[17] E. B. Holt in *The New Realism*, p. 366.

nor that there is any sense in which the entity "Charles I dying in his bed" can be said to be, other than the sense that it may conceivably be talked or thought about. The very notion of a sort of "being" that is distinct from "being real," and equally distinct from being perceived or imagined, is to the natural man exceedingly tenuous and elusive. It is not necessarily the worse on that account; what I am suggesting is merely that this type of realism is not entitled to make the best of both worlds. It cannot claim the virtue, or supposed virtue, of metaphysical naïveté, and at the same time make use from the outset of a refined and subtle distinction and an abstract speculative theorem, of which even the meaning escapes the grasp of those not philosophically initiated.

The introduction of this concept of a realm of "being" which includes "unreal" as well as "real" beings created a new logical situation in which, as the proponents of this view believed, certain of the usual arguments for dualism lost their force. It made it possible, for example, to admit the validity of the reasonings which had led dualists to maintain the unreal and non-physical status of (at least) the types of content usually recognized as non-veridical, without admitting that such content is therefore "mental" or "subjective," i. e., generated by the mind of the percipient and confined in its being to the occasions on which it is experienced. The dilemma which had usually been taken for granted by the dualist—*either* physically real *or* mental—was no longer assumed to be unavoidable; there remained the third possibility that data, or some of them, may be unreal and yet "objective," in the sense in which everything that can be thought of was declared to be objective. Thus when the realist of the new fashion made the seemingly paradoxical generalization that "as things are perceived so they are," he presently explained that he by no means signified by this that "as things are perceived *so they really are, i. e.,* all perceived things are real things." [18] His thesis thus appeared to be no paradox, but rather to verge upon the innocuously platitudinous; for it is obviously impossible for any experienced

18 Holt in *The New Realism,* p. 358.

datum to "be" other than what *it* is experienced as being. But the thesis, of course, did not wholly reduce to this platitude, for it was meant to imply that the same datum has also some significant status called "being" over and above its being perceived.

This doctrine, then, that everything that can possibly be thought or imagined has a sort—albeit a tenuous and ghostly sort—of objectivity *seemed* to present a possible alternative to the older dualistic view concerning the status of such data as are admittedly unreal—the objects of error, illusion, dream, hallucination and imagination. Whether it was in fact significantly different from that view we shall inquire shortly. Meanwhile we have to ask what its bearing was upon the cases in which perception is supposed to make us acquainted with real and physical objects. The type of realism with which we are just now concerned did not, of course, question that there are such objects nor that they are perceived by us: it was a physical as well as a logical realism. What, then, is the nature of the entities which not only "are" but also "really are," and in particular of those which have physical existence; and what is their relation to the percepts through which we know them? If both object and percept were assumed to consist of pure subsistents, to have only "being" and not existence, they might—supposing the percept to be veridical—be conceived to be identical, in the sense in which any logical essence is necessarily identical with itself. That physical objects *are* so constituted was sometimes asserted by some of the American neo-realists, notably by Mr. Holt, who declared that "matter analyzes out completely into mathematical entities, and leaves no residue by way of material brickbats." [19] But if "mathematical entities" means entities having only the sort of being ascribed by pure mathematicians to the universals of which they discourse, such a thesis, a sort of ultra-Platonic doctrine which would reduce even sensible things to timeless and placeless essences, amounts to an obliteration of the physical world and of the distinction between "real" and "unreal" objects of thought. To be "real" must be

19 *The New Realism*, p. 368.

conceded—and, in fact, despite occasional utterances which seemed to say the contrary, was by realists of this school commonly conceded—to be a great deal more than to subsist as a mathematical entity. The "real" world was defined as the system of objects having situations and relations in a common space and time and causally affecting one another, while the "unreal" consists of all the actual or possible objects of thought which have no place in the spatio-temporal system and are "sterile of consequences," acting neither upon entities of the former, or physical, sort, nor upon the mind so as to cause it to become aware of them.[20] But, as Mr. Holt observed, time and space are the "great individuators"; and since real things have spatial and temporal determination and belong to the causal nexus, they are not universals but particulars. But as particulars having diverse dates, situations, and rôles in the dynamic processes of nature, physical things, of course, could not be existentially identified with one another. "Within any whole we find that no part can be identically repeated. The molecule of water so far as its being goes can be and is repeated indefinitely, but the molecule of water that is part of a coherent system, as it is in the chemist's test-tube, is just itself and no other."[21] But, for analogous reasons, percepts also must be held to be particulars. They too "exist," and cannot be assigned to the limbo of pure timeless being; they have dates and—at any rate in the case of vision and touch—relative spatial positions, whether we say that they are in the same space with physical objects or in private spaces; and though they do not appear to have the same sort of causal efficacy, conforming to the same laws, as physical objects, it is at least not undisputable that they have none at all. And if it is granted that they too are particulars, then the long recognized and often repeated reasons for denying that percepts and their respective *cognoscenda* can be identical existents retain their force. A given percept also "is just itself and no other." The argument, outlined in the first lecture, for epistemo-

[20] Montague in *The New Realism*, pp. 255ff.
[21] Holt, *The Concept of Consciousness*, p. 43.

logical dualism thus remained wholly unaffected by the introduction of the theory of the eternal extra-mental subsistence of
logical entities. And this was, on occasion, apparent even in the
writings of philosophers most zealous for that theory and most
insistent upon its importance for our understanding of the nature
of perception. No dualist need have the least reluctance to admit
the identity of content and object in the only sense in which it appeared, in the end, to be affirmed by such philosophers—namely,
in the sense of partial, and perhaps merely schematic, resemblance. To maintain *only* that "images are as essentially identical
with a certain portion of the concrete object studied as the engi-
neer's designs are with the concrete particular ship or trestle
that is constructed in accordance with them"[22] was to concede the
truth of the doctrine of representative images—in other words, to
abandon altogether the revolt against epistemological dualism.

Still, it may be urged, the thesis of the objective subsistence of
all possible objects of thought does not leave unaffected the position of psychophysical dualism; it renders that unnecessary by
providing—in the way already indicated—an alternative view
consonant with the admitted facts upon which such dualism had
been based. Percepts, whether veridical or illusory, are not "mental" because all alike have "being," and "being" is not a status
conferred upon things by a mind, or by the accident of their being
attended to. The percept subsists before and after it is experienced; being eternal, it can be no offspring of a percipient event
in time. Yet there was, I think, even here no significant difference
between this new variety of realism and the old psychophysically
dualistic view with regard to content. It is not necessary for a
consistent dualist to deny—if it gives anyone satisfaction to assert
—that his percept of a table or his dream-image of a hippogriff
both "were" before his perception or his dream began—in the
sense in which *Hamlet* was before Shakespeare was born, or the

---

[22] Holt, *op. cit.*, p. 271. In Professor Montague's contribution to *The New
Realism* the theory of knowledge propounded was frankly and consistently dualistic,
though it was associated with an original and interesting theory of the physical
status of percepts, somewhat akin to that later advanced by Mr. Bertrand Russell.

Panama Canal before it was dug. For it manifestly does not follow from this that the *existence* of the percept or of the image
is not dependent upon the occurrence of a percipient act and limited to the time during which and the context in which the percept
is by an individual being experienced. The eternal subsistence of
the Idea of the Panama Canal did not, before 1914, make it unnecessary for ships to go round the Horn in order to pass from the
Atlantic to the Pacific, nor render superfluous the labors of Goe-
thals and his associates. As little does the supposed eternal subsistence of a universal of which a given percept is a concrete
instance or particularization make it unnecessary for that percept
to be brought into existence in the temporal world, nor render
superfluous the assumption of some generating cause of its existence. It is wholly with the world of existence, not with that of
subsistence, that the contentions of the historic dualists, as of their
present-day successors, are concerned. And between subsistence
and existence there is not merely all the difference in the world;
there is all the difference between being in and of the world and not
being in or of it. Now, not only was there nothing in the notion
of the subsistence of percepts to imply that a given bit of content,
e. g., a dream-image, had a physical existence when unexperienced; if *all* that was maintained with regard to its objectivity
was that it subsisted before and after the dream, it was by implication admitted *not* to have had physical existence when unexperienced.[23] And in any case the fairly evident reasons for not attributing to it such existence remained untouched. I am not, for the
moment, insisting that those reasons are conclusive; I am merely
pointing out that the doctrine of the subsistential objectivity of
essences had no bearing whatever upon that issue. That doctrine,
in short, did not imply either that data, *when* they exist, are *not*
mental or that they *are* physical.

　　We must conclude, then, that the attack of those who pro-

[23] "Before" and "after" are, of course, not properly applicable to subsistence; to
pure being time-determinations are simply irrelevant. If this is borne in mind, the
conclusion above becomes still more evident. But I have not thought it worth
while to dwell upon this consideration.

claimed so enthusiastically the objectivity of the subsistent was not in reality directed against the dualistic position at all—either against its epistemological or its psychophysical portion. The whole episode, whatever its interest or importance in itself, was irrelevant to the issue with which these lectures are occupied. I have dealt with it here only because it has been commonly supposed to be a part of the revolt against dualism, and is by some supposed to be the most significant and most effective part of it. But the tactics of a genuine insurgency must be more radical; the true goal of the revolution was to establish the contentions that (a) data are not merely in essence but in existence identical with the entities which they enable us to know, and (b) percepts and all other content can legitimately be regarded as "real" and physical existents.

That this goal has not been and cannot be attained is one of the clearest results of the philosophical discussion of the past twenty-five years. The first phase of the revolt has been a failure. No effective or credible way has been found for reconciling pan-objectivism,[24] in its strict and literal form, with those familiar facts of experience and those (by the objectivist) undisputed assumptions on which natural dualism rests. This will become evident when we recall to what strange shifts the would-be consistent monistic realist was compelled to resort, what extraordinary corollaries he was constrained to accept, in his efforts to reconcile his doctrine with these facts and assumptions, and what lapses from his own creed he has in the end been unable to avoid.

(1) Let us consider first what could be done in such a theory with the fact of the finite velocity of light. What was to be proved by the monistic realist was that, in spite of this fact, the visual percept is identical with part of the perceived object, which is to say, also, that it is a true part of the material world. But this statement of the theorem is not definite. With *what* physical object is the percept to be identified? There are three conceivable

---

[24] This word is exasperating to philologists; but I know of no other equally convenient brief designation for the general type of theory here under consideration.

variants of the theory of identity, with respect to this point. By the physical object perceived might be meant, first, a causal object such as physical science already recognizes, *e. g.,* a distant star, acting through stimuli upon our nerves and through these upon our brains, and thus giving rise to a perception—according to the monistic view, a perception of itself. But to make the meaning of "object" here really precise we must give the object a date; *i. e.,* even if we conceive of it as a perduring thing, we must designate the particular transient state or phase of it which is to be shown to be identical with a given moment's perceptual content. When, then, the date is added, the first possible interpretation of the theory of identity would be that the visual percept is qualitatively and existentially identical with the external causal object as it is at the moment when the light is emitted from it.

But this form of the theory was, on the face of it, incapable of reconciliation with the admission of the finite velocity of light—as it is perhaps hardly necessary to repeat. The percept comes into being after the object—in this sense—has ceased to exist; and if, as this way of construing the theory of identity assumes, the percept now exists at the place where the supposed perduring object was when the light-ray left it, it exists at a place at which neither that object nor, usually, any like object known to the inventories of physical science is present. Thus the identification of the percept with *this* object was absolutely excluded. It could only be with some *other* object—or some other state of the same postulated perduring object—that the percept could conceivably be identified. It was, in other words, necessary to transform the meaning of the theorem of identity, so that "object" might mean something strictly coexistent in time with the percept at the place—or in the direction relative to the eye of the observer—in which the percept appeared. This necessity was not, I think, generally recognized by those who were active in the early polemic of the new realism; like most philosophers, no doubt, they were not always very prompt to observe the remoter, weirder and less welcome implications of their hypothesis. But the necessity was apparent to some of them, and at least one, Professor Dawes Hicks, clearly and frankly insisted upon it as a plain implication of a monistic theory of perception. The specific view which he proposed, in order to carry out this implication, was to the effect that the visual percept experienced at the present moment is identical existentially and in its qualities and relative position with the perduring object from which the light came, *as that object now is.*[25] Such a view, of course, requires a very extensive revision of the usual conception of the rôle of the stimulus. It is commonly assumed that the light-waves in some fashion transmit at least some approximation to the momentary two-dimensional geometric pattern of the complex of moving particles by which they are set in motion, and imprint this pattern upon the retina, much as they do upon a camera-plate; and that the character of this retinal image—itself thus predetermined by the stimulus—determines in turn, under ordinary circumstances, the characters of the perceptual content. No one, so far as I know, has ever maintained that camera-plates are somehow automatically post-dated—that photographs show the true appearance of the object represented not at the instant when the light left the object, but at the instant—which in the case of astronomical photographs may be many thousands of years later—when the light reaches the camera. Yet in the case of perception, the proposed solution implies, there occurs precisely such post-dating. What we actually perceive is *not* the pattern which the light-wave conveyed to the retina, but a substitute therefor, which is somehow mysteriously made to match an object synchronous with itself, from which no stimulus has yet reached the end-organs. This would mean either that the stimulus—at least so far as concerns its specific quality, such as wave-length, or the like—is essentially otiose; or else that it has a curious prophetic gift—that it can, when setting out from or passing through a region of space, receive, or be affected by, the pattern of something that is not there, and possibly does not yet exist. It was substantially

[25] *Proceedings of the Aristotelian Society,* 1911–12, pp. 165–183.

the former alternative that Mr. Hicks adopted; but he observed that a certain rôle in the affair can be assigned to the stimulus if we distinguish between the event or act of perceiving and the perceived content. The latter, consisting of specific qualities, such as color, is not "mental." The act of perceiving, on the other hand, "is certainly mental"; it is "the mental act or state of consciousness in and through which there is awareness." Now the various physical and physiological phenomena antecedent to the occurrence of a perception—"the wave-motions, the retinal image, the nerve-change, the cerebral disturbance"—doubtless are necessary to evoke or prompt the act of perceiving; but "there is no reason whatever for saying that they in any way intrude into the content apprehended." The "conditions involved in the genesis of the cognitive act" are not identical with "the conditions involved in that act's relation to the object." This relation is not mediate but direct; the "act of perceiving is directed upon the real thing," though it is always a process of selection and "can never exhaust the wealth of detail of concrete reality." Because of this partial and selective character of the perceptive act we may, if we like, distinguish between percept and physical object; "but this is not a distinction of two existences." "The percept is not a *tertium quid* between the act of perceiving and the real thing."

In accordance with this general view, then, Professor Hicks concluded that the time-interval required for the transmission of light is no evidence that the visually perceived content is not identical (so far as it goes) qualitatively and existentially with the distant physical object apprehended. From the fact that eight minutes elapse between the beginning and end of the process by which a ray of light passes from the sun to the retina, "it does not at all follow," he contended, "that the sun we are perceiving is the sun of eight minutes ago. Although the wave-motions set out on their journey eight minutes ago, there is no reason whatsoever why, by the act of perceiving to which those wave-motions give rise, we should be incapable of apprehending the sun as it now is." What really happens in these cases Mr. Hicks explained as follows. "Let A represent a certain star as it existed a hundred years ago, and A¹ the same star as it exists now. Wave-motions have been transmitted from A to B, the bodily organism of a percipient subject. They have taken a hundred years to reach B. The influence which they exert is conveyed by the optic nerve to the brain and, in conjunction with the brain change, a state of consciousness, C, ensues, the act, namely, of perceiving the star." Now—observes Mr. Hicks—"there is nothing in the mere recital of what has taken place between A and C to prove that C is the act of perceiving A, rather than A¹'"; and there are, he finds, "psychological reasons" for holding that it *is* A¹, rather than A, that is perceived by means of C. These reasons appear to consist in the assumption that epistemological dualism cannot be true, at least with respect to sense-perception. The specific character of the stimulus, then, has no part in determining the specific character of the perceptual content. A light-wave from an object which (since the objectivity of secondary qualities is also implied) is actually and objectively blue reaches the eye and affects the visual receptors in the manner of what we may call a "blue stimulus"; and these in turn presumably transmit to the optic nerve the impulse which is the distinctive effect of that particular sort of stimulation. If the distant object has continued to be blue during the interval, a sensation of blue will thereupon emerge in consciousness. But it is not in consequence of the "blue" quality of the stimulus that the blue sensation arises. For if, in the meantime, the same object has turned red, precisely the same stimulus which in the former case was followed by a sensation of blue will now be followed by a sensation of red. The stimulus does not convey any information to consciousness; it merely acts as a releasing mechanism. It is the pressure on the button, or the spark which touches off the powder; "consciousness" thereupon does the rest. All kinds of stimulus may be followed by the same kind of sensation; and the same kind of stimulus may be followed, on different occasions, by wholly dissimilar sensations. In defense of the legitimacy of these suppositions Professor Hicks further pointed out that it has not been shown empirically that we in fact see now non-existent objects or states of objects.

That a star extinguished a century ago, the wave-motions from which take (say) two centuries to reach me, would still be visible in the heavens, that if I were to travel for the next 50 years at the rate at which the ether waves have been traveling from it to me, but in the reverse direction, toward the position once occupied by the star, I should not only go on perceiving the star as object, but that it would appear larger and larger to me as I proceeded, and that its features would be discriminated with constantly increasing accuracy—all this, I submit, is not established scientific fact, but unverified hypothesis based on the equally unverified hypothesis that what I perceive consists either of ether vibrations or of the effects of ether vibrations.[26]

This bold and ingenious hypothesis is, perhaps, the less strange of the two imaginable ways of attempting to reconcile the finite velocity of light with a genuinely monistic theory of perception. But it can hardly be regarded as a successful means of accomplishing that end. For it has a number of implications which are not only extremely odd, but plainly inconsistent either with admitted empirical facts or with assumptions which physical science is hardly likely to abandon even for the sake of escaping dualism.

For example, there should, I take it, upon such a hypothesis, be a marked discrepancy between the results reached in astronomy by direct observation and by photography. The photograph, it seems to be admitted, shows a planet or a group of stars as it was when the light-waves left it; but the percept, according to Professor Hicks, shows each of these bodies "as it is now." But each has by now changed in various ways, some of which should be appreciable; some stars may have split in two, others have become extinct; and the more rapidly variable stars have been going through their periodic fluctuations in brightness. The astronomer should consequently see with the naked eye—and presumably also through his telescope—a very different aspect of the heavens from that which he sees in his photographs taken at the same time. No such discrepancy, of course, is found. The only way

[26] *Op. cit.*, p. 180.

out of this embarrassment, for the theory in question, would seem to be through the setting-up of a supplementary hypothesis, to the effect that photographs and reflections, unlike other material objects, are perceived by us, not as *they* are now, but as they ought to be in order to depict the present appearance of the objects they image!

Again, consider what must be supposed to happen, on this hypothesis, when a star *does* become extinct. It may be that monistic philosophers are prepared to assure astronomers for "psychological reasons" that no such phenomenon as the extinction of a star ever occurs in nature. This would certainly be a novel and important contribution to astronomy from an unexpected quarter. But if the possibility of extinction—for example, by disruption—is admitted, what then happens to the astronomers or to other percipient organisms whose eyes are at that moment turned towards the star? If they are to be saved from seeing that region of space as it is *not,* their sensation of light from the place occupied by the star at the moment of disruption must instantaneously cease. Yet, admittedly, light from that place will continue to beat upon the retinas of astronomers for days, years, or generations, thereafter. Either, then, the stimulus will during all this period evoke no sensation at all; or else the astronomers will immediately see the star "as it now is," in the sense that they will see its fragments, large and small, luminous or non-luminous, scattered in many directions through the immensities of celestial space. Either alternative seems to lack plausibility. A similar difficulty is suggested by the famous observation by which the finite velocity of light was originally demonstrated by Roemer. The moons of Jupiter in their orbital revolutions periodically disappear from the astronomer's view behind the shadow of the planet and after a time emerge on the other side. It is evident that some singularly considerate behavior on the part of the moons would thereupon become requisite, by the present hypothesis, in order that the terrestrial astronomer may observe one of these satellites just peeping from behind its planet at precisely the instant at which it is actually in that position, relatively to the earth. It is not supposed in that hypothesis, as we have seen, that the light-wave is absolutely superfluous. It is necessary to touch off the "act of perceiving." Now at the moment when a satellite first emerges from eclipse, or at least at some corresponding moment, no light-wave from that point is reaching the astronomer's eye. Consequently there is no stimulus to release the "act of perceiving." Consequently the satellite must pause in its revolution until the light reaches the eye. If there happen to be astronomers on other planets, i. e., at different distances, this would be an especially difficult requirement for the satellite to live up to.

Plainly, the hypothesis proposed as indispensable in the interest of a monistic psychology of perception would require the astronomers and the specialists in optics to discard virtually the whole of their present sciences and start over again on an almost completely new set of presuppositions. For example, the theory of refraction would necessarily go by the board; for that theory is an explanation of the supposed fact that, in certain cases, we do not see bodies in the direction in which they actually lie (or lay), but in other directions. If we always saw things as and where they are, there would be nothing to explain. Again, the test of the correctness of Einstein's theory of gravitation by measurement of the deviation of a light-ray in consequence of its passage through the gravitational field of the sun would, upon this hypothesis, be impossible. That there is a deviation, observation could never discover. It really seems simpler to give up the theory of the identity of perceptual datum and physical object than to reconstruct optics and astronomy so extensively.

Nor is it only with the assumptions of astronomers that the suggested hypothesis would conflict; it would be equally evidently at variance with the most familiar facts of every-day terrestrial experience. We know, of course, by the most abundant evidences, that there is a uniform concomitant variation between changes in the specific character of the stimulus and change in the "content apprehended." The fact is known to every child in the nursery who has ever seen the light from a luminous object passed through a colored glass. But upon the present hypothesis it should not be a fact. For if the "cognitive act" has the wonderful power of discerning remote objects just as they now really are, undisturbed by such circumstances as the wave-length of the light-stimulus or the character of the retinal image, how should other media sometimes intervening before that act occurs—a bit of glass, a drop of water—be able to rob it of that power?

What all this serves to illustrate is the extreme lengths to which those adherents of the monistic view who were clear-sighted enough to discern its less obvious implications were compelled to go, by the immanent logic of their, at first sight, seemingly innocuous and attractive assumption. Either this, or an alternative which is hardly likely to be preferred, must necessarily be adopted by anyone who, without denying that light is transmitted with a finite velocity, affirms the identity of any extra-corporeal physical object with the visual percept.

The alternative would be to hold that the present content of a visual perception is identical, not with the present state of a perduring object from which, in some previous state, the light emanated, but with some *other* physical object, some real character-complex, now actually occupying the position in space which the perceptual datum appears to occupy. As compared with Mr. Hicks's hypothesis this supposition would, for the purposes of the monistic philosopher, have some advantages and some disadvantages. It would have the advantage of permitting bodies which we usually designate by the term "stars" to retain the characteristics and relative positions which astronomy assigns to them; for it would have no implications whatever as to the present state and arrangement of the stars which are entered in the catalogues of the astronomers. And it would be free from the rather arbitrary and, in its implications, embarrassing assumption that, though the light-stimulus conveys no information as to what and where a star was when the light set out from it, it is nevertheless always some subsequent state of what we call the *same* star that perception reveals. But on the other hand, such a supposition would imply that we can know nothing at all, at least through perception, about the particular stars which astronomers are accustomed to talk about—since, once more, those stars are supposed *not* necessarily to exist, at the moment of perception, in the places or directions in which the perceptual star is observed, nor to have, at that moment, precisely the characters which the perceptual star exhibits. The only stars we should ever see would be quite unknown to astronomy. This seems an inconvenient supposition to entertain. And even if—inconsistently—the existence of the astronomer's stars were also assumed, it would still be implied— as in the hypothesis previously mentioned—that the specific character of the original light-emitting object, or of the stimulus, or of intervening media, had nothing to do with the nature of the resultant experience—in spite of the considerations both theoretical and empirical which oblige us—or at least should oblige a monistic realist—to believe the contrary. Finally—not to prolong unduly the recital of the peculiar consequences of such a hypothesis about perception—these luminous objects scattered about in space, though unknown to astronomers, would not be, in any full-blooded sense, physical: that is to say, they would not conform to any of the physical laws which have been reached through inferences from experience tested by observation of the congruence of their implications with further experience; nor would they, in particular, have any inferrible dynamic interaction either with one another or with scientific objects. The empirically grounded equations of the physicist would not hold good of the countless purely optical entities supposed to exist at any given moment in the regions where the perceptual objects of the innumerable percipients appear. Thus the hypothesis would not even accomplish the end for which alone it could be designed; it would not justify the assertion of the identity of percepts with what could properly be called physical objects. On the whole, then—if a choice is in such a case possible—Mr. Hicks's hypothesis is rather to be recommended for adoption by epistemologically monistic realists who have some concern for consistency.

Beyond the three mentioned, there seem to be no further possible ways of particularizing the meaning of "object" in the proposition "the perceptual (visual) datum and the external real object (or some physical part of it) are identical."[27] In one of these ways, then, the proposition must be understood; and I take it to be more than sufficiently clear that, when any definite meaning is thus assigned to it, the proposition is untenable. Taken in the first way, it directly conflicts with the fact of the finite velocity of light; taken in either of the other ways, it does not do this, but it entails ulterior conclusions and requires supplementary hypotheses which it is impossible to believe.

(2) This result alone is sufficient to make evident the failure, and the inevitability of the failure, of the first phase of the revolt. If it is impossible, for the reasons already indicated, to reconcile a thorough-going monistic realism with what we know—or with what a believer in that theory must assume that we know—about optical phenomena, then the fate of this type of realism is settled. The hypothesis has been subjected to a logical *experimentum crucis* and has been shown thereby to be inadmissible. It is, therefore, logically unnecessary to pursue the question further. But it is, perhaps, inexpedient to rest a conclusion so important upon a single argument, however decisive it may seem. It is possible to show that the neo-realistic enterprise broke down at other points also; and it is worth while to notice the nature and causes of its failure in at least one of these other instances.

Let us, then, turn to that class of experiences which first gave rise to the belief in a realm of being consisting of apprehended but non-physical, and at least in that sense "mental," particulars —the experiences of illusion, dream, hallucination, creative phantasy. The content of these also must, of course, in a realistic

[27] It might, of course, conceivably be held that the percept is a physical object inside the body of the percipient organism—presumably in the brain. This theory, in the three different forms in which it has been propounded by Mr. Bertrand Russell, we shall examine in lectures six and seven.

philosophy untainted with metaphysical dualism (with respect to content) be given a place among "real" and "physical" existents. But the question here too necessarily arose: with *what* physical realities *where,* are the illusions of the senses, the appearances in dreams, the visions seen or voices heard by paranoiacs, to be identified? Of what sort is the "objective" and "physical" reality which can be attributed to these things? Upon these questions two differing views seem to have been held by different groups of representatives of monistic realism.

(a) It was obviously desirable, if possible, to avoid construing the hypothesis in such a way as to bring back into the "physical world" all the troublesome monsters which, to the great convenience of natural science, dualism had extruded from it. To suppose that that world includes—in a single sense of "includes" —not only scientific objects and ordinary perceptual objects (the objective reality of every perceived feature of which this philosophy necessarily affirmed), but in addition all the stuff that dreams are made on, all the airy nothings which the poet's imagination bodies forth, and all the phantasms of madness and delirium— this seemed a way of taking one's pan-objectivism which was to be accepted only if no alternative was available. And an alternative seemed to suggest itself—the view, namely, that delusions, dream-content, the creatures of imagination and the like, are not additions to the physical objects recognized by science or common sense, but are the same objects, or parts of them, somehow apprehended as present in the wrong places. The kinds of data experienced in dream or hallucination are the same as those given in normal sense-perception; and these latter, according to the principles of monistic realism, are parts of the physical world. Thus it appeared possible to conceive of delusive or imaginative content as made up of "real things"—the identical real things which constitute the world of science—with merely a change of position or arrangement in space and time. "The world of illusions," Professor Samuel Alexander has written, "is identical with what we call the real world, but dislocated, its parts taken from their proper places and referred amiss. That dislocation is the mind's own work. Illusion is due to the intrusion of the mind's own idiosyncrasies into the apprehension of reality. But it does not create but only rearranges what is already there. . . . Thus all the materials of illusory percepts are real." [28] When you look into your face in the mirror, it is "the real face" that you see, but there has been a shift of the "real position" of the face—in consequence, it would seem in this case, less of the agency of the mind than that of the mirror.[29]

Now, if the "real world" here referred to is the physical world, and the "real face" is the physical face, this way of dealing with the illusory seems to credit physical objects with a somewhat surprising mobility. We may illustrate this by applying the same sort of explanation to dream-content. If an architect in Chicago, after dining too well, dreams of a structure having the façade of the Church of the Madeleine and the nave of Cologne Cathedral, surmounted by the dome of the Capitol at Washington culminating in a Chinese pagoda, the physical reality of this picturesque edifice is supposed to be shown by the fact that all four of the parts composing it are physical realities. But they are all in different places, and none of them in Chicago. It will, perhaps, be suggested that the searchlight of consciousness can direct itself upon any place, however distant—even upon places antipodal to the body by the functioning of which it is conditioned; and that it can likewise direct itself upon many places at once. In his dream, therefore, the architect would literally be looking simultaneously—though not, of course, with his bodily eyes—at a place in Paris, and a place in Cologne, and a place in Washington, and a place in China. But, unfortunately, this clearly is not what happens. For the parts of this architectural nightmare do not remain in the places, i. e., the positions relative to one another, in which the parts of the physical world with which they are identified are found. In the dream they are, in empirical fact,

28 *Space, Time and Deity*, II, pp. 216–217.
29 *Mind*. N. S. XXXIII (1923), p. 9.

in immediate juxtaposition to one another, which is to say, in the same place—though whether we ought to say that this is Chicago or one of the four other places concerned it may be left to the monistic realist to determine. If the fragments of other buildings of which the dream-structure is composed are real objects, then at least three of those fragmentary real objects have been moved—by the agency of the mind of a sleeping architect. But they also remain unmoved; for nothing, I take it, is supposed to have occurred in Paris, Cologne, Washington or Pekin, in consequence of the dream. The same "real objects" must, therefore, —if we are to accept this account of the metaphysics of dreaming and of illusion in general—be assumed to be capable of being in two places at once.

One cannot but ask, therefore, whether those who express themselves in such terms as I have quoted from Professor Alexander mean to accept literally these curious consequences which their language seems to imply. Are "real things" *really* "dislocated" or "rearranged"? Is my "real face," when I look into the glass, in the place where what is more commonly called the mirror-image of it is perceived—namely, in the space behind the mirror? And is there any real meaning in the proposition that the visible face which is perceived there is existentially identical with the tangible face which is in front of the mirror? It does not, in fact, appear that Professor Alexander intends these expressions to be taken literally. For he uses, for example, "referred amiss" as synonymous with "dislocated." What is it to "refer amiss"? In what terms, psychological or physical, is the act to be described? When object A which is really at place B is "referred" to place C, is there, or is there not, anything actually presented or apprehended as *at* place C? In the actual experiences in question it is quite certain that there is. In the case of the mirror-image I *see* something in the space behind the mirror, and this something is not the tangible face which is before the mirror. And in the architect's dream, a façade like that of the Madeleine is perceived as immediately contiguous with a nave like that of the Cathedral in Cologne; the "wrong reference" consists in this perceived contiguity, not of parts of the two churches, for they are not contiguous, but of objects resembling them. (In the usual sense of the expression there would, of course, be no wrong reference unless there were a judgment that bits of the two real churches are thus contiguous and intermixed.) In dream and hallucination, then, there empirically exists a set of characters in a place where the real thing (or fragment of a real thing) with which those characters are (by the monistic realist) said to be identical does not at the same moment exist—unless it is in two places. And the employment, of the term "referred amiss" appears to be an obscure way of expressing this fact, of saying that no real dislocation of any "real object" has occurred, but that something supposedly like a certain real object has been perceived in a certain place (*i. e.,* in a certain configuration) in which that object is not itself present. What is implied, in short, is not a dislocation but a (partial) duplication of the object. But if the particulars which are experienced in dream, etc., are duplicates, even if these, too, are assigned to "the real world," they are additions to that world, over and above the commonly recognized "real objects." But this last was the way of taking pan-objectivism which was to have been avoided.

That Professor Alexander does not really conceive of delusive data as identical with the percepts (*i. e.,* for the realistic monist, the real physical objects) which they may resemble and of which they are often quasi-memories, is further shown by the fact that though he calls such data "real," they apparently do not fit his definition of "physical." "A percept of a physical thing" is physical because it "obeys the laws of physics." Now the percepts in dreams and hallucinations for the most part do not—and it is recognized by Mr. Alexander that they sometimes do not—obey the laws of physics. Hence they are not physical. If the dome at Washington is physical, it is a non-physical and therefore another dome which the sleeper in Chicago beholds in his dream. And if another, then there is no occasion to talk of any "dislocation" of an object; "dislocation" once more proves to be only another name for duplication. And in what sense can the non-physical dream-dome be said to be also non-mental—especially since its status is admittedly not that of a subsistent universal? It can hardly be denied to be a private object, accessible only to the dreamer. And there is no cogent reason (since it admittedly does not belong to the world in which physical processes regularly and continuously operate) for supposing that it exists as a particular when nobody is dreaming of it. Unless at all events it is thus gratuitously assumed to have a "real" yet wholly inactive existence before the dream began or after it ended, or both, the non-physical dome must be classified as "mental" in the sense in which dualistic philosophy has so described it.

The pressure of certain unescapable considerations thus seems to make it impossible, even for philosophers who at first tell us that the world of illusions is simply the world of real objects with its parts dislocated, to adhere unequivocally and consistently to such a view. A further example of this may be seen in the interesting chapter in which Professor Laird has inquired into the status to be assigned in a realistic philosophy to "the stuff of fancy"—*i. e.*, to all classes of so-called non-veridical data.[30] The common-sense (and dualistic) view that the images in imagination, hallucination and dream "are unreal and merely mental things . . . the dreamer's private mind-stuff," is, he thinks, "by an unhappy chance quite untenable." For "these mimics of sense which we call images must have the same status as percepts. If the latter are objects, the former are, too. . . . The imagined St. Sofia is domed and minaretted and shapely just as the perceived St. Sofia is, so that . . . if the perceived St. Sofia is not mental the imaged St. Sofia cannot be mental either: and even common sense must accept the logic of this situation if it hopes for consistency." (Why consistency should impose this obligation upon common sense is obscure; but it undeniably imposes it upon the monistic realist.) Now such a realist holds "that things perceived and re-

[30] *A Study in Realism*, p. 63 ff.

membered are independent of the mind and directly apprehended by it." This, then, must also be true of images. "Independent and directly apprehended" is not, of course, necessarily equivalent to "physical"; but the simplest and most reasonable way of construing the objectivity of images seems to Mr. Laird to lie in supposing "that they are physical facts forming part of the world of physical things"—though with a qualification to be noted presently. When, then, Mr. Laird comes to the difficult case of "creative imaging," especially as it is exemplified in dreams, he too suggests that in this phenomenon the images are compounds or rearrangements of experienced percepts—the compounding being the work of the mind. If so, the argument proceeds, we are not obliged to hold that even a seemingly novel object—"the gorgon or the dream-palace or whatever it may be"—is "mental." "A house is not more mental than a glacier, although a glacier is constructed by nobody and a house is a combination of material which human beings have brought into existence; and it is hard to see how anything must be mental if its elements need not be." But the "elements" are, by the hypothesis, not merely non-mental but physical, since they are percepts; hence, in this case also, the images are made of physical stuff.

Nevertheless it is clear—and is recognized by Mr. Laird—that they cannot be simply and literally made of physical, i. e., perceptual, stuff. Though they have some they do not have all the properties and relations characteristic of such stuff; the two do not behave in the same manner. "The meaning of imaged things is different from the meaning of perceived ones." Though the images themselves, since "they have extension, figure and duration" are "thoroughly particular," their "meaning is emancipated from any particular context in space and time. . . . In a word, images are precisely what they appear to be, spatial, temporal and physical, yet without a home in the perceived order of space and time." They either lack definite localization or, if localized, are situated where perceived objects are not; and they have not the same sort of sequelae. If the drunkard expects the crawling serpents he sees to strangle him, he is simply mistaking the kind of "meaning" possessed by images for that possessed by percepts.[31] Now the physicality here ascribed to dream-images and the like is manifestly quite different from that ascribed to the objects of normal perception. The "difference in meaning" amounts to a radical difference in nature and status. By virtue of this difference the images admittedly lack even the primary advantages commonly credited to physical objects, *viz.*, precisely, "a home in the perceived order"—which is for a monistic realism the objective order—"of time and space," a causal efficacy which is a function of their relative situations in time and space, and the habit of conformity to the laws discovered by the investigations of physicists. The "world of physical things" of which perceptual objects form a part does not, then, include these images among its members, nor does it include, as particulars, the "elements" of which the images are compounded. If the image as a whole has no local habitation in the spatio-temporal and causal order of the physical world, its component parts evidently cannot do so. Its elements could be merely qualitatively, not numerically, identified with the true physical objects supposed (by realists of this way of thinking) to be directly apprehended in normal perception. Thus no identification of the images with these objects is accomplished.

(b) It proved, then, impossible to put the "stuff of fancy" into the physical universe by conceiving of it as composed of dislocated fragments of the entities usually recognized by common sense or by physical science as legitimately belonging therein. In such a theory the notion of existential identity was subjected to a strain so insupportable that it broke down into pure meaninglessness. There remained for the monistic realist the alternative mentioned —to put the wild data into that world as additions to its previously accepted membership-list. Though this alternative was scarcely ever, I think, adopted whole-heartedly and applied rigorously in detail, it was sometimes carried pretty far. Thus we were told, by a philosopher sensible of the genuine implications of the

[31] *A Study in Realism*, p. 68.

monistic theory that things objectively are what they appear to be, that when the same water appears warm to A and cold to B, we ought to "attribute literally" both temperatures to the water; and we were assured that there is no more contradiction in this than in attributing to the same water at once warmth and acidity. Again, it was affirmed by the same writer that the stick thrust into the pool (and not merely the retinal image of it) "does not simply *appear* bent; it *is* bent." This, however, it was recognized, can hardly be true unless we suppose the stick to have two dissociable sets of real geometrical characters, those apprehended visually and those apprehended tactually. The stick is really straight, but this is a tactual straightness; it is just as really bent, but this is a visual bentness. The "same stick," it was thus implied, has its geometrical characters in different places; and its real visual and tactual characters sometimes coincide (*e. g.,* those of the part of the stick not under water), and sometimes diverge. This, perhaps, seemed a little curious; but the essential point was that there exists under the surface of the water an actual "objective" stick, joining the stick above the surface at an angle.

It is evident, however, that this alternative—in view of the failure of the other—must be applied to experienced content rigorously and universally, if dualism is to be avoided. All the wild data, and not merely some of them, must have the same status as the theory ascribes to veridical percepts, which is to say, the status of independent realities present in the regions of space in which they appear to be present. The monistic doctrine made it necessary (so far as its representatives had the courage of their premises) to crowd into the so-called "physical world" all the weird and jarring creatures of hallucination, delirium, dream, illusion and imagination, until that world became the objectified sum of all nightmares, where tables, trees, ghosts, gorgons and hydras and chimeras dire, straight sticks that are bent and round coins that are elliptical, things present and things to come, the drunkard's pink rats and the physicist's colorless atoms and electrons, all dwell together in the same space and time, when no man perceives them.

And when all this was done, the end desired remained unaccomplished. The wild data continued to behave in a wild manner. They were still refractory to the laws of the realm of physics; they refused to do any physical work; and they lurked in the privacy of individual fields of consciousness, resisting incorporation in any world of public objects accessible to common knowledge. The physical status ascribed to them was not that ascribed by monistic realism itself to the objects of normal sense-perception or to the imperceptible entities of theoretical physics. Though the program of pan-objectivism had been inspired in part by the feeling that dualism was incongruous with the preconceptions of natural science, the men of science proved unappreciative of the labors performed in their behalf by monistic philosophers. The biologists remained unimpressed by the objectivity of dream-fauna; the physicists continued to explain the bentness of the image of the stick upon the assumption that there is below the surface of the water only one stick (if any), and that a straight one; and the psychologists still assumed that the Zöllner effect or the Müller-Lyer illusion had no counterpart in the physical lines which they commonly believed to be actually drawn in ink upon the paper of their text-books, and that the physicists could give them no aid in the explanation of these phenomena. The only possibly significant consequence which could be deduced —though it apparently was not—from the thesis of the objectivity of all content was an affirmation of the metaphysical uses of inebriety. For it followed from this thesis, when it was applied to a certain phase of human experience, that the consumption of large quantities of alcohol or other intoxicants is a means of becoming acquainted with a class of "real" and "extra-mental" objects which are unhappily hidden from the more abstemious.

We may conclude from all this, I think, that the second alternative method for attempting to reconcile the existence of delusive and imaginative content with the requirements of the theory was no more fortunate than the first. And with this conclusion I shall end our examination into the logical practicability of a rigorous and consistent epistemological and psycho-physical monism of a realistic sort. For enough seems to me to have been said to show that—at least so far as the methods of this first phase of the revolt went—a dualistic counter-revolution was possible and was certain to be successful. If we should take the time to inquire whether pan-objectivism could meet the other essential arguments of the dualist—the physico-physiological argument, that from the general possibility of error, and that from the experience of retrospection—we should, I think, find this conclusion confirmed. But it does not appear to stand in need of further confirmation. We have compared the monistic and dualistic hypotheses at two crucial points and have, as it appears to me, found the monistic alternative incredible and incapable of being consistently carried through.

Even the external fortunes of the movement make sufficiently evident the complete breakdown of the first grand offensive against dualism. The revolt had little more than started before it began to disintegrate; in the earliest methodical formulations of the new doctrine, lapses at precisely the crucial points into epistemological dualism were manifest; and many rival explanations of the nature of error were devised, none of them capable of commanding any general agreement even among the faithful. Some of the most redoubtable early champions of the cause of naïve realism have now apparently abandoned it; formidable new adversaries have multiplied in recent years; and judicious observers far from unsympathetic with the purposes of the revolt have candidly pointed out its ill-success thus far, and the ineffectiveness of the weapons hitherto employed in it. Thus Mr. Bertrand Russell, while still averse to psychophysical dualism, nevertheless declares that the falsity of "the view that perception gives direct knowledge of external objects . . . appears as certain

as anything in science can hope to be." [32] (Whether, when epistemological dualism is thus rejected, psychophysical monism can still
be effectually defended, must be a question for later examination.) Professor Mead, also, has lately borne testimony, the more
impressive because it is regretful, to the failure of all the offen-
sives hitherto undertaken against dualism in general.[33]

The metaphysical assault upon the dualism of mind and nature, that has
been becoming every day more intolerable, has been made in regular formation by Bergson's evolutionary philosophy, by neo-idealism, by neo-
realism, and by pragmatism. And no one can say as yet that the position
has been successfully carried.

Yet, while the first advance against the old entrenched lines of
dualistic realism has failed to fulfil the high hopes with which it
was begun, fresh attacks, with quite different weapons, have been
preparing in other quarters, and have of late been launched with
much energy and *élan*. There has thus arisen in philosophy, as
Professor Mead has said, a new "strategic position of great importance"—which, as some acute philosophic minds believe and
hope, may yet make possible the final overthrow of dualism. It
is with some aspects of this new situation that the three following
lectures will deal.

[32] *The Analysis of Matter,* p. 196.
[33] *Proceedings of the Sixth International Congress of Philosophy,* 1927, p. 75.

III

THE SECOND PHASE: OBJECTIVE RELATIVISM

The second phase of the revolt precisely reverses the strategy of the first. Those who have formulated its principles concede, or rather insist upon, the relativity of the content of perception (and apparently of other cognition) to a situation in which the perceptual or cognitive act is an essential, and the proximately determinative, factor. So far from making the logical doctrine of the externality of relations the basis of their philosophy, they tend to assume the essentiality of all relations; and even where this principle is not expressly adopted as a generalization, it is at least applied to the special cases of sentiency and knowledge. The existence and character of experienced data depend upon the occurrence of percipient events and therefore upon the nature and situation of the organism which has the experience; and it is only "in relation to" a given organism that the object known possesses the character exhibited by the datum. Nevertheless, all perceptual content is still stoutly declared to be "objective"—in some sense or senses yet to be defined; and the dualistic "bifurcation of nature" is condemned not less vigorously than by the revolutionists of the older school. To this general type of doctrine the name "objective relativism" has appropriately been given.[1]

The influences which have contributed most to the development in our time of this form of ostensibly realistic philosophy seem to be three, two of them rather old, the other new. The first was the survival of a way of thinking which, in philosophers who had

[1] The name was, I believe, first suggested by Mr. Arthur E. Murphy (*Philosophical Review*, XXXVI, 1927, p. 122).

been reared in the tradition of objective idealism and thoroughly initiated in the Hegelian logic, had become a habit of mind that persisted after their emancipation from both the temper and the dogmas of that system as a whole. Many of the ablest philosophic minds of an entire generation, in America and Great Britain, were exercised in their youth in a subtle and powerful dialectic which demanded, above all, that the relations of things should always be conceived as entering into their essential natures; and this dialectic has continued to work potently and in diverse ways, even after the idealism with which it had seemed inseparably connected was overwhelmed by the rising tide of realism. To those who approach all problems with this general preconception, the supposition that even the relation of content to the percipient organism can be barren and unconstitutive of the character of what is experienced, is naturally repugnant; and to such minds, therefore, the turn first taken, for the most part, by the realistic uprising of the beginning of the century seemed a mistaken one. Yet to regard the data of perception as "relative" to the percipient was not —the same dialectic seemed to suggest—equivalent to making them "subjective"; for does not the objectivity of rational thought, according to that dialectic, consist precisely in apprehending things in and through their relations?

Nevertheless, when the presumption of the essentiality of relations was given this turn, it led to a consequence opposite to that which, in the logic of objective idealism, had been derived from the same principles. By that logic a thing can be truly understood only in the light of *all* its relations. Knowledge is more "objective" in proportion as a fragment of reality is viewed from many standpoints. Any such fragment has aspects as numerous as the other fragments with which it is diversely related; and "truth" is approximated in so far as these diversities of aspect are taken account of in all their multiplicity, yet synthetized into a coherent unity. Consequently, an aspect peculiar to a single point of view presents the minimum of objective validity. The full truth about any part would be possessed only by an intelligence capable of simultaneously grasping in an exhaustive synthesis the concrete whole of organically interrelated elements—an achievement beyond the reach of any temporal and finite mind. But by the objective relativist of the new type this reasoning is—or tends to be—curiously inverted. While the assumed relevance of every relation of a thing to the determination of its nature is the ground on which he seems chiefly to base his inference as to the relevance of the percipient or cognitive event to the determination of the nature of what is apprehended, this inference is now construed as meaning that that nature must be peculiar to each individual point of view. For, in the first place, the character of every distinguishable part of reality, just because it is the product of a unique convergence and interplay of relations, must be itself unique. And it is, in the second place, at such a unique focus of convergent relations that the perceiver or knower at every moment stands. If he should disregard the special aspect which reality wears from that standpoint and seek to place himself in some extraneous or generalized or "eternal" point of view, he would not thereby come nearer to the concrete truth of things; he would, on the contrary, simply ignore or falsify that particular manifestation of the whole nexus of relations which distinguishes his own situation therein. But—the objective relativist usually declares—it is in fact impossible for the individual percipient or knower thus to escape from his own situation. The reality which he can know is always the aspect in which reality in general presents itself from his standpoint—a standpoint determined by his constitution as a knower and by the time and place and juncture in experience in which he finds himself.

By this inversion, then, of the dialectic of what may be called the older (*i. e.*, the neo-Hegelian) "objective relativism," the new variety, somewhat paradoxically, arrives at much the same outcome as another philosophical tendency to which it at first seems antithetic—the type of scientific positivism represented by Mach and Petzoldt. The affinity between the two may be illustrated by quoting Petzoldt's summing-up of the fundamental principles of positivism:

> We can think things only in the form in which we find them presenting themselves to us, never in a form in which they present themselves to nobody. We can apprehend the world only from the standpoint in which we actually stand, not from a standpoint in which we cannot think of ourselves as standing, or from no standpoint at all. There is no absolute standpoint, and there is no exemption from standpoints; there are only and always relative standpoints. . . . I can in reality think of no absolute whatever; I always tacitly place myself upon the scene as the observer who is beholding things in their relation to himself.[2]

The new relativism often sounds like an echo of this familiar strain. Yet its representatives still continue to assert a kind of objectivity in knowledge which the positivist cannot consistently admit—though he too has not always been able to refrain steadfastly from assuming it.

These older influences have of late been powerfully reënforced by the implications—or the supposed implications—of certain important new developments in natural science, especially in physics. A part of Einstein's special theory—not, in fact, the most significant or most characteristic part—has seemed to show that even the properties of natural objects and events which had most commonly been conceived, even by science, as inherent and absolute —their metrical properties, and especially their dates and durations—are "relative" (in a sense which we need not, just yet, attempt to define), and that certain relations of which the variations had been supposed to be dissociable from and irrelevant to certain other relations and properties, in fact "make a difference." This appeared to afford fresh and striking evidence of the general relativity of things; while at the same time, just this world in

2 "Wir können die Dinge nur so denken, wie wir sie vorfinden, nie so, wie sie niemand vorfindet. Wir können die Welt immer nur von dem Standpunkt aus denken, auf dem wir wirklich stehen, nicht von einem Standpunkt aus, auf dem wir überhaupt uns gar nicht stehend denken können, oder von gar keinem Standpunkt aus. Es gibt keinen absoluten Standpunkt und es gibt keine Standpunktslosigkeit, es gibt allein relative Standpunkte, diese aber auch stets. . . . Ich kann in Wirklichkeit gar nichts absolut denken: im Stillen stelle ich mich noch immer als der Beobachter vor, der die Dinge sich gegenüber sieht." (*Das Weltproblem von positivischem Standpunkte aus*, p. 142).

which things own their properties only in their diverse relations to other particular things is by some relativistic physicists conceived as the true objective order of nature. According to the physical theory of relativity, as it is frequently expounded, an identical body has many different lengths, in the direction of its rectilinear unaccelerated motion, depending upon the state of relative motion of the reference-body with respect to which its motion is defined; it has therefore many different shapes; and these effects, the Lorentz-Fitzgerald contractions, are often described by physicists, not as illusory ways in which the body merely "appears" to different observers, but as physical properties of the body, any one of them as "real" as any other.[3] Thus a character which a material thing has only in a special context, only in its relation to another individual thing, it has none the less objectively and physically. This suggested that a character which exists only in relation to an individual sentient organism, or to an act of perception, may be in like manner objective and even "physical."

This is, no doubt, only an inadequate indication of the principal elements in the background of ideas out of which objective relativism emerged. But into this matter it is unnecessary, for our present purpose, to enter more minutely. Our concern here is, first of all, with the polemic of the objective relativist against dualism. This polemic sometimes, and most characteristically, takes the form of an attempt to trace the historic origin of modern dualism to the influence in an earlier age of a general non-relational way of thinking about reality. Here again the decisive aberration is blamed upon the philosophers of the seventeenth century (in this case chiefly upon Locke), though the nature of the error ascribed to them is quite different from that discerned by some other critics of seventeenth-century ideas. Modern

---

[3] It is perhaps unnecessary to insist that this is only half the story about the physical theory of relativity, and not an entirely correct version of that half; but it is the half, and the version of it, which helped to promote the philosophical relativism with which we are concerned.

philosophy has been wandering in the wilderness for some three hundred years largely because Locke and his contemporaries, in approaching the problem of knowledge, were dominated by "the old notion of separate, independent substances, each of which has its own inner constitution and essence,"[4] apart from its relations to other things. The objects aimed at by knowledge were conceived as such isolated substances; it was, and by subsequent dualists habitually has been, assumed that "those characters which the mind attributes to reality must either belong to such reality absolutely or not at all."[5] But seventeenth-century science had already begun to show, what later science has made increasingly evident, that the characters of things are not absolute but relative, and, in particular, that the characters given in perceptual experience are dependent on physical conditions varying with the diverse relations of perceivers to the object, and upon the special constitution of the perceiver or knower. Given, then, this non-relational conception of the *cognoscendum*, on the one hand, and this undeniably relative character of perceptual content, on the other, dualism legitimately and inevitably followed; the self-contained, self-subsistent object, and the dependent qualities arising from its relations to other things, and especially to minds (or to the physical and physiological conditions of perception), remained irreconcilable, and thus it was that the world became bifurcated into subjective "sensations" and external realities; "in final analysis, the opposition between the inner constitution and essence (which Locke retained from prior metaphysics) and the relations which are knowable (his own contribution) is the source of the opposition which we are familiar with as the Lockian contrast between idea and object."[6] And such a dualism inevitably was forever

[4] Dewey: "Substance, Power and Quality in Locke," *Philosophical Review,* XXXV, 1926, p. 23.

[5] A. E. Murphy, "Ideas and Nature," *University of California Studies in Philosophy,* 1926, p. 195.

[6] Dewey, *op. cit., Philosophical Review,* XXXV, 1926, p. 23; *cf.* also Lamprecht, "Sense Qualities and Material Things," *Philosophical Review,* XXXVIII, 1929.

lapsing implicitly or explicitly into phenomenalism or agnosticism. "Knowledge which grasps only relations—such as were the staple of the new physics—cannot grasp an inner essence, which remains accordingly hidden and mysterious." [7]

The doctrine of the subjectivity of the secondary qualities is the most familiar historic example of the effect of this combination of a non-relational conception of the object to be known with a relativistic conception of the content of experience. The primary qualities were defined by Locke as "such as are utterly inseparable from the [external] body, in what state soever it be"; they were thus by definition not functions of the diverse and mutable interactions of that body with other bodies, or with minds. The secondary qualities, on the other hand, by definition—though the definition was not merely verbal, but had behind it, for Locke, specific reasons—were essentially relational; they were "powers in bodies by reason of the particular constitution of their insensible primary qualities" to produce certain effects in other things —and in the case which concerns us, to produce through their action upon "us" such "sensible qualities" as colors, sounds, tastes, etc.[8] Being thus relative to other bodies (such as our brains) or to our minds, these "sensible qualities" must be regarded only as subjective "ideas in the mind," while the primary qualities were "modifications of matter in the bodies that cause such perceptions in us." [9] If Locke, however, had carried out his own logic more consistently—the objective relativist observes—he might have seen, even from the standpoint of the science of his time, though still more clearly from that of the physics of today, that the qualities which he called primary are relational too, not the absolute, immutable, intrinsic properties which he supposed them to be.[10]

[7] Dewey, op. cit. Dewey points out, however, in the same paper, the influence in Locke's thought of another, relational mode of thought, which remained for the most part barren in him and his successors.

[8] Essay Concerning Human Understanding, II, chap. viii, §§ 10 and 23. There are some waverings in Locke's definitions, which it is not essential to consider here; cf. Dewey, op. cit., and the article of R. Jackson in Mind, January, 1929, pp. 56 ff.

[9] Locke, op. cit., II, viii, § 7.

[10] Dewey, op. cit., p. 26.

If he had remarked this he would have been led by his assumption about the nature of the objects which knowledge should be concerned with to admit the pure subjectivity of *all* the qualities we perceive or conceive.

Such, in brief, is the objective relativist's account of the historic origin and the logical source of modern dualism. That source—from which such evil consequences, as it seems to him, have flowed—he finds to be a preconception not only gratuitous but transparently false. There is no justification for the assumption that "the characters which the mind is entitled to attribute to reality belong to it absolutely or not at all." For a character which an entity has by virtue of its relation to some other entity none the less "belongs to" it. In so far as the dualist has insisted upon the relativity of sense-data—even upon their relativity to percipient events—he has been the spokesman of an important truth, missed by the naïve realist, and neglected by the leaders of the first phase of the revolt against dualism. It is, for example, manifestly true that, if the book I see is red, "its redness characterizes it only under conditions"; it "would not be red in the dark, it would be less red under an electric light, and if I were color-blind it would not be red at all." [11] But it does not in the least follow from this that the redness "does not characterize the book at all," that the sense-datum, because it cannot be imputed to the object absolutely, "tells me the nature only of itself." Things are what they are in their relations; in the reality of the isolated, self-contained Lockian substances we have no reason to believe. Nature is a complex of characters which not only are interconnected, but are determined by their interconnections; and to experience a relative character of a bit of reality (an "event," as the objective relativist prefers to call it) is not to experience something subjective and extraneous to nature, but to apprehend a part of nature as it truly is. Knowledge *is* perception of relations or relational attributes; and "if knowledge is to have to do with real natural existence, then Locke"—and all other dualists—"should have con-

[11] Murphy, *op. cit.*, p. 195.

cluded that existence, as the subject-matter of knowledge, is inherently relational."[12] When this truth is grasped, the old assumption of "the ultimate incompatibility of objectivity and relativity" is destroyed; it becomes plain that "the objective facts of the world of nature and of reality are the very 'apparent' and relative happenings disclosed to us in perception."[13]

Relativity, then—and specifically relativity to a perceiver or thinker, or to the special conditions determining the content of his perception or thought—is so far from implying subjectivity that it is rather (objective relativists frequently insist) the very essence of that objectivity in the understanding of the nature of things which science has always sought to attain. Error in science mainly arises, it is observed, through neglect of some relevant factor in a problem under investigation; a duly critical scientific procedure therefore "requires that all the conditions of a given event be taken into account." Now, the relation of the event to the perceiver, "what it is experienced as, must be accounted as one of the objective conditions." It was the disregard of this type of condition by the older theoretical physics that Einstein noted; he pointed out how certain contradictions which experiment had disclosed arose precisely from a failure to recognize that measurements of time, and of the linear magnitudes of bodies, are relative to the standpoint of the observer's particular reference-system. In calling attention to this oversight he was not lapsing into subjectivism, but, on the contrary, was carrying forward "the high tradition of scientific objectivity." To him especially, then, "belongs the credit of having shown that what the world is perceived as from any and all possible physical points of view constitutes the essential part, if not all, of its objective nature for physical science."[14]

12 Dewey, *op. cit.,* p. 23.
13 A. E. Murphy, "Objective Relativism in Dewey and Whitehead," *Philosophical Review,* XXXVI, 1927, p. 122.
14 M. C. Swabey, *The Monist,* 1927, pp. 310, 313; the passage is a good illustration of the inversion of the older logic based upon the principle of the essentiality of relations.

What can the dualist legitimately say in defense of his position against this new and impressive attack? He can, I think, say a number of not irrelevant things; and first of all, he may call attention to a simple distinction which, though it is not wholly rejected nor invariably overlooked by objective relativists, is by most of them rather lightly regarded and only intermittently observed: the distinction between (a) conceiving of external objects as possessing properties by virtue of their relations to one another, and (b) conceiving of those objects as possessing their properties by virtue of their relation to a particular mind, or organism, or percipient or cognitive event.   It has not, I believe, been especially characteristic of dualistic philosophers to deny the former sort of relativity; certainly they have not been so utterly unmindful of the interrelatedness of things as some now widely current accounts of them might lead one to suppose. We are told by a recent writer that "dualistic realism, no matter how much it may be supposed to have outgrown the limitations of its seventeenth-century ancestry, has retained the (usually uncriticized) assumption that reality is non-relational. It has supposed that whatever 'really' or externally exists, is a 'substance,' in the sense of a self-determined and self-contained thing dependent for its nature on nothing outside itself." [15] But Herbart is the only important dualistic philosopher, so far as I can recall, in whom this notion that "reals" must be absolutely unrelated things is exemplified. And certainly there is no good reason why a dualist, as such, should adopt it. Objective things may, so far as the essential logic of his view is con-

[15] S. P. Lamprecht, *Philosophical Review*, 1929, p. 28; italics mine. How little such a remark holds good of Locke may be judged from *Essay Concerning Human Understandings*, Bk. IV, ch. 6, sec. --: "The great parts and wheels, as I may so say, of this stupendous structure of the universe, may, for aught we know, have such a connection and dependence in their influences and operations one upon another, that, perhaps, things in this our mansion, would put on quite another face, and cease to be what they are, if some one of the stars or great bodies, incomprehensibly remote from us, should cease to be or move as it does. This is certain, things however absolute or entire they seem in themselves, are but retainers to other parts of nature, for that which they are most taken notice of by us. Their observable qualities, actions, and powers, are owing to something without them: and there is not so complete and perfect a part that we know of nature, which does not owe the being it has, and the excellences of it, to its neighbors."

cerned, be precisely as variously and intimately related, and as much conditioned by their relations—as they happen to be. All that a dualistic realism need assume, on this point, is that "what 'really' exists" is independent of a *particular* relation, that it is not a function of the percipient or cognitive event.[16] And this has hitherto been taken as the common assumption of all realism.

The objective relativist's account of the historic and logical origin of dualism is, in truth, a complete misconception—as should be sufficiently manifest from the first of these lectures. It is true that Locke talked of certain inherent or primary qualities of bodies, "such as in all the alterations and changes a body suffers, all the force can be used upon it, it constantly keeps"; by these, however, he usually meant the defining qualities of "body" in general, and he did not imply that the particular instance of one of these qualities—e. g., the particular extension or figure—characterizing a given body at a given time, was possessed by it unconditionally or apart from all relations. And in any case his dualism did not result from such a conception. Mere relational dependence was not the essence nor the basis of the notion of subjective existence, any more than independence of all relations was implied by the notion of objective existence. Neither Locke nor, I suppose, any other dualist, ever called anything subjective or mental merely on the ground that it was causally, spatially, or otherwise related to a physical object. He did not designate as "ideas" the effects produced in one material body by the action of another body. And if the relativist said no more than that *this* kind of interaction and interrelation in the universe was objective,

16 Professor Lamprecht (*Philosophical Review*, 1929, p. 29), in a reference to the part of these lectures which was delivered at a meeting of the American Philosophical Association, seems to impute to me a view similar to Herbart's, and adds that "if the requirements we are supposed to demand of the physical order," *i.e.*, those mentioned in the latter part of the first lecture, "are not permanence and independence of relations," it is difficult to understand the reasons for my "relegation of sense-data to another realm." I take occasion, therefore, to observe that I have never suggested that "independence of relations" is one of the characteristics which I suppose to belong to the physical order—but only independence of relation to sentiency or cognition. The distinction seems hardly negligible.

he would be saying nothing which the dualist has any occasion to deny.

It has, in short, never been a premise of epistemological dualism that "the characters which the mind attributes to reality belong to such reality absolutely or not at all"—if by absolutely is meant unconditionally. There has, it is true, been a certain general and usually unexpressed preconception underlying dualistic theories of perception, and specifically the Lockian theory of the subjectivity of what are commonly called the secondary qualities; and it is through a confusion of this with the notion of the subjectivity of the relational that the objective relativist's misconception has arisen. What the dualist has actually assumed is that the things which are the subjects of discourse, and the presumed objects of knowledge, have definite situations and boundaries, spatial and temporal, of their own, that their attributes lie within those boundaries, and in particular, that the effects produced by one thing through its action upon another are not necessarily attributes of the first thing—in other words, that the qualities of an effect are not *eo ipso* qualities of its cause. A candle-flame has, while it exists, certain qualities of its own; it has also, as Locke would have said, a "power" of melting a piece of sealing-wax at a certain distance. The "power" also may be called, as it was by Locke, a "quality" of the flame. But we do not call the molten state of the wax a quality of the flame. A hunter with a gun has the power to kill a rabbit; but if he exercises it, it is not customary nor convenient to ascribe the resultant deadness to the hunter. And it is merely this simple and elementary distinction which is the really indispensable presupposition of epistemological dualism. If the *cognoscendum* is a determinate somewhat—not necessarily a "substance," but a complex of concrete characters—and if it and the qualities which characterize or constitute it are contained within certain limits of time or place or both, then any effects which arise at other times or in other places in consequence of its being in that time and place are not *it,* and are not *its* qualities. (They may, of course, be other instances of the same kind of qualities.) The specific reality-to-be-apprehended is the distant star, or the event of yesterday, or the emotion in my neighbor's bosom; anything extraneous to that, even though dependent upon it, is another entity, though it may possibly be a means of inferring something about the first. Now that in, e. g., the case of the star, it and the sense-data by which we are informed about it do not exist at the same time and place, the epistemological dualist has believed for the sort of reasons already explained. And Locke and others who have maintained the objectivity of primary and the subjectivity of secondary qualities have done so because they thought it possible to determine which classes of characters the object probably had within its own limits and which were rather the effects of its "power to produce modifications in other things." But there is in this specification of the locus and limits of the object of reference nothing that implies that the characters which the object has within those limits are possessed by it absolutely or unrelatedly— any more than, when we do not describe the flame as melted, nor say that the hunter in killing the rabbit has killed himself, we imply that the flame or the hunter is a pure absolute. And, of course, it is on the other hand obviously implied that the characters which are *not* attributed to the object of knowledge *are* attributes of some other object or locus, conditioned by an interraction between the former object and the organism. Yet the objective relativist is apparently unable to see this; to him the innocent and useful practice of directing your cognitive enterprises upon definite and limited objects, and, as a means thereto, of distinguishing causes from their effects, seems equivalent to the complete negation of the causal, and of every other, interconnection of things.

Thus far, then, the relativist's polemic against dualism seems doubly irrelevant. He has assumed that the delimitation of the intended object of knowledge, and the exclusion from the number of its properties of its effects upon other entities, is the same as a general denial of its (or else of their) relatedness or relativity; and he has assumed that the undisputed truth that many things which are (in one sense or another) relative to other things are objective, has some bearing upon the real question at issue between himself and the dualist, *viz.*, whether things which are relative *specifically to percipient events* are, or can be, "objective." And both of these assumptions we have now seen to rest upon confusions. The influence of the latter confusion may be seen in a mode of reasoning which, if I am not mistaken, is recognizable in more than one of the lively assaults upon the dualistic position in which objective relativists have of late engaged. It seems, namely, to be sometimes supposed that if it is granted, or can be demonstrated, that "all characters belong to existence *in some relation or other,*" the blight of subjectivity is, by this alone, somehow removed from the characters which are relative to percipient events. If any object possessed any properties whatever which were not functions of its relations to something, perceptual data would, no doubt, by comparison with those absolute properties, have an inferior, a "merely subjective," status. But where all the characters of the object are relative, those which it has relatively to a given percipient are, it is suggested, in no worse case than the rest. It is objectively true that the object has them in that relation, just as it has others in other relations; wherein, then, are they any less objective than the others? And where, in such a relational world, does any bifurcation of nature manifest itself? It is, of course, impossible to be sure just what this argument is supposed to mean so long as "objective" is left undefined; but it *looks* as if it came, when reduced to its logical skeleton, to the following inference: Things which are relative, but not relative to percipient events, are objective (in the sense of "independent of percipient events") ; *ergo,* things which are relative to percipient events are objective (viz., *not* in the sense of "independent of percipient events").

However, the case of the objective relativist does not really resolve itself into this ingenuous argument. If we eliminate the confusions and irrelevancies which have been pointed out, we come to the question which, as I have said, is the real issue between this type of philosophy and dualism: can the things which are by both doctrines declared to be "relative to percipient events" be considered "objective"? But, as so put, the question is still full of ambiguities. Before discussing it, therefore, we must scrutinize more closely the meaning of its essential terms.

(1) At least three distinct, though not necessarily inconsistent, senses of the term "relativity" seem discernible in the objective relativist's reasonings. (a) The first and most obvious we may call "conditionality." As applied to the case of perception, it consists in the dependence of the existence of a character, or set of characters, actually given in experience, upon the existence or occurrence of something else. The empirical datum which is declared to be so conditioned we shall, for brevity, simply call "the character." If that by which it is declared to be conditioned is supposed to be itself a single existent, for example, a brain and nervous system, considered apart from *its* other relations, we have a simple asymmetrical two-term relation, in which the character would be one term and the brain the other, and in which the character would be conceived as dependent on the functioning of the brain, but not conversely. In fact, however, the objective relativist, in agreement with dualism and with common sense, regards perception as involving three factors; in other words, the relativity which he ascribes to the character is relativity to a relation between two other terms; this we may call the "conditioning relation." What, more precisely, the terms of the conditioning relation are conceived to be we have yet to inquire; so far as the general relativistic conception is concerned, they might be any one of several pairs, such as a body not necessarily organic and an organism, or a region of space and an organism. But in any case, one of them appears to be conceived as more closely related temporally and causally (though not spatially) to the character, and also as more closely connected (if not identical) with the percipient organism; it is the pole of the conditioning relation which takes the place, in objective relativism, of the subject-end of the traditional subject-object polarity, while the other term corre-

sponds roughly with the object-end. We may therefore call the two terms of the conditioning relation the proximate and the ulterior relatum. Objective relativists usually appear to maintain, further, that the character does not "belong to" the proximate relatum, or is not situated where that term is, but is an attribute, or occupies the position, of the ulterior relatum.

(b) With the relativity of the character that consists in its conditionality the relativist usually associates, for reasons which have already been suggested, a second sort of relativity. The proximate relatum, though commonly described as a percipient event, is also referred to as a "standpoint"; and it is asserted that the character "belongs to" the ulterior relatum, or occurs at the same place with it, and can be perceived to do so, only *from* this standpoint. This apparently contains two distinguishable affirmations. Partly, I suppose, it expresses the fact of the numerical distinctness of the data of different percipients. My percept and your percept of the reading-desk are two things, not one. But the proposition seems also, and chiefly, to be intended to assert the necessary *qualitative* disparity of the content present to different percipients, even when they are said to be dealing with a common object. Because you and I have different points of view —not only in the literal, visual sense, but in an extended sense— and because the point of view determines the nature of the content present, we cannot experience the same kind of data. The hypothetical common object will exhibit different aspects of itself to each of us.

To assert this is manifestly to say more than that the character exists only by virtue of the conditioning relation and is to be allocated to the ulterior term of that relation. It might conceivably exist, and be so situated, "from" all possible standpoints; for there is nothing in the notion of the dependence of a character of an existent, A, upon the relation of the latter to another existent, B, which implies that the position of B constitutes the sole "point of view" from which the character of A can be observed. The development of objective relativism, however, has been much influenced by the notion of perspectives; these tend to be taken as the best example, in familiar experience, of the type of logical situation in which the relativist believes perception, and knowledge in general, to consist. The perspective distortions of the visual images of objects—the convergence of the railway tracks, the elliptical shape of the penny—according to ordinary optical theory, are characters which I can perceive only by standing at certain distances and angles with respect to the "real" non-convergent tracks, or the "real" circular penny, and which I must perceive when so situated; and this may be, and by the objective relativist would be, expressed by saying that from those standpoints, and from them only, the tracks *are* convergent, or the penny *is* elliptical (though common sense prefers to say that, *e. g.,* the tracks are not convergent but only appear so). The kind of relativity which involves, besides the general idea of conditionality, the further notions of the existence or appearance of the character exclusively from the standpoint of the percipient, and of the necessary diversity of the characters experienced by percipients having different standpoints, we may call "perspectivity."

(c) The third type of relativity which it is needful to keep in mind in considering objective relativism may be termed "respectivity of the meaning of characters," or more briefly, "respectivity." A character is said to be "respective" when the term designating it has no meaning, as a possible predicate of a subject of discourse, unless, besides that term and the subject, some definite third term is implicitly or explicitly specified. A "respective" attribute, in short, always, by its logical essence, implies a triadic, not merely a dyadic, relation. Common sense and traditional logic have not been ignorant that certain characters are respective and others absolute. It has doubtless always been evident to the plain man that it is meaningless to say that one thing is "large," or at any rate to say that it is "larger," without mentioning something else with which the size of the first is compared; or to say that an object is "to the left" without indicating what it is to the left of. But it has not usually been supposed by the plain man that it is meaningless to say that a thing is blue or square without referring to another thing with respect to which it has those properties; on the contrary, such reference would probably seem to him meaningless. In short, the distinction between respective and absolute (which does not, in this context, necessarily mean unconditioned) predicates has commonly been identified with the difference between relations and qualities; that any terms except those designating relations are respective in meaning at least requires proof.

Between the supposedly absolute and the respective predicates of things, important differences in logical properties have always been recognized. The former have been supposed to be of a much more jealous and monopolistic temper; in other words, qualities, because of the assumed absoluteness of their inherence, have seemed more liable to fall into mutual contradiction. Even they, it is true, have been generally held to be readily classifiable into certain obvious genera between the members of which contradiction cannot subsist; but of no one subject or place could two positive qualities of the same genus be asserted without absurdity. A coin—it has seemed evident to the human species, until certain recent developments in philosophy—could not be at once circular and elliptical, though it could be at once either circular and yellow, or elliptical and yellow; a stick could be objectively straight and objectively tapering, but not objectively straight and objectively bent; a liquid could be warm and sweet, but not warm and cold or sweet and sour. How such a relation of mutual repugnance can obtain between simple positive concepts has seemed to some philosophers a mystery. Leibniz, for example, in spite of the importance in one part of his system of the assumption of an inherent *a priori* incompatibility between many separately conceivable characters, and in spite of his faith in the principle of sufficient reason, admitted his inability to explain the reason of the incompatibility of different simple attributes, or how it is that purely positive natures can be opposed to one another.[17] But how-

17 *Philos. Schriften,* ed. Gerhardt, VII, p. 195.

ever odd this peculiarity of certain groups of concepts may appear to some logicians, common sense, science, and most philosophy have unhesitatingly accepted it as a solid and indispensable basis for their inferences about things. Relations, however, have usually been regarded as less liable to these oppositions. They, too, it is true, so long as they were taken abstractly, as mere universals, fell into sets of which the members were antithetic to one another, though not to members of the other sets; but one thing or locus might without contradiction be simultaneously in any number of objective relations, even of the abstractly antithetic sort, with respect to different relata.

The relativity which Einstein's special theory emphasized, as usually interpreted, appeared to show that a great many more characters are essentially respective than had hitherto been supposed. Thus, for example (in the words of a typical exposition) the difference between the classical definition and the relativity definition of simultaneity may be expressed concisely in the following way. According to classical mechanics simultaneity is a dyadic relation, a relation between two terms. According to the relativity theory, simultaneity is a triadic relation. . . . According to the classical theory one would say, "A is simultaneous with B"; according to the relativity theory, "A is simultaneous with B with respect to K." [18]

Again, the theory of Einstein showed that "physical length, instead of being a dyadic relation between two intrinsic lengths, is a triadic relation between the intrinsic lengths and the reference-system used"; and so in general with the metrical characters of bodies. Thus the properties ascribable to the concrete entities in nature seemed to be very widely and deeply infected with respectivity of meaning; and it was because of this that it became possible to predicate of a single thing so great a variety of properties previously assumed to be mutually exclusive.

There is, consequently, in at least some forms of the theory now

[18] V. F. Lenzen, in *University of California Studies in Philosophy*, V, 1924, p. 44.

before us, a tendency to extend this notion of the respectivity of meaning, if not universally, at least so widely as to cover all the attributes of sensible appearances. Such attributes would thus come to enjoy that degree of comparative immunity from the constraints of the principle of contradiction which relations have always by general consent enjoyed. If shape or color are predicable of an object only with respect to something else, then the same coin may be both truly circular and truly elliptical, the stick thrust partly under water may be as objectively bent as it is objectively straight, the same surface of a material object may literally possess the color which is perceived by an observer having what is called normal vision and that which is perceived by a color-blind person —different relata, or loci of reference, being in each case presupposed.

The two previous senses of relativity, it is evident, do not include or imply respectivity. Conditionality, as defined, may be merely an empirical relation of causal dependence of the existence of a particular having a certain character upon the existence of another particular having another character, neither character being necessarily destitute of logical import apart from a reference to the other. And a perspective appearance of a thing is not necessarily a character which, by its very meaning, contains a reference to the standpoint from which it appears. To say that a penny has an elliptical shape from a certain point of view does not obviously imply that "elliptical shape" in general cannot be so much as conceived unless one is thinking of a point of view and of the phenomena of perspective distortion. The from-ness, so to say, which is a part of the generalized notion of perspectives is neither interchangeable nor reciprocal with the to-ness which is involved in the notion of respective attributes. It is therefore essential to be on the alert against illicit substitutions of one of the senses of relativity for one or both of the others, in the objective relativist's reasoning.

(2) "Objective" and "subjective" are vague and equivocal terms, which philosophers ought not to use without definition.

The apologetic of objective relativism has, however, been much facilitated—as it seems to me—by a neglect of this precaution. There are in fact four essentially distinct senses of the antithesis which are pertinent to the relativist's theorem. When these are discriminated, it becomes apparent that, in one sense, any form of the doctrine which admits that sense-data are particulars is equivalent to the affirmation of the subjectivity of the data; that with respect to another sense the doctrine is often vaguely and equivocally stated, but can be best construed as implying subjectivity; that in a third somewhat elusive sense, peculiar to this doctrine, the objectivity of data is maintained; and that in the fourth sense, their subjectivity is plainly implied.

(a) In a sense which we shall call "causal subjectivity," anything is described as subjective when it is assumed to have as a necessary condition of its existence the occurrence of a percipient event. This kind of subjectivity is obviously a special case of the sort of relativity which we call conditionality—the case in which a percipient event is the proximate relatum of the conditioning relation. Such conditionality of the character is, presumably, what any relativist who regards data as particulars intends to affirm;[19] the proposition that data are "relative" is, so far, simply equivalent to the proposition that they are subjective. To accept this proposition is to concede *ab initio* the crucial article of the dualistic creed. It is also to concede something which, if true, is philosophically important. It means that percipient events (however these be themselves further defined) are no barren virgins, but give birth to entities which, in a world in which perceiving did not occur, would have no being—and therefore did have no being in our own planetary system before sentient organisms appeared in it. If such characters admittedly exist, they form a class distinct in a specific and significant way from all the characters which are dependent upon relations to terms other than percipient events— the class of mind-begotten, or at all events of brain-begotten, ex-

[19] With the form of objective relativism which rests upon the assumption that data are universals or essences I shall deal in the following lecture.

istents. A radical bifurcation of nature results in either case; though how radical it is will not become fully apparent until a later point in our analysis.

(b) Particular things or qualities (more precisely, instances of qualities) may, secondly, be said to be "existentially" or "psychologically subjective," if they are assumed to exist only as data for awareness, only when and in so far as they are being perceived or thought. Causal and existential subjectivity have commonly been supposed to go together. If a character (as a particular) owes its being to a percipient event occurring in me, it has usually been thought evident that it exists only *for* me, that its appearing in my experience is the only sort of being it has. This, however, does not strictly follow. Whether it does or not depends upon precisely what is understood by the generative "percipient event." If such an event is defined in purely physiological terms—for example, as a particular change in the arrangement of molecules in a cerebral cortex—it might conceivably generate characters which, though usually accompanied by awareness, could sometimes exist without that accompaniment. Or again, even if the occurrence of an awareness were taken to be an essential element in the percipient event which gives birth to the characters, the latter might possibly persist after the awareness of them had ceased.

To persons unfamiliar with recent theories of perception these last will, no doubt, seem possibilities too odd and improbable to be entertained; but to some who have reflected long and acutely upon the problem they have not appeared undeserving of consideration. It has been suggested by more than one recent writer that "the traditional manner of regarding the relation of mind and body" needs to be restated, "as involving two quite distinct problems"—that we "shall have to ascribe to the brain a two-fold function, as conditioning the sensa and as conditioning awareness. Since these two functions are fundamentally distinct, there must be two sets of brain-processes."[20] If there are, it is evidently not

[20] Norman Kemp Smith, *Prolegomena to an Idealist Theory of Knowledge*, 1924, p. 79.

inconceivable that the sort of brain-process which generates sensa may sometimes occur unaccompanied by the process which conditions awareness, and that, consequently, sensa (*i. e.,* brain-begotten particulars) may exist unsensed. That they do not do so, it has been maintained, we have no reason for supposing. "In support of the contention" that "consciousness is inseparably bound up with sensa . . . we have no sufficient evidence," observes Professor Kemp Smith. Doubtless, "when they are known to exist, consciousness is there bearing witness to their existence. But this is no proof that consciousness is what makes them possible of existence, and that they are unable to exist where consciousness is absent." [21] It is evident, then, that the discrimination of the notion of causal from that of existential subjectivity is logically possible and important, and that we shall need to inquire whether it is open to the objective relativist to deny the latter, with respect to the particulars which we at times sensibly experience, while asserting the former.

(c) The third sense of the antithesis "objective-subjective"— though it is the former term that is here chiefly pertinent—is a specialty of objective relativism, yet it has never (so far as I know) been distinguished from the preceding senses by any appropriate designation. I shall, for want of a better name, call it "attributive objectivity." A character, even though it is admitted to be causally, or even existentially, subjective, might nevertheless be said to have attributive objectivity if it is *ascribable to the object of knowledge* as an attribute, *or to the place which that object occupies.* It is, of course, not immediately apparent that a character which exists only as a consequence of a percipient event in me, and only while I am perceiving it, *can* legitimately or intelligibly be said to be an attribute of an object or an "event" assumed to exist independently of perception; or even that such a relative character can be held to be truly situated at the locus

<hr>

[21] *Ibid.,* p. 74, Mr. C. D. Broad arrives at the same conclusion, but thinks that the question whether it "in fact ever happens" that sensa exist unsensed is one which can be "decided by empirical considerations" (*The Mind and Its Place in Nature,* 1925, p. 177).

(spatial, temporal or spatio-temporal) of such an object or event. But here that general relativistic conception of the nature of things of which I spoke at the beginning of this lecture comes into play. If "existence, as the subject-matter of knowledge, is inherently relational," and if, therefore, all the attributes of realities belong to them only in and through their relations, then (the relativist may argue) a character which arises, or becomes "ingredient into nature," through the relation of an object to a percipient event in an organism may nevertheless be a true attribute of the object—or at all events of *some* reality "in nature" external to the organism. The conception may be illustrated by a passage of Whitehead's:

> Qualities, such as colors, sounds, tastes, etc., . . . can with equal truth be described as our sensations or as qualities of the actual things which we perceive. These qualities are thus relational between the perceiving subject and the perceived things. . . . We may not directly connect the qualitative presentations of other things with any intrinsic characters of those things. We see the image of a colored chair presenting to us the space behind a mirror; yet we gain thereby no knowledge concerning any intrinsic characters of any spaces behind the mirror. But the image thus seen in a good mirror is just as much an immediate presentation of color qualifying the world at a distance behind the mirror, as is our direct vision of the chair when we turn round and look at it.[22]

"Intrinsic characters" here seem to be characters not conditioned by the functioning of a percipient organism. Though the mirror-image is not such an intrinsic character, but "relational" to the perceiving subject, it is nevertheless described as "qualifying the world" in a space external to the organism, and is thus an attribute of an "actual thing."

(d) From all of the foregoing must be distinguished what may be called epistemological objectivity or subjectivity. An experienced datum is conceived as epistemologically subjective if it is not assumed to possess, and therefore to be capable of exhibiting, any "intrinsic" quality or relation which the intended object of knowledge has within its own spatio-temporal limits. It is obvious that a character might conceivably be subjective in this sense without being either causally or existentially subjective. If, for

---

[22] *Symbolism, its Meaning and Effect*, pp. 22–24.

example, we should assume that the immediate datum in my visual perception of the railroad tracks is one of the retinal images, and should regard that image, after the manner of naïve realism, as a physical reality having the same qualities as are perceptually given—then the datum would not be conceived as subjective in either the causal or the existential sense. It would not be assumed to exist either solely by my percipient event or solely for my perception. Yet it would be epistemologically subjective. For the *cognoscendum,* the object which is at once the source of the images and the existent about which I am supposed to be seeking information, consists in this case of the assumed "real tracks"; and these are by hypothesis parallel, while the lines corresponding to them in the retinal image are convergent. Of course, if I, the particular percipient in question, am supposed to know that the real tracks are not convergent, I must have "before my mind" some datum which is epistemologically objective—in other words, an image of straight tracks; but, in the case supposed, this will not, at any rate, be the retinal image. If that were my only source of information and my sole content, *I* should not know the tracks as they are. The ordinary theory of perspective is, of course, simply an assertion of the partial epistemological subjectivity of both the retinal images and the visual shapes of things.

On the other hand, a character might conceivably be both causally and existentially subjective, and yet be supposed to be either objective or subjective in the present epistemological sense. This may be illustrated by recalling once more the traditional dualistic view about the primary and secondary qualities. According to that view even the primary qualities *as given*—i.e., the particular "ideas" exhibiting them—are subjective in the two first-mentioned senses, but they are epistemologically objective, for they are supposed to disclose the attributes of objects of knowledge other than themselves. The qualities of these perceptual data, even when they were said to be "in the mind," were not, in this view, held to be determined to be what they are solely by the constitution of the mind, or of the physiological organs of perception. Not only could qualities *of that sort* exist unperceived, but also the data which manifested those qualities were taken as being, at least in some cases, representations, untransformed by the percipient event or *its* conditions, of properties belonging to extra-experiential realities independently of any relation between those realities and a sentient being. Of the secondary qualities, in the usual seventeenth-century view, this could not be said; they were subjective in all three of these senses. Both generically and as individual existents they were what they were in consequence of the constitution of the perceiver; and, indeed, the *particular* primary qualities of shape and size, as given in visual perception uncorrected by thought, were in each case determined (in part) to be what they were experienced as being by virtue of the spatial relation between the body of the perceiver and the external body—in other words, by the perceiver's point of view—as well as by the peculiarities of his optical apparatus; and for this reason they could not be supposed to be direct manifestations of the qualities possessed by an object apart from and prior to these conditions. Reflection could, however—it was assumed—using these triply subjective visual data, together with other data, chiefly tactual, as grounds of inference, arrive at representations which though, once more, causally and existentially subjective, were not epistemologically subjective.

The distinction between attributive objectivity and epistemological objectivity may not at first be obvious; but if the definitions given are considered, it will be seen to be two-fold. On the one hand, to say of a datum that it is attributively objective is to say that the very same entity (whether it be regarded as an existent or a subsistent) which is the datum is also an attribute of the object of knowledge, of the "actual thing." This is not implied by the definition of epistemological objectivity. A datum may be epistemologically objective and yet be an existent distinct from the character of the object with which it makes us acquainted. And on the other hand a datum is, by definition, epistemologically objective only if it serves to give us information about a character that the object has within limits of time or place, or both, which do not include the percipient event, and independently of the occurrence of that event; whereas a datum said to be attributively objective is not thereby said to belong to the object thus prior to and apart from the percipient event.

The special pertinency which the notion of epistemological subjectivity has to our general topic is due to the objective relativist's emphasis upon the relativity of data in the second of the senses of that term which we distinguished, *viz.*, perspectivity. It is apparent from the definitions that perspectivity seems directly to imply epistemological subjectivity. To say, as the relativist appears to do, that all data are nothing but perspective aspects, that they are determined to be what they are by the special standpoint of the perceiver and the nature of the individual percipient event upon which they depend, seems equivalent to saying that no datum can ever inform us about the nature of anything not itself, *i. e.,* of anything not relative to and conditioned by the particular "standpoint" from which it appears. And even if, introducing the concept of attributive objectivity, we should add that the datum nevertheless truly "belongs to the object" *from* that standpoint, it would still seem to be implied that we can know nothing of any attributes which the object has from any other standpoints or in relation to any other percipient events. And this would appear to leave us, at best, an extremely meager possibility of knowledge— and with respect to what is called the external world, no possibility of knowledge at all. The objective relativist, however, does not usually recognize these agnostic consequences of the doctrine of the perspectivity of data; and it will therefore be necessary for us to try to determine whether it is in fact possible for his theory to escape them.

These definitions and distinctions are, I think, indispensable, if in discussing objective relativism we are to deal with clear-cut and unequivocal issues. With these distinctions in mind, we may proceed in the next lecture to examine the position of that theory *vis-à-vis* the dualism earlier outlined. We are to seek to determine more precisely what the two have in common, and, where they differ actually and not merely nominally, what the merits of the proposed relativistic alternative to dualism are.

IV

THE OUTCOME OF THE SECOND PHASE

That there is much in common between objective relativisim and dualism has doubtless become sufficiently clear in the course of the preceding lecture. The dualist, like the relativist, recognizes three factors as essential in perception. There is, as ulterior relatum, an external causal object or event. There is, as a *part* of the proximate relatum, a physiological event in an organism possessing certain special organs, such as eyes, optic nerves, and cerebral cortex. And the character experienced is an existent conditioned upon an interaction between the external object and the organism. Both theories, in short (except in that form of objective relativism which denies that data are particulars), are at one in affirming at least the causal subjectivity of the character. And with respect, at all events, to the characters which he regards as epistemologically subjective, the dualist agrees that these are peculiar to individual standpoints and to the particular constitutions of perceivers, and are not disclosures of the attributes which things have apart from such standpoints..

In all these respects, then, relativism is identical with dualism; but beyond these lie certain points of apparent or possible, though not, as we shall see, in all cases of actual or necessary, divergence. These have to do with the following five issues: (1) The existential subjectivity of the characters which constitute our perceptual content. (2) Their physicality. (3) The legitimacy and significance of the notion of the attributive objectivity of characters, if their causal and existential subjectivity is admitted. (4) The presence in experience of data which are not (in the generalized sense of the term) perspective aspects, and are therefore epistemologically objective. (5) The pertinency to the problem of perception, and of knowledge in general, of the concept of respectivity.

(1) Historic dualism has always declared—rightly, I think—that while the occurrence of certain physical processes is doubtless a necessary, it is probably not a sufficient, condition for the existence of the particulars which enter into experience; it has, in other words, denied that entities generated by "percipient events" exist unperceived. What is causally subjective is also existentially subjective, or at any rate cannot be known or reasonably assumed not to be so.

Does "objective relativism" imply or affirm the contrary? If we consult the utterances of contemporary philosophers who adhere to that doctrine—who, that is to say, insist upon the compatibility of "relativity" with some, usually unspecified, sort of "objectivity"—the answer is not clear. The proximate relatum in the relation which conditions the existence of a percept is by these writers usually called, as we have seen, "the percipient event"; but that expression is equivocal, and we have hitherto not attempted to eliminate the equivocality. Does the term, then, for the relativist signify a mental event—a perceiving, regarded as a psychical act of consciousness—or a purely physiological event, cortical or other? As the relativistic doctrine has been interpreted by Professor Mead, in an important paper, what it asserts is that "the sensuous qualities of nature are there in nature, but are there in their relationship to animal organisms"; to which he adds (as some adherents of the doctrine perhaps would not) that even "the spatio-temporal structure of the world and the motion with which exact science is occupied is found to exist in nature only in its relation to percipient events or organisms."[1] But this leaves the ambiguity unremoved; the terms "animal organism" and "percipient events" are not, in their usual senses, synonymous, yet they appear

---

[1] "The Objective Reality of Perspectives," in *Proceedings of the Sixth International Congress of Philosophy*, 1927, p. 82. Mead is, from the context, apparently taking the term "percipient event" over from Whitehead; on its meaning in that writer's usage, see the following lecture.

to be used interchangeably. More explicit is another relativistic writer who tells us that "in general so-called sense-data are the characters which belong to events in relation to a human body." This presumably means in relation to, *i. e.,* in consequence of, a particular functioning of a human body; but the event to which the sense-data are here declared to be relative seems, at any rate, to be supposed to be a purely bodily event, involving no consciousness of the data.[2] It is this second conception of the proximate relatum that the spokesmen of objective relativism appear in the main to wish to convey. But since either view upon the point is possible, we must consider both.

If the objective relativist holds that the event by which the existence of a perceived character is immediately conditioned is the event of somebody's being aware of the character, then, of course, he is simply restating the usual dualistic view on this issue; he is affirming, in his own fashion, that the character is existentially as well as causally subjective. It is to consciousness, or to a relation of which consciousness is a term, that the particulars which enter into our experience are admitted to be relative. Upon the objective relativist who interprets his theory in this sense the benediction of the spirits of Descartes and Locke may be supposed to fall.

An issue thus far arises, then, as between dualism and the new relativism, only if the alternative interpretation of the latter is adopted. So interpreted, objective relativism declares that the proximate condition necessary for the existence of, *e. g.,* the particular that is the elliptical penny I am now seeing, is solely a physiological, presumably a neuro-cortical, process. And this proposition, if accepted, appears to some to be sufficient to vindicate the objectivity—in the sense of the physicality—of the sense-data thus generated. If a mind, as a qualitatively unique thing, or consciousness as a qualitatively unique type of event, were a

---

[2] A. E. Murphy in *University of California Publications in Philosophy,* 1926, p. 204. But the same writer in a paper published since the above was written declares that "the body *and mind* of the observer enter as factors in the situation" (*Journal of Philosophy,* XXVI, 1929, p. 288).

necessary condition for the occurrence of data, the latter might, no doubt, be called "mental" in the sense that they are those parts of the constitution of nature which are relative to minds or to consciousness, in distinction from the parts of that constitution which are relative to entities of other sorts. But if the proximate term of the conditioning relation be taken as itself a physical organism, or as the position which an organism happens to occupy in the system of spatio-temporal relations, then no reason remains for attaching to sense-data, or to any other content of experience, the supposedly honorific epithets of "mental" or "psychical." This hypothesis of the exclusively physical character of the events by which data are generated has, as has been remarked, commended itself not only to objective relativists but also to several recent philosophers who can hardly be so classified; so that an inquiry into its tenability will be pertinent to more than the special doctrine which is the primary theme of this lecture.

A very short and easy method is sometimes used for disposing of the matter. We are simply told that it is manifestly impossible that the occurrence of the mental event of perceiving should be a condition of the existence of anything. Thus Mr. Broad, in discussing, from the standpoint of his own theory of sensa, the question whether colors are "mind-dependent," answers that "the pervasion of a certain place by a certain color from a certain region of projection is not dependent on this color being perceived by the mind which animates the organism that occupies the region of projection"—because *"nothing* depends for its existence upon being perceived."[3] But how anyone can possibly know this last to be true, I am entirely unable to imagine. The particular data, *e. g.,* the patches of color seen, are admitted to be existents conditioned by the occurrence of certain bodily processes in the organism—by percipient events in the physiological sense. Empirically,

[3] *The Mind and Its Place in Nature,* p. 177. I find it difficult to reconcile this passage with Broad's statement elsewhere (*ibid.,* p. 169) that "since we cannot get a brain and nervous system like ours working properly without a mind like ours, it is obviously impossible to be sure that the latter is irrelevant for the present purpose and that the former is sufficient by itself."

these processes and the resultant data are always accompanied by awareness; the sensa *are* sensed. Through what revelation is it disclosed to us that they *could* exist unsensed—in other words, that what is empirically an invariable concomitant of their occurrence is not an indispensable condition of it? It will perhaps be replied that it is the postulate of the realistic philosophy that nothing can depend for its existence upon being perceived. I suggest that a realistic philosophy which postulates so much as this is laying up a great deal of unnecessary trouble for itself. All that it is essential for realism to maintain is that *some* things can exist unperceived—namely, things which are *not* conditioned by percipient events, even in the physiological sense, and are antecedent to and causal of our percepts. But the familiar reasons for believing in *such* metempirical realities afford no justification for the dogma that entities which (by hypothesis) are begotten, along with consciousness, by the brains of individual organisms, and manifest their existence solely by appearing as items in the private fields of awareness of those organisms, could exist outside those fields.[4]

The proposition that they could thus exist can be seriously considered and discussed, it seems evident, only if taken to mean that they sometimes do so; that the existents, such as this copper-colored elliptical shape before me, which are (so far as experience shows) produced by my brain concomitantly with an awareness of them, *are* sometimes produced without that concomitant, or continue in existence after the awareness has ceased. To say merely that they *might* exist unperceived, but never in fact do, would be, I can't but think, a wholly barren and unimportant, a highly improbable, and an obviously unprovable assertion.

But the theory that particulars "relative to brain-events" do exist unperceived would surely be a very queer one. It would be a gratuitous and an extremely inconvenient addition to physics and

---

[4] The curious prevalence of this dogma, especially in British realism, seems to be traceable to the influence of the non-sequitur in a celebrated early essay of G. E. Moore's ("The Refutation of Idealism"), to which reference was made in the first lecture. Even those who recognize that it *was* a non-sequitur, apparently continue to accept the conclusion as if it were an axiom.

physiology to assume that a process in the brain can not only produce, *e. g.,* an elliptical copper-colored entity without mass, and
can (as seems to be further implied) project this instantaneously
out to some more or less distant region of space, but also that this
imponderable brain-begotten particular can and does exist when
nobody is aware of it.   For, it will be observed, if characters "relative only to (physiological) percipient events in individual organisms," are assumed to be present (though unperceived) at the
places (whatever precisely these may be) assigned to them outside
the organism, nothing results elsewhere in the physical world
from their being there.   These unsensed sensa would be otiose
members of the physical universe. Unless our physics is *all* wrong,
they could not be supposed to play any part in the dynamic
processes of nature; and they would thus be entirely useless for
the theoretical explanation of the phenomena which we actually
experience.

The queerness of such a hypothesis becomes the more apparent
when we take note of a previously unmentioned implication of
objective relativism.   Whatever kind or degree of objectivity is
ascribed by this theory to any sense-data of the sort commonly
called veridical must *a fortiori* be ascribed to non-veridical data—
i. e., to dream-content and hallucinations.   For these are, more
undisputably than any others, relative to percipient events or the
conditions of individual human bodies.   Everyone, except the
consistent pan-objectivist, admits that *they* are thus relative; and
the objective relativist can least of all deny it.   And since his
principal thesis is that such relativity is perfectly compatible with
what he calls objectivity, and is even of the essence of it, he is debarred from setting up any invidious class-distinctions between
these two types of content, in the matter of objectivity or physicality.   And empirically, of course, there is just as much evidence—
which is to say, none at all—for the existence of wild as of tame
data when unperceived.   In fairness, then, the objective relativist
also (if his somewhat protean doctrine should take the general
form we are now supposing) ought apparently to hold that there

are present in the external world the objects of dream, fancy, and hallucination, even when no one is experiencing them. Nature would hardly be simplified or rendered more intelligible by such a supposition.

It will meanwhile be observed that if the brain-generated entities which sometimes *are* experienced—the percept of the extinct star, the visual after-image, the convergent railway-tracks, *etc.,* are assumed to be capable of existing, and therefore sometimes actually to exist, unperceived in nature outside the organism, as effects there of brain-events, the result is not only still a dualism, but an especially difficult sort of dualism to accept. "Physical" nature itself is bifurcated into two very curiously dissimilar classes of objects or events. It is not evident that this type of dualism is preferable to the other and more usual sort, that it does not rather, by filling physical space with a multitude of strangely incongruous neighbors—elliptical and intangible pennies mixed with circular and solid ones, dream-palaces really beside (or perhaps inside) real hovels, quasi-hallucinatory sea-serpents really swimming, unmarked by any mariner, in real seas—give us a peculiarly complicated, confused, messy, and improbable picture of the constitution of nature. The difficulty here is even greater than the analogous one which was pointed out in the case of pan-objectivism; for, upon the hypothesis we are just now considering, all these supernumerary members of the physical world are not there (so to say) in their own right, but are supposed to be thrust into it through some extraordinary potency of molecular motions in the brain to give birth to these anomalous additions to the "physical" sum of things—which, once born, are further assumed to be capable of supporting themselves without the assistance of their progenitors.

Taking, then, one consideration with another, the second horn of the dilemma—in the interpretation of the equivocal term "percipient events"—seems one which it would be inexpedient for the objective relativist to adopt. But, as we have seen, the alternative to doing so is the acceptance of the dualist's contention with respect to the first of the five points under consideration. In other words, unless we are to construe objective relativism as implying a peculiarly grotesque piece of pseudo-physics, that doctrine must be taken as an assertion of the existential as well as the causal subjectivity of content—if content consists of things that "exist" at all, *i. e.,* of particulars.

(2) It immediately follows from this that objective relativism also implies the non-physical status of whatever characters it declares to be relative to percipient events—in any sense of "physical" in which dualistic philosophy, or natural science, or common sense, has ever been accustomed to employ the term. Indeed, this is true even if the relativist denies the existential subjectivity of data and asserts only their causal subjectivity. For a thing is *not* proved to be physical in any ordinary sense, even if you prove that the sole necessary conditions of its existence are physical. To be physical means (to repeat our definition in part) to be, at the least, a factor in the executive order of nature apart from being perceived; to be potentially common to the experiences of many percipients, as an external cause of their sensations if not as an actual datum; and to conform to the laws of physics. But the putative offspring of the brain have none of these accepted marks of physicality. They are destitute of causal efficacy, at all events unless they are perceived; they give no evidence of continuing to exist and undergo regular changes when unperceived; they are strictly private affairs, accessible only to the consciousness connected with the brains that severally beget them; so far as we have any knowledge of them, they do not conform to physical laws. They are much more like "ideas" than they are like anything that has ever previously been called a physical object.

This is fully recognized by Broad in his exposition of his theory of sensa: those entities are "particular existents of a peculiar kind; they are not physical," even though "there is no reason to suppose that they are states of mind or existentially mind-dependent. In having spatial characteristics, color, *etc.,* they resemble physical objects as ordinarily conceived; but in their privacy and their dependence on the body, if not on the mind, of the observer they are more like mental states." "Objective relativism" thus, when you try to extract a definite meaning from it, seems, so far, to be identical with this theory of brain-generated sensa—if it is taken as excluding existential subjectivity. But since we have seen that it cannot be so taken without implying rather preposterous, and to its adherents presumably unacceptable, consequences, the distinction between its "characters-relative-to-percipient-events" and the dualist's "ideas" becomes still more elusive.

(3) But it is, I suppose, upon the third point that the most significant issue arises, in the opinion of most of those who see in objective relativism a new and clarifying insight which solves the old epistemological problem. Even though—as some of these would apparently agree—the proximate term to which the sense-datum is "relative" is, or includes, an actual perceiving of the datum, it still may be maintained that the datum "belongs to" the ulterior relatum or at all events to some real object or event; and this attributive objectivity is the essential matter. The sort of dependence upon the percipient event which the character has is no bar to the ascription of it to the object of knowledge. It was in failing to recognize this sort of objectivity, we are told, that the essential error of the dualist lay. He took the datum to be a kind of substance or thing instead of an attribute or adjective; and he was therefore unable to bring it into connection with that other substance or thing, the real object, which by hypothesis was *not* relative to the event of perception. In Professor Murphy's words, "an adjective never occurs in the same way as a substantive, and it is not possible to make either do the work of the other"; but this is precisely what dualism has attempted. It has assumed that "the character of redness must belong to something, and belong to it simply. Hence enters the idea, not as *apprehended quality, but as substantive,* as that which owns the quality. It is this which is really red; my idea then tells me the nature only of itself. . . . If ideas are (thus) substantives, characters of themselves, so to speak, they cannot be characters of anything else—duplicates, per-

haps, or symbols, but that is all." [5]   Thus it is that datum and
cognoscendum, which nature (with the aid of percipient events)
has joined together, are unlawfully put asunder.

This would seem to presuppose that the universe is composed of
two mutually exclusive classes of entities, substantives and adjectives, that one can always easily and confidently distinguish them,
and that sense-data are manifestly and indubitably of the adjectival
class. Now, one desires first of all an elucidation of the meaning
of this distinction. Just what is it to be an adjective, and by what
criterion are adjectives and substantives to be infallibly discriminated? The answer given to this question by the very competent
interpreter of objective relativism whom I have last cited, and less
clearly by some others, is that adjectives are by nature universals.
The proposition that data are adjectives consequently signifies that
data are universals or essences. This last theorem, put forward
by some of the contributors to the volume of *Essays in Critical
Realism,* and still stoutly defended by at least two of them,[6] thus
would appear to be for some the heart of the doctrine that relativity to a percipient is entirely compatible with objectivity—
though for others of its adherents that doctrine seems to include
no such article. We must, then, attempt to determine whether
this theorem, if tenable, would establish the "objectivity" of data,
in any sense in which dualism has been accustomed to deny it,
and also whether, or in what sense, the theorem *is* tenable.

The *prima facie* advantages of the adoption of the view that
data are essences, for the purposes of a would-be objective relativism, are fairly evident. For, in the first place, it seemingly puts
all of our previous criticisms out of court. They all took it for
granted that data are particulars which at certain times come into
existence, and that their relativity to percipient events means that

---

[5] *Op. cit.,* 1927, pp. 202, 195–6; italics mine.
[6] By Santayana and Drake. Strong seems to have abandoned it; *cf.* his articles
on "The Genesis of Sensible Appearances," in *Mind,* N.S., XXXVII, in which
sense-data are unmistakably treated as particulars. Strong's earlier article from
which I shall quote nevertheless remains one of the clearest and most concise expositions of the conception of data as essences.

their existence is generated by those events. But if data are essences, they do not "exist," and therefore cannot be generated by anything. What, according to the present version of relativism, "we directly perceive are qualities, and any such quality is timeless in the sense that, being just that quality irrespective of the circumstances of its occurrence, it is repeatable and so far universal. Its nature as quality is not constituted by the circumstances of its occurrence, and hence we may call it an 'eternal object.' "[7] With this assumption, the causal subjectivity of data is excluded; and since the foregoing arguments for their existential subjectivity and non-physical status presuppose their causal subjectivity, the whole case thus far made out against their objectivity seems to collapse.

And the identification of data with universals also offers an apparent way of escape from epistemological dualism. If the color which I perceive when I look at the back of a book is simply "the character of redness" in the abstract, then identically this abstract quality may also "belong to" the physical book. It is, in the words of one of the critical realists who have best expounded this hypothesis, "precisely because it is a mere universal that the essence given" in experience "and the essence embodied in the object may be the same, and that the mind in sense perception may therefore be able to rest directly upon the object"; and for this reason, also, "the *same* datum exactly might be given to another person, or to the same person at a different time and place."[8] Hence, "unless the essence given misrepresents the object . . . epistemological monism—in this carefully limited sense—is the truth; whereas the view that the datum is an existence," *i. e.,* a particular, "inevitably leads to the fallacy of representationism."[9]

Let us consider, then, the first of these two arguments, *viz.,* that data, being "eternal objects," are not "existences"; that they are therefore uncaused; and that their relativity to percipient events

[7] Murphy, *op. cit.,* p. 200.
[8] *Essays in Critical Realism,* 1920, pp. 241, 231.
[9] *Ibid.,* p. 241.

consequently cannot be construed to mean their causal subjectivity. What, indeed, one naturally asks, *can* it, upon these assumptions, be construed to mean? After all, percipient events *are* events, that is, happenings in time. And how, or in what sense, can an "eternal object" be "relative" to a happening in time? Surely, if it is so, the happening must, by its occurrence, and when it occurs, do something to the eternal object. Something befalls "the character of redness" when, by virtue of the present functioning of my neuro-cerebral mechanism, an oblong red patch is transiently presented in my visual experience. What befalls it, however, in the formula of the critical realists who adhere to the doctrine of essences, is merely that the redness is "given." The givenness is a temporal incident in the life of an organism, an incident which is supposed (too lightly, I think) to leave *what* is given uninfected with its own temporality. When I perceive the red book, I am momentarily contemplating the pure Platonic Idea of redness, of which the timelessness is quite unimpaired by its becoming an object of my contemplation. The present version of objective relativism apparently requires some such conception as this. Its theorem must, that is, be put thus: the givenness of a datum, though not the datum, is relative to (*i. e.,* caused by) a percipient event in the organism.

Now if Platonic realism is assumed, we are by hypothesis concerned with a sort of objective reality when we contemplate a timeless essence. This type of logical realism we have already encountered in the doctrine of certain pan-objectivists discussed in the second lecture. But is it no more than this that the relativist intends to affirm when he speaks of the objectivity of the datum? Does objective relativism surprisingly resolve itself into nothing but logical realism? Manifestly not, at least by the intent of those who propound it. Their contention is that data are both relative to percipient events and present *"in nature,"* which presumably means, in the world of spatio-temporal existence. And since merely being "given" is assumed to leave an eternal object still outside that world, the relativist has yet to explain to us how he proposes to fetch that object into it. And it is, I think, sufficiently evident he cannot offer any such explanation, because the thing itself is, in the nature of the case, impossible. You cannot convert Platonic Ideas into natural things without first divesting them of the abstractness which gave them their status in the World of Ideas; you cannot make temporal "events" out of "eternal objects" without impairment of the eternality of those objects. If the datum is no more than a timeless extra-mundane subsistent, it is not objective in the sense required by the theory; most obviously of all, it is not physical.

But this objection, it will perhaps be said, still ignores the fact that essences are, in this theory, held also to be *characters* of existents. "The essence as such," Murphy observes, "is abstract, to be sure, but it is a quality, and hence has an inescapable reference. . . . The error arises from the assumption that qualities do not characterize their objects but only themselves, and that existence has some other nature than the qualities that belong to it. The qualities are not the existent, to be sure, but they are its whole nature, and it has no other." [10] There underlies this reply that curious conception of the nature and relations of qualities and existence which appears also in the philosophy of Whitehead. "Existence" consists of "events," in the sense of that term in which "events" are "the relata of the fundamental homogeneous relation of 'extension,'" the "situations" to which "eternal objects," that is to say, qualities, are "referred." [11] Thus an event is not a universal but a unique term or locus in a mesh of purely spatio-temporal relations; and it has as such no character whatever, unless its position in that system be a character. Qualities, however, may be "ingredient" into events; and after their ingredience, it appears to be supposed, they remain just as truly "eternal objects" as before. But this is precisely what, I suggest, they cannot conceivably do. If a quality characterizes an "event," it does so by acquiring the temporality and the localization of the

[10] *University of California Publications in Philosophy*, 1926, p. 202.
[11] *Principles of Natural Knowledge*, pp. 61, 67.

event—in short, by assuming the properties by which "existence" has been defined. If, then, the ingredience of a character is declared to be conditioned by a percipient event in an organism, the character is thereby declared to be a particular of which the existence has been caused by the occurrence of the percipient event. No escape, then, from the admission of the causal subjectivity of data is to be achieved by objective relativism through the adoption of the device of identifying data, and characters in general, with "eternal objects." And on the other hand, if it is still insisted that qualities *do* remain "timeless" and "merely subsistent," despite their so-called ingredience—then, once more, they have no place in "nature."

We, turn, then, to examine the other argument, *viz.*, that data are universals, and that therefore a datum and an attribute of "the object" may be identical. Here the emphasis is not upon the timelessness and ingenerable nature of essences, but merely upon the sameness of any essence in each of its embodiments. Indeed it is a necessary part of the argument here to assume that essences are capable of repetition, of turning up again at various times and places—which seems a notion not wholly uncontaminated by the concept of time. If, however, they are identical with themselves in each repetition, this, it is argued, makes it permissible to say that my perceptual datum, *e. g.*, red, is not a duplicate or representation of a character of "the object"—at least it is not when the object happens to have that character, and the percept is therefore veridical—but *is* just that character itself. Thus again, it is concluded, data can be credited with at least an attributive objectivity.

Now there is at the bottom of this argument, I think, an undeniable and, indeed, sufficiently obvious truth—which, however, has been inflated into a conclusion which it does not justify. It is, of course, the fact that the same kind of quality may appear in numberless instances or repetitions. And it is also true that when I judge that a quality which is now a datum in my experience—*e. g.*, some character of a present memory-image—was also a quality of the event which I believe myself to be remembering, I am not judging that the present datum *quâ* particular was an ingredient of that event.   Professor Drake is surely quite right when he observes that, if "the character that I ascribe to an external existent" is, say, "the character of being-a-tree-ten-feet-away," and if I assume that "such an essence (since everything you can mention is an essence) may conceivably exist in external space, as we naturally suppose," then "it is *impossible* that that essence" (which Drake supposes to be "my datum") should "be a character of my perceiving organism, which is not ten feet away." [12]   But it does not follow from this that the datum is a *mere* essence—an essence not dated, located, or particularized. On the contrary, this very argument of Drake's manifestly implies that the datum is *not in that sense* an essence.   For the proof that it is not a character of my perceiving organism is drawn from the assumed difference of spatial position between my organism and the so-called essence.   An "essence" that has a position in space is not a "mere essence"; it is precisely what is commonly called a particular, inasmuch as it exists at a particular time in a particular place, and not elsewhere.   And that the datum is this kind of "essence," namely, an essence particularized, the epistemological dualist agrees.   Only, just because it is particular, it cannot, he assumes, be in two places at once; and therefore it cannot be identified with any coexistent state of, *e. g.*, a "tree-ten-feet-away." But though the tree is not the datum, and though neither can possibly be a "mere essence," they none the less "have," *i. e.*, repeat or embody, a common essence.   The obvious truth, then, that qualities when predicated of two or more things are necessarily dissociated in thought from the particularity of each of those things, does not warrant the conclusion that, *as really characterizing each thing* (or, if that phraseology is preferred, as "ingredient in each event"), the qualities do not "exist," or are not particulars.   Existences may resemble one another; in so far as they do

---

[12] "That Elusive Doctrine of Essence," *Philosophical Review*, XXXVII, 1928, p. 55.

they exemplify or are characterized by the same universals; and in any judgment which attributes the same character to two existents it is necessarily the character *quâ* universal that we attribute to them. When, therefore, I take a percept as giving information about an external object, I am attributing to the object the character of the percept taken as a universal, *i. e.,* as repeatable. But I am not thereby implying that there are *not* two repetitions or instances of that universal, one in the percept, the other in the object; nor am I implying that each instance of that universal is not a concrete existent, in the only sense in which anything can be said to be a concrete existent. And the "identity of datum and object," which epistemological dualism denies, is primarily identity of repetition or instance, not identity of *mere* essence or universal (*i. e.,* likeness of·kind). Two pennies fresh from the Mint are as alike as it is possible to make them; they have, so far as ordinary observation shows, virtually complete identity of essence (in the sense of the term in which *not* "everything you can mention is an essence"). And when I ascribe any quality of the one to the other, it is the abstract quality, *e. g.,* copper-color, that I am ascribing. But it does not occur to anyone, not even to philosophers, to say that, since the pennies have the same essence, they must be the same coin, and that, if you have one in your purse and I have one in mine, we must not permit ourselves to fall into a pecuniary dualism with respect to them, but must regard it as a case of a single penny being "given" in two purses. There is no more reason (there is, in fact, less) for saying that your visual percept of a penny and mine are an identical datum "given" in two awarenesses, or that both are identical with a real, physical penny. In one sense the proposition that the two data have, or are, in some respects one essence is a harmless truism; in another sense it is patently contrary to fact; and the air of philosophical importance with which the proposition has been invested arises through treating the two senses as if they were one.

Perhaps in this last I shall seem to have forgotten the delicate gift which is, in this theory, supposed to be possessed by consciousness, namely, that of leaving the essences which it contemplates undisturbed in their aloofness and timelessness. No doubt in order to enter the purses, the essence "penny" must become two particular pennies; but it need not, in order to become content of consciousness, cease to be a pure and eternal universal. About this, however, one must observe in the first place that it cannot, at any rate, be true of sense-awareness. If there is anything whatever that is certainly dated and localized (whatever be the nature of the space in which it is localized), it is the content of perception—the penny that I see and touch. This, more indubitably than anything else, is here and now. And it is not an abstract "event," as a mere "situation" of qualities, that is here and now; it is the patch of color seen, the tactual *quale* felt. But even if it were not so, the case of the objective relativist would not be bettered. For if data when given remained thus outside this bourne of time and place, it would follow that they do not belong to objects in the way in which unperceived qualities do. An inanimate thing or a bare "event" presumably has not the power merely to contemplate eternal essences. If it is to acquire them as its actual properties, it must, as I have suggested, drag them down into the particular region of the spatio-temporal order which is its own abode. There would thus be a radical contrast between the characters which "belong to" the object or event, and the data, *i. e.,* the eternal essences, which would by hypothesis be "given" in the peculiar sense that they do not belong to anything. In such a view, then, data would, even more conspicuously than before, be left isolated in a supra-mundane realm of being, and would least of all be capable of performing the office of adjectives of natural existents.

We may, then, sum up our discussion of this point as follows: (a) Data are not essences (in the sense of that term which is required). (b) If they were, and if the unperceived characters of physical reals were not, then the data would not be "adjectives" of physical reals in the sense in which those characters are adjectives. They would, and so long as they remained essences could, only be given for awareness; and such givenness would leave them unattached to objects. (c) In any case they would as *mere* essences remain external to "nature." Hence they would not be objective in the sense in which their objectivity appears to be affirmed by the objective relativist. They would have, at most, merely the other-worldly sort of objectivity which every Platonic Idea is held by logical realism to have. We must conclude, in short, that the assertion of the attributive objectivity of data ought not to be identified with the theory that data are mere essences, for two sorts of reasons: first, because that theory is not true; and second, because, if it were true, it would not justify objective relativism.

We revert, then, to the general interpretation of this doctrine with which we began. The content of perception is assumed to consist of particular existents; these are "relative to," *i. e.,* conditioned by, percipient events in the organism; this means their causal subjectivity; and this renders at least highly probable their existential subjectivity. They are, in short, cerebrally or mentally generated entities, *viz.,* sensa. And we have now to ask what meaning accordant with *this* understanding of objective relativism can be assigned to the proposition that sensa are adjectives, or true attributes, of objects or events "in nature."

One possible meaning is evident—namely, that the universal which is embodied or particularized in a sensum may be the same universal that is embodied in an object existing independently of perception. That in this sense identity of essence between datum and *cognoscendum* may be affirmed we have just seen. But this is not equivalent to attributive objectivity, as that term has been here defined; and such identity has, of course, always been recognized and emphasized by epistemological dualists, in the case of those data which they have regarded as genuinely veridical. How many and which data should be so regarded, has been a question about which there has often been a wide difference of opinion among dualistic philosophers. None have been quite so naïve as to think that all sensible appearances are representations of the characters of external objects; but there has been no unanimity as to where the line should be drawn. The most familiar view may again serve as an illustration sufficient for our present purpose. According to this, certain essences which are called the primary qualities are embodied as particulars both in sensa and in material objects; hence, though the sensa themselves cannot properly be said to be attributes of the material objects, this class of their attributes and those of the objects can be said to be the same, while other attributes of sensa, *viz.,* the secondary (or in Locke's awkward terminology, the "sensible") qualities are not ascribable to the objects. If, now, this is all that the objective relativist means when he affirms the attributive objectivity of experienced characters, his doctrine, up to this point, merges completely with one or another of the historic forms of dualism. With which one would depend upon the relativist's own decision as to the number and kind of sensible characters which are objectively attributable to physical reality. This would be a detail, important in itself, but leaving the general nature of the doctrine unaffected. The relativist manifestly could not hold that *all* characters are in this sense objective without denying the possibility of perceptual (and other) error.

This, however, is not the only possible interpretation which could, without conflict with the general outlines of the doctrine, be given to the theorem of attributive objectivity. It might conceivably be held that the sensa *as particular existents*—not merely the universals characterizing them—are attributes of "the object," provided that the object were itself so defined that it would be capable of having particulars as its attributes. And this would be conceivable if we understood by "the object," not another concrete particular, but merely an "event" in the sense already mentioned—a locus or region of space at a time. So construed, the theorem we are considering would come to this: the character (a particular) which is my sensum, though generated by the percipient event in me, exists at the present time "out there" in a certain determinate region of space. It is a character now actually present in that region (or, in the terminology of Whitehead, actually "ingredient into that event"). And this is, I think, sometimes the kind of attributive objectivity which objective relativists intend to affirm with regard to the content of perception. Most of the expressions of the doctrine with which I am acquainted are couched in such general and equivocal terms that I am not sure that this is what is usually meant; and in some cases such an interpretation would seem to be excluded. But we are trying to extract *some* definite and distinctive meaning out of objective relativism; and since this is a possible meaning, and since such a view appears to be actually held by some adherents of that doctrine, and also by other philosophers innocent of any general relativistic bias, it will be worth while to consider a little more precisely what it signifies, and whether, even if it were accepted, it would be inconsistent with the essential contentions of philosophical dualism.

We observed in the first lecture that the early modern dualists fell into an unhappy confusion of terminology, if not of ideas, when they defined "mental" entities as unextended and non-spatial, and at the same time included "sensations" (*i. e.*, sensa) among mental entities. That visual and tactual and perhaps auditory content is given as located and extended in *some* space or other we have accepted as a primary fact of experience. That, in this general sense, space-occupancy is attributable to some sensa seems beyond reasonable dispute. But this alone does not go far towards vindicating their "objectivity." For there are recognized in recent philosophy and physics not merely many possible kinds of space, but many possible separate spaces of a single kind. It is not evident that your visual sensa are given in a space identical with that in which mine are given, or even that your own visual and tactual sensa are both given in a common space. It is, furthermore, not evident that *any* sensa exist in the space in which physical objects are commonly supposed to exist—or at all events, that if we say they exist there we are using words of the same meaning as when we say that the physical objects exist there.

Broad has lucidly set forth the considerations which make it seem
"clear that either (1) sensible determinates (such as some particular shade of red) do not inhere in regions of physical Space-
Time, but in regions of some other Space-Time; or (2) that if
they do inhere in regions of physical Space-Time, they must inhere
in the latter in some different way from that in which physical
determinates (like physical motion) do so."[13] We appear to be
confronted with this dilemma: "either there is one sense of inherence and many different Space-Times, or there is one Space-
Time and many different senses of inherence."[14] And aside from
these difficulties about the localization of sensa in the same space
with one another and with physical objects, there are the (logically prior) difficulties attaching to the supposition of a single
absolute space in which to locate physical objects themselves.
These difficulties have been notorious for more than two centuries; and the results of the Michelson-Morley and kindred experiments, with the reasonings of Einstein concerning them, have,
it is now even more notorious, seemed to most mathematicians and
physicists to give the notion of an absolute space its *coup de grâce.*
But if there is no absolute space even for physical objects, to *what*
space are we to assign sensa in order to invest them with the desired objectivity? It will perhaps be answered that they may be
assigned to the Minkowskian four-dimensional continuum of
space-time which in relativity physics has taken the place of the
Newtonian absolute space. But visual sensa are *not* in this space-
time. For, as Mr. Bertrand Russell has remarked, "in the world
of percepts the distinction between space and time does really
exist, and space does really have certain properties which [Ein-
steinian] relativity denies to physical space,"[15] that is to say, to
space-time. The "events" of relativity physics are thus not even
in the same kind of space, or quasi-space, with our percepts.[16]

Before, then, we could assign any specific meaning to the ob-

[13] *Scientific Thought,* p. 543.
[14] *Ibid.,* p. 544.
[15] *Analysis of Matter,* p. 338.
[16] This point is further dealt with in Lectures VII and VIII.

jective relativist's general thesis—as we are now interpreting it—
we should need to know what in that thesis is meant by the space,
or the space-time, in which (some) sensa are declared to be situated. Such information is not, so far as I can recall, usually
afforded us by those who propound this philosophy. To deal
thoroughly with it we should therefore be obliged to reconstruct
for ourselves all the views which might conceivably be held about
physical space or space-time and the relation to these of the space
of perception, and examine into the tenability of each of these
views. This would demand an exceedingly long and complicated
analysis. But, happily, it does not appear necessary, for the purposes of this lecture, to attempt this. Our concern is primarily
to determine whether the objective relativist has overthrown the
essentials of dualism or presented a real alternative to it. And, in
so far as psychophysical dualism is at issue, it can easily be shown
—in consequence of the results reached earlier in this lecture—
that the relativist cannot escape that doctrine, whatever specific
theory he may adopt as to the nature and relations of physical and
perceptual space. Let the theory which would be the most favorable to his general view be assumed. This would be the theory
that, despite the physicists, there is a single absolute space, that
this is identical with the space of perception, and that in it, therefore, both our visual data and physical particulars have determinate positions. Nevertheless, the data are still sensa and exist
only for awareness. In other words, it is, we assume, conceded by
the relativist—since we have shown that it must be—that the
character which I perceive is both causally and existentially subjective. Even though it be "out there" somewhere in space, it is
there only as an effect of a percipient event in me and only while
I am conscious of it. The sole mode of "being there" that it has
is that of being perceived there by me. It is not there in the sense
that it exercises any physical action upon material bodies, or upon
other entities of its own kind, i. e., the sensa of other percipients;
and it is not there, even in this tenuous sense of "being there,"
for any other percipient. And it is, moreover, according to the

implications of the theory, not "objectively" there in any sense in which the contents of hallucinations and illusions are not equally objectively there. Consequently, no definite meaning is here left for the distinction between "really being there" and "appearing there for an individual subject of awareness"; in other words, the import of the former expression, when it is so applied, reduces to what dualistic philosophers, and people in general, have usually meant by "subjectively appearing." That visual objects have an *apparent* existence in space can hardly have been unknown to any dualistic philosopher who had eyes.

It may, however, at first seem that, by means of the assumption about space and the presence of sensa therein which I have mentioned, the objective relativist might escape epistemological dualism. The sensum, being after all, by hypothesis, in some fashion out there where the physical object is, is to that extent ingredient into the "event" which the object occupies; the character, or a character, of that event is thus known directly, since the sensum *is* that character. A very little reflection, however, is enough to make it evident that there is no way out of epistemological dualism here; if it seems otherwise, it can only be through a neglect to specify the locus of your *cognoscendum.* If what is ordinarily called the visual image of a distant star is (as we are assuming) supposed really to be present—though in the peculiar and tenuous sense mentioned—in space outside the observer's body, and even if it is supposed to be as distant as the star was when the light left it (a supposition for which there appears to be no ground), it is nevertheless not identical with the star about which the observer is, according to the usual belief of astronomers, getting information. For in consequence of the finite velocity of light—not to repeat the other familiar considerations recalled in the first lecture—the astronomer's star is no longer there. The sensum was not begotten by the observer's brain until centuries or millennia after the remote causal event which it makes (in some small measure) known to the astronomer. It is extremely unlikely that the same kind of event is now occurring in that place, and it is quite certain that the same *particular* event is not now occurring there. The sensum, then, would at best be present (in its peculiar non-physical fashion) only at the place where the astronomical event *did* at some previous time take place. To maintain, then, that the two are existentially identical would be much like maintaining that because King George can visit a place where one of his ancestors lived—say Henry VII—he is therefore identical with Henry VII. Nor, of course, is this the worst of it. If the direction in space in which the star-character *appears* to lie is admitted by the relativist to be that in which it does lie (and he, at least, can hardly deny this), then the supposed locus of the percept is often one at which the ulterior causal event did not occur. For the light before reaching us may have been, and perhaps in some degree always has been, refracted. We may not see the star in the precise direction in which it lay when the light now reaching our eyes was emitted from it. All that the relativist's thesis can come to, then, is that the percept is *somewhere* out there in space, its situation having indeed some relation to that of the ulterior causal event, but being determined also by the refraction of light, and, indeed, by many other modifying factors which it is not needful here to enumerate. That it occupies even a former residence of its remote ancestor remains questionable. It is, in short, clear that if the sensum is to give the astronomer any knowledge of a distant event, it can do so only by virtue of being apprehended as a duplicate of some character (which may be merely a quantitative or relational character, *i. e.,* a spatio-temporal pattern) of that event. The result, then, even when we postulate the theory about physical and perceptual space which is best adapted to the needs of a would-be-objective relativism, is pure dualism in the epistemological as well as the psychophysical sense —if, at least, such relativism is assumed to be consistent with the belief that perception affords us any knowledge at all. But we now turn to another clause of this theory which, as I have already intimated, raises a doubt whether it is not equivalent to a wholesale negation of the possibility of knowledge.

(4) That clause is to the effect that data are perspective aspects or appearances of objects—or of "events" in Whitehead's sense. The characters perceived or otherwise given as content are, it is especially insisted, "relative to the standpoint" or "point of view" of the percipient or knower. I will first state what I understand these propositions, as employed by objective relativists, to mean. The notion of a standpoint or point of view apparently implies, in the first place, a situation in which *some* element is initially taken as *not* relative to the percipient. It is assumed that a standpoint is a point for viewing something external to the standpoint, and that many points of view may somehow have a common locus of reference. From my point of view the penny may appear elliptical, from yours, circular; but the phraseology implies that the same object, or at least the same region of space or space-time, is in some sense being viewed by both of us; if this were not implied, the term "point of view" would be meaningless. This postulated antecedent, non-relative factor in the perceptual situation we may call, for short, the "object of reference," the word "object" being used in this expression to cover loci or any other conceivable containers or possessors of attributes.

The proposition that data are perspective aspects is not, of course, meant to apply merely to visual data, nor exclusively to spatial perspectives. "Perspective" designates any relation between a percipient event and the object of reference which makes the content given by means of that particular event unlike the object as it is apart from that relation; and "my standpoint" consists of the total set of conditions which gives to that "aspect" or "appearance" of the object which is my datum a special character that does not otherwise belong to the object, and does not belong to its other aspects or appearances. The constitution and condition of my sense-organs and my brain—and of my mind, if the mind is admitted to have any rôle in the affair—is thus a part of my standpoint; and as the *proximate* factor determining the nature of the content experienced, it may be called the "immediate standpoint."

We need not here again consider the question just where the character which is due to the standpoint is, according to objective relativism, situated. Let it, so far as the present issue is involved, be situated where it may—at the starting-point of the process which is the necessary condition for the production of the datum, or elsewhere in physical space outside the organism, or inside the brain, or in a private space. What now concerns us is that, if a datum, whatever its supposed situation, is *only* a perspective appearance, if it is what it is solely from the standpoint of the percipient and only for him, and, in the last analysis, only by virtue of his individual constitution, then his experiencing of it would not appear to afford what is commonly understood by knowledge. Is, then, epistemological objectivity reconcilable with perspectivity?

That it is not has hitherto usually been considered obvious. Just so far as data are regarded not only as causally and existentially subjective but also as having their *nature* determined by a particular standpoint (including the constitution of the percipient), they have commonly been admitted to be subjective, in the sense which is significant for the theory of knowledge. Helmholtz long since gave typical expression to the doctrine of the complete relativity of the character of our sensory content to the physical antecedents and especially to the physiological conditions of sensation; but he did not imagine that in emphasizing this he was vindicating for us an objective acquaintance with the nature of the external world. A little reflection, he wrote in the *Physiological Optics,*

reveals that all properties attributable to objects in the external world may be said to be simply *effects* exerted by them either on our senses or on other natural objects. . . . Each effect, as to its nature, quite necessarily depends both on the nature of what causes the effect and on that of the person on whom the effect is produced.

Upon this last point Helmholtz was especially insistent. That the kind of effect produced by the action of one body upon another depends always upon the peculiarities of both bodies is a thing that "we never even doubt for an instant when it is a question of two bodies in the external world." But in the case of properties depending on the mutual relations between things and our organs of sense, "people have always been disposed to forget that here too we are concerned with the reaction towards a special reagent, namely, our own nervous system, and that color, smell, taste, and feeling of warmth or cold are also effects quite essentially depending on the nature of the organ that is affected." [17] Not only the physiological conditions, but also "our consciousness," as the final term of the process, the proximate relatum, must have a part in determining the nature of those effects which are "our perceptions and ideas." Hence,

to expect to obtain an idea which would reproduce the nature of the thing concerned, that is, which would be true in an absolute sense, would mean to expect an effect which would be perfectly independent of the nature of the thing on which the effect was produced; which is an obvious absurdity. Our human ideas, therefore, and the ideas of any conceivable intelligent creature, must be images of objects whose mode is essentially co-dependent on the nature of the consciousness which has the idea and is conditioned also by its idiosyncrasies.[18]

The general philosophy implied by these principles, it seemed to Helmholtz, is a pragmatic phenomenalism. Our ideas "enable us to adjust our actions so as to bring about the desired result." "Not only is there *in reality* no other mode of comparison at all between ideas and things—all the schools are agreed in this— but any other mode of comparison is entirely unthinkable and has no sense whatever." [19]

This is, I suppose, the classic statement of the agnostic implications of the view that all the attributes of the content of perception are determined ultimately—and to a degree to which limits cannot be set—by the "nature of the thing on which the effect is produced," that is to say, by the "standpoint" of the percipient

[17] *Op. cit.*, III, p. 21. That any claim to knowledge implies that there is something in experience which is *not* due to the nature of the ultimate organ affected— this Helmholtz failed to see.

[18] *Ibid.*, III, p. 19.

[19] *Ibid.*

organism. And it is a view similar to this, but still farther-reaching, that the professedly "objective" relativist often seems to be enunciating—and enunciating not regretfully but jubilantly. Not merely some but all content, he appears to tell us, is affected with perspectivity. Everything of which I am aware is what it is solely because I, the experiencing organism, am just now occupying a unique place in the general frame of things and am just now constituted in the particular manner in which I happen to be. Alike in perception and memory and thought I apprehend nothing but appearances due to my special standpoint, and therefore not identifiable with any characters otherwise belonging to the object of reference, nor with the appearances presented from other standpoints. Never, then, can I know things as they are, or would be—or past events as they were—if I were now unaware of them, and if my body were not now functioning in the special manner which causes this particular character to be presented to me. Consequently, in the doctrine of the universal perspectivity of data —if consistently carried out—any reality as it is apart from the special circumstances under which it is perceived or thought of becomes completely unknowable. The "object of reference" becomes a mere x, like the Kantian *Ding-an-sich,* and is in the end likely to suffer the same fate. For if the nature of all the content (whatever it be) through which the subject of experience represents that object or locus is itself determined by his special standpoint, the latter swallows up even its own object of reference, and the knower is left confined within a "point of view" from which nothing whatever outside that point can be viewed. And even if the relativist does not carry out his characteristic logic so thoroughly, he still is committed to the proposition that what appears from *any* standpoint is "objective," and that all such appearances are equally objective. Hence, unlike the epistemological dualist, he retains in his universe no standard objects or facts, even in theory. Everything truly *is* all the things that it appears to any and all percipients (or concipients) to be, and no one preferentially "objective" object or event, from which the appearances are distinguished, and with which they can be in thought compared, is provided.

Thus the outcome to which the doctrine of the perspectivity of the apprehended characters of things logically tends—and which it often all but reaches—is a general deliquescence of the notion of factual truth and falsity; and the influence of that part of objective relativism which consists of this doctrine in promoting such a tendency is widely apparent in contemporary American philosophy. "What is a 'fact'?" asks a recent writer; and he answers, putting the position with admirable candor and clarity:

There are no facts at large; at least science knows no such facts and is ready for a reconstruction at any point in the field of facts. Facts are facts *for somebody;* they lie within experience and get their meaning there. They are by no means equivalent to "existence" or "reality," but are *correlations of data within perspectives.* This is to say that it is necessary to note where, when, and how they are given. Close observation will show that they are neither prior, independent existences, nor yet an immediate "datum" which comes, as it were, self-labelled; they have to be attained or determined in the context in which they are relevant. Accordingly, for the ancients it was not a belief, it was a fact, that the earth is flat. *For us* it is not a fact, and never was a fact, because our correlated data are different. The difference is a difference of perspectives and of data. . . . That the earth was flat *was* a correlation of data constituting fact and truth. By the same token it is *now* a fact that the earth is round and was so in the past, and the belief in this fact *is* true.[20]

Another writer has had the acumen and the boldness in paradox to "extend radically the doctrine of perspectives" so that it may apply—as in consistency it unquestionably should—to the concepts of time and evolution. The doctrine, in general terms, is thus formulated:

Whatever is found empirically to happen always involves the compresence of an intelligent organism, and (which is more important metaphysically) the way in which it happens is, in the last analysis, *the way in which it comes to play the part that it does play in the development of the perspectives or centers of experience through which it gains its place in the objective order that we call the world.*[21]

20 Donald H. Piatt, in *The Journal of Philosophy,* XXV, 1928, pp. 324–5.
21 Edwin A. Burtt, in *Proc. of the Sixth International Congress of Philosophy,* p. 174; italics mine.

Now the "standpoint" which determines any actually given "perspective" is always a present standpoint. What, then, is the past from the standpoint of the present? Are not its nature and the order of the events composing it those which it empirically exhibits *within* the standpoint, *i. e.*, within the present "from" which it is viewed? If this question is answered, as the "doctrine of perspectives" seems to require, in the affirmative, it follows that "the world always takes shape from the present outward. It expands into the past as knowledge of the past is needed to satisfy present desires. . . .: But it remains within the present all the while, in fact it only generates a vastly larger present." Thus "real time" begins only with organisms whose presents include temporal perspectives of the past; the "time of science," conceived of as something independent of such perspectives and prior to the existence of the intelligent organisms experiencing them, is a mere "abstract time." It "does not characterize the world at the beginning, it only emerges when the expanding process of real time has gone far enough for the meaning of a successive continuity to be clearly seized and the habit acquired of fitting events into it. Real evolution is thus not a temporal process if we mean thereby the time of physics." [22] And this, generalized, means that "the order of discovery is the order of reality." [23] No doubt "in abstract time the ages the geologist studies preceded the days of his own childhood." But then abstract time is not "empirical reality." "No past event becomes an empirical reality until it has taken its place in the order of discovery"—which appears to mean that its date of existence is the date when it was first discovered, or rather, when *anybody* discovers it. For of course, if all that were meant by its "empirical reality" were its *being* discovered, the seeming paradox would come only to the tautology that the date of the discovery of the event was the date when it

[22] *Ibid.*, pp. 172–3. The reference to the "expanding process of real time" which went on *before* the organisms, apparently by a sort of fiction, conferred "successive continuity" upon what preceded their present, is a little puzzling; there would seem to have been a fairly "real time" before real time began.
[23] *Ibid.*, p. 176.

was discovered. Since this can hardly be what is intended, the consequence here deduced from the doctrine of perspectives seems to be that the being of the past is entirely contained within the present, and its characteristics (including the sequences of its events) entirely determined by present organic conditions—needs, interests, purposes, beliefs. Nothing could illustrate better than this deduction—which seems to be quite correctly drawn from the premises—how meaningless the very notion of objectivity becomes when the principle of the perspectivity of all so-called "knowledge" is taken seriously, and how completely in such a philosophy the concept of the knowledge-process as an attempt to apprehend the nature of realities apart from and prior to the knowing has disappeared. For pastness, as has more than once been remarked in these lectures, is the primary and most indubitable mode of the non-relativity of fact both to the cognitive event and to the vehicles through which facts get reported; and retrospection exhibits the transcendent reference of the data of knowledge in its clearest and most obvious form. The irrecoverable and irremediable past has always been the arch-example of independence, in the epistemological as in other senses, an example upon which countless proverbs and apophthegms and passages of reflective poetry have dwelt. But it, too—even the very pastness of it—is now made dependent upon present standpoints which nevertheless are conceived to be themselves forever changing and forever lapsing into the past. In this kind of relativism the last vestige of sense disappears along with the last vestige of objectivity, and the *reductio ad absurdum* of the "doctrine of perspectives" becomes complete.

There is, I am well aware, a reply which the "objective" relativist has ready to hand for meeting the charge that his doctrine is a pure subjectivism. I will quote the best statement of it with which I am acquainted.

Given a specified standpoint, and the truth is quite final and ultimate. A body is at rest in a given system of reference. The fact that it is moving through another in no way contradicts the final and indisputable fact that it is not moving in this system. The question is not one of subjective caprice; given the conditions, there is one true judgment on the matter, and no other. No absolute could alter or supplant this fact nor need any rational person be skeptical about it. If you were trying to treat motion as absolute and predicate it of things in themselves, there would be contradiction. Here there is none whatever. . . . If ultimacy were the property of reality "in itself," then our judgments, being obviously less than such an absolute, would be false in respect to it. If ultimacy attached to events in their relations, then predication is valid for a given context, and in that context is quite ultimate. . . . Hence the metaphysical ultimacy which we claim for events—the ultimacy of the determinate fact. If I like cucumbers now it is eternally and indubitably true that I do like them. The different taste. of my neighbor, a house cat, or the absolute mind does not render this fact false or unreal. . . . The instance is trivial but the fact is not. Concrete occurrences in their relations are facts which no further information can discredit. We may go farther and higher, but we cannot be content with less. Upon this rock we found our metaphysics, and the forces of bifurcation shall not prevail against it.[24]

The reply is here put as clearly and effectively as the nature of the case permits. Yet it fails to meet the issue, as can be shown by an examination of the three considerations upon which it chiefly rests.

(a) In the first place, when it is said that a predicate which is purely relative is not for that reason a thing of "subjective caprice," the observation is true but irrelevant; for "capricious" and "subjective" are not interchangeable terms. What is capricious may be subjective, but the subjective, even in the epistemological sense, is not necessarily capricious. When, for example, the dualist has called the secondary qualities subjective, he has not meant that there is any caprice about them. The color a visual observer sees he cannot help seeing, be it what it may; its presence in his experience is presumably as rigorously determined causally as any other natural fact. It does not follow, for the dualist, that it gives him true information about any property which objects have when unseen, or even about any property which they have for all possible or all actual visual observers.

[24] A. E. Murphy: "Substance and Substantive," in *University of California Studies in Philosophy*, IX, 1927, pp. 83–4.

(b) The chief point of the reply, however, seems to lie in the observation that if a thing has such and such a character from a given standpoint and in a particular perspective, then it has that character from that standpoint and in that perspective. This tautological proposition is beyond dispute—and wholly irrelevant. The question at issue is whether the awareness of a character found only in one perspective and determined by a private standpoint is *enough* to constitute what is commonly understood—by science as well as by common sense—as knowing. And it is manifest that it is not enough—that such awareness is precisely the sort of experience which the word "subjective" was invented to designate. It is no evidence of the epistemological objectivity of a character which is discoverable from a "specified standpoint" that *from* that standpoint the nature and the givenness of the character is an "ultimate fact," beyond the reach of doubt for anyone who is standing there. The epistemological dualist has always asserted with regard to all immediate appearances that they are, in one sense, ultimate and absolute. About *their* characteristics, he has been accustomed to say, not only need there be no error; there *can* be, at the moment of their sensible presence, no error —in so far as inference, introducing elements not sensibly present, can be excluded. He has regarded this sort of ultimacy as the very mark of the subjective in the epistemological sense. When immediate data are simply taken as ultimate—as not claiming to express a character of something beyond them which is not determined to be what *it* is by the percipient event or its specific conditions—they are *eo ipso* taken as "mere appearances," innocent of epistemic pretensions. Even the idealist, in so far as he has sought to vindicate the possibility of objective knowledge, has denied the perspectivity of data, has affirmed that the individual knower can sometimes apprehend characters which some determinable portion of reality possesses, not from "a specified standpoint," but irrespective of any differences in the standpoints of finite knowers.

(c) Consequently, the analogy drawn between the relativity— more precisely, the respectivity—of rest and motion and the assumed relativity—more precisely, the perspectivity—of perceived characters, is inapposite. No one questions that a body A may be moving with respect to one system of reference, S_1, and at rest with respect to another, S_2; and there is assuredly nothing in *this* fact which implies that "moving" and "at rest" are not equally objective and physical characters of the same body. But the proposition "A is in motion" is in that case not true solely from the standpoint of an individual observer or knower; it is true of A *with respect to S_1* regardless of standpoints. Respective characters may be as objective as any others; and when they are, they are not merely perspective aspects. We should have a situation parallel to what the complete relativist conceives to be the knowledge-situation only if we made at least three additional assumptions about A and its relation to S_1 and S_2: (i) that an observer P on S_1 could know *only* the character, *viz.,* "in motion," which A has *relatively to his own system;* (ii) that A would not have this character *even relatively to P's system* for any observer or knower having a different perceptual or cognitive standpoint; (iii) that the proximate necessary condition for A's having that character relatively to P's system was a *percipient event* in the observer on S_1; in other words, that A would not be in motion relatively to S_1 if that percipient event had not occurred. The point that needs to be especially emphasized here is (ii). If you assert the cognitive ultimacy of every standpoint, then, if an observer on S_2 should (because of some peculiarity of his psycho-physical constitution) declare that A is at rest with respect to S_1, and even that it must be so perceived by P, it would follow that he is uttering a "truth quite final and ultimate." From the "specified standpoint," namely, his own—in other words, in virtue of his particular make-up and the consequent peculiarity of his content—that is the way in which the relations of A and S_1, with respect to rest or motion, present themselves; such is their perspective appearance to him. And since any perspective appearance is said to be as objective as another, it would be the objective fact not only that A both is and is not in motion with respect to S_1, but also that it is perceived by the observer on S_1 to be both moving and at rest relatively to the same system of reference.

What has made it possible for eminently sensible persons to suppose that the relativity of all content to particular standpoints (in the sense above defined) can be affirmed without thereby denying the epistemological objectivity of any content, is partly, I suppose, that such persons have failed to recognize that this consequence—proposition (ii) in the preceding paragraph—is necessarily implied by their premises. They appear to assert the perspectivity of our data universally, but tacitly assume an exception—or several exceptions—and it is the exceptions which permit this kind of relativism to appear "objective." This is interestingly illustrated in the passage last cited. We were told that, after all, there is a "metaphysical ultimacy" belonging to any event that actually happens; and it was quietly assumed that the event may be *known* from many standpoints, and *is actually known by anyone only in so far as the character which it has irrespective of all external standpoints is apprehended.* If even a relativistic philosopher likes cucumbers, "it is eternally and indubitably true that he does like them" and "no rational person need be skeptical" about it—or about any other "concrete occurrence in its relations." This manifestly means that the event "this-philosopher-liking-cucumbers" has a fixed character which does not vary with standpoints. To be sure, it involves a relation between the philosopher and the cucumbers; it is from his standpoint, and perhaps from that only, that they are likable. If, therefore, the question about which knowledge is sought were that of the absolute gastronomic virtues of cucumbers *überhaupt,* we should find no answer to *this* question in the philosopher's eccentric taste. *De gustibus non disputandum est* because purely gustatory propositions claim (it is assumed) no epistemological objectivity. But since it is only the merits of cucumbers from one philosopher's standpoint that are in question, and since it is a fact that from that standpoint they are desirable vegetables, *this* fact is—even by the relativist—exempted from the reign of relativity and set up as an absolute on its own account. If other minds, animal, human, or divine, are to know truly the philosopher-cucumber relation, they must know it as that philosopher knows it—be *their* standpoints, with respect to him or with respect to cucumbers, what they may. If a rival philosopher, having a different taste in both epistemologies and edibles, were to declare: "It is inconceivable that anyone, even a relativistic philosopher, should like cucumbers," he would not be excused by the relativistic philosopher on the ground of the ultimacy of his standpoint; he would be set down as a dogmatist asserting an untruth about a matter of fact. And in so describing him, the relativistic philosopher would, no doubt, on the one hand, be rightly asserting the indefeasible reality of his own taste in edibles; but he would, on the other hand, be asserting the correctness of his rival's epistemology.

To "know" is thus implicitly admitted, even by the would-be relativist in epistemology, to mean apprehending a fact of which the character is *not* relative to the special standpoint of the organism in an individual perception or judgment. If or in so far as you really know, you become acquainted with the object of reference as it is, or was, or will be, untransformed by the accident of your present knowing of it—and untransformed by *any* factors not operative within the limits which you implicitly defined when you made *it*, and not something else, your object of reference. That is the essence of the knowledge-claim; and it is plainly what objective relativists, like other men, really conceive themselves to be doing when, and in so far as, they credit themselves with actual knowledge of anything in particular. Their supposition that they are doing something different from this appears to be due largely to a habit of unconsciously shifting the object or locus of reference. If that object initially is, say, a now extinct star, you know *it* only if you apprehend the characters present when and where it existed, and in the physical context which co-existed with it; and any characters which arise outside of that situation—which, that is, are due to external standpoints, even in the physical sense—do not inform you truly about *that* object. But of course, if you forget that this was your original object of reference, and (while assuming that you are still dealing with the same question) ask, *e. g.*, what is the character of the retinal image of the star, then about this substituted object you may suppose yourself to have genuine knowledge—provided that you assume that no factors intervening between *it* and your actual percept have caused the character of the percept to deviate from that of the retinal image (*i. e.*, if you assume that there is here *no* perspectivity). But if, on the other hand, you further assume that your percept is determined by intra-cortical factors which alter to an indeterminable degree the effect of the retinal images, you once more imply that you do not know even those images. This game of jumping from one object of reference to another while assuming that you are throughout dealing with one only, can be played as long as you like; and if the successively substituted objects are conceived as stages in a continuous causal sequence, and if the *ultimate* effect is supposed to be not a perspective appearance but a reality apprehended just as it absolutely is, the epistemological objectivity thus imputed to your apprehension of *it* comes to be transferred, by what is, no doubt, a natural illusion, back to the prior members of the series, and finally to the original member. But however natural, it is (by the logical implications of the theory of universal perspectivity) still an illusion. The only object of reference of which you can legitimately claim, under the circumstances assumed, to know the character (beyond that of being *something* belonging in that causal series), is the ultimate effect, *i. e.*, the percept conceived as a strictly private possession of your own. And even the abstract property of being a member of the causal series you can be said to *know* only if your judgment about the existence of an original causal object and of other members of that series is assumed to be not relative to your standpoint, to be itself innocent of perspectivity.

The (in this sense) non-relativistic implications of the notion of the objective are, of course, copiously illustrated in the history of science, and nowhere better than in recent theoretical physics, despite the potent influence therein of some contrary tendencies. In the scientific investigation of nature, men have been looking for views of things which have, at the minimum, *some* degree of generality, and are *not* relative to particular contexts or standpoints. You approach the truth about a thing, both common sense and science have usually supposed, only when, after changing your standpoint, you find some of the characters of the thing remaining the same; the more changes of standpoint you make, the more justification you have for identifying the characters found to be common in all with the sort of object knowledge aims at. The perspective appearances of physical objects, with their diversities of shape and size, have been treated as subjective, not because they did not truly appear, but because they varied with standpoints. The *cognoscendum,* in short, has always been regarded as a sort of constant—in the sense that it is not a function of variable relations to knowers or to conditions of knowledge external to its own spatio-temporal region of existence.   And it is precisely in our time and in what is miscalled "relativity physics" that the craving of the scientific mind for such constants or absolutes has been most strikingly manifested.   It is true that the earlier steps in the reasoning of Einstein's special theory seemed to reduce the whole of the world of the older physics to a sort of relativity which looked very much like universal perspectivity.   All of the characters previously supposed to be "primary" and truly physical were resolved into conflicting appearances presented from the standpoints of different reference-systems; no one reference-system was any more true or real than another; and apparently a reference-system could be determined only by an arbitrary setting-up of coördinates, *i. e.,* by an act of a mind.   But so far from being content with this sort of world, physicists were profoundly dissatisfied with it; and the greater and more characteristic part of Einstein's effort, as has often been remarked, was a "quest of the absolute," which he found in the Minkowskian four-dimensional continuum with its absolute space-time magnitude, the "interval."   The constructive part of Einstein's reasoning, in short, has throughout been determined by the principle that "the test of objectivity is invariance for all observers"; and it was through the application of this test that his reasoning led to the conclusion that, "unless we wish to continue to talk about such shadows as space and time, it is in the space-time world and there alone that we shall obtain universal objectivity." [25] It is precisely in the degree in which he denied that "what the world is perceived as from any or all" potentially *differing* "points of view constitutes the essential part of its objective nature for physical science," that Einstein really continued "the high tradition of scientific objectivity." In so far as objective relativism in philosophy has been inspired by the theory of relativity in physics, it has been by the part of that theory which is regarded (though, undeniably, with much wavering and equivocation) by its author and by most physicists as proving that the world of actual appearance, at least in those respects in which it varies with standpoints, is *not* "objective."

The business of knowing, then—if by the word we mean anything more than bare sensation or pure revery—is the business of transcending standpoints; it is the quest of content which can be believed to have some character identical in nature (if not in existence) with a character which belongs to (or is present in) the specified object or locus of reference independently of the knowing and within its own limits. That precisely this achievement, which to some epistemologists seems so paradoxical, is the essence of that practical application of knowledge to life, which we name wisdom is a truism—but it is one which the "doctrine of perspectives" plainly contradicts. What we call, in the practical or moral sense, "seeing things in perspective" is in fact seeing them out of perspective—correcting the foreshortenings and distortions which arise from their temporal proximity to us, or from their differing relations to our transient moods or preoccupations or passions. It is equally evident that the transcendence of standpoints is the essential of that kind of reasonableness which makes man (to some small extent) a social being. In Professor Mead's words:

25 D'Abro, *The Evolution of Scientific Thought*, 1927, pp. 222–23.

It is only in so far as the individual acts not only in his own perspective but also in the perspectives of others, especially in the common perspective of the group, that a society arises and its affairs become the object of scientific inquiry. The limitation of social organization is found in the inability of individuals to place themselves in the perspectives of others, to take their points of view. . . . The social perspective exists in the experience of the individual in so far as it is intelligible, and it is its intelligibility that is the condition of the individual entering into the perspectives of others, especially of the group. In the field of any social science, the objective data are those experiences of the individuals in which they take the attitude of the community, *i. e.,* in which they enter into the perspectives of the other members of the community.[26]

Now when a man, through an effort of the imagination, learns to place himself in the perspective of another with respect to any object of reference, he not only transcends the confines of his original restricted standpoint; he also becomes aware of a property or relation of the object which it does not owe even to his present standpoint. And in so far as he fails to become thus aware of the properties (for example, the values) which objects have for his fellows independently of his own perspective—and fails to recognize that they *are* thus independent—he fails to perform successfully the characteristic function of either a cognitive or a social animal. For only a cognitive or standpoint-transcending animal is in any genuine sense a social animal.

The transcendence of one perspective may, however, be merely the disclosure of a character present in another perspective; that is to say, the object of reference may itself be a perspective aspect. For this reason epistemological objectivity may be considered a matter of degrees. I am, for example, attempting to recall an incident in my experience yesterday. What I wish to know—if it is in fact at knowledge and not delusion that I aim—is something which did not get its then character from the fact that I am today trying to remember it, nor from my present mood, nor from any peculiarity of the act of retrospection in general. But since it is an experience of *mine* that is the object of reference, its nature must no doubt have been determined, in greater or less degree, by per-

[26] *Proceedings of the Sixth International Congress of Philosophy,* 1927, p. 78.

manent peculiarities of my personal standpoint—*i. e.,* of my individual psychological constitution. I may, in turn, seek to transcend this without transcending the standpoint of the human species in general. I do so, for example, if I say that any light-wave falling upon a human eye normally functioning will produce a color-sensation which will be gray (including under this term black and white), or one of the color-tones lying in the spectrum between violet and red, or some mixture of these—but that none of these qualities can be known to belong to the light-waves or to the sources of light. The judgment here is, or purports to be, epistemologically objective in so far as it (a) transcends both my present and my permanent individual standpoint, and (b) has reference in part to objects, *viz.,* light-waves and light-sources, which are assumed to exist apart from the visual sensations to which they give rise, *i. e.,* independently of relations to percipients. But the judgment is epistemologically subjective in so far as it also relates to properties which are dependent upon a "standpoint," *viz.,* the optical constitution of the human animal. It is, in short, an objective judgment partly about an epistemologically subjective existent; it is the usual modern way of putting the thesis of the subjectivity of color. The objectivity belongs to it in virtue of its asserting something which is not relative to a standpoint, the subjectivity in virtue of its asserting something which is so relative. And so far as the objectivity is assumed to reach, so far knowledge is claimed; so far as the subjectivity (in this sense) is assumed to reach, so far the claim to positive knowledge is denied. To assert the relativity of color to sense-organs is to say that we are in certain respects ignorant of the real qualities of light-waves and luminous objects. If we should assert that we actually know that the waves and the objects do not possess color, we should be claiming a negative objective knowledge about those entities, *i. e.,* about what they are not, apart from any relation to a percipient and his standpoint. But however manifold and complex the mixture of the elements of epistemological objectivity and subjectivity in a judgment, the former always attaches to a predicated character by virtue of its assumed non-perspectivity, the latter by virtue of its supposed existence exclusively in some special perspective or class of perspectives.

A different sort of example of this may be seen in the Kantian type of idealism, which makes all the formal characters of experience and thought relative, not to single percipient events, nor to individual knowers, nor to the physiological peculiarities of the human organs of sensation, but to some generic psychical constitution of knowers as such. In the world of such a philosophy there is a socially objective order, since in certain matters there are supposed to be no possible individual differences in experience. Those features of it which are, as Kant would have said, grounded in the universal and necessary conditions of the possibility of experience in general, are the same for everybody, which is to say that they are to this extent not of the nature of perspectives. Nevertheless, since it is to something peculiar to the particular class of beings called knowers that even these elements in experience are relative, human experience in its entirety is here regarded as a sort of perspective; and these doctrines therefore have commonly and properly been described as theories of the subjectivity of the elements in question (time, space, the categories). They are, in short, consistent, at most, only with phenomenalism. Since there is nothing in experience which is not infected by these pervasive formal conditions of the function of experiencing, realities as they are in themselves are necessarily, for such a philosophy, wholly beyond the reach of knowledge and conjecture.

If, now, the objective relativist really intends to assert only some *partial* perspectivity of the data of perception or thought, he may, precisely so far, claim that his thesis does not imply an epistemological subjectivism. But the objectivity which he seeks can begin only where the perspectivity ends. He, too, may, for example, conceivably intend to say, not that all characters are relative to the standpoint of an individual percipient event, but only that they are relative to certain physiological conditions of perception common to the human species. If so, he leaves room for objectively valid

judgments by one knower about events which are not his own perceptions, nor determined to be what they are (or were) by his private point of view—events, namely, which are the percepts of
other or all individuals. But if this is all that the relativist means
by his doctrine, he is not leaving room for any knowledge whatever of physical reality; he is merely again giving utterance to a
form of phenomenalism.   Objective relativism often, however,
has the air, not only of being a physical realism, but of offering us
reassurance as to the possibility of a knowledge of the qualities
belonging to physical things, or present at determinable places in
an objective or public space or space-time.   These realistic pretensions manifestly are possible for the relativist only to the degree in
which he restricts the scope of the thesis of the perspective relativity of perceptual content.   But as soon as he thus abandons the
assumption of universal perspectivity, his doctrine once more
proves to be identical with that of the dualist. And it encounters,
of course, the same difficulties. It too must have some criterion for
determining which data are to be taken as possibly or probably
mere perspective aspects and which are to be taken as epistemologically objective.   And, in the case of the latter, it too has the
task of explaining *how* existents which are causally and existentially subjective can disclose without falsification characters of
existents not themselves, and what is implied by the supposition
that they do so.   As our review of the relativist's theory thus far
shows, it offers no means whatever for evading these problems.

(5) It is evident from some examples already cited—and
others might be given—that the plausibility of objective relativism
for some contemporary philosophers has owed a good deal to a
current tendency to read into the notion of conditionality, and
especially into that of perspectivity, the logical implications of
what I have named "respectivity."   It is easy to confuse the proposition that an object exhibits such and such a character from the
standpoint of a given relatum with the proposition that it has that
character "relatively," *i. e.,* respectively, to the same relatum; for
the former expression *may* mean the same as the latter. I look

north and see a water-tower of which the shape, as visually presented to me, is elliptical. We say that the tower—a common compass being assumed—is truly north with respect to me and as truly south with respect to a person on the far side of it; and we express the same fact by saying that it is north from my standpoint and south from the standpoint of the observer on the other side. Here the phrase "from the standpoint of," being a synonym of "with respect to," carries no implication of subjectivity. We also sometimes say that the water-tank "is" elliptical from my standpoint, and circular from the standpoint of an aviator flying over it. Here "from the standpoint of" is not obviously synonymous with "respectively to"; but if it is assumed to be so, it follows that the tank is truly elliptical with respect to me, or to my position, and truly circular with respect to the aviator or to his position. Thus when the two categories are treated as equivalent, any individual perspective appearance seems legitimately predicable of the object of which it is said to be an appearance, in spite of the obvious reasons, already indicated, for assigning it rather to the other terminus of the process through which it arises—to the "immediate standpoint." And it similarly appears legitimate to predicate all manner of formally antithetic characters to the same object or to suppose them to occupy the same region. If there is no difficulty about a body's being truly in motion relatively to one reference-system and truly at rest relatively to another, why should there be any difficulty about its being truly, and without duplication, of one shape relatively to one moving body and of another shape relatively to another; or again, about its being truly of one color relatively to one percipient and truly of another color relatively to another percipient?

Is, then, the distinction between perspectivity and respectivity which was provisionally set up in the preceding lecture tenable? Or, supposing that a formal distinction expressible by these terms can be made out, are there at any rate reasons, as some seem to suppose, for extending the concept of respectivity to cover characters commonly supposed to be absolute, *i. e.,* non-respective, in meaning—in such a way that the case for dualism is weakened through the undermining of one of the familiar grounds of it set forth in the first lecture? The proof that perceptual data are—at least for the most part—not existentially identical with the objects believed by realists to be known through perception has, it will be recalled, rested partly upon the assumption that *certain kinds* of qualitative difference are irreconcilable with existential identity. If the many visual observers of the penny have as their data many differently shaped objects, then, the argument runs, these data cannot be the one particular which is the physical penny, nor can they be identical with one another. If the mountain is purple to those who gaze at it from a distance and green to those who look up at it from its base, the visual content of at least one group of observers cannot, it has been inferred, be any part or attribute of the actual mountain, which, if it has, physically, any color at all, has in any determinate region only one color. But, now, if shapes and colors are respective characters, the differences of shape and color between the data of different percipients will afford no proof that these data are entities distinct from the physical object of knowledge; they may mean only that the percipients are severally observing the various characters which the one object truly has with respect to different relata.

Before inquiring more particularly into this proposed extension of the concept of respective attributes, we must recall that, even if it were conceded, the dualistic position would not necessarily be damaged. For only one of the arguments by which that position is supported would be affected. And if the remaining arguments were sufficient to establish the conclusion—as I think it will be seen that they are—the logical situation would obviously remain as before. Nevertheless, it is desirable to determine whether this particular argument may still be kept in the armory of the dualist or whether it should be discarded as obsolete.

What, then, is the criterion of that respectivity which enables a character to belong to an object, or to inhere in a locus, without excluding the possibility that other characters of the same mode, formally antithetic to it, may also belong to the same object or in-here in the same place? I answer that the criterion of respectivity is—respectivity. If a term possesses this logical attribute, it must be evident to anyone who understands the term that to predicate it of a subject means nothing at all unless a third relatum, of a definite kind, is specified. Do, then, the characters customarily referred to in the argument for dualism which is here in question have this triadic implication? And if they do, what is the third term to which they are respective? Is, for example, the adjective "purple" destitute of meaning, incapable of being intelligibly predicated of an object or place, until you add "with respect to" some other thing or other place? There have, of course, been idealistic, and even some realistic, philosophers who have said so. Any idea of color, they have declared, contains an implicit refer-ence to a seeing eye (at least in the sense in which idealists may suppose that they have eyes); so that the expression "an unseen color" would be as meaningless a combination of words as "a father to whom no one stands in the relation of son or daughter," or "a body in motion with respect to no other body or frame of reference." For the idealist this, of course, is merely a part of his general theorem that we can conceive of no existent which is not "for" a conscious subject. But when that to which a character is asserted to be respective is a knowing subject or a percipient event involving awareness, respectivity manifestly has precisely the same logical consequence as perspectivity; it implies that the character which is declared to be *thus* respective is also subjective—causally, existentially, and epistemologically. When, then, a realist asserts that indeed not all, but some, specific classes of characters, such as colors, are respective to percipient events, he is simply telling us in an indirect way that characters of this sort are purely subjective, and cannot so much as be conceived as having any other status. Now for our philosophical relativist, as we have seen, percipient events apparently *are* the relata to which characters in general are respective—if it is respectivity that he means by "relativity." The notion of respectivity, thus applied, can evidently help him not at all to vindicate the objective reality or the cognitive validity of data, as he conceives of them.

I cannot, however, see why any realist—or anyone who has seen through the fallacy of the egocentric predicament—should admit that the idea of a color (as characterizing an object or pervading a region) is meaningless apart from a reference to a percipient event or an organ of sense. He may, indeed, hold, in accordance with the traditional view, that colors do not in fact exist, or cannot be known to do so, except as effects of percipient events; but thus to assert that they are conditioned by such events is not equivalent to asserting their respectivity, while it *is* equivalent to asserting once more, though on different grounds, their causal and there-fore, as a probable corollary, their existential subjectivity. There is, however, nothing except percipient events to which it is even plausible to affirm that colors are respective; and I do not recall that anyone has in fact affirmed their respectivity to any other re-latum. But if this class of characters are not respective in mean-ing—if they may conceivably be present in a region or belong to a particular existent absolutely, though not unconditionally—then the usual dualistic argument from the discrepancies of the colors of different visual percepts of an assumed common object appears —so far, at least, as this consideration is concerned—to retain its force.

There is, however, another possible contention, sometimes con-fused with the assertion of the respectivity of color (or other sensible characters), which should be mentioned and considered here. It is to the effect that (a) while these characters are *not* re-spective *in meaning,* two or more of them may nevertheless con-ceivably occupy a single region of space (which may be called the region of pervasion); that (b) they may do so in consequence of the presence in another region (which may be called the region of projection) of a brain and nervous system; that (c) if they both thus pervade the whole of the same region, each will be per-ceived to do so only by the organism whose brain and nervous system occupy the region of projection; and finally that (d) it is reasonable, since this dual—or rather multiple—pervasion of a single region is conceivable, to assume that it is a fact, since the two or more observers do *appear* severally to see the different colors in one and the same place.[27] This, it will be observed, is very similar to one of the possible versions of the notion of "attributive objectivity" which has already been examined. It differs only in the specific assertion of the conceivability of the multiple pervasion of a single region by *many* colors (or other characters). Now this assertion—proposition (a), when taken without the qualification contained in (c)—I shall not discuss. I seem to myself to be unable to attach any consistent meaning to the statement that one and the same surface not merely appears to different beholders to be, but actually *is,* both purple and green. Nevertheless, I am told by persons of logical acumen and practice in introspective discrimination that they find no difficulty whatever in thinking of such simultaneous dual or multiple coloring of an identical surface; and I feel bound to admit the possibility that they do in fact achieve this, to me, elusive feat. This may seem to be tantamount to admitting that the dualistic argument from the diversities of the perceived colors of a hypothetically single object, or "event," is invalid. If it be granted that any number of colors can be compresent in the same place, which is that of the physical object, or be "ingredient into the same event,"

---

[27] I follow here in part the terminology of Broad in his exposition and partial defense of the "Theory of Multiple Inherence" (*The Mind and Its Place in Nature.* pp. 160 ff.). This is, I think, the most illuminating discussion of the topic which has appeared; but it seems to me, nevertheless, to leave undistinguished, if not to confuse, the two theories here discriminated; *viz.,* that of the respectivity of color, shape, *etc.,* to percipient events, and that of the merely factual "multiple inherence" of these characters, as effects the presence of which in the region of pervasion is conditioned by brain-events. If the characters are respective in meaning, so that they can be conceived as occurring in a region only *for* percipients in other regions, and as being what they severally are only relatively to the several positions and constitutions of the percipients, then their multiple inherence is necessary—but also necessarily subjective, as has been shown. If they are not respective in meaning, then a proof is required that they are capable of multiple inherence, and that they do in fact thus pervade the same regions. Even so critical and penetrating a reasoner as Mr. Broad has here, if I am not mistaken, not invariably succeeded in keeping the distinction between respectivity and conditionality in view. It should be mentioned that Broad in the end rejects the theory on the ground that it implies the assumption of a single absolute space.

is not this, it may be asked, equivalent to saying that they can all be true components of that object or true adjectives of the event? We have but to recall some considerations already mentioned to see that it is not. The various colored shapes apprehended by the several observers are not the less distinct particular existents merely because they have all, in theory, been crowded into a single region. Existential identity means identity *both* of character and of space- and time-locus. Where you have either identity of locus without identity of character, or identity of character without identity of locus, you are not dealing with one particular but with two. In the case supposed there is identity of spatial locus; but the several colored shapes are not identical either in color or in shape, and (because of the finite velocity of light) they are not in fact even present in the same place at the same time. The comparatively small purple shape which is the percept of the mountain from a distance is not the same item in nature as the comparatively large green shape which is the percept of the mountain from near-by, even though they are (at *almost* the same time) in the same place. And, by the hypothesis, each of these separate particulars comes to be in this place only by virtue of the functioning of individual sentient organisms in various distant places, and each has no other mode of being there than that of appearing there for such an organism. They are thus (as has already been pointed out *à propos* of "attributive objectivity") both causally and existentially subjective. The several colors (still by the hypothesis) are not real characters or parts of the object or event in the physical realist's sense of "real"; by experiencing them you do not learn what the object supposed to be in that place is, nor yet what it was, independently of the various percipient events in the several organisms. The colored shapes, in other words, would not cease to be perspective appearances, and therefore epistemologically subjective, through being assigned, in all their multiplicity and diversity, to a spatial position common to them all and to the postulated real object—supposing it were possible to assign them to such a position. The theory of merely factual multiple inherence, in short, when not confused with the (for other reasons) untenable doctrine of the respectivity of color, proves to be simply the generative theory of sensa *plus* the hypothesis of the projection of the sensa out to the place once occupied, in absolute space, by the causal physical object; and it has already been sufficiently shown that the latter hypothesis is inadmissible, and that if it were not so, it would offer no avenue of escape from either epistemological or psychophysical dualism.

With regard specifically to shapes the same conclusions are even more plainly evident. Shape is a predicate of a region of space occupied or bounded by some other character, such as a sensible color or some form of energy. It has often been argued, and may plausibly be maintained, that the notion of an *existent* shape is inseparable from that of some such other character. But this does not mean that shape is a concept respective in its import. And it is mere contradiction to say that, in a given space-system, the same region is of two shapes; for the shape is one of the defining characters of the region which is in question. Take its singleness of shape away from it and it loses its identity as *this* particular extension rather than that. And, for the same reason, a merely factual multiple inherence of shapes in a region is excluded.[28]

Let us turn to the proof of the respectivity of certain characters supposed to be offered by the physical theory of relativity. That theory is often said to have shown that a single body may have two or more unequal lengths in the direction of motion, and therefore two or more shapes, as functions of the differing velocities of its unaccelerated motion relative to different frames of reference

[28] Broad, *loc. cit.*, makes a distinction between "geometrical" shape and "sensible form." The "geometrical" circularity of an area and its "sensible" circularity are two distinct properties. "If an area is geometrically circular it is so intrinsically, and there is an end of the matter"; but "it does not follow that the sensible form of an area" (*i.e.*, apparently, of the same area) "is an intrinsic property of it." Hence "it may be that one and the same area is 'informed' by one sensible form from one place and by a different sensible form from another place." I am unable to understand what is meant by one and the same area being of two shapes, or to conceive how an area can be sensibly circular without also being geometrically circular; nor do the reasons which Broad gives for supposing that it can seem to me persuasive. I have, therefore, not thought it necessary to consider this distinction in the text.

—the appearance of contradiction being avoided by the assumption that shapes are respective—not to percipients, but to the velocities of frames of reference. A man six feet tall in one frame may be three feet tall in another; a body which is spherical in a system relatively to which it is at rest, will be an oblate spheroid in a system relatively to which it is in motion. Does, then, relativity physics actually demonstrate that shape is a respective property, and that the same physical entity may therefore without contradiction have many actual shapes at once—in so far as, in relativity physics, we are permitted to say "at once"? (If it did, it is to be noted, the respectivity of the ordinary perspective diversities of shape would not be vindicated, for they are not "relative" to velocities.)

Before directly considering this question, it is pertinent to note that a good deal of confusion and misunderstanding have arisen in recent physics as well as in philosophy in consequence of the equivocality of the term "relative." One of the things most to be desired—though doubtless hardly to be expected—in the discussion not only of the philosophical doctrine we are now considering, but also of the physical theory of relativity, is the discontinuance of the use of this ambiguous word, and the substitution in each case of one or another of the expressions "caused" or "conditioned by," "respective to," or "appearing from the standpoint of." The present fashion of employing a single term masks the fact that differing sorts of "relativity" are in question in different parts of the theory or in different interpretations of it. Two familiar instances of relativity recognized by classical science and presupposed by the Einsteinian doctrine—the mathematical relativity of the measurement of magnitudes to standards, e. g., of lengths to measuring rods, and the kinematical relativity of unaccelerated motion and velocity to frames of reference—are obvious cases of respectivity. The so-called relativity of simultaneity is primarily also a case of respectivity—though of a respectivity made-to-order. To the notion of the simultaneity of two events occurring at a distance from one another a certain meaning is arbitrarily assigned by definition, such that the events can be said to be simultaneous only if light-rays from each arrive at the same instant at a point situated before their arrival midway between them; but since this point must be in some determinate frame or reference-body, and since a reference-body in which a point midway between the places of occurrence of the events could be thus determined may move during the motion of the two light-rays, in which case the criterion of simultaneity will in it not be satisfied, a reference to the state of relative motion or rest of reference-bodies is made an essential part of the meaning of simultaneity.[29] But a pair of events which are thus simultaneous relatively to one reference-body and not simultaneous relatively to another, are, of course, also simultaneous from the standpoint of an observer on the one body and not simultaneous from the standpoint of an observer on the other. But this, again, apparently is not intended by Einstein to signify that the character "simultaneity" is merely of the nature of a perspective aspect. By anyone acquainted with the space-relations of the places of occurrence of the two events to the two bodies, and the state of relative motion or rest of each body after the emission of the light-signals, the two events would, by virtue of the respectivity put into the definition, be rightly judged to be both simultaneous and non-simultaneous, relatively to the two specified relata.[30]

The confusion of the senses of relativity appears chiefly in the expositions and discussions of the status in the special theory of the phenomena mathematically expressed by the Lorentz transformation-equations—the contractions of lengths in the direction of unaccelerated relative motion and the retardations of ₊chronometers. Is the "relativity" of length (and consequently of shape) and of duration in this part of the theory conditionality, perspectivity, or respectivity? In other words are, e. g., the contractions of rods on a system S_1 real and non-respective *effects* caused by its

[29] The logical procedure by which this relativity of simultaneity is supposed to be established seems to me fallacious; but with this question I am not here concerned.
[30] There seems, however, to be some wavering or obscurity on this point in Einstein's argument.

motion relative to another system, S, so that it would be false to
say that the rods are uncontracted; or are they merely ways in
which the rods in S_1 will appear to observers on S, so that it would
be false to say that they *are* contracted; or are the rods to be said
to have two (or more) real lengths, one with respect to the system S_1, the other with respect to the system S, *etc.?* To this question, and to the corresponding question about the retardations—
in so far as it is definitely faced, and not merely covered over by
the use of the word "relative"—curiously conflicting answers are
given or implied by different competent writers on the subject, and
frequently by the same writers in different passages. Thus we are
told, in a recent and able exposition of the theory, that in consequence of the relative motion of two Galilean frames, "nothing
would have happened to the cubes and the clocks; only the conditions of observation would have been changed." [31] Upon such
an interpretation the relativity of length, *etc.*, is a case of mere
reciprocal perspectivity, analogous to the ordinary illusions of
visual perspective in which two men appear to one another to
grow smaller with increasing distance. But the same writer elsewhere vehemently assails Bergson for suggesting this analogy, and
declares that "in Einstein's theory the rod *is* contracted"—but
adds: "This contraction holds only in the space of the frame with
respect to which the rod is in motion. In the space of the frame
accompanying the rod in motion no contraction would occur." [32]
According to this account there would be an actual duality (or
rather plurality) of the lengths of each rod and of the shapes of
each body. "Relativity" now, in short, means respectivity. But
in the case of the retardations the same writer, with many others,
employs the term in a third sense; the proposition that there is a
slowing-up of chronometers, natural and artificial, in the system
S_1, and that this slowing-up is "relative to" the velocity of the
system, means—as the theory is usually set forth—that a physical
effect upon the action of chronometers in S_1 is caused by its rela-

[31] D'Abro, *The Evolution of Scientific Thought*, 1927, p. 145.
[32] *Ibid.*, p. 220; my italics.

tive motion, and that only *one* effect on the speed of any one chronometer is produced. For nearly all the expositions of the special theory set forth the celebrated paradoxes of the clocks and of the twins-of-unequal-age as among *its* necessary consequences; and these imply that unaccelerated relative motion has an actual physical effect upon the movement of clock-mechanisms and upon the physiological processes of the "travelling twin"—and not upon the clocks or the physiological processes of the twin who stays at home. This "relativity," in short, is not, by orthodox physicists, admitted to be merely a matter of perspective appearances. Nor is it treated by them as a case of respectivity. When the traveller returns home he has not—if the tale as commonly told be true—two physiological ages, one relative to one frame of reference and another to another frame, but only one age. To introduce the notion of respectivity in dealing with the retardations would obviously be absurd. The retardations, then, at least as they usually figure in this deduction from the theory, exemplify "relativity" only in the sense of conditionality; they are treated as if they were real, unilateral, unequivocal, and absolute changes caused by relative motion. This is, no doubt, somewhat curious, since the status of the contractions and retardations admittedly ought to be the same; and in fact we are (elsewhere) often told that they *are* the same, and that the retardations are therefore bilateral.[33] But with this we are not just now concerned. What cannot, I think, be denied is that "relativity" is often asserted, not only in different parts of the theory, but even in the same part and with respect to the same matters, in quite different senses, and that, whatever be the consequence of this upon the logic of the doctrine, it is not favorable to clarity and precision of exposition.

[33] When the retardations are regarded as actual physical effects and *also* as bilateral, the paradox of the twins becomes pure nonsense; each twin, it would follow, would at any given moment of his existence, during their unaccelerated relative motion, be physiologically both older and younger than the other. There is no real escape from this consequence; but as physicists usually maintain that there is, and offer a number of arguments to prove it, it would be necessary to review all these arguments in order to justify the contrary opinion. I have prepared such a review, but find it too long for inclusion here. I therefore do not, in the text, assume that the paradox involves the absurdity in question.

This lack of discrimination in the use of the term by physicists appears to be one of the causes of some confusions which seem to me characteristic of "objective relativism" in philosophy.

The particular way of construing the Lorentz-Fitzgerald contractions and the resultant modifications of shape of relatively moving bodies which is pertinent to our immediate theme is that which represents a single body as actually characterized by a diversity of shapes, and seeks to eliminate the apparent resultant contradiction by means of the assumption of the respectivity of shape to the motion of frames of reference. But there is in fact, I think, nothing in Einstein's reasoning which enables us to conceive of an identical physical particular as truly having many shapes, in the ordinary sense of that term. The "travelling twin" either has a three-dimensional body or he has not. If he has not, his two (or more) shapes are not physical realities but merely appearances in the fields of consciousness of different percipients. If, on the other hand, he has a three-dimensional body, the identity or particularity of the body presumably consists partly in its shape, *i. e.*, the ratio of its length to its breadth; and it is not apparent that this can be conceived to be respective to the two frames of reference, and therefore dual. Paul's actual body, then, if he is supposed to have one, is presumably of a single shape. Where there are two shapes, there are either two physical bodies, or else at least one of the shapes is a perspective appearance of the physical body —in other words, a character, not of that body, and not where that body is, but of some other entity at some other place, and perhaps in some other space. But no one, I suppose, holds that a man possesses two—or rather, incalculably many—real physical bodies, each having a different set of real physical properties and a different rate of senescence. The first of these alternatives may therefore be disregarded.

This is so evident that physicists in their interpretations of the theory of relativity usually (so far as I have observed) end by regarding the disparate magnitudes and shapes *not* as respective real characters, but as perspective appearances—even though they usually begin by insisting upon the equal "rightness" of the differing judgments of length, shape, *etc.*, made by observers moving with different relative velocities, concerning the same body—a practice which has greatly promoted objective relativism in philosophy. This equal rightness, it turns out, means simply the equal wrongness of all of these judgments, their epistemological subjectivity. Thus Max Born, while maintaining that the retardations are real and unilateral, observes that "the contraction is only a consequence of the way of looking at the event (*Betrachtungsweise*), not a change of a physical reality." [34] Eddington, while finding that it is "not altogether easy to give a plain answer" to the question whether it is "really true that a moving rod becomes shortened in the direction of its motion," nevertheless gives an answer. The proposition is "*true* but it is not *really true*." And this somewhat oddly phrased distinction signifies that the proposition "is not a statement about reality (the absolute), but is a true statement about appearances in our frame of reference." [35]   This, it should be observed (though the point lies a little aside from the special issue just now before us), means for Born, Eddington, and most physicists who express themselves in a similar manner, not that one of the lengths or shapes is a reality and the other an appearance, but that both are mere appearances.   Paul's impression that he is six feet tall is no more right than Peter's impression (when the unaccelerated relative motion of their apparent bodies is at a certain velocity) that Paul is three feet tall; and if Paul were able to bring his projectile to a velocity equal to that of light, his impression that he was still six feet tall would be no more right than Peter's impression that Paul had no height at all. And this, of course, means that Paul has no physical body in the ordinary sense. The "reality that lies behind the appearances" is the four-dimensional space-time manifold. "Thanks to Minkowski, a way of keeping the accounts of space has been found which

[34] *Die Relativitätstheorie Einsteins*, 1922, p. 192.
[35] *The Nature of the Physical World*, pp. 33–4. This, of course, is not the whole story concerning Eddington's metaphysical theory in this work.

exhibits realities (absolute things)."[36] Born similarly tells us that "a material rod is not a spatial thing, but a spatio-temporal structure (*Gebilde*)." The "adequate conception" of a rod with respect to length is not that of a one-dimensional magnitude along, say, the x-axis of a set of coördinates. It requires the inclusion of the t-coördinate, and is therefore two-dimensional; it consists of the strip (*Streifen*) of the plane defined by xt. "The contraction, however, does not relate to such a strip, but only to a distance along the x-axis. . . . Only the strip as a manifold of world-points or 'events' has physical reality."[37] Thus it is that the length of the rod from the standpoint of the observer travelling with it is no more "real" than any other. For one more typical expression— d'Abro remarks that through the special theory,

real shape was removed from the status of a primary quality, and there was no sense in speaking of the shape of an object in a world devoid of all observers. Similar conclusions applied to size, duration, and all the other primary qualities, with the sole exception of electric charge. . . . Of course, had the theory of relativity deprived us of the possibility of conceiving of a sufficient number of primary qualities, hence of an objective world, it would have led us to a stone wall. . . . But the theory has merely modified the list of the primary qualities of classical science, assigning the same fundamental rôle to others in their stead. These are given by the space-time intervals, and, more generally, by space-time configurations and tensors. In other words, the objective universe disclosed by relativity is no longer one of shape and duration, of space and time, but of space-time.[38]

On the question whether this is in fact the true philosophical interpretation of the theory of relativity I shall not here express an opinion; for any adequate discussion of the point would demand a long inquiry which would take us far from our immediate topic. I point out here only that *if* this is the outcome of the theory—and it is, I suppose, the one accepted by most physicists —then, so far as philosophers are concerned, the general result of the work of Einstein is simply a vindication of dualism. For obviously the data of perception do not consist of the characters

[36] Eddington, *op. cit.*, p. 34.
[37] Born, *op. cit.*, p. 192.
[38] *The Evolution of Scientific Thought*, p. 420.

which, upon such a view, constitute "the objective universe disclosed by relativity"; they differ from it far more widely than from the objective world of the older physics. And yet the characters not given in sense-perception are still conceived somehow to underlie and connect together the data of experience. Thus the physical doctrine of relativity is a bifurcation of nature of the most extreme sort. The scheme of things which it puts before us is in essentials the scheme of the seventeenth-century philosophers, except that, in d'Abro's apposite phrase, it gives us a radically expurgated and revised "list of the primary qualities." This difference is, no doubt, extremely important, but it leaves the broad outlines of the older view unaffected. It is not to the new physics that the philosophic insurgents against dualism can hopefully look for support.[39]

It is, at all events, sufficiently clear, I think, that relativity physics gives no real justification to the idea that the shapes of bodies are respective characters, in such wise that different shapes (in the usual sense of the term) may truly belong to identical particulars in the objective physical world. In this regard also, then, the old dualistic assumption that where such difference is recognized existential duality must be admitted seems to remain unrefuted.

As this examination of objective relativism has been lengthy and involved, and not free from digressions, it is perhaps desirable to recapitulate, in a somewhat different order, the results of it. As a key (primarily) to the solution of the problem of knowledge this philosophy propounds the principle of the objectivity of the relative, ignorance of which is supposed to have begotten and sustained historic dualism. Taken in a certain sense this principle is undisputably true; but in that sense it is merely a formal truism.

[39] While the account of the nature of the physical world drawn from this interpretation of the theory of relativity does not seem to me convincing, it is clear—when the above-mentioned confusion about respectivity is eliminated—that no other interpretation is *more* favorable to epistemological and psycho-physical monism; and this is the only point that concerns us here.

It tells us that if a thing (or event) has a certain character in or by virtue of a certain relation, then it "objectively," *i. e.,* truly, has that character; in short, that what exists "relatively" nevertheless actually exists. But from this platitude no consequences bearing upon any controverted philosophical issue follow; nor is dualism, epistemological or psychophysical, reducible to the denial of any such barren tautology. What dualism has affirmed is (a) that there is a certain class of things, namely, physical things, which exist without dependence upon a specific kind of relation to a specific kind of events, namely, brain-events accompanied by perception or other modes of awareness; and (b) that there are certain other things, namely, all (or, in a restricted form of the doctrine, most) immediate perceptual and other data, which exist only by virtue of that kind of relation to that kind of events. It has (sometimes) called the former things "objective," in a particular sense of that word in which it means not merely "actually existing," but "existing independently of the specified relation and with certain specific properties"; and it has (sometimes) called the latter things "subjective" in a particular sense of that word in which it means, not "non-existent," but "existing in dependence upon the specified relation and without those specific properties." In so far as objective relativism has anything to do with the case, it must be supposed to controvert these theses of dualism and—if it has any positive content—to offer alternative views upon the same matters. If it is intended to be a form of realism—as, by first intention, it apparently is—it cannot consistently controvert proposition (a). Does it, then, controvert proposition (b)? Does it, in other words—in addition to the harmless tautology mentioned—maintain that perceptual and other data are "objective" in the sense of "*not* dependent upon brain-events accompanied by perception or other modes of awareness"? We found some difficulty in answering this question, because of ambiguities in the meaning of all four of the terms in the proposition in which the relativist's view is expressed, *viz.,* that "data are relative to percipient events but are nevertheless objective." It was not wholly

clear whether (1) perceptual data were conceived to be particular
existents or universals which have mere "subsistence." It was not
wholly clear whether (2) "percipient events" meant "brain-events
accompanied by awareness" or "brain-events not necessarily accompanied by awareness." It was not immediately clear (3) in
which or how many of four possible senses "objective" (or its
opposite) was to be understood, or (4) in which or how many of
three possible senses "relative" was to be understood. We were
therefore compelled to consider several different conceivable ways
of construing this general and equivocal thesis. The interpretation of it as assuming that data are universals we set aside, both
because this view appeared untenable, and also because it seemed
inconsistent with the manifest intent of the proponents of the
doctrine to maintain that data exist in the spatio-temporal world.
When this interpretation was excluded, objective relativism was
seen to be, in any case, a form of the generative theory of sensa;
in other words, to be in accord with dualism in the crucial point
that it regards data as particulars having brain-events as the proximate causes or conditions of their existence. This view, it was
found, cannot be held, without highly improbable and paradoxical implications—which, for the rest, it does not appear that objective relativists intend—unless it is also held that the existence
of data is conditioned by perception or other modes of awareness
—that sensa probably *are* only when and in so far as they are
experienced, and only for the individual organisms which experience them. With this the distinction between objective relativism
and dualism began to appear rather elusive. But a further contention of some relativistic as well as of some other philosophers
seemed at first to imply a small margin of difference between the
two views: the contention that visual and tactual data, at all
events, though causally and existentially subjective, are located in
the same space with physical objects. Waiving the difficulties
arising from the implication, in this thesis, of the notion of a
single absolute space, we observed that visual data certainly cannot occupy the same positions in space as the more or less distant

causal objects which are (by philosophical realists) commonly regarded as the objects of perceptual knowledge; while the assertion that some data are merely *somewhere* in space, and solely
while they are being perceived there and by virtue of the occurrence of individual acts of perception, is not in conflict with any
essential point of the dualistic doctrine.

Thus far, then, objective relativism seemed upon analysis to
break down completely into dualism; nor was there discoverable
any virtue in the concept of respectivity to save it from this fate.
The outcome was, indeed, inevitable from the start. This philosophy began as an attempt to avoid "the bifurcation of nature"
while rejecting epistemological monism—partly because of its
manifestly preposterous consequences—and while doing justice to
the empirical considerations which lead to the conclusion that the
data of perception are "relative to percipient events." But there
is, within the limits of realism, no way in which this conclusion
can be given any precise meaning, not entailing the same prepos-
terous consequences, which does not itself radically bifurcate nature into a subjective and an objective order (in the sense which
these terms have historically had in dualistic philosophy) and exhibit the former as the ground and instrument of whatever knowledge we may have of the latter.

One further way of construing the "relativity" of data to percipient events there was, however, in which we found the relativistic doctrine overshooting the limits of realism altogether, and
landing in an extreme and self-contradictory form of subjectivism.
Certain factors which have been operative in the genesis and
development of this general fashion of thought—partly the Hegelian presumption of the internality of relations, partly remin-
iscences of Leibniz, partly misunderstandings of the physical
theory of relativity—have resulted in a tendency to conceive of
all data as perspective appearances, determined as to their nature
wholly by the unique set of conditions and relations characteristic of the special "standpoint" of each knower, and even of each
percipient or cognitive event, and thus as incapable of revealing

anything except the character which reality happens to take on in that particular perspective and from that standpoint. Rigorously and universally applied, this conception, it was evident, amounts to a complete denial of the possibility of knowledge. But happily, of course, it seldom is quite rigorously and universally applied. How wide an application it is meant by most contemporary relativistic philosophers to have, it appears difficult to determine. There are, in fact, two logically distinct sorts of current relativism, in one of which the asserted "relativity" of the content of perception and thought means essentially perspectivity, while in the other it means merely conditionality—*i. e.*, the dependence of the *existence* of the particulars constituting such content upon the functioning of sentient or thinking organisms. When the latter doctrine is not confused with the former, radically subjectivistic type, it may legitimately be called, in a definite sense, an "objective" relativism; but in this sense the designation is simply a synonym for dualistic realism.

This, however, does not prevent those who profess this philosophy from continuing to proclaim that dualism has at last been vanquished. And this phenomenon—the prevalent fashion, among philosophers whose doctrines, when assayed, prove to be in both their epistemological and their metaphysical content radically dualistic, of denouncing the conclusion which their arguments plainly establish—seems to me one of the oddest as well as one of the most characteristic features of the philosophy of our time. Another example of it may be seen in a recent theory which has in its conclusions much in common with the latter kind of objective relativism, but rests partly upon different premises— the theory set forth in Professor Kemp Smith's *Prolegomena to an Idealist Theory of Knowledge.*[40] This seems to me a significant and illuminating expression of the position, on certain crucial is-

[40] Kemp Smith's theory of knowledge, it should perhaps be explained, is in fact a realist theory of knowledge, the term "idealism" being used by him in an unusual sense which is not antithetic to "realism."

sues, to which the reflective experience of our generation legiti-mately leads. That the simple epistemological monism char-acteristic of the earlier phase of the revolt against dualism is impossible, Kemp Smith also recognizes—chiefly on the ground of the physico-physiological argument. Since "sensa are complexly conditioned by antecedent physical and physiological processes" and "thus occur as terminal members in very lengthy series, they cannot be known to be qualities inherent in the physical objects in which the series originate,"[41] and therefore cannot be the same particulars as *those* physical objects: "the physiological processes have the function of conditioning the existence of sensa as well as that of conditioning our awareness of them." Kemp Smith is even willing to grant (as I have mentioned in another connection) that "psychical processes" may *possibly* have some part in the affair.[42] However that may be, the sensa produced by the functioning of the individual percipient are also presented only as objects for the psychical processes of awareness of the same percipient: they are "private" and "discontinuous."[43] "Nothing that we experience," then, "exists independently, precisely in the form in which we ex-perience it. Indeed, since imagination is tied down to the sec-ondary qualities we have to admit that, while the independent constitution of objects may be conceptually apprehended in the light of the results established by the sciences, such concepts can never be rendered precise by the employment of images."[44] We have no means of "determining how far, or in what manner, any of the (sensible) qualities may precisely match those with which the independently real is intrinsically endowed."[45] Yet this view is conceived by its author to be free from all taint of "subjectiv-ism"—that deadly infection which he finds in all the historic forms of dualism. "The sensa, though always private to each

[41] *Op. cit.*, 1924, p. 179.
[42] *Ibid.*, p. 90.
[43] *Ibid.*, p. 187.
[44] *Ibid.*, p. 228.
[45] *Loc. cit.*

percipient, are not for this reason subjective, but are objective happenings." [46] Nor does the generative theory mean that what is
generated is other than "physical," or even that it is not "independently real." [47] Galileo and Descartes still figure as the orig-
inators of the arch-error of modern philosophy; Kemp Smith
declares himself to be of one mind with Whitehead in rejecting
"that fatal doctrine of bifurcation, whereby Descartes distinguished between the psychical, conceived as comprehending all
the 'secondary qualities,' and physical entities conceived as endowed with merely mechanical properties, . . . a contrast of the
most amazing and incredible kind." Yet we are at the same time
told that "in locating the secondary qualities in physical objects
we are almost certainly subject to illusion," and that over against
all the sensa there stand space and time, and the "scientific
objects" existent therein, which are not generated in the course of
the perceptual process, and are *not* "private to the individual."
Thus "our conscious experience is a function of two distinct factors.. . . . Through the constant factors [space and time] a public
world is revealed; through the sensa, in terms of which alone this
public world can be actually experienced, it is apprehended in a
perspective suited to the individual's practical needs." [48] The dualistic character of the conclusion is evident.

It is, of course, plain that in such expressions as I have been
citing, the terms "bifurcation," "objective" and "subjective,"
"physical" and "mental" are employed in unusual and highly attenuated senses. "Physical," for example, does not, for Kemp
Smith, even imply "being in space," since the sensa, though particulars, are described as "extensionless." Most of the connotation customarily carried by the word "subjective" has plainly been
transferred to "objective"; and when the latter term is applied to
the sensa, the only vestiges which appear to be left of what I sup-

[46] *Ibid.*, p. 198.
[47] *Ibid.*, pp. 90, 225.
[48] *Ibid.*, pp. 24, 187.

pose to be its usual meaning consist of two implications which no dualist need deny, and which scarcely any, from Descartes on, have denied: (1) that sensa afford an indirect and limited means of acquaintance with reals existing independently of the percipient event, and (2) that they are certainly not generated by psychical processes occurring alone, *i. e.,* apart from neuro-cerebral processes.

Now it is evident that hypotheses in which "objectivity," "physicality," *etc.,* are used in these novel and evanescent senses should not be credited with the advantages, real or supposed, of doctrines which ascribe a quite different and far more thorough-going objectivity and physicality to all content. And credit is thus wrongly given, to the great confusion of many readers' ideas, whenever any generative theory of sensa is represented as avoiding the bifurcation of nature. That the naïve realism characteristic of the first phase of the anti-dualistic movement did avoid this is undeniable; its initial allurement and also the chief cause of its ultimate failure lay precisely in its obliteration of distinctions of status among the various kinds of existents. All of them were to be put upon the same level: ontologically all were to be treated as equally "independent," epistemologically all were to be regarded as equally directly known. But any theory which describes all sensory content as private and relative to, *i. e.,* conditioned by, the percipient act, and at the same time asserts the existence of realities not thus conditioned, is obviously dualistic. The most significant line of cleavage, in short, with respect to theories of perception, is that which divides *all* generative theories from all others. If, in the act of perceiving, each of us makes temporary additions of his own to reality, it is a question of secondary though not of negligible consequence whether these are supposed to be psychically or psychophysically or purely cerebrally generated additions; it in any event remains the admitted fact that (most or all) of the things I actually, immediately, sensibly perceive, exist only in so far as I, an individual organism, exist and exercise a function of a biologically very peculiar sort. And if all the immediate content is thus engendered by and relative to the perceiver, the epistemological situation remains the same, whatever variety of the generative theory be adopted. If I am at any given moment to have knowledge of events or entities independent of my individual constitution and momentary condition, I must reach these ulterior realities through present and private data; and the ultimate justification, if any, for doing so, must be found either in a reasonable faith or in some process of probable inference. The traditional reproach against historic dualism has been that this penetration through and beyond the immediate to the not-immediately-given is impossible and inconceivable. If this be a difficulty, it is a difficulty shared by all generative theories, except when they reserve some residuum of strictly independent reality of which an unmediated apprehension is claimed. And even in these cases, the difficulty remains with respect to all the supposed objects of knowledge except this meager residuum.[49]

Not only in these instances but in numerous others one may note the same tendency to play loosely upon these terms. It has become almost the established custom to use the language after rejecting the substance of naïve realism, or pan-objectivism; sternly to condemn "dualism" while accepting its essentials; to express the utmost horror of "bifurcation" and then—the proprieties having thus been duly observed—to proceed cheerfully to bifurcate. This, of course, is a sort of phenomenon common enough in human behavior, especially in the history of religions. The progressive transformation of the import of the terms in the religious vocabulary is a familiar story. Among philosophers "objective" is one of the blessed words, while "subjectivistic" has

[49] A very small margin of the theory of direct apprehension finds a place in Kemp Smith's doctrine—in the form of the thesis that of space and time we have a direct non-sensory intuition—that, e. g., "real, independent space in its own person" makes "entry into the 'conscious' field." This, however, admittedly affords us no information about concrete existents in space, our knowledge of which must still, upon this hypothesis, be reached through the brain-generated—or brain-and-mind-generated—sensa. The dualistic character of the doctrine as a whole thus remains unaffected.

come to be an abusive epithet in the current philosophical vocabulary. It is not unnatural that philosophers, like other men, should put new wine into old verbal bottles, should wish to express their creed in formulas of which the terms are no longer taken in their natural or historic senses. But however much justification there may be for such a practice in the case of symbols of which the value and function is in great part that of expressing an emotional attitude and a moral temper, it can hardly, I think, be considered desirable in philosophy. I venture to suggest that it would make for better understanding if, instead of reducing almost to the vanishing point the signification of these words, we should agree that, when any item in the content of experience is asserted to be conditioned by the occurrence of the processes of sensation, perception, or thought (even though these be themselves called physical) and to be directly accessible as a non-inferential particular existent only to one individual, that item is thereby declared to be existentially "subjective"; that we should deny the adjectives "objective" and "physical" to any content so conceived; and should uniformly and plainly attach the label "epistemological dualism" to every account of perception which assumes that one bit of reality is known through the presence in the individual field of experience, not of its identical self, but of something spatio-temporally and numerically separate (even though not causally independent nor perhaps logically isolable) from it. How words are used by philosophers is not, after all, a negligible matter; the formulation of a doctrine in phrases which historically have expressed, absolutely or approximately, the opposite of that doctrine, produces confusions, not only in the minds of the unsuspecting laymen who may read the philosophers' works, but in the reasoning of the philosophers themselves, and especially in the picture which they and others form of the relations of current to older theories. The present prevalence of the notion that the hypothesis of ideas has been superseded appears to be largely due to a neglect to define what is meant by "objective" and "physical," *i. e.,* to distinguish be-tween their several possible meanings. The recent and current phase of the revolt against dualism is in fact carried on almost exclusively by dualists.

Of this curious phenomenon in contemporary philosophy we shall observe some further illustrations in the lectures which are to follow.

V

MR. WHITEHEAD AND THE DENIAL OF
SIMPLE LOCATION

Any such analytical inquiry as we are attempting into the
present state of the argument respecting dualism must necessarily
give especially full and careful attention to certain aspects of the
philosophy of Professor Whitehead. No one has more impres-
sively asserted the utter incredibility of the hypothesis of the
"bifurcation of nature into two systems of reality which, in so
far as they are real, are real in different senses"—into a "nature
apprehended in awareness," which "holds within it the greenness
of the trees, the song of the birds, the warmth of the sun," in
short, the whole world of sensible appearances, and a conjectured
"nature which is the cause of awareness" and consists solely, at
least for our knowledge, of the meager and abstract entities of
physical theory. To showing the impossibility of such a view, the
character of the initial errors which historically have given rise
to it, and the way of escape from it, Mr. Whitehead has devoted
a great part of that series of volumes, distinguished alike by their
literary grace, speculative originality and logical subtlety, with
which he has enriched the philosophy of the past decade. He has
urged the necessity of the adoption of a set of fundamental concepts and assumptions radically different from those hitherto commonly employed in dealing with these issues; so that, if this
necessity is shown, the whole discussion enters a fresh phase and
must henceforth be conducted upon a new *terrain*. Contentions
so important, put forward by so distinguished a figure in contemporary thought, must manifestly receive close examination before

any conclusion can legitimately be reached with respect to the questions with which these lectures are occupied. But before attempting to decide what Mr. Whitehead has proved regarding these questions, it is necessary to devote some pains to determining precisely what it is that he has asserted. This will involve rather lengthy exegetical inquiries, which I would gladly avoid. But I am unacquainted with any method for judging of the tenability of a hypothesis without first ascertaining what it means; and in this case, the meaning is not at all points immediately apparent. In general, it is evident, the doctrine is a variety of objective relativism—of which, indeed, Mr. Whitehead is one of the major prophets. But it is a variety characterized by certain distinctions and emphases of its own; and it cannot, therefore, be assumed to have been sufficiently dealt with in the two preceding lectures.

What, precisely, is the "bifurcation of nature" which is by Whitehead denied? To this question a full answer can be given only at the end of our analysis; but certain things which this negation might be thought to mean, but clearly does not, and certain points in which its meaning is not clear without somewhat minute analysis, may be pointed out at once. It is not, in the first place, a denial of psychophysical dualism in general; there is, on the contrary, a fundamental and peculiarly sharp cleavage of reality as a whole into mind and nature. What "mind" is conceived to be remains to me a little obscure; it is, however, said not to be "in time or in space in the same sense in which the events of nature are in time"; and it is manifested in the functions of sense-awareness and thought, which, while temporal processes, are by definition distinct from "nature," which signifies only what is *for* awareness. "Nature" is, indeed, frequently defined in such a way that all unperceived entities must, purely by definition, be excluded from it—if the language employed were to be understood in its usual sense. "Nature is that which we observe in perception through the senses";[1] but it seems that, on the one hand, "observe" here in-

[1] *The Concept of Nature,* pp. 3–4.

cludes the meaning of "infer"; while, on the other hand, not all immediate content is said to be in "nature." Memory-content, for example, is apparently excluded; and dreams are also ruled out, on the ground that they are events of which the time and place cannot be specified in any coherent system of spatio-temporal relations common to them and the objects of waking experience.[2] Whether, in the later development of the doctrine, delusions are similarly barred from "nature," it is difficult to determine;[3] in some statements of it, at all events, they are not, presumably on the ground that (for the victim of them) delusive objects are located in the same space and time with the objects of normal perception.[4]

The denial of "bifurcation," then, so far as it is pertinent to what actually enters experience, seems to relate solely to sensory content, and only to a part of that—namely, to normal sense-data and perhaps to the illusions of waking life. Of such content, what is most clearly and most frequently asserted is that it does not consist of "psychic additions to nature"; the mind must not be "dragged in" as "making additions of its own to the thing posited for knowledge by sense-awareness." But this, as a previous lecture has made evident, is a proposition in no way incongruous with epistemological dualism, nor even with the theory of the non-physical nature of the immediate data of experience, in the usual and natural sense of the word "physical." The questions of most importance, we have seen, are not whether sense-data are "psychic," i. e., mind-made additions, but whether they are *additions,* to a nature which, in the absence of organisms carrying on the peculiar organic function called perceiving, would contain no such entities—whether in the total process of perception (as a physiological if not as a mental event) some or all of the objects of our direct apprehension are generated, and, if so, whether the existents thus produced are private, i. e., limited to individual

---

2 *The Concept of Nature,* p. 68; *Principle of Relativity,* p. 63.
3 *Symbolism, etc.,* pp. 54–5.
4 *Concept of Nature,* p. 155.

fields of experience, and whether they lack the distinguishing properties (*e. g.,* direct causal efficacy in the interconnected processes of nature) ascribed to the realities not thus generated or conditioned by the perceptual function. If Whitehead answers these questions in the affirmative, he is not an adversary of the dualism with which we are here concerned, but only a dualist with a difference; and it would remain only to examine into the nature, importance and justifiability of the difference. But that his answers *are* in the affirmative, or that the revision of certain fundamental assumptions which he proposes would logically lead to affirmative answers, is not initially clear; on the contrary, his expression of opposition to bifurcation-theories seem frequently to be directed against epistemological dualism, and also to imply that there is no material difference in status, or in their relation to the perceptual function, between the actual contents of perception and the constituents of the physical world not immediately given in perception. What is, at least sometimes, denied is not the potency of "mind" in the causation of content, but, more generally, the "concept of nature as bifurcated into causal nature and apparent nature"—into "individual experience and external cause." We are, it is maintained, not warranted "in assigning a superior reality in nature to material inertia over color or sound. So far as reality is concerned all our sense-perceptions are in the same boat and must be treated on the same principle." [5] "Subjectivism" is rejected not merely in its extreme but in its "halfway" or "intermediate" form—*i. e.,* the view that "our perceptual experience does tell of a common objective world, but that the things perceived are merely the outcome for us of this world, and are not *in themselves* elements in the common world itself." [6] Especially strong antipathy is expressed to the notion that nature, apart from "ourselves," is a dull affair, "soundless, scentless, colorless." These utterances are all, it is true, highly ambiguous; even they might be interpreted dualistically. But

[5] *Concept of Nature*, p. 44.
[6] *Science and the Modern World*, p. 124; italics in original.

they so naturally may be and, if I am not mistaken, so generally have been, construed as repudiations, in some significant sense, of *both* epistemological and (with respect to content) psychophysical dualism, that I shall provisionally take them as such, and proceed to inquire just what alternative to those theories is proposed, and what reasons are presented for accepting it.

The logical source and the historic origin of the error of bifurcation Professor Whitehead finds in what he terms "the fallacy of simple location." This was "the very foundation of the seventeenth century scheme of nature"; it "underlies the whole philosophy of nature during the modern period"; and it is by it and the conceptions associated with it that "modern philosophy has been ruined." The thing first and chiefly needful at present, for both the theory of knowledge and natural philosophy, is the elimination of this notion, and of the habits of mind which it has engendered, from our thought. For "among the primary elements of nature as apprehended in our immediate experience there is no element whatever which possesses this character of simple location"; the belief that there is has resulted from making a methodologically convenient abstraction from the complexity of reality and then treating the abstraction as a correct description of the reality. In its place we must now make "the ultimate concept of organism" the foundation of our scientific scheme.

What, then, is to be understood by "the idea of simple location"; what is the "organic view of nature" which is to be substituted for it; and what epistemologically significant consequences would follow from the abandonment of the one and the adoption of the other? It is not possible to answer briefly, for at least seven distinguishable senses of "simple location" and its antithesis seem to me to be intimated. I do not mean that these are all inconsistent, but only that it is important to avoid confusing them, if we are to estimate the logical force of the argument. I do not mean, either, that in all of these senses simple location is actually denied in the doctrine in question; but only that in each of them it *seems* at times to be denied, and that it therefore appears necessary to determine in which sense or senses it is actually rejected, and what the most significant aspect of the alternative view is.

(1) The formal definition of the notion gives it a comparatively narrow scope. To ascribe "simple location" to any entity, *e. g.,* "a bit of matter," is to assume that the entity "can be said to be *here* in space or *here* in time, or *here* in space-time, in a perfectly definite sense, which does not require for its explanation any reference to other regions of space-time." [7] The question, so stated, relates wholly to the *definition* of spatial, temporal, or spatio-temporal, position. The supposition attributed to the believers in simple location does not appear to be that a "here" or a "now" can be defined without a reference to *any* region of space or time—an absurdity which few, if any, have held; but only that any limited region, whether given in perception or defined in thought, is conceivable without reference to ulterior regions. Whitehead makes two remarks which I find puzzling about the logical affinities and historic rôle of this conception. He observes that the idea of simple location thus defined can be equally consistently applied from the standpoint of either the relational or the absolute theory of space and time; and that, taken in one way or the other, this is the idea which has dominated modern science since the seventeenth century. Now the relational way of conceiving time or space is usually distinguished from the absolutist way in that the former, in Broad's phrase, regards any (*e. g.*) temporal relation between two events as "simple, direct and unanalyzable, uniting the two events in question and nothing else"; while the latter holds that relation to be "a complex compounded out of other relations which involve other terms in addition to the two events." [8] The prime merit of the relational view, for

---

[7] *Science and the Modern World,* p. 69. Another definition is given at p. 81: "To say that a bit of matter has *simple location* means that, in expressing its spatio-temporal relations, it is adequate to state that it is where it is, in a definite region of space, and throughout a definite finite duration of time, apart from any essential reference of the relations of that bit of matter to other regions of space and to other durations of time." This is presented as a restatement of the definition cited in the text.

[8] *Scientific Thought,* p. 89; *cf.* also p. 91.

those who prefer it, is that it does *not* implicate the whole universe in the notion of every event or every locus. It enables us to take our space or time piecemeal; when two or more events or objects are empirically given or postulated, certain unique spatial and temporal relations are apprehended as subsisting between just those terms, without any indispensable reference to ulterior (or even to interior) "regions"—while, according to the absolutist view, the ulterior regions are implied in the very concept of any such relation and must be assumed to have whatever degree of reality is attributed to the events or objects in question and their *particular* relations *inter se*. Thus the definition of the relational theory of space, *etc.*, seems to correspond to Whitehead's definition of "the fallacy of simple location," and the definition of the absolutist theory to correspond to the organic view of the nature of spatial relations. I cannot see, therefore, how "simple location" can be said to be formulable in terms congruous with the latter view, as well as with the former. Nor do I see how it can be said that the philosophy of the seventeenth century, or the "whole philosophy of nature during the modern period," has attributed "simple location," in the sense defined, to objects in space. It is true that modern mechanics and kinematics have usually recognized what Birkhoff has termed "geometric relativity" —"a relativity present in the application of the geometery of Euclid to nature which allows us to start from any particular rigid body of reference, as defining a space of its own, and then to locate the position of other material objects at any time relative to that space." [9] If recognition of the possibility of defining position and motion in this particularistic or relativistic way—and, indeed, the unavoidability of doing so, in any concrete instance—is, as the definition above would suggest, the idea of "simple location," then that idea has, no doubt, pervaded modern science; but it is difficult to suppose that this, which is obviously no fallacy, can be the conception which we are called upon to abandon. If, however, the belief in simple location is the supposition that there is

[9] *Origin, Nature and Influence of Relativity*, p. 8.

no logical implication of the concept of existent ulterior spaces in the concept of any limited space as existent, then modern science between Newton and Einstein has not, for the most part, been given over to that belief; it has usually, I take it, accepted geometric relativity as a practical methodological necessity rather than as a metaphysical or cosmological principle. It has, in other words, assumed that a bit of matter could not truly *have* location exclusively with reference to some one (or even some three) other bodies, but that it must at the same time have determinate (though not by us determinable) location with respect to all bodies and to all regions composing the totality of space. One of the first steps in the Einsteinian doctrine of relativity, on the other hand, was the proposal to get rid of this assumption of a single and absolute space altogether, and thus to make all purely spatial location "simple," *i. e.,* isolable, a private affair of a particular reference-system. Thus "simple location," in the first sense of the expression, is a conception commonly absent from the older physics, so far as space—and, subject to some non-essential qualifications, so far as time—is concerned, while it is, in the same respects, of the essence of the new relativistic physics. When, then, Whitehead denies "simple location," in the spatial sense, he is only denying what the traditional absolutist theory of space has always denied, and is affirming what is most distinctive of that theory. This is exemplified in his remarks about volume. "The volumes of space have no independent existence. They are only entities as within the totality; you cannot extract them from their environment without destruction of their very essence."[10] It is just this reasoning that the relational theory rejects. And it is not apparent how the errors of the seventeenth century are to be escaped, and the theory of knowledge and the philosophy of nature to be reconstituted on an essentially new basis, by accepting such reasoning. It is, however, possible to read into this first definition more than it explicitly says; what this potentially implicit signification is we shall see later.

[10] *Science and the Modern World*, p. 91.

(2) It is true that the relational theory, though it in the main asserts the logical isolability of particular spatial or temporal relations from other such relations and from Space and Time conceived as simple, continuous, organic wholes, nevertheless implies the essentiality of the relation between two terms which the absolutist theory treats as only accidentally connected—*viz.,* between space and matter. More precisely, it implies that there cannot be *any* case of a spatial relation where there are not some concrete existents—bits of matter, in the traditional physics—having other attributes than purely spatial ones. And, if I am not mistaken, the "fallacy of simple location" sometimes is identified with, or treated as including, the negation of this view. It is apparently because of this use of the expression that Whitehead regards his own "organic" conception as akin rather to the relational than to the traditional absolutist theory;[11] and in this particular, indeed, it is so. But the unisolability of the conception of spatial position from that of matter in the relational theory is simply the consequence of its rejection of any "organic" view of spatial relatedness as such; it is, in other words, an implication of geometric relativity, when that is regarded as *more* than a provisional methodological device. In short, "simple location" in this second sense has been denied mainly in order that "simple location" in the first sense might be maintained. There seems, then, to be a measure of incongruity in using the same term to designate both conceptions; and in any case, it would appear that the relationist's "admission that we cannot know space without matter" cannot legitimately be treated as correct in principle and at the same time be cited as evidence of the truth of the view from the assumed falsity of which it is inferred.

[11] *Cf. The Concept of Nature,* p. 141: The "conception of entities whose characters are capable of isolated definition . . . admittedly breaks down when we come to the relations of matter and space. The relational theory of space is an admission that we cannot know space without matter or matter without space." The last sentence is, I take it, an overstatement. *Both* the usual absolutist and the relational theory recognized the implication of the notion of space in that of matter; but the former did not regard this dependence as mutual. *Cf.* Broad, *Scientific Thought,* p. 88.

(3) In neither of the foregoing senses does the belief in "simple location" seem to have played an extremely significant rôle in the philosophy of the past three centuries; nor does the rejection of such a belief, in those senses alone, offer any manifest solvent for our present philosophical difficulties, or any alternative to either epistemological or psychophysical dualism. One is compelled to surmise, therefore, that these senses do not adequately express the essential point of opposition between the older way of thinking which we are to abandon and the new, "organic" conception of nature. And in fact, the question of "simple location" seems often to have to do with a much more general issue: not merely with the conceptual or existential isolability of a given region of space or time or space-time from ulterior regions, nor merely with the isolability of the concept of position from that of matter or concrete objects, but with the isolability of anything whatever from anything whatever. In other words, the alternative to "simple location," the "organic" view, is frequently expressed in terms which might naturally be construed as asserting the essentiality of *all* relations, the complete and inextricable logical entanglement of every least fragment of reality with every other—in short, the familiar flower-in-the-crannied-wall type of metaphysics, translated from idealistic into realistic terms. "The relation of part to whole has the special reciprocity associated with the idea of organism in which the part is for the whole; but this relation reigns throughout nature." [12] "Nothing in nature could be what it is except as an ingredient in nature as it is." [13] "*Any* factor, by virtue of its status as a limitation within totality, necessarily refers to factors within totality other than itself. It is therefore impossible to find anything finite, that is to say, any entity for cogitation which does not, in its apprehension by consciousness, disclose relationships to other entities, and thereby disclose some systematic structure of factors within fact." [14]

[12] *Science and the Modern World*, p. 208.
[13] *The Concept of Nature*, p. 141.
[14] *Principle of Relativity*, p. 17.

What appears to be asserted in numerous passages of this type is the determination of the existence and of every character of any concrete entity in space and time by its relations to other such entities, and reciprocally—so that if a single relation were different, everything else would also necessarily be different or non-existent. If this conclusion were affirmed and vindicated, the result pertinent to our present problem would be not a refutation of dualism but a refutation of realism. For nothing that in any moment of cognition is apprehended would be what it is apart from its relation to the knower. Leave him, as he at that moment is, out of the reckoning, and the whole universe would be different or non-existent. The doctrine of the essentiality of all relations can lead to nothing but idealism.

But this, it turns out, is not the real meaning of the "organic view" which is proposed. If the assumption of "simple location" means the theory that there are some external, unessential, or non-constitutive relations, then, in this sense, Professor Whitehead does not himself appear to deny simple location. For the dogma of the universal essentiality of relations is elsewhere emphatically repudiated. There are "contingent" as well as "essential relationships of a factor in fact," *i. e.,* of an element in the whole of nature; the former are relations "which might be otherwise without change of the particular individuality of the factor. In other words, *the factor would be what it is even if contingent relationships were otherwise.*"[15] So again we are told that what is termed "the physical field" is "luckily atomic," *i. e.,* "we can discriminate in the four-dimensional continuum regions or events, such that each exhibits a physical character which is entirely independent of the physical characters of other events or of the other physical characters of that event." This atomicity "involves a breakdown of relatedness." It is this feature of the constitution of nature which alone makes possible the "intelligibility of the apparent world to a finite mind with only partial perception." Without it we could not isolate our problems; "every statement would re-

[15] *The Principle of Relativity,* p. 23.

quire a detailed expression of all the facts in nature." [16] Precisely
which relations are contingent and which are essential, and in
precisely what sense, it is not, for the moment, needful to inquire;
it is clear, at all events, that the hypothesis now before us assumes
only a limited liability for the establishment of essential relations.

(4) And where it assumes that liability it does so with a difference. The concept of essential relations presents diverse facets to
different eyes. To some its significance lies in the implication that
the part lives only in and for the whole; hence the cult of the Idea
of Totality in orthodox neo-Hegelianism. To others the same
conception, when generalized, exhibits everything as in the act of
deliquescing into everything else, so that nothing in particular remains; the universe, to change the figure, is resolved into an encyclopaedia consisting exclusively of cross-references, and therefore devoid of any real content. But for Whitehead the notion of
essential relations serves, not for the humiliation of the mere part,
still less for its annihilation, but rather for its aggrandizement;
the point chiefly emphasized is not the inclusion of the part in the
whole, but a sort of inclusion of the whole in the part, or at least
—when the restricted applicability of the notion is borne in mind
—the reciprocal inclusion of *certain* parts in certain others, to
their mutual enrichment. Frequently that is expressed in a completely generalized way. Thus we are told that "in a certain sense
everything is everywhere at all times." [17] The individual fact "is
only itself as drawing into its own limitation the larger whole in
which it finds itself." [18] "Science and philosophy have been apt to
entangle themselves in a simple-minded theory that an object is at
one place at any definite time, and is in no sense anywhere else,"
whereas in truth "each object is in some sense ingredient throughout nature. [19] The way of thinking about the physical world which
even science must now learn to substitute for the one which has
been dominant since the seventeenth century, was intuitively felt

[16] *Ibid.*, p. 73.
[17] *Science and the Modern World*, p. 128.
[18] *Ibid.*, p. 132.
[19] *The Concept of Nature*, p. 145.

by the Romantic poets: "a sense of that mysterious presence of surrounding things which imposes itself on any separate element that we set up as an individual for its own sake."[20] But this again, in view of the passages already quoted, must apparently not be literally construed; it means only that *some* things are, in some sense, *somewhere* else.

Here, then, the suggested alternative to the assumption of simple location seems to be, not—at all events, not primarily nor chiefly—the doctrine of the mere inextricability of part from whole, nor yet that of the dependence of some parts upon others, but the attribution to certain elements in nature of a sort of duplicity or multiplicity of spatial situations, the assertion that they are—with the all-important saving clause "in some sense"—in two or more places at one determinate time (presumably in a single reference-system); while the "fallacy of simple location" would be the denial of the possibility of such a plurality of simultaneous positions in a defined system. In short, "simple location" would now seem to mean "single location." And it is, in fact, against the belief in the singleness, "in some sense," of the location of the components of the physical order that the chief attack is apparently directed.

There is a tendency, natural enough to metaphysically imaginative minds in certain moods, and not infrequently exemplified in the history of philosophy, to rebel against the notion of the baffling mutual externality of things—a feeling that there is something intolerable in the picture of a universe sundered wholly into *partes extra partes,* as any universe conceived under rigorously spatial or quasi-spatial categories seems inevitably to be sundered. There is an appealing and psychologically comprehensible sort of metaphysical pathos in the idea that

> Nothing in the world is single,
> All things by a law divine
> In one spirit meet and mingle.

[20] *Science and the Modern World,* p. 117.

The tendency of which I speak was apparent, of course, long be-fore the Romantic poets. The classic example of it is the Neo-platonic conception of the *anima mundi,* an entity which was, indeed, entirely innocent of simple location, since it was completely present in one place without being any the less completely pres-ent in all other places—as Pope concisely put it, it "spreads undivided." But a like ubiquity was sometimes ascribed by Neo-platonism to things in general: thus Plotinus writes: "All things see themselves in others. . . Every one has all things in himself and again sees in another all things, so that all things are every-where, and all is all and each is all, and infinite the glory."[21] The thought is echoed in the fifteenth century by Nicholas of Cues with a Latin vigor and conciseness of phrase: *Omnia in omnibus esse constat, et quodlibet in quolibet; . . . et ita quodlibet recepit omnia, ut in ipso sint ipsum contracte*[22]—not a bad Latin equiva-lent, I take it, for Mr. Whitehead's "prehensive unity." In our own time something of the same tendency may be seen in Berg-son; witness his despatialized *durée réelle* revealed in the *intui-tion philosophique,* an existence "made up of a thousand diverse elements which fuse and interpenetrate, without definite contours, *sans la moindre tendance à s' extérioriser les uns par rapport aux autres.*"[23]

Of this ancient and recurrent tendency, then, the contemporary revulsion against the idea of "simple location" is plainly one manifestation. But it is rather the expression of a velleity to escape from that idea than an actual escape from it. The mysti-cal paradox of the ubiquity of the things in space and time is not, in fact, seriously maintained; on the contrary, Mr. Whitehead sanely insists that mutual exclusion is an essential property of real things and the recognition of it an essential characteristic of

[21] *Enneads,* V. 8, 4. T. Whittaker's translation.
[22] *De docta ignorantia,* II. 5. The passage in full is as follows: Cum constet Deum quasi mediante universo esse in omnibus, hinc omnia in omnibus esse constat, et quolibet in qualibet. . . . In qualibet enim creatura universum est ipsa creatura, et ita quodlibet recepit omnia, ut in ipso sint ipsum contracte; cum quodlibet non possit esse actu omnia, cum sit contractum, contrahit omnia ut sint ipsum.
[23] *Essai sur les données immédiates de la conscience,* 1909, p. 100.

rational thought.   The "mere fusion of all that is" into the "non-
entity of indefiniteness" is above all things to be avoided. "The
salvation of reality is in its obstinate, irreducible matter-of-fact
entities, which are limited to be no other than themselves. Neither
science nor art nor creative action can tear itself away from obstinate, irreducible, limited facts." [24] And this self-containedness
and otherness of existents is manifested primarily in their spatial
situations and attributes: "Everything which is in space receives a
definite limitation of some sort, so that, in a sense, it has just that
shape which it does have, and no other, also in some sense, it is in
just this place and no other"; the same is true, *mutatis mutandis,*
for time.   Nor, in the hypothesis now under consideration, is the
equivocality of the notion of simultaneity, asserted by the relativity
theory, employed to modify this proposition. A "simultaneous
spread of the whole of nature" is postulated; in any distinguishable
part of any duration, the locus of any object, in a single spatial order, is seemingly conceived to be single and definite. The concept
of "events," fundamental in the doctrine, clearly implies such reciprocal exclusiveness.   Events are "the relata of the fundamental
homogeneous relation of 'extension'" of which both space and
time are derivatives.   They are, in short, loci, or regions in space
at determinate times; they could be described as point-instants
except that they are neither literally punctual nor literally instan-
taneous.   Mutual externality is thus of their essence.   "An event
is there and not here (or here and not there) ; it is then and not
now (or now and not then)"; it "is a fundamental property of
events" that they "can only be in one place at a time." [25] Events,
however, are described—though apparently with some implicit
addition to the connotation of the term—as the true substance of
nature; in any case, their properties define its structure; and consequently simple location—in our present sense of the term—is
the first law of nature. Events must, indeed, possess qualities
(which Whitehead prefers to call "objects") as well as situations;
but in so far as its qualities actually qualify an event, they must

[24] *Science and the Modern World,* p. 132.
[25] *The Principles of Natural Knowledge,* pp. 62, 65.

(as we have seen in the preceding lecture) share its individuation and localization; *as* ingredient they are where it is and not elsewhere, they are separate *instances* of the ingredience of an object, not to be identified with any other instance.

Since, then, the sense in which "everything" is asserted to be "everywhere at all times" is no literal sense—is, on the contrary, entirely compatible with the proposition that every concrete reality, *i. e.*, every qualified event, is in one place only at any time—the meaning of the "simple location" which is denied, and of the alternative which is affirmed, is still to seek.[26]

(5) Occasionally the point at issue seems to concern, *not* events in their concreteness, but "objects," in the special sense given to the term in this theory; it is of the latter that simple location is now denied. For an "object," in this sense, is, of course, a universal. And the same universal can be simultaneously embodied in many particulars at different places. Thus it is remarked that "the chief confusion between objects and events is conveyed in the prejudice that an object can only be in one place at a time." This prejudice is simply "a misplacement from events to objects" of the fundamental property of the former; and through it "the theory of natural objects" has been "wrecked."[27] In truth, "the self-identical object is there and then, and it is here and now; and the 'it' which has its being there and here, then and now, is without equivocation the same subject for thought in the various judgments which are made upon it."[28] In the light of such expressions, the "fallacy of simple location" would seem to consist in

[26] Russell seems to have overlooked these essential negations of the literal doctrine of multiple location; he writes that "Dr. Whitehead's fallacy of simple location leads, when avoided, to a world-structure quite different from that of common sense and early science. But his structure depends upon a logic which I am unable to accept, namely the logic which supposes that 'aspects' may be not quite alike and yet may be in some sense numerically one. To my mind, such a view, if taken seriously, is incompatible with science and involves a mystic pantheism" (*Analysis of Matter*, p. 340). The view is *not* taken seriously by its author; his real denial of simple location has neither the charm, nor the dangers for science, of the mystical pantheism with which some of his expressions have the air of identifying it. It is unfortunate that such expressions, capable of leading even Mr. Russell into a misapprehension, should have been used.

[27] *The Principles of Natural Knowledge*, p. 65; cf. *The Concept of Nature*, p. 145.
[28] *Principles of Natural Knowledge*, p. 63.

the proposition that a single universal can *not* be present or "in-gredient" in more than one event at a time—that no two blades of grass can simultaneously be green, no two coins circular.

But this is a fallacy which no one commits. Something like it, indeed, was apparently asserted by some of the Greek Sophists; and Leibniz's principle of the identity of indiscernibles bears a superficial resemblance to it, but is at bottom a negation of it. Modern science in general has obviously been prone to no such absurdity. If it has attributed simple location to "objects," it has done so in quite another sense of that word: the imputation to it of the supposed confusion seems plausible only when the word is used with two different meanings in the same sentence—first as signifying universals, second as signifying particulars, or "events" *with* their qualities. And, on the other hand, that mood of the Romantic poets which is pointed to as an historic illustration of the intuitive repugnance of profound minds for the idea of simple location can hardly be supposed to have consisted merely in a conviction common to all or nearly all the human species. Words-worth's "sense of something far more deeply interfused," what-ever else it was, was surely not a sense of the undisputable truth that there is green at once in the tree and in the grass, blue in the sky and in the mountain lake which reflects it.

The technical logico-metaphysical problem of the relation of es-sences to particulars, or to the spatial and temporal loci in which they are manifested, has, to be sure, been a troublesome one for philosophy, modern and contemporary, as well as ancient; and there is a type of answer to it, discussed in the last lecture, which does, in a sense, deny simple location. It is the theory that all the characters which are ascribed to things are mere essences, having no genesis, no date, no place, and no dynamic relations. To this theory Whitehead in his account of the properties of "objects" often seems to incline. "Objects" are said to be "without space and time"; hence "it is an error to ascribe parts to objects, where 'part' means spatial or temporal part."[29] This, however, is a case

29 *Ibid.,* pp. 63, 65.

of throwing out the baby with the bath; it denies simple location to "objects" by denying location to them altogether. The "event" is left as a bare region of reference in an abstract quasi-geometrical scheme of formal relations; the "object" is bereft of extension and elevated to the eternal world; and the elementary fact of experience that we perceive, e. g., extended, bounded, and thus individuated, patches of color *in* definite spatio-temporal relations, remains not merely unexplained but unacknowledged in this account of the situation. Such a view, however, is not only, in itself, the very negation of a solution of the problem, but it is not really congruous with a theory of the type we are examining; it does not, so to say, accord with its distinctive genius. For, in the first place, the theory after all declares that "objects," *i. e.,* qualities, *are* "ingredient into nature," that is, into the system of which the relata are events. And to insist that the "objects" are wholly and literally "eternal" and extra-spatial would be simply a way of denying the empirical fact of their genuine ingression. Moreover, the "events" without their qualities actually pervading them are admittedly pure abstractions; the essentiality of the relatedness of the two we have seen to be one of the other senses in which simple location is denied. Most of the things said of "objects," on the one hand, and of "events," on the other, plainly hold good only of the two conceived together as a unity of logically distinguishable but concretely inseparable aspects of the same fact. There is, indeed, it seems to me, a confusing dual use of both terms; in the first use each is sharply antithetic to the other, while in the second use the two approach equivalence of meaning, "event" signifying a locus really pervaded by qualities (or "objects," in the other sense), and "object" signifying a group of qualities actually pervading a locus. Finally, it is clear that the alternative to simple location which Whitehead is desirous of establishing has *some* connection with the doctrine of the internality of relations. That doctrine, if not affirmed without qualification or restriction, is still the first and great article of the creed. But of "objects" (in the first sense) we are told that their relations are non-constitutive; "two objects, being what they are, have no necessary temporal and spatial relations which are essential to their individualities." [30] Hence "objects" (in that sense) are of all things the most repugnant to any "organic conception of nature." The mere presence of one universal in different situations has manifestly nothing in common with the notion of reciprocal determination— which is part, if not the whole, of what is to be proved; it is a mere iteration of the same, not an interconnection or interfusion of the distinct. For all these reasons (among others), we must conclude that the error which we are called upon to abandon is not the (virtually non-existent) notion that universals are incapable of multiple simultaneous manifestations in space, nor yet the logical theorem that universals are not truly ingredient into nature at all.

(6) It is sometimes suggested that the alternative to "simple location" is a notion, long familiar in physics, which may be called the concept of the universal diffusion of the physical object—illustrated by Faraday's remark that "his theory of tubes of force implies that in a sense an electric charge is everywhere." [31] Since theoretical physics has been more and more resolving the hypothetical ultimate units of what, in its sensible apparitions, we call matter into electric charges, the outcome has been that those ultimate units, instead of being the smallest of things prove to be the biggest; the electron, conceived as merely a unit negative charge is, as sometimes defined, if not everywhere, at all events immensely extensive. The definitely limited atom of the older physics has been broken up into parts larger than itself. In this and other ways in recent science the idea of nature as a collection of sharply bounded "things" has tended to give place to the idea of nature as a multiplicity of "fields," not bounded sharply nor perhaps at all, and not mutually exclusive. In the phrase of Professor H. C. Brown, "the concept of the physical object has taken

30 *Ibid.*, p. 65.
31 *The Concept of Nature*, p. 146.

on a new meaning; it no longer denotes the character of a region, as such, but the 'totality-effect' of a region." [32]

But such a conception of physical objects manifestly does not do away with simple location. For an electron, or any other "field," unlike the *anima mundi,* does *not* "spread undivided"; whatever its spread, one part of the energy which constitutes it is, at any determinate time and in any determinate space, present in one region, another part in another, and so on. We are still confronted by a world of *partes extra partes.* It is true that the fields of two or more electrons, so conceived, may and, indeed, must overlap spatially and temporally; but this means only that the sum of energy present in a given region is resolvable into components, which may severally be referred to different centers or causally connected with energy-conditions existing in various other regions. What is concretely present in any empirically definable region is nevertheless just this sum of energies and no other, taking just this form and no other, and just here and not elsewhere. The idea of the infinitely diffused electron—from which the idea of the seemingly mysterious interpenetration of these entities arises—is itself, in fact, simply an abstraction reached by considering certain connections between what is found in these limited regions. You discover that the energy measurably present in one region at a given moment is a function of that measurably present at various others at other moments; you then hypostatize the law of these correlations into a collection of quasi-substances spread through space or space-time; and, not surprisingly, you conclude that they must jointly occupy the *same* space or space-time. The entities you started with, meanwhile, retain all the simple location which they had empirically at the outset.

And consequently the case for epistemological and psychophysical dualism is in no degree weakened when a "physical ob-

---

[32] It is in this sense that Professor Dewey also has recently denied that physical objects have simple location, and has sought in this view an answer to the question concerning "the whereabouts of illusory objects" which is presented by the dualist as "the final clincher to demonstrate the psychical character of the characteristic objects of perception." (*Journal of Philosophy,* 1925, pp. 596–605.)

ject"—whether of science or of common sense—is thus deprived of any local habitation; the case for psychophysical dualism is, in fact, somewhat strengthened. For even though my percept of the distant star of which I am assumed to know by means of that percept were itself merely a portion of the total physical field which, by definition, constitutes the "star," it could not be the same as the portion of the field from which the light was emitted —unless the doctrine of the finite velocity of light were assumed to be false. The local separation, and consequently the existential duality, of content and *cognoscendum* remain as indubitable from the point of view of field-physics as from any other. Nor does such a point of view alleviate the difficulty of finding a place in the orderly system of physical nature for "the ghost that isn't there," or "the imaged tree which moves when the eyeball is pushed." Every region of a field is occupied by its own events, taking place, by hypothesis, in accordance with physical laws; and to no such region, at a given moment (in any given time-system), do those laws assign any events having the particular properties of either the wild or the veridical sense-data experienced at that moment. There is nothing in the conception of objects as "fields" which serves either to rehabilitate ghosts or to multiply the number of stars in the heavens by the number of observers. On the other hand, if there is supposed to be nothing in the physical world except fields, and if no field has any sharp edge or definable boundary, then the physical world must be extremely unlike the world of sensible appearances. Obviously, the more you reduce physical objects to pure energy-systems, and the more you insist upon their lack of definite spatial limitations, the more you set them in contrast with the immediate data of perception, which are not describable in the terms in which energy is described, and are, in vision and touch, characterized by spatial limitation and mutual exclusion. It is not, then, in the conversion of the notion of physical things into that of indefinitely or infinitely diffused fields of force that a way of escape from dualism is to be found; nor does this, despite some indications to the contrary, appear to be the way really proposed to us in the philosophical doctrine which we are examining. For, as has been noted, it is characteristic of this doctrine that its interest is not, so to say, in diffusion but in concentration; not in spreading out the individual object throughout the universe, but rather in conceiving of the individual object, without loss of its definiteness and limitation of locus or character, as in some sense embracing or manifesting the whole universe within itself.

(7) The sense in which "everything is everywhere" (or more precisely, some things which are somewhere are also elsewhere) seems finally to be expressed in the proposition that the "aspects" of one entity (or qualified event) are present in others, or at the places which are the situations of the others. What, then, is an "aspect"—a term which in past philosophy has had a devastating career. The notion at first appears to involve that of perspective, of which a good deal was said in the last lecture. In the ordinary sense, a perspective aspect is a set of characters, A, situated in L_1, which is related to another set, B, situated in L_2, in a specific manner; *viz.*, A's presence in L_1 is dependent (in part) upon B's presence at L_2; A is quantitatively or qualitatively different from B in some degree, though not necessarily wholly or in all respects; and the nature or degree of its difference from B is a function of its spatial relation to B, such, *e. g.*, that at successive distances from B the degree of difference of its perspective aspects will vary uniformly. Now the fact that in common speech we sometimes say that A is B "from the standpoint of L_1" seems in part to be the basis of the supposition that in the case of perspectives "simple location" has been transcended. But so long, at all events, as we do not add to the ordinary and empirically familiar conception of perspectives there is manifestly no such transcendence. A is *not* B, and it is not where B is, at the time when B is there; there is merely a special type of causal relation between them. It is true that an observer of A, having some acquaintance with the laws of perspective, will be—or would have been, according to the suppositions of common sense and the older physics—able to infer

the character of B; and this fact may be expressed by saying that A is the way in which B appears from L_1. But "appear" here signifies only the particular dual relation of conditionality and partial similarity, *plus* the fact that, given a knower, B can be known through A. It is also probably true that if any observer stands at L_1 and looks in the direction of L_2 he will see in his visual spatial field in that direction an object having a size and sometimes a shape which are not those of B as perceived by observers in other positions nearer to it; and these peculiarities of the size and shape of the visible object at or in the direction of L_2 will correspond somewhat with the peculiarities of the physical "perspective aspect" of B which might be found on a camera plate at L_1. This special sort of perspective effect which is projected back into (roughly) the supposed locus of the original object seems sometimes to be what Whitehead has in mind: thus he speaks of a sensible object as located at L_1 with the "mode of location" at L_2. But this projection of the perspective aspect towards the region of emission of the light-ray is, so far as we know, a unique phenomenon dependent upon the occurrence of a perception; it does not, presumably, happen in the case of physical perspective aspects. The image on the camera plate is on the plate, with no "mode of location" anywhere else.   Thus when Russell seeks to build up a universe out of "perspective appearances" which do not necessarily appear to anybody, he conceives these appearances *not* as all present at their common center, but as scattered throughout space. But it is an alternative to simple location which can be supposed to hold good of nature apart from "apprehension" that Whitehead is seeking; and no such alternative is offered by the concept of perspective.   Nor, even in the case of visual perception, is there any justification for saying that the object seen, with its perspective, is spatially coincident with either the pair of retinal images, or the brain-configuration which was its proximate condition. There is, then, no magic in "perspectives," in the ordinary sense of the term, which will enable us to escape "simple location," and with it, epistemological dualism.   Dualists have not, after all, been unaware of these phenomena; on the contrary, they have often pointed to them as illustrations of the truth of their contentions.

Something more, then, must be supposed to be conveyed by the term "aspects." An "aspect," it would seem, need not resemble, in any definite manner or degree, that of which it is an aspect. An observation of it, even if supplemented by a knowledge of the laws of perspective, would not give information as to the nature of that of which it is an aspect; its difference therefrom is not a function of the distance; it need not be a member of a group constituting a graduated series of differences. We are told, for example, that "the Tower of London is a particular aspect of the universe in its relation to the banks of the Thames"; what this seems to signify is that the constitution of the rest of the universe is determinative of the fact that there is such a structure at that place. It would appear that, in the sense of the term which is distinct from that of perspective, any event is called an "aspect" of another if its character (*i. e.,* its ingredient "object") is partly conditioned or determined by the character of that other (*i. e.,* by the ingredience of a certain other "object" in the other event); and if, further, this determination is not merely contingent and empirical but logically necessary, inherent in the essence of the former event. That there are events or objects which are actually conditioned by other events, or the situations of other objects, has not, of course, been often denied; so that the point at issue obviously lies not in the first but in the second clause of this definition—it concerns, not the fact that there exists a functional correlation between many events or their characters, but only the logical and metaphysical interpretation of that fact. The essential thesis propounded, in short, seems to be that such relations are of the nature of pure logical implication, are somehow involved in the very quiddity of their terms, while the theory of "simple location" would be the view, held by Mr. Bertrand Russell and many others, that what is called the determination of one event by another is "merely causal or inductively derived from empirical correlations."[33] To this issue the difference between the assertion and the denial of simple location appears now to reduce.

The denial of simple location in this sense is obviously difficult to reconcile with the conception of the properties of events and objects which has already been mentioned. "Internal" relatedness, necessary mutual implication, usually seems, in Professor Whitehead's universe, to belong only to spatio-temporal regions or loci —to "events" in the stricter sense in which they are merely "relata in the relation of extension," and are *not* "colored with all the hues of their content." It is this alone, as we have seen, that the formal definition of the opposite to simple location, cited at the beginning of our analysis, includes. Every "here" and "now" was declared to have a necessary reference to other "heres" and "nows"; but it was not in that case and is not usually maintained that the *qualities* which are *here* determine what qualities shall be *there*. On the contrary, qualities, *viz.*, "objects," we have seen to be defined as having no necessary relations *inter se;* they are personified in the Miller of Dee of the nursery rhyme. Doubtless they can figure in "nature" only as ingredient in events; but the relationship of any "object" even to the particular event it qualifies is contingent,[34] and must *a fortiori* be so to any other event. The two *"regions"* in which the objects are situated may be "aspects" of one another, in the sense that each refers to the other or to the whole of space, time, or space-time, of which both are essential parts; but to say that the meaning of the location of an object A at L_1 can "be explained" only in terms of the relations of L_1 to other loci is not equivalent to saying that the presence of A, rather than some other sort of object, at L_1 is logically possible only because B, rather than some other sort of object, is at L_2, and so on.[35]

[33] Russell, *Analysis of Matter*, p. 247.
[34] *The Principle of Relativity*, pp. 24–5.
[35] *Ibid.:* "When we perceive green, it is not green in isolation, it is green somewhere, at some time. The green may or may not have the relationship to some other object, such as a blade of grass. Such a relation would be contingent. But it is essential that we see it somewhere in space related to our eyes at a certain epoch of our bodily life. The detailed relationships of green to our bodily life and to the situations in which it is apparent to our vision, are complex and variable and partake of the contingence which enables us to remain ignorant of them."

If, then, we should interpret the notion of "aspects" in the light of the previous account of the nature of events and objects respectively, we should be compelled to conclude that that notion is applicable only to the interrelations of spatio-temporal regions, apart from their content; and our seventh sense of "simple location" would be identical with the first, which in turn seemed to be identical with the denial of the absolutist theory of space. But it seems clear that the internal relatedness expressed by the word "aspect" is frequently supposed to subsist between "objects" (*as ingredient*) and not merely between the places and moments they occupy; and it is with this new thesis that we are now concerned. Its apparent inconsistency with other parts of the doctrine need not trouble us, if it should appear to be supported by sufficient reasons, and to have significant consequences for natural science and, in particular, for epistemology.

But that it has no significant consequences for science is evident. The acceptance of one of the alternatives in question rather than the other could have had no possible effect upon the actual development of modern science. For there is no difference between the two which would affect the procedure of the investigator or the theorist in dealing with any concrete problem. Those who deny "simple location" in this last sense do not maintain that any *particular* correlation between natural happenings can be known *by us* otherwise than empirically; the supposed necessary logical inherence of the relation in its individual terms is discoverable by no mortal through any mere inspection or analysis of the terms. The point has already been well put by Mr. Russell: "Given a group of events, the evidence that they are 'aspects' of one thing must be inductive evidence derived from perception, and must be exactly the same as the evidence upon which we have relied in collecting them into causal groups."

Nor does the difference between denying and affirming "simple location," in the present sense, appear to have significant consequences for epistemology. Call the character of an object A at the locus L_1 an "aspect" of the object B at L_2 rather than a contingent effect of the presence or action of B at L_2, and nothing is changed; all the definable and specific qualities and relations of A and B designated by the one form of expression are precisely the same as those designated by the other. The one phrasing may, indeed, appear to afford some slight gratification, which the other denies, to that natural craving, of which I have spoken, to transcend in thought the reciprocal externality or stand-offishness of things. It at least *sounds* more like Cusanus's *quodlibet in quolibet*. An "aspect" of A being by definition essential to A, something without which it could not logically subsist, may seem to be, if not A itself, at all events in some sense a part of it. Yet even in this case the satisfaction given to our human propensity to break down walls of division is more nominal than real. For an "aspect" is still one term of a real relation; and if it is the office of a relation to unite terms, it is just as truly and essentially its office to keep them apart. If it did not do so its occupation would be gone; it would be in the position of a professional go-between who indiscreetly allowed his principals to meet. This separative function of relations is not annulled when they are declared to be internal or constitutive—unless the notion of their internality is construed in the impossible Bradleian fashion which notoriously results in the disappearance of terms, relations and all; and from this strange and self-destructive dialectic the doctrine now under consideration is entirely free. An "aspect" is a definitely bounded and spatio-temporally located event-object which is not fused nor identified with that of which it is an aspect; and even the internality of the relation between the two, though affirmed, is not exhibited in any particular instance. No one, to repeat, could simply by looking at an "aspect" in its own situation tell of what particular event in another situation it is an aspect. The observable characters constituting an aspect need in no degree resemble, or be a faithful revelation of, their counterpart, the other term of the relation. It is, indeed, said, in Leibnitzian phrase, that whatever is at one place "mirrors itself" in other places; but the mirror admittedly not only is a dim but may be a completely transforming one. Obviously

the particular and distinguishing characteristics of the other parts
of the universe are not present on the banks of the Thames; nor
does imprisonment in the Tower of London of itself afford much
information about the world beyond its walls.

I have said that the denial of "simple location," in the sense
now in question, has no important bearing upon the epistemological problem. What this means, with reference to the special
theme of these lectures, is that the proposed "organic view" of
nature leaves the usual arguments for epistemological dualism
essentially unaffected. This becomes the more clearly evident from
the fact that the theory of perception associated with this view is
itself a form of epistemological dualism—which can, moreover,
be distinguished from psychophysical dualism only if the word
"physical" is used in that unusual and questionable sense mentioned in the preceding lecture. A percept—called in the terminology of the theory a "sense-object"—is, of course, described, as
is everything else in nature, as an event which is an "aspect" of
another object or other objects, ingredient in other events. What
has just been said of "aspects" in general holds true of it: it has,
when it exists, its own inalienable space-time locus; it is therefore
existentially distinct from the events of which it is an aspect or
"prehensive unity of aspects"; it need not, and in the main does
not, qualitatively resemble those events or their ingredient "objects"; and its character is therefore no plain and direct disclosure
of theirs. It has, however, certain peculiarities, especially with
regard to its relations to consciousness, on the one hand, and to the
other components of nature, on the other hand. The sense-object
is, of course, emphatically declared not to be dependent upon mind
or the function of awareness; but it is not apparently denied that it
has a distinctive and especially intimate relation to that function.
It is called the "object of immediate appearance." With it, cognizance is directly concerned. It is, in other words, through *this*
sort of aspect of themselves that all physical events enter, at least
primarily, a field of individual experience. Its existence and na-

ture, however, are held to be an aspect of two classes of other events; more precisely, it may be said to be an aspect of an aspect. At a given time, the rest of the physical universe "mirrors," or, rather, disguises, itself "at some places in those" prehensive unities of aspects "commonly called organisms," and, in particular, in neurocerebral systems—just as at other places it mirrors itself in other prehensive unities such as the Tower of London. Let us now call the locus, at some definite time, of a sentient organism, L_1; let us call the aspect of things at L_1, which is a special kind of event in the history of that organism's brain and nervous system, a "percipient event" or, for short, P. Let us call the qualities which make up the concrete character of this event QP; let us designate the "sense-object," or perceptual datum, by S; and finally, let W stand for the rest of the world outside the organism, or for those parts of the world—if not all the parts be concerned in the business—of which the organism, and, specifically, its percipient event, is an aspect. Then S is, according to the present theory, primarily an aspect of P, though it has not the qualities QP; it is determined by and "has a necessary reference to a percipient event." But since P is an aspect, or a unity of aspects, of W, S is also indirectly an aspect of W. It is, however, said to be in a peculiar sense, or *par excellence,* an aspect, not of all of W—though P *is* the aspect of W as a whole—but of a particular, singled-out part of W, called the perceptual object. And it is of the nature of the perceptual object rather than of P—or the rest of W—that S is somehow and in some degree revelatory; its qualities are apparently conceived to be more or less like those of the perceptual object; in any case, it is of it, and not of P, that it is specifically significant.

Such, in brief résumé, is what I understand to be the account of perception connected with the denial of simple location. I have, it is true, indicated a distinction which seems to me to be clearly implied, but which is not always made explicit. Some of Whitehead's expressions on the subject might perhaps, at first sight, be construed as identifying the sense-object with the percipient event, and as making the assumed logical reference of the percipient (bodily) event to the perceptual object of which, among many other things, it is an aspect, equivalent to the occurrence of a cognition of that object. For example:

> You are in a certain place perceiving things. Your perception takes place where you are, and is entirely dependent on how your body is functioning. But this functioning of the body in one place exhibits for your cognizance an aspect of the distant environment. . . . If this cognizance conveys knowledge of a transcendent world, it must be because the event which is the bodily life unifies in itself aspects of the universe."[36]

And again:

> The distant situation of a perceived object is merely known to us as signified by our bodily state, *i. e.,* by our percipient event. In fact perception requires sense-awareness of the significations of our percipient event together with sense-awareness of a peculiar relation (situation) between certain objects and the events thus signified.[37]

Such passages, if isolated, could perhaps be given a semi-behavioristic interpretation, as meaning that the bodily processes—in other words, the molecular movements in the neuro-muscular system—are the only "aspects" of "the distant thing" (there are, of course, innumerable distant things of which, by the hypothesis, they are aspects) which are essential to cognition. But this, clearly, is not what is really intended. The conception proposed is more nearly expressed in such passages as the following:

> The modes of ingression of sense-objects in nature are the outcome of the perceptual objects exhibiting themselves. The grass exhibits itself as green, the bell as tone, the sugar as tasting, the stone as touchable. Thus the ultimate character of perceptual objects is that they are Aristotelian adjectives which are the controls of ingression.[38]

Only one must bear in mind here a rather constant peculiarity of Professor Whitehead's way of putting things—his custom of speaking of that which is cognized indirectly or inferentially in terms which would ordinarily be regarded as appropriate only to

---

[36] *Science and the Modern World,* pp. 128–9.
[37] *The Concept of Nature,* p. 188.
[38] "Uniformity and Contingency" in *Proceedings of the Aristotelian Society,* vol. XXIII, pp. 1–18.

the "objects of immediate appearance." It is not directly but by
deputy that the bell or the grass or even the stone "exhibits itself";
this is, on occasion, fully recognized and insisted upon. The percipient event "signifies" the perceptual object *"for cognizance"*
only through its determining the "ingredience into nature" of a
sense-object. "There is no apprehension of external events apart
from recognitions of sense-objects as related to them." [39]

The reasons why the distinction of sense-objects from perceptual objects is recognized as necessary seem to be chiefly those, or
certain of those, mentioned in the first lecture as the perennially
regenerative roots of epistemological dualism: *e. g.,* the time-
interval between the existence of the datum and that of the *cognoscendum,* and their difference of spatial situation, in the case of
illusions of perspective. "When the astronomer looking through
a telescope sees a new red star burst into existence, he sees redness
in some event which is happening now." "We say that what he
really sees is a star coming into being two centuries previously,"
but the relations of the two "stars" to the percipient event are
entirely different. The mirror image is seen behind the mirror,
the perceptual object, that which is "really perceived," is not
there. [40] The physico-physiological argument appears to play an
equally important part.

Clearly there is in all this no intimation of an alternative to
epistemological dualism; there is only a re-enunciation of it in
novel terminology. Essentially what is propounded by Mr. Whitehead is another generative theory of sensa. The aspect of B at (or
from) L_1 is due to the interaction between what is "modally" at
L_1, *i. e.,* is simply located there—namely, the organism—and what
is "modally" at other loci, and in particular at L_2. In so far as
the present hypothesis is nominally distinguishable from the generative theory, the difference consists in the strain of Platonic
realism in it—its description of "objects," *i. e.,* the qualities *at*
the several *loci,* as "eternal." But to one to whom the "ingredi-

[39] *Principles of Natural Knowledge,* p. 83.
[40] *Ibid.,* p. 85.

ence" of a universal or "eternal object" at a time into a spatial locus seems only a round-about way of describing what is commonly meant by the coming into being of a particular, the distinction between the view outlined and the hypothesis of brain-begotten sensa is a vanishing one. And in any case, the "sense-objects" are explicitly subjective in that they are unfavorably contrasted with another class of existents designated by a term synonymous, by definition, with one of the usual meanings of "objective"—*viz.*, "adjective." An "adjective" is defined as a "character which an event has for itself alone"; and there are, as we have seen, events which possess such a "contingent" character, one which "marks a break-down in relativity by the very simplicity of the two-term relation it involves." Now "a sense-object, such as the color red, is not a true adjective of its situation, since there is always a necessary reference to a percipient event."[41] Sense-objects "only simulate adjectives for an observer who in his intellectual analysis of the situation forgets to mention himself."[42] On the other hand, the perceptual objects, which are signified by the sense-objects, *are* true Aristotelian adjectives of the events they qualify; "this relation of adjectives to subject requires no relation to *anything* else."[43] Such an expression as the last is, it is true, regarded as an inadmissible overstatement by other adherents of objective relativism, who think it essential to maintain the relativity of everything to something else.[44] This difference, however, as has been already pointed out, is of no pertinency to our present question. Even though perceptual objects "never transcend relativity or centeredness in some form," they still admittedly "transcend relativity to human beings,"[45] that is to say, to the percipient events occurring in the lives of individual human beings, and are

[41] *The Principle of Relativity*, p. 33.
[42] *Ibid.*
[43] "Uniformity and Contingency," p. 17; italics mine.
[44] Cf. Stebbing, *Jour. of Philosophy*, XXIII, 1926, p. 209, and Murphy, *Philosophical Rev.*, 1927, p. 137. It is, indeed, difficult to reconcile the sentence quoted with other utterances of Whitehead's own, *e. g.*, *Science and the Modern World*, p. 217.
[45] Murphy, *op. cit.*

thus incapable of identification with sense-objects, to which the latter relation is essential. And the distinction between the existents which are and those which are not relative to individual human or other percipients, between public objects and private sense-data, is precisely the historic philosophical distinction between the objective and the subjective orders of being.

The profoundly dualistic character of this hypothesis, whether regarded as a theory of knowledge or a philosophy of nature, becomes still more apparent with the progressive clarification, in the sequence of Whitehead's writings, of the concept of the perceptual object. This has more and more become identified with the highly abstract entities of theoretical physics, for the same reasons which have brought about a like result in the history of previous dualisms; "under the pressure of the need for exactness in thought, which demands simplicity in the logical relations involved," as Miss Stebbing has put it, the "perceptual" and "physical" object "gives way to the final substitution of the scientific object." [46] And this last, of course, is extremely unlike the perceptual datum which actually appears. "A scientific object differs decisively from a sense-object viewed as a pseudo-adjective," for one thing, in its duration; it is "permanent," it "qualifies a [temporal] region extending from the present into the future." But the sense-object is transitory: "it qualifies events in the present," is "confined to a spatial region with the minimum of historicity requisite for the duration of the moment." [47] The scientific object, again, has a causal efficacy in the temporal order, it "affects future contingency," as the sense-object does not.

In Mr. Whitehead's more recent little book on *Symbolism* the dualistic character of his philosophy becomes, if possible, even clearer than before. There are, it is true, what appear to be renewed denials of "bifurcation"; the conceptions presented are said to "do away with any mysterious element in our experience which is merely meant, and thereby behind the veil of direct per-

[46] *Op. cit.*, p. 207.
[47] *The Principle of Relativity*, p. 34.

ception." The "doctrine of direct experience of the external world" is still formally professed. Nevertheless, two types of objects of experience, and two corresponding modes of apprehension, are sharply contrasted, and the contrast is, in essentials, if I have correctly grasped it, that which dualists have always insisted upon, between the immediate data of perception and the external causes or conditions of the genesis of these data. The first type of content, "pure presentational immediacy," affords one sort of knowledge, but this is "vivid, precise and barren." It is barren "because *we may not directly connect the qualitative presentations of other things with any intrinsic characters of those things;*" [48] this seems meaningless unless things are supposed to have "intrinsic characters." So long as we are limited to presentational immediacy there is no possibility of error. Such content "refuses to be divided into delusions and non-delusions"; it is all upon the same footing, actually and immediately present. But it is impossible for beings constituted as we—or even as organisms far below us in the scale of intelligence are—to be content at any moment of experience with what is then directly given. We must apprehend—our way of adjusting our action to the practical necessities of existence consists in apprehending—a beyond. We do so, or attempt to do so, by treating some components of our direct perception as symbolic of other things not perceived in the same sense, or at the same time—symbolic, at the least, of other experiences of our own, ultimately of a causal order of events in which the settled past controls the character of the present, and the present will control the future. This symbolic reference, since it is not the actual presence of the object intended, is liable to error in its details; but of the reality of *some* external world of causal efficacy we have, it is maintained, a "direct" and therefore, presumably, an infallible perception. But this, it would appear, is a "perception" of the "that," not of the "what," of the external order; it is but a dim sense of something-there-to-be-conformed-to, of the "vague relata 'oneself' and 'an-

[48] *Symbolism*, p. 24.

other' in the undiscriminated background."[49] While the world of causal efficacy and the world of presentational immediacy must obviously be apprehended as in some manner and at some points actually intersecting, the chief emphasis is upon their mutual exclusion. Few previous dualists have ever insisted more clearly and emphatically that percepts are articles of domestic manufacture, added to the stable and impersonal system of causally efficacious realities—enriching and adorning its surface but, for the most part, forming no true part of it. The content of presentational immediacy "displays a world concealed under an adventitious show, a show of our own bodily production." Direct perception exhibits to us "a world decorated by sense-data dependent on the immediate states of relevant parts of our own bodies."[50] Yet it is to the elusive reality behind this façade of sensible appearances that we seek to penetrate. That paradoxical craving of man as knower, of which I spoke in the first lecture, to understand something of the *être intime* of things that are no psychic offspring of his, to understand what they are out of relation to himself, is admirably expressed by Mr. Whitehead: "For all their lack of definition, these controlling presences, these things with an inner life of their own, with all their richness of content, these beings with the destiny of the world hidden in their natures, are what we want to know about."[51]

What meaning, then, can any longer attach to the denial of the "bifurcation of nature into causal nature and apparent nature"? Is it not in all this clearly admitted that, in a perfectly definite and important sense, "a superior reality in nature" must be "assigned to material inertia over color and sound," and that "the things perceived," so far as either their existence as particular entities or their characters are concerned, *are* "merely the outcome for us

---

[49] *Ibid.*, p. 43.
[50] *Op. cit.*, pp. 44, 14.
[51] *Symbolism*, p. 57; cf. p. 58: "The bonds of causal efficacy arise from without us. They disclose the character of the world from which we issue. . . . The bonds of presentational immediacy arise from within us. . . . The sense-data represent the conditions arising out of the active perceptive functioning as conditioned by our own . natures."

[individually] of a common objective world and not *in them-selves* elements of the common world itself"? Do not Mr. White-head's real conclusions, in short, illustrate anew the ineluctability of what he calls "half-way subjectivism" for a realistic philoso-pher, however intense his original aversion to it—if he but keeps in view those facts of common experience which are the primary and the perennial source of dualism?

It may, however, still be asked whether this amounts to a *meta-physical* bifurcation of nature *i. e.,* of that part of reality upon which awareness is directed. Must one who accepts the conclu-sions indicated hold that perceptual content is "mental"? White-head's answer to this question appears clear without any long analysis. He holds that it is still possible to maintain that sense-objects and physical or scientific objects are "real" in the same sense, that they are merely distinguishable elements in an essen-tially homogeneous order, and, therefore, that the former are not to be set over against the latter as composing an isolated mental world. For this opinion three reasons seem to be offered: first, that sense-objects are dependent not upon mind or mental events, but only upon bodily ones—are, in the terminology of the two preceding lectures, causally but not existentially subjective; sec-ond, that those objects have situations in the same Space as well as the same Time with the physical objects; third, that when for the concept of matter we substitute, as we must, that of events in which qualities, or "eternal objects," are ingredient, sense-objects and the rest of nature are seen to be composed of the same types of elements.

(1) Of these three propositions, the first has been dealt with in the preceding lecture. It may be worth while to recapitulate briefly the criticism there made. The proposition, we have seen, is in the first place inherently incapable of proof. Acts of aware-ness as well as neuro-cerebral events admittedly occur whenever sense-objects are produced—or "become ingredient in nature." Of two empirically invariable concomitants of a class of phenomena we cannot arbitrarily single out one and declare it alone to be a

necessary condition for the occurrence of such phenomena. Least of all, I should suppose, could anyone inclining to believe in the essentiality of relations accept such an inference. Why sensa should not be "aspects" of the awareness, as well as of the bodily events, with which they are associated, it is difficult to see. It is very true, as Whitehead remarks, that physicists did not adopt the wave-theory of light because it struck them that "waves are just the sort of thing which ought to make the mind perceive colors."[52] But it is also true that physicists did not adopt that theory because it struck them that waves are just the sort of thing which ought to make the nervous system and brain give birth to sense-objects possessing colors which the waves are not supposed to possess, and *not* possessing energy or causal efficacy in nature, which the waves *are* supposed to possess. If the latter consideration offers no reason for denying that the brain does give birth to such objects, the former offers no reason for denying that the mind, or its function of consciousness, may have a necessary part in the genesis of the same objects. Brain-begotten sensa, in short, are just as alien to the world of unperceived entities and processes devised by the physicist to explain certain uniform sequences and correlations in our experience, as are mind-begotten sensa; and if you admit the one, there is no presumption—on these grounds at least—against admitting the other. After the physicist has conducted his waves to the retinas, and the physiologist has conducted his nerve-currents from these to the optical centers in the cortex, it still remains for somebody—whether you call him psychologist or epistemologist—to take account of the fact, extraneous to the physicist's province, that there do thereupon jointly occur the peculiar natural event called an awareness and the perhaps even more peculiar natural event called the coming into being of a sensible appearance—or once more, in Whitehead's terminology, the "ingredience of a sense-object"—upon which the awareness is directed, an object which itself bears no resemblance to the cortex, the nerve-current, or the wave, and which, finally,

[52] *The Concept of Nature*, p. 41.

is experienced as at a place external to the perceptible body—and usually at a place from which the wave is not supposed by the physicist to have been emitted. If we are to mean by "nature" the world of scientific objects, that, undeniably, *is* "closed to mind"; but it is equally undeniably closed to what are—and if I have understood him, are by Whitehead recognized to be—the immediate objects of mind in perception. Meanwhile it remains a part of the business of science, if not to account for these last, at all events to state, as well as it can, the conditions under which they arise. And one of the universal and the most certain of these conditions—more certain than the occurrence of the cerebral event—is that they are accompanied by awareness. By what principle of inductive logic are we authorized to infer that this is a wholly irrelevant condition? When it is further recognized that these entities have no discoverable status or rôle in nature *except* that of being objects of individual states or acts of awareness, it becomes evident that, in all probability, sense-awareness and its immediate objects are generated together and are incapable of existing separately. Of these objects (as conceived not merely by historic dualism in the past, but by Whitehead also) Berkeley's argument holds; the distinction between *esse* and *percipi* ceases to have meaning with respect to things which exist only relatively to a percipient and so only at times when they are perceived, and have efficacy (if at all) only through being perceived. Additions to nature of which this can be said may, surely, be not inappropriately described as "psychic additions."

(2) But sense-objects, it is maintained, are in space as well as time, and in the same space with all the other components of nature, *e. g.,* scientific objects; and thus, whatever the conditions necessary for their existence, when and so long as they exist they take their place in a common world—common to all classes of objects except those of dream, and also to all percipient (bodily) events, and containing the visual and tactual and (perhaps) the auditory fields of all observers. The reason "why the bifurcation of nature is always creeping back into scientific philosophy," ob-

serves Whitehead, is "the extreme difficulty of exhibiting" sense-data, such as "the perceived redness and warmth of the fire, in one system of relations" with the physicist's entities, such as "molecules, electrons and ether." [53] But "the all-embracing relations which the advocates of the philosophy of the unity of nature require" are provided by time and space; "the perceived redness and warmth are definitely related in time and in space to the molecules of the fire and the molecules of the body" of the percipient.[54] The denial of bifurcation here reduces to the theory of a single space and a single time and of the location therein of sense-objects and physical objects alike. Being thus established in a public spatio-temporal order percepts seems *less* private than the "sensations in the mind" of which the older psychology and epistemology were accustomed to speak; they retain a certain residual objectivity. Just where in space they are to be understood to be—whether in the situation of the brain-event, or in that of the perceptual object, or in neither—it is unnecessary for our present purpose to ask; I take Whitehead's eventual view to be that they are, in vision and visual imagination, projected by the brain into regions outside the body which vary with physical and physiological conditions. Wherever any one of them is, the point is that it is there, and thus is in real and unequivocal spatial relations with the objects that are not dependent upon the perceptual process for their ingredience.

This point also has been already considered in the fourth lecture; but here too a brief restatement of the argument is perhaps advisable. That some percepts are in space in some sense is undeniable. The Cartesian form of dualism which excluded all "ideas" from among the *res extensae* has long been obsolete. If we accept the assumption that there can be only a single or public space, in which all things extended must perforce be localized, it is true that sense-objects gain some slight relief from the privacy in which the older dualism confined them. But it is very slight. They still,

[53] *Concept of Nature,* p. 32.
[54] *Ibid.,* p. 33.

by hypothesis, are accessible only to the individual perceiver to whose percipient events they are relative; no one of them is public property. They still have, of themselves, no dynamic relations to the causal "scientific" objects with which they are reputed to have spatial relations; when sentient beings began to appear upon the earth and project from their brains countless particular existents not (upon the present theory) there before, the mass of our planet is not assumed by the physicist to have been increased. The sense-objects, in short, are, at best, only private appearances in a public space with the publicity of which they remain uninfected. Their "being in space" is their being perceived in space; we do not find, and cannot infer, that they have any other being there. It is, moreover, apparent that even this inadequate device for avoiding bifurcation presupposes the acceptance of the absolute theory of the nature of space. If "space" signifies only a mode of relatedness between particular entities, the "all-embracing relations required by the advocates of the philosophy of the unity of nature" disappear; there is no longer any reason to suppose that, because the objects in my visual field are spatially related *inter se,* they are also related in the same way in the same space-system to the objects in my neighbor's visual field, or to the constituents of the world of physical theory. That all these fall into a single, interconnected spatial pattern, or "mesh" of relations, becomes, upon the relational theory, a thing to be proved, not to be assumed; and the proof has not been formulated by Whitehead. Thus the tenability of the supposed alternative to bifurcation cannot be said to have been shown; while even if it can be established, the bifurcation does not disappear, but is merely shifted to another point.

(3) I come to the third and last of the considerations that might seem to mitigate the dualism which, it is clear by this time, cannot in essentials be denied. In the older dualism the division of nature was into matter and some sort of immaterial entities, such as sensations or ideas. In Whitehead's universe material *substance* seems at first to disappear; all that we have is qualities

and their spatio-temporal loci—"objects" and "events." "It is not the substance which is in space, but the attributes. What we find in space are the red of the rose and the smell of jasmine and the noise of cannon. . . . Thus space is not a relation between substances but between attributes." [55] With the vanishing of the substrate of the qualities belonging to the world independent of perception, the sharpness of the contrast between it and sensible appearances diminishes. Both are just sets of attributes grouped into events in different regions and durations, one no more substantial than the other. Yet we have found that, in the eventual outcome of Whitehead's reflection on these matters, "physical objects" are not wholly unlike "substances" as Locke defined them. They are not, it is true, defined as mere carriers of attributes, having no attributes of their own; they too are complexes of characters ingredient into "events." But they nevertheless are "something we know not what"; for of their qualities we have only a symbolic knowledge. They are the realities underlying the groups of attributes which are our "sense-objects"; and the essential difference, qualitative and existential, between the two sorts of entities remains undiminished.

Thus we once more see the "bifurcation of nature" roundly denounced in the preamble and plainly affirmed in the conclusion. The assailant of dualism becomes its defender and elaborator. Despite the introduction, not merely of a formidable new terminology, but of some new fundamental concepts, we still have before us, in essentials, the picture of the events called perceiving and knowing which historic dualism has always drawn: an organism confined at each moment within its own spatial bounds; in its field of awareness certain data or sense-objects which are private, transitory, conditioned by both the generic nature and the individual character of the percipient event, and existentially dependent upon this event; over against these sense-objects a world of reals not *thus* conditioned or relative, numerically distinct, and

[55] *Concept of Nature*, p. 21; *Symbolism*, pp. 22 ff., pp. 53 ff.

in all probability qualitatively different, from the sense-objects; between the organism and the external realities such a relation that the latter partially determine the character of the sense-objects, though only as terminal products of a long series of intervening events; and these terminal products apprehended by the percipient as somehow "signifying" the external reality and affording him the only basis for any knowledge of its existence and of the pattern of spatio-temporal and causal relations which characterizes it.

VI

MR. BERTRAND RUSSELL AND THE UNIFICATION OF MIND AND MATTER: I

The reputation and influence of Mr. Bertrand Russell among contemporary philosophers writing in English, and the persistency and originality of his efforts to find a way of escape from at least one of the forms of dualism, make it seem desirable, for the purpose of these lectures, to devote to his philosophy, as to Mr. Whitehead's, an especially careful examination. His position is the more interesting, in relation to our theme, because it is against only half of the so-called Cartesian dualism—and perhaps the less important because the less fundamental half—that he is in revolt. His conclusion that epistemological dualism is "as certain as anything in science can hope to be,"[1] has already been quoted. He has not, it is true, remained at all times quite unmoved by the tendencies adverse to that view; but he never seems to have yielded to them very far,[2] and in his latest work he adheres as uncompromisingly to the dualistic theory of knowledge, and to a form of the correspondence theory of truth, as in his *Problems of Philosophy* of 1911.[3]

[1] *The Analysis of Matter*, p. 197.
[2] In *The Analysis of Mind*, 1921, p. 20, Mr. Russell, using the term "realism" as equivalent to epistemological monism, or the view "that we know objects directly, in sensation certainly, and perhaps also in memory and thought," says that he had "been a realist in the past," and remained one "as regards sensation, but not as regards memory or thought." Yet even this was an overstatement of his actual concession to epistemological dualism at that time; for, as will appear from the subsequent review of the psychophysical doctrine of *The Analysis of Mind*, a sense-datum was not for him identical with the physical object known, but only with a "part" of it, and even this in a very peculiar sense of the expression.
[3] *Cf. op. cit.*, p. 32.

It is worth while, before passing to the main topic of this lecture, to note the grounds upon which the present epistemological dualism of Mr. Russell rests. Though only cursorily and somewhat casually indicated, they seem to coincide with the first four of those set down in the opening lecture as among the natural and perpetual bases of such dualism. (1) In recollection, knowledge is necessarily indirect, because "the event which occurs when I remember is quite different from the event remembered. . . . There is no mystic survival of the past when we remember," and the "correctness of memory" can consist only in a "similarity of quality and identity of structure" between a present image and a previous perception.[4] (2) The finite velocity of both sound and light "make it very difficult to accept a naïvely realistic view" with respect to either auditory or visual perception.[5] (3) "Percepts come at the end of a causal chain of physical events leading, spatially, from the object to the brain of the percipient"; and "we cannot suppose that, at the end of this process, the last effect suddenly jumps back to the starting point."[6] And (4) there is real contradiction between the visual percepts of different observers, which shows that they are never actually perceiving an identical object, but only diverse private effects of a common but unperceived "causal object."[7]

On the other hand, Mr. Russell finds in psychophysical dualism a real aberration of seventeenth-century philosophy. "The divorce between perception and matter" which was, from the point of view of the student of philosophy, "the chief thing that happened in that century,"[8] must be annulled; "it is not metaphysi-

---

[4] *Philosophy*, 1927, pp. 198–9.
[5] *Analysis of Matter*, pp. 209, 155.
[6] *Ibid.*, p. 320.
[7] *Ibid.*, p. 198. I have thought it pertinent thus to bring together connectedly Mr. Russell's reasons for his main epistemological doctrine, partly to illustrate further the observation in Lecture I that the roots of dualism there mentioned, in spite of vigorous efforts to extirpate them, perennially regenerate the same conclusions. But it is an amusing example of the present state of philosophical opinion that Mr. Russell thinks it "would be a waste of time to recapitulate the arguments" against that naïve realism which apparently seems to Professor Alexander, and such neo-realists as remain true to the faith, the prime certainty of philosophy.
[8] *Analysis of Matter*, p. 156.

cally defensible."[9] Thus Mr. Russell is ostensibly, with respect to the psychophysical problem, a more uncompromising enemy of "bifurcation" than Mr. Whitehead. While the latter "still allows a bifurcation of nature and mind," Mr. Russell wishes "to include nature and mind in one single system, in a science which will be very like modern physics, though not at all like the materialistic billiard-ball physics of the past." It is, accordingly, to what he conceives to be an especially characteristic and urgent task of contemporary philosophy, that of "showing in detail how the data of sense are to be fitted into physics," that he has increasingly devoted his philosophic effort. Whatever the success of the effort— into that we are to inquire—it is one of his great merits among contemporary adversaries of the older psychophysical dualism that he at all events realizes the necessity, and accepts the obligation, of making it—of offering a definite alternative hypothesis to make clear *how* the data of sense, and other content, can be identified with parts of the physical world. Most of those who proclaim the obsolescence of "Cartesian dualism" seem to have no sense of the fact that such a task is incumbent upon them. The "traditional distinction of the mental and physical," and the belief that entities or events of both sorts exist, are not to be overthrown, like the walls of Jericho, by a blast of the trumpet, for they rest upon the definite empirical observation that certain classes of content (at least) and a certain type of phenomenon, namely, awareness itself, do not appear to possess the properties or to conform to the laws commonly implied by the term "physical." The attempt to reduce the mental to the physical, or to membership in a class of "neutral entities" which may be either the one or the other according to circumstances, calls for a painstaking effort of reconstruction. The terms "physical object" and "physical event" must be given clear and consistent definitions, some reason must be offered for substituting these for the older senses of the terms so far as they differ, the generic laws holding good for such objects or events must be explicitly formulated in the

[9] *Analysis of Mind*, pp. 108, 137, and *Analysis of Matter*, p. 10.

light of modern physics, and the characters and spatio-temporal relations of each species of experienced content, and of the phenomenon of experiencing, must be compared, point by point, with these definitions and postulated laws, before any pretension can be made to have overcome psychophysical dualism. It is this that Mr. Russell has recognized; and it is because he has done so, and because he is a writer of great logical resourcefulness and (for a philosopher) unusual scientific learning, that it is especially to our purpose to inquire carefully in what way, and with what success, he has carried out his design of proving that the distinction of mind and body lacks "any fundamental philosophical significance." [10]

Mr. Russell has, in fact, gone about this enterprise in two, or more precisely, in three ways, the first represented chiefly by his Lowell Lectures on *Our Knowledge of the External World* (1914), and *The Analysis of Mind* (1921), and the second and third by *The Analysis of Matter* and the volume entitled *Philosophy* (both published in 1927). Even if the later methods were presented as definitely superseding the first, it would be of some interest to review the earlier effort as a remarkable and somewhat celebrated episode in the revolt of which we are here recalling the vicissitudes. If it were admittedly a failure, it should be an instructive failure. But that such an admission is intended is not clear. The theory propounded in *The Analysis of Mind* seems to be still defended in *The Analysis of Matter;* whether it is congruous with the new conceptions which appear in that work is another question. [11]

This lecture will therefore be devoted to an examination of the strategy and the outcome of Mr. Russell's first movement against the dualistic position. I shall use the historical present in describing this, without implying thereby that the reasonings of the later writings are wholly in accord with those here set forth.

[10] *Philosophy,* p. 17.
[11] Since the above was written Mr. Russell has (1929) republished *Our Knowledge of the External World* without alteration of the passages pertinent to the theme of the present lecture.

The initial and decisive measure is the adoption of a new definition of a "physical object" or a "piece of matter." Common sense, which is to say, the simpler sort of dualistic realism, as we know, assumes that when (for example) several persons look at what is called a table, there is one "real table," which is not strictly identical in shape and texture and size with any of the perceived tables of the different observers, and is at a place other than the places occupied by the observers; but that this central or nuclear table is the common source or cause of all the differing perceptions of the observers, the differences being explained mainly by the laws of optics: and, further, that this "real table" is the *cognoscendum,* the object-to-be-known by the several observers by means of these discrepant perceptual contents. By the older physics the object was supposed to differ in its qualities very widely from any of the appearances, *i. e.,* from all the tables actually perceived; but it was still conceived to be a real entity in the region of space defined by the convergence of the directions of vision of the observers, and to be the chief common factor in the determination of their visual content. With some modifications, important in themselves but not in relation to the present issue, a similar notion of what happens when we perceive appears to be held even by many post-Einsteinian physicists. But this view we are called upon by Mr. Russell to abandon. Though natural, "it was mistaken to regard the 'real' table as the common cause of all the 'appearances' which the table presents (as we say) to all the observers." Doubtless there is involved in the situation *some* real table distinguishable from any single appearance and "neutral as between the different observers." But "instead of looking for an impartial source, we can secure neutrality by the equal representation of all the parties." In other words, instead of meaning by "the table" a central causal object, we may mean by the term simply the whole variegated collection of the "appearances" situated at the several places occupied by the observers—"the set of all those particulars which would naturally be called 'aspects' of the table from different points of view."[12] A number of appearances constitute *one* object, according to this definition, when they form a group "related to each other approximately according to the laws of perspective." A collection of appearances not correlated in this manner is not a single physical object, but a miscellany of bits of many objects.

An "appearance," therefore, is not an external effect of the object; it is "actually part" of the object, "in the sense in which a man is part of the human race";[13] and over and above the sum of the appearances there is no "real" object. This, so far, sounds like pure phenomenalism; but Mr. Russell hastens to add that by an "appearance" he means something that does not necessarily appear; *i. e.,* he includes under the term not only actual percepts, but also "aspects" of the object—which, in the phraseology of the causal-object theory, would have been called the actual and potential effects of the object—at places where there do not happen to be any brains and nervous systems, nor, consequently, any sentient observers. Entities having essentially the same characters as visual sense-data, except that they are not "sensed" (however that participle be defined), are thus extrapolated into all the circumambient space (or space-time) ; in Mr. Russell's own words: "I think that when I see (say) a penny, what I perceive is one member of the system of particulars which is the momentary penny, that it is that member which is situated (according to one meaning of 'situation') in a certain part of my brain. I think that, very near this part of my brain there are closely similar unperceived particulars which are other members of the momentary penny; there is no solution of continuity in passing from what I perceive to the outside particulars dealt with by physics."[14] That such "aspects" can and do thus exist where there is no brain and no mind was apparently evidenced for Mr. Russell by the fact that a photographic camera-plate, when properly exposed, exhibits

[12] *Analysis of Mind,* p. 98.
[13] *Analysis of Mind,* p. 134.
[14] "Perception and Physics" in *Mind,* N. S., 1922, p 483.

them. If the number of such unperceived appearances making up (along with possible perceived ones) each "single object" is not literally infinite (that would depend upon rather complicated considerations about space which it would be confusing to introduce here), it is at any rate enormously great;[15] for "in every place at all times" there must be at least one such aspect "for every physical object which can be seen or photographed from that place."[16] "Matter" being thus, by definition, composed of sets of entities all of which are similar to sense-data and some of which *are* sense-data, the materialization of this large and primary species of so-called "mental" content seems achieved; again in Mr. Russell's own words, if this definition of "matter" is accepted, it "shows that what we call a material object is not itself a substance, but is a system of particulars analogous in their nature to sensations, and in fact often including actual sensations among their number. In this way the stuff of which physical objects is composed is brought into relation with the stuff of which part, at least, of our mental life is composed."[17]

Before proceeding further we must stop to ask what is meant by "place," and in general by the spatial terms used in this account of the nature of matter. Some misconception may arise here in consequence of a peculiar use of terms by Mr. Russell, which makes his notion of space seem less simple than (at least in the present context) it is. As is implied by what has been said, he assumes, with the epistemological dualist, that the entities con-

---

[15] According to Mr. Russell it is infinite: *Analysis of Mind*, p. 134.

[16] *Analysis of Mind*, p. 100. Mr. Russell neglects to specify the power of the eye or camera of which the purely hypothetical or potential presence in a place would entail the actual presence of a "part" of a given physical object there; but since the magnitude of such an object, at least for Mr. Russell, can hardly depend upon the state of the art of the makers of telescopes and cameras, we must suppose that he means "seen or photographed by an ideally perfect eye or camera." Consequently, parts of any visible object would be everywhere in space-time, except where the view of it was cut off by intervening opaque objects. Meanwhile, how opaque objects can "intervene" between a "place" and an "object" when the object is a collection of appearances scattered through the infinity of space, is an obscure point, on which see below. I am not, I may add, sure that the expression "ideally perfect eye," *etc.*, means anything; but Mr. Russell's theory appears to me to require that we should suppose it to mean something.

[17] *Analysis of Mind*, p. 108.

stituting the momentary complexes of sensory content experienced by several observers are not identical particulars. This assumption, when combined with the relational theory of the meaning of "space," leads Mr. Russell to say that the data of each percipient are in "private spaces." If "places can be constituted only by the things in or around them," then, where you have entirely separate sets of things you will also, obviously, have separate "places." Thus, the world as seen at a given moment by one observer "contains no place in common with that seen by another."[18] This, however, would not seem to prevent us from connecting these separate places in thought with one another, by imagining spaces—or spatial relations—continuous with them and intervenient between them, or the things in them. And this, in fact, is what Mr. Russell does; he postulates "one all-embracing perspective space" in which all the "places" of the perspectives are contained. The term "private spaces," however, would seem to imply that the space (e. g.) of my visual field when I look out of the window is not spatially continuous (i. e., can be related to no common set of coördinates), or is not metrically comparable, with perspective-space. At one point—in connection with the thesis that data, and therefore the perceived extension of the visual field, are "in my head"—this view might offer advantages, from Mr. Russell's standpoint; but in the main it clearly would not do. For if the space—or mesh of spatial relations—belonging to my actual visual content could not be located in, or regularly linked up *spatially* with, the "all-embracing space," there would evidently be an extreme "breach of continuity in passing from what I perceive to the outside particulars dealt with by physics"; and there would be no meaning in the assertion that the perceived content and those outside particulars form a single system of appearances differing from next to next in accordance (primarily) with the principles of geometrical perspective. Thus the "private spaces" must be conceived, and in his actual reasonings are by Mr. Russell conceived, simply as parts or "elements" of perspective-

[18] Cf. especially Our Knowledge of the External World, pp. 88–9.

space; they might less equivocally be called merely separate regions in that space. They are private only in the sense in which the spaces occupied by two camera-plates are private—*viz.*, that they do not overlap. You can pass in thought from a private into perspective space with no jolt whatever; an orientation performed in the one holds good in the other. We are told, for example, that if you look at a penny from such an angle (as it is commonly expressed) that it appears circular, and then move towards the penny so as to perceive "a graduated series of circular aspects of increasing size," each of the perceived aspects will be in (or will constitute) a private space; but "the perspectives in which the penny looks circular will be said to be on a straight line in perspective space, and their order on this line will be that of the sizes of the circular aspects." [19]

There is a further peculiarity of Mr. Russell's terminology, when speaking of the spatial relations of the various elements in his scheme, which tends still further to obscure its meaning to the reader. He offers, namely, a definition of "the place (in perspective space) where a thing is"; and this, upon close scrutiny, oddly turns out to be a definition of the place where the thing is not. It is reached as follows. We again consider the penny which we found appearing in many perspectives. "We formed a straight line of perspectives in which the penny looked circular, and we agreed that those in which it looked larger were to be considered as nearer to the penny. We can form another straight line of perspectives in which the penny is seen end-on and looks like a straight line of a certain thickness." These two lines, "if continued will meet in a certain place in perspective space, *i. e.*, in a certain perspective, which may be defined as 'the place (in perspective space) where the penny is.'" [20] Put more briefly, this appears to mean that "the penny" is at the center in the "one all-embracing space" upon which lines drawn through each of the series of similar (but unequal) "aspects" of it would converge.

[19] *Our Knowledge of the External World*, p. 90, 2nd ed., p. 95.
[20] *Ibid.*, pp. 90, 91.

But we have seen Mr. Russell elsewhere insisting that the penny is not in any one place, but is simply the complete set of aspects scattered through space. This seemed to be the great point in the enunciation of the new definition of a physical thing; but it is manifestly inconsistent with the definition of the place "where a thing is." At most only a *part* of a thing—*i. e.,* one of its aspects—could be at that (or any other) place.

And, if we consider the Russellian conception of a "physical object" yet more closely, we shall see that not even a part of such an object can properly be said to be in the place where (in the definition cited) "the object" is said to be. This is evident not only from Mr. Russell's statements but also from the implications of his premises. It is, in the first place, the consequence, in the terms of this theory, of the empirical fact which common sense would describe by saying that an object (as a whole) cannot be seen or photographed from the place it occupies. Since potential visibility or photographability is, for Mr. Russell, the hypothetical test of the presence of an aspect of an object at a given place, the one place of all others "from" which (in the ordinary phrase) an object cannot be seen or photographed is a place where no aspect or appearance of it is present. In Mr. Russell's own words: "As a rule [the reason for the qualification does not appear] even when the center of a group" of appearances "is occupied by a percipient, it nevertheless contains no member of the group, not even an ideal member: 'the eye sees not itself.' A group, that is to say, is hollow: when we get sufficiently near its center it ceases to have members." [21] That the same conclusion is implied by Mr. Russell's

[21] *Analysis of Matter,* pp. 211-212. The passage occurs in an exposition of what a phenomenalistic way of taking the perspective-aspect definition of a physical object might be; but the difference between the phenomenalistic way of taking it and the realistic way is not in the nature of the definition itself, but only in the denial or assertion of the "real existence" of the sort of entities it describes. The fact that there is no aspect of a penny at the center is also recognized in *The External World,* p. 91. That this is of the essence of the hypothesis has been recognized and dwelt upon by Mr. C. A. Strong: "What first strikes one in this theory is the curious reversal of the spatial position of objects which it seems to involve—objects apparently being everywhere except in the place where we see and feel them. It is . . . a paradox that light should have to proceed from a place in which there is no constituent of the object, as a condition of the arising of a perspective of it." ("Mr. Russell's Theory of the External World," in *Mind,* 1922.)

objections to that "unnecessary thing in itself," the "real table" of common sense, is equally evident. If there were a central *aspect* of the table, it would be a mere quibbling over words to refuse to call it *the* table; for it would have all the attributes ascribed by common sense to the definitely located causal object which Mr. Russell has repudiated. It would be a material reality emitting or reflecting light rays and would also have the property, which the other appearances would not have, of intercepting or refracting light; and changes in the other appearances would be functions of prior changes in it. Mr. Russell plainly intended to deny the existence of *something* which people generally have believed in; but his denial would have come to nothing if he had left either central objects or (what, in all but name, would come to the same thing) central members of groups of aspects, in the places assigned to the "real" tables, pennies, *etc.,* of common sense. The only adequate reason, in short, for redefining the "physical object" as the diffused collection of all the aspects lies in the assumed disappearance of any reality of the kind at the middle of that collection. All material things, then, in Mr. Russell's world, are built around holes.

If we are to understand the nature of Mr. Russell's logical procedure in all this, we must try to determine how much of the reasoning which has been outlined consists of what the logic-books call "real" and how much of "verbal" propositions. The whole argument, we have seen, rests upon a definition of "a piece of matter" or "physical object." But mere definitions neither prove anything, nor themselves require proof. A nominal reduction of sensory contents to "matter" by means of a redefinition of the latter term would obviously be all too easy and entirely unimportant; it would express nothing more than a preference of Mr. Russell's for using an old word in a new and peculiar (and misleading) way. It is evident, however, that the definition proposed is meant to be *something* more than this, that it is intended to convey certain factual propositions, capable of truth or falsity and logically susceptible of verification. But precisely what are these propositions? Is the definition, for example, to be taken as asserting the *real existence* of particulars of the sort it mentions? Though expressions already cited might seem clearly to imply an affirmative answer to this question, there are other passages in *The Analysis of Mind* which might as naturally be construed in the opposite sense; on the metaphysical status of the unperceived appearances, and therefore of what *he* calls "matter," Russell's language is very elusive. Sometimes the whole theory has the air of a mere *Philosophie des Als-Ob;* matter (as defined) is, we are told, "a logical fiction invented because it gives a convenient way of stating causal laws," and "psychology is nearer (than physics) to what actually exists." [22] If this meant what it might seem to mean, and if it expressed his final view, Mr. Russell's reconciliation of matter and mind would be of an old and familiar sort— none other than that propounded long ago by Berkeley. But closer analysis shows that the term "matter" here is equivocal. Mr. Russell apparently has two definitions of matter, both different from any previously current; and it is only one of these that is held by him to express merely a logical fiction. In the first sense a "piece of matter" is a "system of *regular* appearances," *i. e.,* appearances which vary from next to next in accordance with the purely geometrical laws of perspective projection, the refraction of light and other possible "distorting effects of the medium" being excluded. "Matter" in this sense is a fiction, not on phenomenalistic grounds, but because we are supposed to know empirically that no such perfectly regular systems of perspective aspects exist. Every group of actual appearances contains more or less "irregular" members, since no group can be in every part—or perhaps in any part—entirely immune against the effects of refraction or other distortions. The "regular" set of aspects is thus simply the ideal limiting case which real sets may be conceived as approaching; appearances in fact approach it increasingly, says Mr. Russell, as they are situated nearer to the center of their

---

[22] *Op. cit.,* pp. 300, 308; cf. also p. 306, "those fictitious systems of regular appearances which are matter."

group.[23] We may, however, also speak of "laws of perspective" in a second and "generalized" sense, in which the term would include the laws of refraction, diffraction, and reflection, in short, "all the intrinsic laws of change of appearance."[24] And in correspondence with this Mr. Russell, clearly, often means by a "physical object"—*i. e.,* "a set of appearances varying in accordance with the laws of perspective"—a set which includes appearances irregular to an indefinitely great degree. "In order that a particular may count as an irregular appearance of a certain object, it is not necessary that it should bear any resemblance to the regular appearances as regards its intrinsic qualities. All that is necessary is that it should be derivable from the regular appearances by the laws which express the distorting influence of the medium."[25] Now, that the separate "appearances," both regular and irregular, do exist where and when they are not perceived, Mr. Russell plainly holds; and therefore the "pieces of matter" of which they may (in the second and looser sense) be considered parts also exist. In this sense, then, matter is *not* a logical fiction: "in so far as physics is an empirical and verifiable science, it must assume or prove that the inference from appearance to matter is, in general, legitimate."[26] When in a more Humian mood Mr. Russell admits that "belief in the existence of things outside my own biography . . . must from the standpoint of theoretical logic be regarded as a prejudice, not as a well-grounded theory"; but he adds that it is a prejudice to which he proposes to continue yielding[27]—not merely, it would appear, in his moments of relaxation from the rigor of philosophy, but in the construction of his scheme of the universe.

23 *Analysis of Mind,* pp. 106–7, 125, 134–6, 305–7. The proposition, of course, is not strictly true.
24 *Ibid.,* p. 106.
25 *Ibid.,* p. 136.
26 *Ibid.,* p. 300.
27 *Ibid.,* p. 133. Cf. also *Mind,* N. S. 1922, p. 485, where Mr. Russell, observing that he has "no doubt sometimes expressed himself as if he were a phenomenalist," explicitly disclaims that view. Being a realist about unperceived aspects, he is also, presumably, a realist about the "perspective-space" in which the aspects are disseminated; this cannot be for him, as Mr. Strong has supposed, "only a mental construction." (*Mind,* 1922, p. 310.)

Assuming, then, that the doctrine is intended to be construed realistically, it is evident that the definition of matter contains at least one affirmative existential proposition, namely: i. There exist everywhere in space (or space-time), independently of the occurrence of percipient events, particulars having generically the sort of properties exemplified by visual appearances (perceptual images) ; and these actually existent particulars fall into groups or systems of which the members vary from one to another, in accordance with their relative spatial arrangement, after the manner described by the "laws of perspective" in the second of the two senses above distinguished, *i. e.*, the perspective variation is not absolutely continuous, but is interrupted by the presence of members "irregular'" in various degrees. It is equally evident that the definition contains at least one negative existential proposition, *viz.*, ii. There exists at the center of any such group—that is to say, in the region which, in the ordinary conception, the luminous or illuminated object of actual or potential vision is supposed to occupy—no member of the group and no *other entity* causal of the existence or characters of the members of the group.

But though so much is plain about the factual and existential import of the proposition which we have called a "definition" of a physical object, there are other essential points which remain in obscurity. When, *e. g.*, it is said that the term "physical object" *means* one of these sets of perspective appearances, are we to understand this as asserting that such sets and their component members, and *no other entities,* are "physical" existents in the *ordinary* fundamental sense of the adjective mentioned in Lecture I? *I. e.*, are (iii) quasi-visual "appearances," arranged in accordance with the laws of perspective (in the "generalized" sense), declared to be the *only* things or "events" which exist in space unperceived as constituent parts of the dynamic system of nature? The statement that "all physical objects are sets of perspective aspects" would by most persons, I suppose, be construed in this way; and it would, on the whole, seem that Mr.

Russell means it to be so construed, though he is, so far as I can recall, by no means clear about it. But if this *is* the import of the proposition, it has, as we shall presently see, some highly paradoxical consequences. On the other hand, if this negation of the (in the usual sense) "physical existence" of things other than sets of perspective aspects is not intended, the new definition of "physical object'" is a verbal proposition, *except* for the two existential assertions previously mentioned; in other words, it permits us to conceive that, besides the supposedly real entities to which Mr. Russell chooses to apply that name, there are other sorts of entities equally physical, in the more familiar sense—and, indeed, with rather less dubious claims to that status. But if there is thus a realm of what would, in ordinary terminology, be called existing physical objects, over and above Mr. Russell's special variety, then (for one thing) the question of the relation of our percepts to these others would remain untouched by his conclusions respecting the relation of percepts to *his* "physical objects."

The principal motives which led to the adoption of this definition—that is to say, of the propositions into which we have resolved its factual import—seem to have been five in number. (a) The first was an attenuated strain of the sceptical or radical-empiricist temper surviving in Mr. Russell in spite of his realism. The central causal object postulated by common sense and by most dualistic philosophers is, by hypothesis, never experienced—at all events, never sensibly experienced—by anybody. The table *"as it is known empirically,"* is, upon the dualists' own theory, "not a single existing thing but a system of existing things," namely, the various tabloid sense-data of the various observers;[28] let it therefore be defined as the *sort* of thing which it is empirically known as being. The "unknown assumed existent" commonly "called a piece of matter," with which the various particulars have "a supposed causal connection . . . would be a mere unneces-

[28] *Analysis of Mind*, p. 97.

sary metaphysical thing in itself."[29]　It was, curiously, this reasoning in the vein of Berkeley which was decisive for Mr.
Russell's new theory of matter; for it was by means of it that the
common central object was eliminated.

(b) Mr. Russell, it is true—as we have already observed—did
not carry out the logic of phenomenalism to the end, since he
next proceeded to assume a whole worldful of things never actually experienced—all the "appearances" that do not appear. But
this admission of one class of metempirical entities, while another
was excluded by the argument from the principle of parsimony,
was not purely arbitrary. The sceptical scruples of the radical em-
piricist could, Russell implied, be in certain cases overcome; the
correct rule of philosophical procedure in this question is to "approach as near to phenomenalism as [one] can without destroying
the whole edifice of science."[30]　But the *particular* reason ordinarily given for departing from the phenomenalistic principle seemed
to him invalid. It rests upon the "notion of cause," and that
notion "is not so reliable as to allow us to infer the existence of
something that by its very nature can never be observed."[31] Hence
the Berkeleian sort of argument held good as against any supposed *causal* object. But the case for the reality of unexperienced
"aspects" stood, it seemed, upon a different logical footing.
Though most of these never *are* experienced, they are (upon Russell's theory) not "by their very nature" incapable of being experienced; they lie about in space, as it were, and any one of them
will empirically manifest its presence there whenever a brain—
or a camera-plate—happens to move into the place where it is.
The extrapolation of analogues of the appearances we experience
into the regions where there chance to be no experiencers did not
seem to involve any dubious reasoning from observed effect to unobservable cause, but was merely an application of the principle
of continuity.

---

[29] *Ibid.*, p. 101.
[30] *Mind*, 1922, p. 482.
[31] *Analysis of Mind*, p. 98.

(c) This reason for affirming the existence of unperceived appearances was apparently reënforced by the consideration that, once causal objects were given up, no alternative way of satisfying the realistic "prejudice" seemed open. It is, as we have observed, assumed that there must be some "neutral" or "impartial" object concerned in the affair, when several persons are said to be seeing the same table. This assumption alone, it is true, might have been fulfilled simply by regarding as "the" object the sum of the actual percepts of the observers; "the equal representation of all the parties" would thus have been fully assured. But this sort of neutrality clearly was not enough for Mr. Russell; there must be a genuinely *objective* object, distinguishable not only from any one but from *all* the contents of individual experiences. This motive is not very harmonious with the rule of being as phenomenalistic as is consistent with the integrity of science; but its influence in Mr. Russell's reasoning seems unmistakable. The curious mingling of phenomenalistic and realistic preconceptions manifest in all this is what gives Mr. Russell's view about the external world (at least that expressed in his volume on the subject and in *The Analysis of Mind*) its unique character. It might not inappropriately be called Centrifugal Realism: with the supposed material core of a group of appearances, the "real object" of common sense, he deals as harshly as any subjectivist, but once away from the middle of such a group, he postulates unexperienced realities even more liberally than common sense is disposed to do.

(d) A definite argument to show that a failure to extrapolate perspective aspects *would* "destroy the whole edifice of science" is not presented; and it could not, in fact, be advanced with much plausibility. For the present fabric of science does not rest upon the supposition that "appearances," in the specific sense which that term has in Mr. Russell's definition, and these only, exist throughout space. Causal objects of the sort which he excludes from his physical world have had, and in the main still have, a part in theoretical physics which imperceptible quasi-visual images do not obviously hold. Nevertheless, his new definition seems to

Mr. Russell to have the merit of according with one conspicuous tendency in recent science—that, namely, to define matter in terms of electromagnetic fields. "What we call one element of matter—say an electron—is," by the physicist, "represented by a certain selection of the things which happen throughout space-time, or at any rate throughout a large region. . . . A piece of matter is only a convenient grouping of occurrences which extend throughout space-time, and it is these occurrences, not matter, that physics accepts as ultimate." [32] Not only in their diffusion but in their interpenetration these fields resemble Mr. Russell's "objects"; just as there are for him "aspects" belonging to many objects in every "place," so for the physicist the fields of countless electrons overlap in each region of space-time. Scientific objects also resemble systems of perspective-aspects in that—as Mr. Russell thinks—they very likely have hollow centers. "We do not," he observes, "know what happens in the center" of an atom. "The idea that there is a little hard lump there which *is* the electron or proton, is an illegitimate intrusion of common-sense notions derived from touch. . . . Modern physics reduces matter to a set of events which proceed outward from a center. If there is something further in the centre itself, we cannot know about it, and it is irrelevant in physics." [33]

That there is, in these respects, a certain analogy between these conceptions of modern physics and the definition of a "piece of matter'" as a system of perspective aspects is undeniable; but the two conceptions are not the same, and the former lends no probability to the latter. If Mr. Russell supposes it to do so, he falls into a fallacy of composition. To ascribe—as he here does—to gross, perceptible objects, such as pennies, tables, and suns, certain structural characters ascribed by the physicist to the imperceptible components of such objects, is not to follow the lead of the physicist, but by implication to contradict him. A penny composed of (possibly) hollow-centered atoms is not a hollow-centered penny. Or

[32] "Perception and Physics," in *Mind*, N. S., 1922, pp. 478–9.
[33] *Philosophy*, p. 157; *cf.* also 159.

again, when a physicist conceives the sun to be made up of electrons and protons, and defines these in turn as vastly or infinitely
extended fields of electromagnetic force, he is not conceiving the
sun itself to be infinitely extended; he regards that body, I take it
—unless he adheres to an essentially phenomenalistic type of
physical theory—as a pretty definitely circumscribed "thickening"
of a set of such fields in the region of space (relative to the
earth) in which the sun is commonly supposed to be. Nothing
corresponding to this thickening appears to characterize the center of a field of perspective aspects.   On the contrary, its center, as we have seen, is supposed to be attenuated to the point of
vacuity; and for Mr. Russell the sun *should* be, not at the center of
the solar system, but everywhere except at the center.   And on the
other hand, a "system of appearances"—whether with or without
"irregular" members—has by definition properties not ascribed by
physicists to a field of electromagnetic force.   An "appearance" is
just *the sort of thing you actually see,* even though it may be in
fact unseen; it is primarily a colored shape,[34] or rather a group of
colored shapes and their spatial relations, such as the group which
constitutes my visual field as I look about the room or out of the
window.   And I cannot but think that any contemporary physicist
would be somewhat surprised if told that matter consists simply
of a collection of colored shapes exactly like those we see—a dense
multitude of quasi-visual little suns and trees and houses and pennies—specimens of each kind being actually present throughout
space where we cannot see them (in addition to the few which
are where we can see them) in such a way that perspectively-
modified sun-aspects and tree-aspects and house-aspects and pen-
ny-aspects all physically occupy the same places, with respect to
any given frame of reference.

The theory of the constitution of matter set forth in Mr. Rus-

---

[34] It is, of course, an essential of Mr. Russell's theory now under consideration
that colors and sounds and secondary qualities generally should not be excluded
from the physical world. "The sensation that we have when we see a patch of color
simply *is* that patch of color, an actual constituent of the physical world, and part of
what physics is concerned with." (*Analysis of Mind,* p. 142.)

sell's earlier doctrine is not merely accidentally but necessarily different from that of the physicist, because it expresses precisely the opposite philosophical motive. The conception of a unit of matter as an electromagnetic field is obviously one of the more extreme results of abstraction from the concrete content of sensation in the interest of the mathematization of physics; the essence of Mr. Russell's procedure as obviously consists in taking the concrete (visual) content of sensation and converting it into "matter," by assuming that analogues of every sense-datum, subject to perspective variations, exist ubiquitously, unperceived. It is only by thus imputing to the "outside particulars," *i. e.*, to matter, all the sorts of properties empirically found in sense-data, that he is enabled to maintain that sense-data *are* matter, or "parts of physical objects." We cannot, then, I think, conclude that Mr. Russell's identification of such objects with systems of perspective aspects finds any support in contemporary theoretical physics. This, however, cannot be taken as equivalent to a proof that the hypothesis is invalid.

(e) The chief attraction of the theory for its author consists, it is fairly evident, simply in the fact that it is—or at all events seems to be—serviceable to his desired end: it appears, in the way just indicated, to reduce at least one class of supposedly "mental" entities to parts of the material world, by first assimilating the properties of the material world to the experienced properties (barring that of *being* experienced) of those entities. Now, if the theory actually accomplishes such a simplification of nature and is at the same time consistent with itself and with the experienced facts or legitimate postulates to which it is designed to conform, it undeniably is, by the criteria usually applied to scientific hypotheses, deserving of provisional adoption. We must now, therefore, proceed to the main question: *does* it satisfy these criteria? Has it, as presented, internal consistency? Or, when reduced to consistency, does it accord with common experience and the better established conclusions of empirical science? Does it give us a simpler, more coherent and more intelligible conception of nature? And does it, in particular, reduce perceptual content to identity with any "parts of the material world'" which we have reason to believe, or can believe, to exist? In scrutinizing the hypothesis with these questions in mind, we shall have to draw out certain consequences of its premises much more fully than does its author; for we shall find that its most essential and most remarkable implications are by him developed only partially, and in some cases not at all.

(1) It must have been evident to every observant reader that Mr. Russell, in his expositions of this theory, was quite unable to dispense with the concepts and modes of reasoning which he professed to abjure. Even the circumscribed central object kept creeping in. There were constant references to "the place where," e. g., "the star is," in the incongruous sense of the definition already cited; whereas, according to the definition of a physical thing, the star is in no "place," though its "members" are disseminated through an infinity of places. Some appearances of the star were described as closer to it than others; and the "irregularity" of certain appearances was said to grow less "as we approach nearer to the object." But of course no appearance could be "nearer to the object" (in Mr. Russell's sense) than any other. If mankind were infinitely or indefinitely scattered through space, we should scarcely speak of one man as "nearer to the human race" than another. It was, indeed, permissible, upon the new principles, to speak of one appearance as being nearer than others to the "hollow center" of the group to which it belongs. But if this form of expression had been consistently used, the fact that the appearances grow (generally speaking) more "regular" as they approach the center would not have been open to the explanation which Mr. Russell, in agreement with common sense, suggested—viz., that the nearer appearances are ordinarily less subject to "the distorting influence of the intervening medium." Why should proximity to the one place where, by hypothesis, no

part of the object is, render distortion less likely?[85] The whole point of this way of explaining the probable decrease of irregularity as you approach the center is the assumption that you are thereby getting nearer to the authentic, uncontaminated, original object—precisely the assumption which the theory excludes.

(2) The phrase last cited illustrates also a second lapse of Mr. Russell into the use of conceptions which he had proposed to banish from philosophy; and this, at least, was clearly a necessary one, and not attributable to carelessness in expression. His aversion to the "notion of cause'" as a means of inference from perceived data to unperceived or imperceptible realities wholly disappears as soon as he begins to deal with the so-called "irregular" appearances. When the appearance A at a given place is, in those features in which it *is* distorted or irregular, declared to be an "effect" of events in the "intervening medium" which are not parts of the system of appearances, or "object," to which A belongs, we have obviously returned to the customary way of conceiving of these matters. The light of a star, Mr. Russell did not deny, might be refracted and otherwise affected "by the matter through which it passes on its way" to the eye. But this elementary commonplace of optics ought to be inadmissible, upon the principles laid down by him; if "the notion of 'cause' is not so reliable" that we are entitled to use it to infer the existence of a common central source or cause of the *similarity* of the appearances, how can it be used to infer the existence of a "distorting medium" as the cause of certain of the *differences* in the appearances? But while condemning the one inference, Mr. Russell unhesitatingly employs the other; he will admit no central causal objects, but freely introduces what may be called eccentric causal objects. Though—by implication—he will not allow the sun to be in the midst of its system, he permits the moon, at an eclipse, to "intervene" between us and the sun that isn't there, or

[85] For the expressions cited, *cf. The Analysis of Mind*, Lectures *V, VII* and *VIII*, *passim.*

the stained-glass window to alter the color of the sunlight before it reaches the eye.

It will perhaps be said that these eccentric causal objects, or interceptors, are not inferred but are actually perceptible: that I *see* the eclipsing moon or the colored window. There is, however, no difference in this respect between the eccentric causal objects, of which the existence is admitted, and the central ones, which are merely "unnecessary metaphysical things-in-themselves." The opaque body or the refracting or diffracting agent, "as known empirically," is, like the table of our previous illustration, "not a single existing thing but a system of existing things," *i. e.,* a set of sensible appearances; and these, on Mr. Russell's principles, are located where the various observers' bodies are, probably in their brains. And if the belief in the existence of a central "real table" as the "common source or cause" of the tabloid percepts is an inference, and an illegitimate one, so must be the belief in a real, definitely located colored window or refracting lens as the common source or cause of the distortions.

(3) It may, it is true, be added that the existence of the interceptors may be inferred on the same ground as that of any other "object" in Mr. Russell's sense (assuming that to be a valid ground), *viz.,* the supposed necessity or legitimacy of extrapolating "appearances" in order to make up "full" sets of these. What is supposed to be so inferred is, however, a collection of perspective aspects diffused through space; and when the supposed interceptors—the opaque body, the microscope, the colored glass —are resolved into "objects" of this sort, they become incapacitated for doing the work of a *causal* object. For, in the first place, if one "physical object" is to cause any effect in another, this, from Mr. Russell's point of view, should mean that the *whole* of the one system of "appearances" acts upon or determines the whole of the other. When I am looking at a dime through a microscope, all the microscope-aspects together (since only they as a group are "the microscope") ought to be enlarging or distorting all the dime-aspects throughout space—including

those *between* what common sense would regard as the place of
the dime and what it would regard as the place of the microscope.
But of course neither Mr. Russell nor anyone else supposes that
a microscope—or any other eccentric causal object—acts in this
multiple way or on this cosmic scale. It is only *one* "part" or aspect of the dime—the one I am perceiving—that is supposed to
be magnified; and all the "parts" or aspects of the microscope but
one (at most) are thus producing none of the characteristic effects
of a microscope upon the light that passes through them. Can
we, however, say that even one part of it has any causal efficacy,
that *any* actual effect is a function specifically of the existence or
locus of that part? Evidently not, if the instrument in question
is still taken as a Russellian physical object. For there is no part
of it present in the one region in which, by the science of optics,
the refracting is supposed to take place. Similarly in the case of
the totally intercepting effect of an opaque body, which offers,
perhaps, an easier illustration of the point. The "center" of the
system of perspective aspects which is, for Mr. Russell, the moon,
is presumably, at a given moment, in that region of space from
the margin of which the light emanates but from within which
the moon could not be seen or photographed—in other words, in
the place in which the moon is ordinarily supposed to be. At this
center, however, there is, according to the theory, no moon-aspect
and no causal object. But in a solar eclipse it is precisely this
"hollow center" of the Russellian object called the "moon" which
passes in front of another hollow center, that of the system of
perspective aspects called "sun." I will not urge that this seems
a strange sort of causality, but will merely point out that, in any
case, *no* "member" belonging to the system "moon" has, on this
theory, any part in causing the eclipse. And the like conclusion
would follow for all other supposed intercepting objects or distorting media; none of them, nor any "appearance" composing
them, would be capable of intercepting or distorting anything.
Thus, for two distinct reasons, in order to conceive of any objects

as causal, Mr. Russell must cease to conceive of them as "physical," in the sense of his own definition.

Among the eccentric causal objects recognized as such by Mr. Russell is the brain of the percipient; that is to say, the presence of this object in the region of space where that "appearance" of (say) the table which is a sense-datum occurs, distorts the appearance, making it, in greater or less degree, different from the pure or perfectly regular perspective aspect of a table which would have occupied the place if no brain had intruded there—and if, also, no distorting influence had been at work in the intervening medium. With respect primarily to the rôle thus assigned to the brain and nervous system, Mr. Broad in his *Scientific Thought* offered a criticism of Mr. Russell's theory on grounds apparently similar in principle to those suggested in the preceding paragraph. He observed that Mr. Russell had "not yet treated the observer's body in terms of his general theory of physical objects," and suggested that the theory owed "some of its plausibility to the fact that, as we read his (Russell's) exposition, we think of our own bodies (and perhaps of other media, such as mirrors and colored glass) as physical objects in the non-Russellian sense, and of all other pieces of matter as physical objects in the Russellian sense." [36] To this criticism Mr. Russell has replied in *The Analysis of Matter*.[37] The reply instructively fails to meet the real difficulty. The objection, we are told, arises from a neglect to notice that (in the theory in question) a physical object has a "twofold character. On the one hand, it is a group of 'appearances' *i. e.*, of connected events, differing from next to next approximately according to the laws of perspective. On the other hand, it has an influence upon the appearance of other objects, especially appearances in its neighborhood, causing these to depart, in a greater or less degree, from what they would be if they followed the laws of perspective strictly." Now "the sense organs have only this second function to perform in the theory of perception, while the object

[36] *Op. cit.*, p. 534.
[37] *Op. cit.*, p. 259.

perceived has the first function. It is this difference of function, in the theory of perception, which makes it seem as if we were treating the percipient's body more realistically than external objects." But in fact "the appearance of an external object is modified also by other external objects—*e. g.,* by blue spectacles or a microscope."

Here we have, it will first of all be observed, Mr. Russell's usual avoidance of the terminology proper to his own theory. A "physical object" cannot possibly, from his point of view, have "an influence upon the appearances of other objects in its neighborhood," inasmuch as it has no neighborhood; it is only the aspects composing the object which can be neighbors to anything in particular—and these only to other aspects, not to other objects. And it cannot be doubted that the theory owes much of its plausibility for the unanalytic reader to this constant employment of familiar expressions which are inconsistent with its most characteristic theses. But there are other peculiarities of the reply which more concern us here. The concluding part of it manifests a complete misapprehension of the point at issue. The objection suggested by Mr. Broad—though his brevity in stating it perhaps gave room for misunderstanding—was not that the body of the percipient *alone* was treated as a physical object "in a non-Russellian sense"; it was that any "objects" *in so far as they were regarded as distorting factors,* including, *e. g.,* mirrors and colored glass, were not (and, indeed, could not be) taken as having the properties of "a piece of matter" as defined by Mr. Russell. It is no reply to this to remark that a "physical object" (in the theory) has "a twofold character"; that fact is the point of departure of the objection. The essence of the objection is that *any* so-called object—the human body or another—must, by virtue of the one "character" ascribed to it have one set of attributes, those of a diffused series of perspective aspects about a hollow center, none of them interfering in any way with the passage of light, and must by virtue of its other "character" have attributes incompatible with these, namely, those of a spatially restricted, relatively sharp-cut, causal object of the old-fashioned sort, at the center of its potential appearances, and capable of obstructing or deflecting light. Nor is it any advantage to the hypothesis to suggest that these two implicitly incongruous "characters" (or "functions") may be allocated to different entities, the one to the "object perceived," the other to the "media" such as sense organs, blue spectacles, microscopes, and the like. For the (external) sense organs and blue spectacles also are, or may be, "objects perceived" (in the sense in which any object is perceived), and, in fact, most of the "objects" (more properly, "aspects") to which a causal rôle in the production of "distorting effects" is ascribed must have both characters—one set *quâ* physical "in the Russellian sense," the other set *quâ* causal—and yet cannot have both consistently. Mr. Broad had, then, as it seems to me, abundant ground (though he did not fully set it forth) for suspecting that the secret of the new theory of matter consisted in operating with two entirely distinct and opposed concepts of a "physical object," using one or the other as the exigencies of the argument required.

(4) It is, however, of some interest to note specifically what, in a physical world composed of perspective aspects, would happen to our brains. Let us first suppose the hypothesis to be applied consistently—*i. e.,* to our bodies in the same way as to other physical objects. In that case, of course, your head would be dissolved into innumerable more or less headlike appearances ranged about a hollow center. If you should sit down in the midst of a converging battery of cameras, and, by pressing a button, should take simultaneous photographs of your head from all sides, you would, if a faithful follower of the principles of *The Analysis of Mind,* be obliged to reason to yourself thus: "Plainly there are real head-aspects where the camera-plates are; and not only in the places where the cameras happen to be, but at all points in the surrounding space. But there is nothing of the nature of a head at the center of this collection of aspects. Yet the head in which I had supposed my brain to be contained was by hypothesis at the center. I seem, therefore, to be constrained

to admit that I have no brain, since a real brain can hardly be inside an unreal head. The only alternative to this somewhat humiliating conclusion is to suppose that a part of my brain is in each of the aspects which together make up my head—including those on the camera-plate. This seems a difficult view to entertain; but if adopted, it makes me out to be, at best, a terribly scatter-brained fellow."

Perhaps, however, someone may suggest that in drawing this modest conclusion you would be overlooking the difference between positions in private and in perspective space. The things you see—the cameras and the rest of the apparatus and the visible parts of your body—are all in your private space, and this, with all its contents, is inside your head, not your head inside of it. This remark, though quite correct (on Mr. Russell's theory),[38] would not show that you had reasoned wrongly; it could be supposed to do so only by one who forgot how many heads that theory requires you to possess. The concentric array of cameras, *etc.*, which you perceive is, to be sure, only an aspect belonging to a particular set of perspectively varied aspects; and if you choose to locate a head hypothetically in the middle of this array—behind the visible tip of your nose, if you have a sufficiently long nose—then the head thus located in relation to a reference-body in your private space cannot contain the things which by hypothesis are external to it, *i. e.*, in front of and around it, in the same space. If these things are to be "in your head," they clearly cannot be in *that* head; it and the things perceived in front of it in your private space, and, in short, the whole contents of that space, must be inside some other head of yours. But what is this other head? We shall try to observe it more closely in the next lecture; but one thing is already clear. Since this head is a physical object, it too must be simply a set of perspective aspects distributed through space, no one of them with any better claim to be the seat of a brain than

[38] *Our Knowledge of the External World*, p. 92: "Our private world is inside our head."

another. Hence it still follows that you have no brain, unless it be one as widely distributed as the head-aspects are.

But what, then, it may be asked, can be the meaning of the proposition that my sense data are inside my head? The answer is evident. Since there is no main or central head, and no aspect which is *the* head to the exclusion of the other aspects, it follows that each of my sense-data is multiplied and distributed about in such a way that a part of it is present wherever one of my head-aspects is to be found. Only in this way could it be said to be "inside my head," in Mr. Russell's sense of the word "head." But at this point the conception becomes really a little odd. For my datum—*e. g.,* the tree which I am now perceiving—is, by hypothesis, not an "object," or collection of aspects, but *one* aspect, the distinctive appearance of the physical tree at one place or "from" a single point of view. If, however, in order to be inside my head, it must be strewn about space in the manner indicated, we must conceive that the aspect or perspective which is peculiar to one place or point of view is also present at many places and discernible from many points of view. This seems to put a certain strain upon the mind as well as upon the brain. Possibly Mr. Whitehead's denial of simple location, in its more mystical sense, might help here; but that is help which Mr. Russell, as we have seen in the preceding lecture, would, with good reason, reject.[39]

If Mr. Russell has not himself remarked these interesting consequences of his own hypothesis, it can only be because, as Mr. Broad has said, he has omitted to "treat the observer's body in terms of his general theory of physical objects." But let us now permit ourselves the same inconsistency; let us, that is, assume that our heads, as eccentric causal objects, have *single* positions in perspective space and that our brains, if any, must be inside them at these positions. On this assumption—which, however, is obviously destructive of the whole theory—we could, it would

---

[39] Some further complications would result if we inquired concerning the *times* at which the brain and the data respectively could be supposed to exist: but it does not seem necessary to go into these.

seem, keep our heads; but even on these terms it is not clear that we should be able (so long as we adhere to the *rest* of Mr. Russell's principles) to preserve our brains, at all events as physical objects. For the brain is completely surrounded by opaque objects (or opaque "aspects"); there is therefore no place from which it potentially could be "seen or photographed"; hence it is not a member of any set of perspective appearances (as these sets have been defined by Mr. Russell), nor, of course, is it the whole of such a set; hence it is no part of any "piece of matter." But a proof that the brain itself is not material seems a somewhat surprising outcome of what was to have been a reduction of psychology to physics. It is to be added that similar considerations would lead to a like dematerialization of other things beside the brain. Whenever a man—say a photographer—goes into a dark room his whole body temporarily ceases to conform to Mr. Russell's definition of a physical thing, as do his clothes and any objects he may have taken in with him. When, in short, "physical" status is made—as it plainly, however incredibly, is by Mr. Russell—contingent upon visibility or photographability, it becomes a very shifty and precarious possession; now you're physical and now you're not. The shutting of a door may be enough to translate you clean out of the material world. The brain, however, during the life of the organism, is continuously excluded from that world—as are presumably, for Mr. Russell, all of man's inward parts, except when the surgeon confers a transient physicality upon some of them.

These latter inferences, however, let me repeat, follow only when, in agreement with Mr. Russell's own practice, you disregard, in this context, the most essential article of his theory. If you keep it in mind, other consequences must be deduced; but they are, as has been shown, equally destructive to our brains.

(5) The most singular implications of Mr. Russell's conception of the nature of a physical object flow, for the most part, from one general peculiarity of that conception—a glaring peculiarity, upon which others have already commented. The theory, as Mr. Broad

has remarked, "seems to have been built up wholly by considering the *optical* constituents of perceptual physical objects." It appears to be "a theory of *complete optical objects and of nothing else"*; so far as could be judged from Mr. Russell's language, he was "thinking only of visual sensa." [40] If this is true, two things evidently follow: (a) nothing has been accomplished by the hypothesis towards resolving non-visual sense-data into "parts of the material world"; (b) no intelligible place has been given in the scheme to this class of data, and no satisfactory account proposed of their relations to the visual sort, and to the "optical objects." To this criticism also Mr. Russell has made reply—but with what seems to me rather extraordinary irrelevancy.[41] The reply appears to be directed against a wholly different contention, namely, that in the case of other senses than sight, inference from sense-data to causal objects is untrustworthy or impossible, that those senses are not valid sources "of the fundamental notions of physics." Presumably as against this view Mr. Russell conjecturally describes what happens, in terms of electrons and protons of the two bodies concerned, when with the tip of a finger we touch an external body; and explains further how, on tactual evidence, we can make some inference as to the shape of the object touched. All this has plainly nothing to do with the point at issue, namely, *whether, e. g., tactual sense-data fit into the proposed definition of a "physical object," or of its component parts.* It is, in fact, patent that they do not. If I look at the table from a certain angle, and then move my head slightly, the whole shape of the sensible table changes in precisely the manner described by Mr. Russell—and by geometrical optics; or if I move backward, the sensible table grows smaller, also in precise accord with the theory. But if I touch the table, and then move my finger gradually away from it, I do not encounter a series of tangible "aspects," filling the space through which the finger moves and "differing from next to next approximately according to the laws of perspective." Yet if such

40 Broad, *Scientific Thought*, p. 533.
41 *Analysis of Matter*, pp. 260–262.

tactual perspective aspects were there, they presumably would be sensible, since tactual qualtiies were sensed when my finger was in the first position—which, upon Russell's hypothesis, ought to mean simply that my brain was then spatially coincident with one of the series of aspects making up the table-plus-finger appearance. We may, therefore, conclude that there are probably no such series of tactual perspective aspects, and that consequently tactual data are not, in Mr. Russell's sense, parts of any physical object, inasmuch as such objects are by definition nothing but collections of perspective aspects. Tactual objects manifestly resist the sort of diffusion through space to which Mr. Russell would subject them. It is, indeed, still *possible* that we may, in the end, be obliged to assign our tactual data to the inside of our heads— though not to the kind of heads here defined by Mr. Russell. But we should even so have no reason for supposing, and definite reasons for disbelieving, that, in addition to those in our heads, there is an innumerable company of counterparts of them—objectified, unperceived, tactual sensa—everywhere else.[42]

Nothing, in truth, can be more apparent to any reader of *Our Knowledge of the External World* and *The Analysis of Mind* than that, in constructing his definition of a "piece of matter," Mr. Russell *was* "thinking only of visual sense-data"; for the definition is couched in terms appropriate only to such data, and is illustrated exclusively from optical phenomena. It plainly reduces physical objects to optical objects; it leaves to what is nevertheless held to be real independent matter only the intangible properties of visual images; and, if consistently applied, it would, as we have seen, require us to remove from the realm of the physical, not to say of the existent, all causal objects, even eccentric ones, and also all objects commonly supposed to occupy regions of space inaccessible to any potential vision, because no light-rays can be emitted from them. The seemingly simple and

[42] I have confined the discussion of this point to the case of touch; but it is, I take it, fairly evident, though for not quite the same reasons, that the data of other non-visual senses are equally unadaptable to Mr. Russell's definition of a physical object.

easy device hit upon by Mr. Russell for bringing our sensory content into the category of material things has, among numerous
unexpected (and by the author unnoted) logical results, that of
formally excluding from that category all species of sensory content but one. This, however, was no merely accidental oversight.
Mr. Russell's hypothesis, however odd, is after all one of the conceivable ways of setting about the subsumption of sense-data
under "pieces of matter"—the essence of it consisting, as has been
made sufficiently evident, in extrapolating analogues of sense-
data into space, assuming these to be independent of percipient
events, conceiving them to constitute systems or groups requiring
the inclusion of actual sense-data for their continuity and com-
pleteness, and thus establishing a close kinship between the data
and the "outside" members of those groups. Now for such a
logical procedure visual content, on the one hand, and the laws
of perspective (as a means of defining the required groups) on
the other, had an obvious *prima facie* suitability; but if the peculiarities of tactual, or of olfactory, data had been taken account
of, the enterprise would, I suspect, have seemed hopeless from
the start—and would never have been begun.[43]

(6) Further consideration of this theory seems hardly necessary; but it is perhaps worth while to add that even if we were
content to define a physical object as a set of objectified visual
sensa arranged according to the laws of perspective, and even
though all the other difficulties previously mentioned were waived,

43 The precise point at which this primary and decisive error occurs can apparently
be recognized: in beginning the exposition of his hypothesis in *The External World,*
Mr. Russell writes: "Let us imagine that each mind looks out upon the world . . .
from a point of view peculiar to itself, and, *for the sake of simplicity, let us confine
ourselves to the sense of sight, ignoring minds which are devoid of this sense*"
(p. 87, 2nd ed., p. 92). The artificial simplification thus introduced nominally for
convenience is never completely corrected; and the whole character of the ensuing
elaborate and curious hypothesis (except for certain inconsistencies which have been
pointed out) is determined by this initial exclusion of the greater part of the facts
by which it should be tested. Mr. Russell does, indeed, attempt to show that auditory
sense-data may be said to differ from next to next in accordance with laws like those
of perspective (*Analysis of Matter*, p. 261); but it is evident that they are not the
same laws, and also that we have no reason to suppose that *tones* are scattered about
in space where there are no percipients, in the manner in which it is assumed that
visual perspective appearances are.

the hypothesis would still be untenable. For there is no such continuity or analogy as it assumes between the visual appearances actually given in perception and any entities (or "events") which the science of optics permits us to suppose to be generally present elsewhere in space or space-time. What is given is, in the optical sense, an image; but *actual* images are not, for optics, strewn about in all places. This objection to the doctrine was pointed out some years ago by Mr. Strong. The formation of an image of an object, he reminded Mr. Russell, is possible only with the aid of a lens; without this, all the points on the surface of the object would send light-rays to every point on (*e. g.*) a camera-plate or the retina, "and all the light-rays would be confused together, and there would be no image or perspective." [44] Since points or areas in space can hardly be supposed to be universally equipped with lenses, there can consequently be no such ubiquitous presence of perspective appearances in nature as Mr. Russell supposed.

To this objection Mr. Russell replied that, admittedly, "the perspectives can by analysis be separated out," and that this was "quite enough for him," since "you cannot by analysis separate out what was not there." [45] The reply is more concise than convincing. For the premise upon which it rests—which is introduced as if it were an axiom—is, as a generalization, notoriously false; and where it is possibly true, it leads to conclusions irreconcilable with Mr. Russell's theory. "Separating out what was not there" is a matter of everyday experience; it happens whenever a chemist analyzes a compound into two simpler substances having positive sensible qualities other than those of the compound, and whenever, by means of a prism, the spectral colors are "separated out" of a beam of white light. It is a commonplace of elementary psychology that those colors are not sensibly present in the light before they are "analyzed" out of it by the prism; "no one," as Woodworth puts it, "can pretend to get the sensations of red or blue in the sensation of white." It may be true that in the ex-

---

[44] *Mind,* N. S., 1922, p. 309.
[45] *Ibid.,* p. 484.

ternal world apart from perception the proposition which Mr. Russell treats as self-evident holds good; the denial by orthodox dualism of the objectivity of the secondary qualities was partly due to a reluctance to admit that in *that* world "emergent" effects —the separating out from a thing of what was not in it—can be possible. But if such effects are excluded from the external world—if, *e. g.*, only the spectral colors exist there, and never a true fusion of these into white light—then our visual data and the unperceived external objects become by so much the more disparate; there appears a marked "solution of continuity in passing from what I perceive to the outside particulars dealt with by physics." And in any case, the hypothesis in question does not admit the subjectivity of the secondary qualities, and for it, therefore, white light must presumably exist, just as it is sensed, in external nature; it must be objectively a genuine fusion of the spectral colors, and must be separable into them again, though it does not contain them, any more than it does in sensation, except *in posse*. In this case, the pseudo-axiom upon which Mr. Russell relies would be true neither in sense-experience nor in nature.

If we turn back to the particular issue raised by Mr. Strong—the question whether quasi-sensory images can be supposed to exist objectively in all regions of space, apart from the usual optical apparatus for producing images—we find that here, too, the principle employed by Mr. Russell in meeting the difficulty tends to precisely the opposite result to that at which he aims. The principle implies that (not to raise a difficulty about geometrical points) in every area in space, however small, there are present perspective images of all the parts of all the objects from which light is reaching that area. But the area which is my visual field is not thus filled with innumerable small images of the same set of objects; thanks to the structure of the optical and neural apparatus of vision, a sensible appearance consists of a single complex image spread out over a considerable extension. A sensible appearance is therefore not at all similar to the insensible "appear-

ance" which would (according to Mr. Russell's hypothesis)' occupy the same space if there were no optical and neural apparatus
there; nor is it similar to the appearances which, by the hypothesis, actually occupy areas of the same extent elsewhere in "perspective space."

How wide the difference is between even visual content and a
"perspective aspect" becomes the more evident when we bear in
mind that the brain and nervous system admittedly. produce additional "irregularities" of their own, over and above any recognized by optical theory—and when we remember, also, how
extensive and peculiar are these irregularities arising solely in
connection with percipient events. It would be true that there is
no breach of continuity between our visual percepts and the "outside particulars dealt with by physics" only if the percept were,
in size and shape, the aspect of an object which would occupy, in
accordance with the laws of perspective and the laws of the modifying effects of the *external* medium, the place occupied at a given
instant by the brain. But in the first place, the laws in question
have pertinency only up to the point in the process at which the
retinal images are produced; the subsequent neural phenomena by
which the retinal excitations are transmitted to the cortical centers
can in no legitimate sense be said to conform to the laws of perspective. And it is a psychological commonplace that the visual
percept is no mere replica of the retinal images, but is greatly modified by the results of previous experience. All these centrally
intiated aspects or components of the percepts, at least, would be
no part of the assumed set of perspective appearances and therefore would not, by Mr. Russell's definition, be physical.

Several further difficulties might be, but no more I think need
be, pointed out in this conception of the nature of "matter." We
may now sum up the results of our analysis; in this brief résumé it
will be convenient to alter their order. The theorem pertinent to
our general topic which is propounded is: Sense-data are physical
objects—or, more precisely, are parts of physical objects. On this

theorem and the proof offered for it the following conclusions seem justified: *i,* The starting-point of the argument is a verbal proposition, a new *definition* of the term "physical object." Mr. Russell says in substance: "If you choose to give to that expression the unusual meaning which I give to it, *then* I can prove to you that sense-data are members of the class defined." But it is *only* in that sense of the term that the theorem is to be taken. It has, therefore, no bearing upon the question whether data are physical in other and more usual senses. *ii.* Nevertheless the theorem appears also to contain implicitly certain existential propositions, to wit, an assertion of the real existence everywhere in space of a species of entities not experienced, namely "appearances," unperceived analogues of our visual images, grouped into sets according to the laws of perspective (in the sense of this last expression, in which it includes the laws of refraction, reflection, diffraction, and other "distorting" processes), and a denial of the existence in space of any other sort of independent reals. Some of the reasons given for these propositions, though not coercive, would not be without force if (a) it were shown that no other way of conceiving of a real physical world is possible, and if (b) the concept of this class of objects could be worked out without contradicting itself or the relevant facts, and if (c) the hypothesis in fact made possible a unification of the mental and the physical, in any significant sense of the latter term. These conditions, however, are not fulfilled. If, on the other hand, the existence of unperceived appearances is not asserted—if, as Mr. Russell sometimes suggests but does not in the end seem to hold, they are merely logical fictions—the identification of data with "material objects" becomes obviously impossible, since the data exist and the material objects (on that interpretation) do not. *iv.* Unperceived "appearances" are, in particular, not identical, in the attributes assigned to them, with the imperceptible entities of theoretical physics; and the sets or systems of such appearances, which are the "physical objects" of Russell's definition, though they have certain broad analogies with some "scientific objects," do not in essentials resemble them. No argument for their existence, therefore, can be drawn from these analogies. *v.* No such existents as Mr. Russell's extrapolated visual images are assumed by the science of optics to be generally present in space; on the contrary, the things that might, from the point of view of that science, be supposed to be so present are extremely dissimilar to the images which are conditioned by the presence, in certain limited regions, of the optical and neuro-cerebral apparatus of vision. *vi.* If the proposed definition of "physical objects" is applied consistently to *all* the objects which are admitted to exist and to *be* "physical," including our own bodies and the media which are supposed to intercept or distort light-rays, a long series of absurd consequences, which need not be recapitulated, results. *vii.* Tactual and other non-visual sense-data cannot be supposed to be members of sets of disseminated "appearances" varying from next to next according to the "laws of perspective"; they therefore could not be brought under the proposed definition of physical objects, even if that definition were in itself unexceptionable.

Such is the outcome of *this* program for "harmonizing physics, the physiology of the sense-organs, and psychology."[46] It remains only to note that, even though it were accepted at its author's valuation, it would accomplish nothing approaching a *general* reduction of experienced content to identify with matter—or with "neutral entities" which are called matter when they are not also content. It would, in fact, imply the impossibility of such a consummation. For, as Mr. Russell himself candidly recognizes, his method applies only to purely sensory content. The new definition of "a piece of matter" not merely leaves the non-sensory data of immediate experience unmaterialized, but formally excludes them from the class of material entities. "Images," that is, the content of memory, imagination, hallucination and dream—all these "belong exclusively to psychology," and cannot be "included among the aspects which constitute a physical thing or piece of

[46] Russell, in *Mind*, 1922, p. 483.

matter."[47] To suppose that when I imagine a centaur or dream of a goblin, perspective appearances of these creatures spread outward from my head through space would be obviously gratuitous and fantastic. This, it will be observed, is only a reason for denying the "physical" status of images in Mr. Russell's special sense of the adjective. It follows from the fact that his definition requires a thing to be a member of a group of aspects having some members outside the brain before it can be called physical.

But the admission of the non-physical character of images is not limited to the special Russellian sense of "physical." In the main Mr. Russell seems to give to the term "physical" (when discussing this particular question) the meaning defined in the first lecture, and to recognize the conclusiveness, with respect to non-sensory content, of those natural grounds of psychophysical dualism which were there summarized. If you attempt to put images into the physical world, *i. e.,* into the class of entities in space which constitute the public causal order of nature investigated by the physicist, you play havoc, in the name of a supposedly scientific dogma, with the regularity and coherency of that order. Mr. Russell's statement of this argument has been cited in Lecture I.

Thus Mr. Russell's "brave pronunciamento" was, as Professor Laird has remarked, "very scurvily fulfilled."[48] A great part of our content of experience was avowedly left outside the physical order. There remained, however, a conceivable hypothesis differing from both that of common sense and that set forth in the writings of Mr. Russell thus far considered, about the nature and situation of *both* sense-data and images; and this, if it should prove logically workable, would justify the inclusion of both classes of experienced content in the "physical world," at least in a certain sense. This is the hypothesis that *all* data are in our heads and constitute parts of those physical objects which are our

---

[47] *Analysis of Mind,* pp. 301–302. The same is apparently admitted to be true also of visual sense-data, when they are very "irregular." "In those cases in which the unity of the system of appearances has to be broken up, the statement of what is happening cannot be made exclusively in terms of matter. The whole of psychology is included among such cases" (*ibid.,* p. 104).

[48] J. Laird, *Our Minds and their Bodies,* p. 94.

brains—in another meaning of "physical," one which does not limit that status to members of groups of quasi-visual perspective appearances, nor necessarily imply that the space outside our heads is full of such appearances. It is, in part, to this seemingly hopeful avenue of escape from psychophysical dualism that Mr. Russell turns in his latest writings. We shall follow his exploration of it in the next lecture.

VII

MR. BERTRAND RUSSELL AND THE UNIFICATION
OF MIND AND MATTER: II

The theories of the nature of matter and of percepts which we have been last discussing still maintain a precarious existence in Mr. Russell's recent works. A "physical object" is again defined, at once circuitously and contradictorily, as the totality of "views of a given physical object from different places,"[1] and any percept which is "objective" is said to be a member of such a group of "views," *i. e.*, perspective aspects, and thus to be a part of a physical object.[2] But it is in the main in an essentially fresh way that the attempt is now made to "bring perception and physics together" so as "to include psychical events in the material of physics" and to show that "from the standpoint of philosophy the distinction of physical and mental is superficial and unreal."[3] To the new argument the old definitions, and the peculiar existential propositions which we have seen to be implicit in them, appear to be in reality not only unnecessary but antagonistic. I shall not attempt to show this by a separate analysis; it will, I think, become sufficiently evident in the course of the exposition of the later theory.

The philosophic basis for the belief in the existence of a physical world of unperceived spatio-temporal particulars is now precisely the reverse of that previously accepted. In his earlier phase

[1] *The Analysis of Matter*, New York, 1927, p. 258.
[2] *Ibid.*, pp. 222–4. This definition of a physical object, and the related conceptions found in *The Analysis of Mind*, are also still defended against the criticisms of Mr. Broad; the passage has been cited and discussed in the previous lecture.
[3] *Ibid.*, 10,402. The last is the concluding sentence of the book.

we found Mr. Russell rejecting the causal theory of perception on the ground that "the notion of cause is not so reliable as to allow us to infer the existence of something that, by its very nature, can never be observed";[4] while, on the other hand, it was assumed to be legitimate, not to say necessary, to postulate by analogy the real existence of unperceived members of the sets of perspective aspects to which our visual data belong. But now the once-rejected notion of cause becomes the corner-stone of Mr. Russell's entire metaphysical structure. "We should accept the usual causal theory of perception," for if, e. g., in vision, "what happens at the surface of the eye is to give us information about the distant object, it must be, in the main, causally determined by the object."[5] "Epistemologically, physics might be expected to collapse if perceptions have no external causes."[6] We cannot, as the earlier theory implied, assume, merely in the name of the principle of continuity, the external reality of analogues of our sense-data, in order to enable us to conceive of sets of perspective aspects as "full"; it would be sufficient to regard the unperceived aspects requisite to complete any such as "ideal" or imaginary. But "it is hard to see how anything merely imaginary can be essential to the statement of a causal law."[7] Unless, in short, reasoning from the existence and nature of percepts to the existence and (to some extent) the nature of their causes were legitimate, physics could give us no knowledge of anything but the content and sequences of subjective experience; and since Mr. Russell still holds that physics must be assumed to give us something more than this, he necessarily accepts as valid the mode of inference whereby alone it can do so.

But aside from this general epistemological indispensability of the causal theory of perception, there are more specific empirical considerations in its favor. One such—an argument which,

[4] *Analysis of Mind*, p. 98.
[5] *Analysis of Matter*, p. 165.
[6] *Ibid.*, p. 197.
[7] *Ibid.*, p. 214.

though "perhaps not very strong," certainly "has some force"—
is the fact that when a number of persons are at differing distances from the place where, *e. g.,* a gun is fired, the time-intervals
between the seeing and the hearing of this event by each of the
several percipients increase with their distance from the gun. The
"natural" way of explaining this fact is to suppose a real space
through which the sound (*i. e.,* something which is the cause of
the auditory sensation) really travels with a finite velocity.[8]
Stronger arguments are derivable from the innumerable familiar
correspondences between the data of different percipients at the
same time (assuming that they can truly convey information about
these to one another by language). These correspondences are
such as to "make it inconceivably complicated and unplausible to
suppose that nothing happens where there is no percipient."[9]

When, however, the ground of inference with respect to the
reality and nature of physical objects or events is thus altered, the
content of that inference must be correspondingly transformed, or
rather, attenuated. So long as you arrive philosophically at your
notion of the external world by the simple method of extrapolating as many analogues of sensible appearances as may be necessary to make up "full" sets of perspective aspects, "matter" and
sensory content, as we have seen, prove—not at all surprisingly—
homogeneous; there is no type of quality belonging to (visual)
sensations which can be denied to physical objects. But the argument from effect to cause yields no such conclusion. A cause may
conceivably be qualitatively quite unlike its effect. We can "no
longer assume, as when we were constructing 'ideal' elements,"
i. e., unperceived members of a set of perspective appearances,
"that what is at the places where there is no percipient . . . is what
we should perceive if we went to them. We think, *e. g.,* that
light consists of waves of a certain kind, but becomes transformed,
on contact with the eye, into a different physical process. There-

---

[8] *Ibid.,* p. 209. This is difficult to reconcile with the views about space later
suggested.
[9] *Ibid.*

fore what occurs before the light reaches the eye is presumably
different from what occurs afterwards, and therefore different
from a visual percept." [10]　This, clearly, amounts to a denial of
the most essential proposition of the earlier theory.　In final analysis Mr. Russell concludes that a realistic philosophy which is
based upon the causal theory of perception can make no claim to
any *qualitative* knowledge of the external world.　We can reasonably refer to the "structure" of that world, relying upon "the
maxim 'same cause, same effect.'　It follows from this maxim that
if the effects are different, the causes must be different; if, therefore, we see red and blue side by side, we are justified in inferring
in the direction where we see red something different is happening from what is happening in the direction where we see blue." [11]
In short, we may assume, in arguing from percepts to their unperceived causes, no more than that "there is roughly a one-one relation between stimulus and percept"; and even this is only
approximately true.　The "intrinsic characters" of the stimuli
remain wholly unknown.[12]　"The only legitimate attitude about
the physical world seems to be one of complete agnosticism as regards all but its mathematical properties." [13]　"We cannot find
out what the world looks like from a place where there is nobody,
because if we go to look there will be somebody there; the attempt
is as hopeless as trying to jump on one's own shadow." [14]

The reader of such passages as these is likely to feel some
astonishment when he also finds Mr. Russell professing "complete agreement with Dr. Whitehead's protest against the bifurcation of nature which has resulted from the causal theory of perception," and declaring that the view he holds is "quite different"
from "Locke's belief that the primary qualities belong to the ob-

[10] *Ibid.*, p. 216.
[11] *Philosophy*, p. 157.
[12] *Analysis of Matter*, pp. 227, 228, 226.
[13] *Ibid.*, p. 270.
[14] *Philosophy*, p. 158; cf. p. 149: "What is called a perception is only connected
with its object through the laws of physics; its connection with the object is causal
and mathematical; we cannot say whether or not it resembles the object in any
intrinsic respect, except that both it and the object are brief events in space-time."

ject and the secondary to the percipient." [15] These expressions concerning the affinities and antipathies of the present doctrine are, indeed, likely to produce a highly erroneous conception of its real character. For, on the one hand, Whitehead himself—if the conclusions at which he arrives are distinguished from the theses apparently announced in his preambles—"bifurcates" nature, as we have seen, pretty widely. Yet, even so, it is not in keeping with the temper and intent of his philosophy to assert that we know nothing of the physical world beyond its mathematical properties. And upon the specific points in which Mr. Russell describes his view as differing from Locke's, he merely goes farther in the same direction; he, too, holds that the secondary qualities "belong to the percipient," but adds that most of those called primary do so also, though there still remain some residual characters which "belong to the object" only.

> The particular bulk [wrote Locke in a familiar passage], number, figure and motion of the parts of fire, or snow, are really in them, whether any one's senses perceive them or no; and therefore they may be called real qualities because they really exist in those bodies; but light, heat, whiteness or coldness, are no more really in them, than sickness or pain is in manna. Take away the sensation of them; let not the eyes see light or colors, nor the ears hear sounds; let the palate not taste nor the nose smell; and all colors, tastes, odors and sounds, as they are such particular ideas, vanish and cease, and are reduced to their causes, i. e., bulk, figure, and motion of parts.[16]

Mr. Russell says essentially the same thing in a more modern idiom—except that he does not profess to know that the causes of our percepts possess even bulk and figure:

> In places where there are no eyes or ears or brains there are no colors or sounds, but there are events having certain characteristics which lead them to cause colors and sounds in places where there are eyes and ears and brains.[17]

And since the same is to be said, according to Mr. Russell, of the entire range of sensible qualities, his philosophy manifestly pre-

[15] *Analysis of Matter*, pp. 257, 258.
[16] *Essay Concerning Human Understanding*, Bk. II, chap. 8, sec. 17.
[17] *Philosophy*, pp. 157-8.

sents a peculiarly wide and radical sundering of "apparent nature" from "causal nature," outdoing even that bifurcation which seemed to Professor Whitehead the most lamentable of all the errors of the seventeenth century—the extrusion from "nature" of "the greenness of the trees, the warmth of the sun, the hardness of chairs, and the feel of velvet."

If, now, we mean by psychophysical dualism simply the thesis that the contents and (or) process of experience have generic properties essentially different from those of unexperienced particular existents, it is plain that, so long as Mr. Russell keeps to the position outlined, he is debarred from maintaining that such dualism is false. He is, in fact, committed to the admission of its probable truth. If none of the sensible qualities can plausibly be supposed to exist where there are no eyes and ears and brains, *etc.*, then the "external" world, the part of reality that is not experienced, and the part that is experienced, are all but completely heterogeneous. Sense-data become a unique class of particulars, occurring in the life of certain organisms but probably unknown elsewhere in the universe. The present hypothesis thus proves to be another variety of the form of dualistic realism known as the generative theory of sensa—a variety distinguished by the extent of its agnosticism about everything *except* immediate data, sensible or other, and therefore by the greatness of the contrast which it admits between perceptual content and metempirical reality.

There is, however, one (and only one) point at which the hypothesis (as at first stated) avoids complete bifurcation; and at this point it differs from the other forms of the generative theory which find adherents among contemporary writers. The difference is summed up in the thesis that "our percepts are inside our heads." This proposition, which is common to Mr. Russell's earlier theory and to his new one—though with an essential difference in its meaning—of course implies that percepts are in "physical space" (*i. e.,* some space common to them and to physical objects), the head in question being, by hypothesis, a physical object. This view differs from the previously mentioned

sensum-theory of Mr. Broad in that, according to the latter, percepts "are not, in any plain straightforward sense, in the one
Physical Space in which physical objects are supposed to be; and
between parts of them which are connected with different observers there are no simple and straightforward spatial or temporal
relations." Thus they "*cannot* be spatio-temporal parts of physical
objects."[18]   This theory, upon the matters at present under consideration, seems to me to be merely a more critical and coherent
reformulation of the essentials of historic psychophysical dualism;
and the question with which the rest of the present lecture will be
largely concerned is whether this account or Mr. Russell's latest
account of the nature and status of perceptual and other content
is the more satisfactory with respect to the points in which they
seem to be at variance [19]—*viz.,* whether such content is or is not in
"physical space," and whether it can or cannot constitute spatio-
temporal parts of certain physical objects, namely, our brains.[20]

The principal reasons offered by Mr. Russell for holding that
percepts are in our heads are four.

(a) If perception occurs at the end of a long causal process
extending from the (qualitatively indeterminate) external object
to the brain of the percipient, it appears (to Mr. Russell) evident
that the percept must exist at the place, as well as at the time, at
which the process terminates and the percipient event occurs.
Otherwise there would be a "spatio-temporal jump between stimulus and percept which would be quite unintelligible."[21]   Thus
"whoever accepts the causal theory of perception is compelled to

18 Broad, *The Mind and its Place in Nature,* p. 181. The subject of these propositions in Mr. Broad's terminology, is "the objective constituents of perceptual situations." But "objective" in this phrase does not have its usual sense; it does not mean
"existing independently of the percipient event." And it does not seem necessary to
examine Mr. Broad's definition and use of the term. "Percept" seems to convey its
meaning so far as is essential for the present purpose.
19 I say "seem to be at variance," because our analysis will exhibit Mr. Russell's
theory as breaking down, by virtue of some of its own contentions, into the doctrine
to which it initially appears to be opposed.
20 There is a pervasive ambiguity in Mr. Russell's use of the term "physical space"
which will, I hope, be cleared up in the course of our analysis. It is, however,
merely a case of carelessness in expression, and not a confusion of ideas.
21 *Analysis of Matter,* p. 336. The same consideration, as already noted, is one of
the arguments offered by Mr. Russell for epistemological dualism.

conclude that percepts are in our heads. . . . We cannot suppose that, at the end of this process, the last effect suddenly jumps back to the starting-point like a stretched rope when it snaps." [22] In so far as this argument rests upon the assumption that the only conceivable alternative to holding that percepts are in our heads is the view that "the last effect jumps back to the starting-point" it, of course, is inadmissible; for there are the two other alternatives which we have already noted, viz., the sort of projection-theory which places percepts in physical space but not at the starting-point of the process, and the view which denies their presence in the same space with the physical object from which the process starts. But the former would doubtless seem to Mr. Russell as impossible as the alternative which he mentions, and essentially for the same reason—that we "cannot suppose" any projection of the percept into physical space outside the brain to occur. This, however, is not self-evident. We have no such knowledge of what is and is not possible in causal processes as to be entitled to lay it down a priori that effects must always be in exactly the same place with the events which are their temporally proximate causes. Taken literally, that proposition would lead to some highly paradoxical consequences. Perhaps, however, Mr. Russell does not mean to imply this (though his way of putting the argument suggests it); his real, though implicit, premise may be the assumption that if the percept were not inside the brain where the physical event immediately antecedent to its genesis is supposed to occur, it could not be known. But there is no reason for supposing this to be true, unless "being known" is assumed to mean the same thing as "being in the brain." This, however, is denied by nearly all adherents of any of the theories of perception opposed to Mr. Russell's, and, of course, is denied by those who believe our percepts to be in external physical space; and since he offers no reasons for accepting it, and, indeed, does not unequivocally accept it himself (inasmuch as he holds that we may in some degree know the extra-cranial causes of our percepts), his first argument

[22] Ibid., p. 320.

must be said to offer no substantial reasons against even the pro-jection-theory of the situation of percepts.

And as against the other real alternative, that represented by the passage I have quoted from Mr. Broad, the argument is wholly question-begging. The causal theory of perception, so far from necessarily implying that percepts are in our heads, can permit that conclusion only if it is first shown that percepts are in physi-cal space; until the fairly familiar objections to placing them there are dealt with, the real issue is not touched.

(b) The notion "that what we see is 'out there' in physical space is one which cannot survive," Mr. Russell thinks, when we grasp "the difference between what physics supposes to be really happening and what our senses show us as happening."[23]   This is true, though not so obvious, in the case of tactual sense-data as in that of visual ones; that the sensation of touch can be produced by arousing the brain-center directly, as well as by stimulating the peripheral nerve-ending, is capable of experimental verification; and this sensation is "something very different from the mad dance of electrons and protons trying to jazz out of each other's way, which is what physics maintains is really taking place at your finger-tip."[24]   This argument, like the preceding, is beside the mark. What it shows is that *if* percepts are physical objects in physical space, they cannot be the *same* objects (or "events") as those described by physical theory as present in certain regions, *e. g.*, adjacent to the finger-tips. But what requires proof is, once more, the antecedent of this proposition, *viz.*, that percepts *are* objects in physical space. And even if they are, it does not follow that they are in our heads; they might, so far as the argument goes, be neither in our heads nor where the "scientific objects" are, but in some other situation in physical space.

(c) The certainty of our knowledge of the existence and char-acter of the immediate datum seems to Mr. Russell to imply the

[23] *Philosophy*, p. 142. This seems to imply that what we see is not in any sense in physical space; but this Mr. Russell elsewhere denies. The point here is that percepts are not *"out there"* in that space, *i.e.*, outside our heads.

[24] *Ibid.*, pp. 142, 143.

intra-cranial situation of what is known. The more distant an object is from our bodies, the longer and potentially the more complex the causal chain from object to percept, and therefore the greater our liability to error concerning the object; hence, where there is no possibility of error—as in the case of our awareness of the purely sensory content of the moment, as distinguished from all inferences—we must conclude that the object and the percept "are in the same place in space-time, or at least contiguous"; "the highest grade of certainty" can belong only to "knowledge as to what happens in our own heads." [25] Is it assumed here that we possess such certain knowledge about *all* that happens in our own heads? No reason for so assuming is given, since, as we have seen, the equation of "being in our heads" with "being known" is unsupported by argument; and in fact it is commonly assumed, especially by brain-physiologists, that a great many things happen in a man's head of which he can never know anything until some physiologist informs him about them. Mr. Russell does not appear to deny this. If, however, the premise of the present argument means that some but not all events in our heads can be known with the highest grade of certainty, it seems a not very probable assertion. If presence in our heads is what makes things immediately and certainly known, why should some things so situated be in fact not directly knowable by the owners of the heads? And if a distinction is suggested between intra-cerebral processes closely related causally to perception, and other such processes, the difficulty still remains; the events in the cortex commonly believed to be immediately antecedent to a particular visual sensation are as little known to the percipient as any other occurrences in his brain.

This third argument of Mr. Russell's contains, it is true, two valid propositions; first: of the existence and character of our purely sensory content in each specious present we have an immediate and certain awareness—though it is questionable whether this should be called "knowledge"; second: the theory that the

[25] *Ibid.*, p. 214.

percept of an object is produced through a sequence of physical and physiological processes in space implies that distant objects cannot certainly be known as they are, because of the possible modifying effects of events in the intervening medium. But that percepts are in our heads does not at all follow from these two propositions. That, once more, could be inferred only if "to be in our heads," and "to be directly apprehended" were known to be merely different names for one and the same fact—which is not generally admitted, and cannot be true unless the whole of brain anatomy and physiology is false. If, then, being in a head is not the same thing as being known, it is possible that *neither* distant events nor intra-cranial ones are known directly and infallibly, and that those which *are* known directly and infallibly are not in-tra-cranial.

(d) The principal reason given for holding that percepts are in our heads is that any other view introduces into nature "a prepos-terous kind of discontinuity." The ordinary account of visual perception, for example, is that "a physical process starts from a visible object, travels to the eye, there changes into another physi-cal process, causes yet another physical process in the optic nerve, finally produces some effect in the brain, simultaneously with which we see the object from which the process started, the seeing being something 'mental' totally different in character from the physical processes which precede and accompany it." But such a view of perception is "miraculous" and "incredible." [26] In this vehement passage it will be observed that Mr. Russell has some-what mixed issues, and damned all dissentients from his view about percepts for the errors, or supposed errors, of some among them. It was not the assertion of the older dualists, nor is it, I take it, of such a contemporary as Mr. Broad, that when the nerve-impulse reaches the brain we thereupon "see the object from which the process started." On the contrary, these philosophers are usually reproached for admitting, as does Mr. Russell, and for the same reasons, that, in the usual sense of the word, we "see,"

[26] *Philosophy*, pp. 140–141.

not that object, but something which is distinct from it existentially and (more or less, according to the special form of the theory adopted) dissimilar to it qualitatively. On the other hand, it is rather curious that the discontinuity from which we are to escape is represented as consisting in the belief that the "seeing" (rather than that which is immediately seen) is "something 'mental,'" wholly different from the antecedent physical processes. For this, though a usual, is not an invariable feature of the theories of perception which do not place our percepts in our heads; it is not incompatible with the view that percepts *are* in our heads; and it therefore, so far as the present issue is concerned, might consistently, and, indeed, with advantage, be adopted by Mr. Russell himself. True, he does not adopt it; he now seems, on the whole, to intend to deny the mental character (in any sense antithetic to "physical") of the —*ings* as well as the —*eds* of sensing, perceiving, thinking, as well as of sense-data, percepts, and thought-content. But the question whether percepts are in our heads is not the same as the question whether perceiving, and awareness in general, is a physical process; and it is a serious confusion to suppose that the considerations which are pertinent to the one question are also pertinent to the other.

The argument is relevant, then, only if it is understood to assert that a "miraculous" discontinuity is implied by any realistic theory which either assigns percepts to places in physical space outside our heads, or denies their presence in physical space altogether, and therewith excludes them wholly from the physical world. The latter thesis undeniably does imply a breach of continuity in the process by which it conceives percepts to be generated or conditioned; it asserts that after the afferent nerve-impulse produces an effect in the brain there comes into being a particular existent, that is, a percept, which is of an essentially different order from the particulars which had figured in the preceding stages of the process, and is not capable of being located, "in any simple and straightforward sense," in the one physical space (or space-time) in which those particulars are assumed to be situated.

Whether this discontinuity is "miraculous" it would be unprofitable to discuss; there are those to whom all discontinuities seem miraculous, in spite of the fact that nature appears to exhibit them in abundance. We need only, in the discussion to follow, consider whether Mr. Russell's hypothesis, when fully developed, itself avoids, or in the nature of the case can avoid, the admission of discontinuity at precisely the same point in the process out of which percepts arise. I will not say an equally great discontinuity, for I do not know that logical discontinuities are capable of measurement and quantitative comparison.

The four arguments which I have been attempting to summarize and appraise relate primarily to the data of sense-perception, and are supposed to establish the same conclusion for all classes of such data. But the inference is not limited to these. Mr. Russell finds it "almost irresistible to go a step further, and say that any two simultaneous perceived contents of a mind are compresent, so that *all* our conscious mental states are in our heads"; and he does not, in fact, refrain from this further step. "A percept," it seems to him reasonable to believe, "differs from another mental state only in the nature of its causal relation to an external"— which seems to mean an extra-corporeal—"stimulus," not in its essential character or spatial locus.[27] Thus Mr. Russell, too, though by a procedure quite different from that of the behaviorists, arrives at an essentially Hypodermic—or more precisely, an Intra-cranial—Philosophy. The world of our experience, if not the whole of reality, is bounded by our skulls; and the assertion of the physicality of percepts, images, and all other content, means primarily that they have such determinate location within our bodily frame, which in turn has position in physical space (whatever this last term may, upon further analysis, prove to signify).

The potency of this conception as a solvent of old and perennial difficulties and confusions, both of common sense and of philosophy, Mr. Russell believes to be very great; it "must be understood if metaphysics is ever to be got straight." The "traditional

---

[27] *Analysis of Matter*, p. 385, italics mine.

dualism of mind and matter is intimately connected with confusions upon this point"; and it is in the development of this new point of view that we are supposed to reach the final justification for the conclusion that the distinction between mind and matter is illusory. This conclusion, however—let us again remind ourselves —is not intended in precisely the sense in which it would have gained the applause of Bishop Berkeley.

In passing to a more analytic examination of the implications of this doctrine, there is a possible misapprehension of its meaning which we must be careful to avoid. The assertion that our perceptual and other content is in our heads and is the "stuff" of our brains might be understood to mean that we already know what brain-states or brain-structures are (chiefly through the labors of the brain-anatomists and physiologists, and the pictures in their textbooks), and that our percepts, *etc.*, are simply that sort of thing. It is apparently in some such way as this that Mr. Broad construes the thesis, when he represents it as Mr. Russell's "view that a percept actually *is* that event in the brain which is usually regarded as its immediate, necessary and sufficient condition."[28] But this, I think, is not what Mr. Russell means to assert; and it is certainly not the conclusion to which his reasonings lead. Percepts, being immediate data and not inferences, have precisely the characteristics which they are experienced as having; they are "just what they are, whatever physics may say."[29] If we are looking at a green patch which we call a leaf, the "patch is not 'out there' where the leaf is, but is *an event occupying a certain volume of our brains during the time that we see the leaf. Seeing the leaf consists of the existence, in the region occupied by our brain, of a green patch* causally connected with the leaf, or rather with a series of events emanating from the place in physical space where physics places the leaf."[30] As for the labors of the anatomists and physiologists, laudable and useful as these have been, they

[28] C.D. Broad, review of *The Analysis of Matter, in Mind,* January, 1928, p. 93.
[29] *Analysis of Matter,* p. 338.
[30] *Philosophy,* p. 281; italics mine.

have, in Mr. Russell's opinion, been performed under a certain misapprehension. These investigators have naturally supposed that they were making observations on other men's brains, when in fact they were simply observing their own. When a physiologist is said to be examining a living brain, "if we are speaking of physical space, what he sees is in his own brain. It is in no sense in the brain that he is observing (*sic*), though it is in the percept of that brain, which occupies a part of the physiologist's perceptual space."[31] It is, of course, implied by this that we have, after all, a first-hand (or first-head) and infallible qualitative knowledge of one part of the "physical world"; but it is, as Mr. Russell assumes, a knowledge which cannot be extended by analogy to the rest of that world. "What we perceive is part of the stuff of our brains, not part of the stuff of tables, chairs, sun, moon, and stars."[32]

It is, then, clear that we are not called upon to understand by "percepts" entities having the properties hitherto commonly ascribed to brain-events, but rather to ascribe to our brains all the properties which percepts are experienced as having. We err, Mr. Russell thinks, when, having first identified (external) physical processes with *our* (*i. e.,* the observers') percepts, we argue that since "our percepts are not other people's thoughts, the physical processes in their brains are quite different from their thoughts." What is proposed, in short, is not a reduction of percepts or thoughts to brains or brain-events, as those are ordinarily conceived, but rather of brains (or portions of them) to percepts and thoughts—though, somehow, without detriment to the "physical" status of brains. Our brains, then, are to be understood literally to consist (at least in part) of such things as patches of color, sounds, odors, ticklings, sensible temperatures, hard spots and soft spots—or more precisely, of these together with the perceived relations whereby they form the connected groups of characters which we call perceived tables and chairs, *etc.;* and to consist,

31 *Ibid.,* p. 140.
32 *Ibid.,* p. 281.

further, of pains and pleasures, emotions, and whatever is our psychological content when we are thinking of such objects as the logical relation "nevertheless," or the square root of minus one.

Are there, however, inside our skulls, besides these extended and definitely located, and in that sense physicalized, "mental states," other entities of the sort more commonly classified as physical? Mr. Russell appears to think that there are. During life, while the contents of the brain consist "partly at least of percepts, thoughts and feelings," they also consist of electrons.[33] But this compresence of "mental states" and electrons in the same place indicates their probable identity, or rather the identity of the former with elements of the latter. If, in other words, an electron is in a human brain, *"some* of the events composing it (the electron) are likely to be some of the 'mental states' of the man to whom the brain belongs." Thus we have, incidentally, a curious division, unknown to the physicist, of electrons into two varieties, one composed partly or wholly of "mental states," the other not so composed. Apparently the electrons not in brains do not contain "mental states" (*i. e.,* sense-data), since the stuff of which the brain is (partly) constituted is not "the stuff of tables, chairs, sun, moon, and stars."

It is perhaps worth while to inquire precisely what is meant by this conception of (some) electrons as composed of mental states. We must therefore determine the special meaning which the terms employed in the proposition have for its author. (a) What is an electron? (b) What is an "event"? (c) How does an event which is a "mental state" differ from one which is not? (d) In what sense are some electrons said to be "composed of" the former sort of events?

(a) An electron (at an instant) is "a grouping of events"; it "includes all the events that happen where the electron is." Whether electrons are of finite size or not is "a matter of indifference." (This is hard to admit, since if our brains are composed of electrons, and the latter are not of finite size, it should follow that

[33] *Analysis of Matter,* p. 320.

our brains are infinitely big—an odd consequence which should be important if true.) However, to "save circumlocution" (surely not a sufficient reason) it is assumed that an electron is a "point." [34] The term "point" or "point-instant" is elsewhere defined as meaning a "place in space-time" which is occupied by a group of events having the two properties that any two members of the group are compresent, and no event outside the group is compresent with every member of it. "Compresence" is a relation between two events such that they "overlap in space-time." The further elaboration of this last definition involves a highly technical mathematical discussion; what is pertinent here is that a "point" can be occupied by a plurality of "events" having spatio-temporal extension. Since, then, an electron may be a complex of events it is hard to understand why its identification with a "point" should be treated as excluding its "finite size."

(b) An "event" is primarily antithetic to the "things" or "substances" of common sense and the older physics in respect of its duration; it "occupies a volume of space-time which is small in all four dimensions, not indefinitely extended in one dimension (time)." But neither its duration nor, apparently, its spatial dimensions can be equal to zero; yet it has (by definition) "no space-time structure, i. e., it does not have parts which are external to one another in space-time." [35] This is puzzling, but we need not dwell upon it. As to its qualities, an event may have any you please, or none at all; the word, that is, relates only to an abstract mathematical element in a spatio-temporal and causal structure.

(c) A percept or other "mental state," if in space-time, will, of course, necessarily be an "event"; if not, it will not be a part of the material world; and until proof is offered, it cannot properly be so classified. Assuming, however, that percepts *are* in this sense events, how do they differ from other events? One difference follows from Mr. Russell's general principles already set forth: percepts possess—or consist of—one or more of the sensible qual-

34 *Ibid.*, p. 321.
35 *Ibid.*, p. 286.

ities, color, sound, odor, *etc.,* while other events are not known, and cannot be assumed, to do so; it is, in fact, often implied by Mr. Russell, as in passages already cited, that we know that scientific objects and sense-data have radically different characteristics. One would naturally suppose that a percept also differs from other events in being perceived. On this point, as has been remarked, Mr. Russell is elusive, since he has at times a tendency to reason as if being in the brain were itself equivalent to being perceived. But he cannot consistently hold this opinion, since he admits unperceived events even within the brain. Hence percepts are events having two differentiae: they possess certain qualities probably foreign to all other events, and they have the peculiar status or relation of being perceived.

(d) We can now see that the statement that "some electrons, in human brains, are composed of percepts, or other 'mental states' " adds nothing to the intelligibility or probability of the original thesis, "our percepts, *etc.,* are in our heads," and nothing of importance to its content. It is merely a re-assertion, with respect to the parts of the brain, of what was first asserted with respect to the relation between percepts and the brain in general. *If* the green patch which I call a leaf "occupies a certain volume in my brain," a part of it will naturally occupy a portion of some of the physical units—protons and electrons—of which it is assumed that the brain is wholly composed, and may be compresent in that small region with other events that lack the two differentiae of percepts. But we have still to determine whether it is possible or probable that percepts and the like *are* in our heads; if they are not, the argument that some electrons, *viz.,* those that are in brains, are wholly or partly made up of them, falls to the ground. It also remains to be determined whether the laws of electronic action, as formulated by physicists, are also the laws of the behavior of percepts, images, and the like—whether, for example, dreams can be explained (in the ordinary scientific sense) by supposing that dream-objects are not merely conditioned by, but are made up of, constellations of electrons.

Whatever the difficulties inherent in the alternative view, it can, I think, hardly be denied that this account of the nature and situation of percepts has some rather curious consequences of its own. Consider, for example, its application to thermal sensations, of which, I believe, Mr. Russell does not make specific mention. It appears to imply that when you drink ice-water a portion of your brain becomes as cold as the water. This will, no doubt, seem surprising to physiologists, who have supposed that the internal temperature of the human body during life cannot go much below 80°; but this, of course, is due to their habitual error in imagining that they were observing objects and bodies outside them and not merely the insides of their own heads. Upon the Russellian hypothesis all observed temperatures must be internal temperatures of the observer—though in an equivocal sense presently to be noted. It will be seen also that, when all classes of sense-data are considered, the stuff of which the brain, or some part of it, is composed must be of a remarkably mixed character. If I should visibly place one hand on a cake of ice and visibly dip the other into, say, hot milk, one part (or some parts) of my brain will literally become hard, glittering, translucent, and almost freezing cold, while another part (or parts) will possess the sensible qualities of an opaque, white, hot fluid.

Again the hypothesis would apparently require us to hold that when (as we say) a surgeon uncovers a tumor in another man's head, he thereby produces a tumor in his own; that the scalpel which he sees and feels in his hand, in so far as it is a perceptible, in other words an empirical, reality, is actually moving from point to point in his own brain; and that the tissues which he perceives it cutting are parts of his brain. These implications cannot be averted by urging that the tumor, in so far as it is in the brain of the surgeon, is merely a percept, and therefore not a "real," or at all events not a "physical," tumor; for that, of course, is precisely what Mr. Russell denies. It is essential to his general thesis to maintain that what the surgeon is observing is as truly a physical reality as anything ever is; and it admittedly is a reality which

looks like a tumor and feels like a tumor and, in short, *is* a tumor
—the only kind of tumor, indeed, according to Mr. Russell's view,
which brain-surgeons ever do or can observe; and upon the same
view, it is "a part of the stuff of the brain" of the observer, that
is, in this case, of the surgeon. Thus it would appear that all sur-
geons operate primarily upon themselves. And on the other hand,
no events of the sort commonly described by the term "brain-oper-
ation" will occur as percepts in the brain of the patient. If unconscious, he will have no percepts at all; if he is delirious, his visions
are not likely to be of an operation; and even if awake, he will not
see or touch his own brain. Yet—what may perhaps seem still
odder—though all the perceptible phenomena of the operation
really happen in the brain of the surgeon, and do not happen at
all in the brain of the patient, it is the latter only who experiences
any physiological effects of them. He alone suffers from the tumor and benefits from the operation; or if the knife slips, it is he,
not the surgeon, that dies.

Other curious consequences of the theory of percepts-in-the-
head suggest themselves if you consider the case, not of the surgeon, but of the brain-physiologist. It is, of course, nominally
recognized by Mr. Russell that there may be percepts *of* brains as
well as percepts in brains, and that the brain which a percept is
said to be "of" is not the same as the brain which it is said to be
in (though it is not explained by his theory why we never have
percepts *of* the percepts that are physical parts of other men's
brains). Now if perception is assumed to have a cognitive function, knowledge of a particular class of objects is to be obtained
by perceiving objects of that class. If the physiologist wishes to
learn about brains, it will not suffice for him to observe the first
object that happens to meet his eye; he must put himself in a position to have percepts of brains—of other people's brains, living
and dead. But according to Mr. Russell's theory this would not
be true; for the essential peculiarity of the theory is the assertion
that *all* the sensible qualities which we experience belong to the
physical organ of knowledge, not, so far as we can judge, to the

external objects of knowledge. Thus all percepts equally give us a direct and infallible acquaintance with one (presumably typical) member of the class "brains"—the only class of physical objects in the world of which such sure and qualitative knowledge is obtainable. The brain-physiologist need not, therefore, trouble to study what are *called* other men's brains; he will accomplish his purpose equally well by playing golf or watching a display of fireworks. He will, indeed, accomplish it better so; for if he seeks to learn about brains by attending exclusively to his so-called percepts of other brains, he will be confusing other brains with his own, or else be substituting an indirect and inferential acquaintance for first-hand observation. Of this advantage the brain-physiologist enjoys a monopoly; the methods of research in other branches of science must, even by Mr. Russell's theory, be at once more laborious and, in their results, much less certain—except in so far as those sciences are regarded as nothing but contributions to brain-physiology, *i. e.,* as descriptions of the brains of the investigators. On its observational side, indeed, no physical science can, for Mr. Russell, be anything more than this. Brain physiology will be the only empirical science.

I cannot think it really prudent that philosophers should thus encourage physiologists to believe that they can learn as much about brain-stuff by playing golf as by dissecting brains—though, doubtless, it is improbable that even Mr. Russell will easily make them believe it. And, indeed, I find it hard to suppose that Mr. Russell himself really believes it. The proposition that our percepts are portions of the stuff of our brain seems, in short, if taken literally, to lead to absurdities—only a few of which have been here suggested; and I am therefore forced to conjecture that Mr. Russell does not, after all, mean it to be taken literally, but only in a Pickwickian sense. To retain it in any sense, without falling into these absurdities, we must take it to relate to a "brain," or a kind of "brain-stuff," which is foreign to the province of physical science. The brain-physiologist must be supposed to be concerned solely with brains about which he must learn, as specialists in other physical sciences do about the objects of their studies, by information obtained through the sense-organs, and consequently to be better acquainted with other men's brains than with his own. It must—if he accepts Mr. Russell's philosophic thesis—be nevertheless the first rule of his scientific procedure to assume that the percepts that are *in* brains give no direct information of any interest to him about the brains which they are in. And the brain-surgeon, likewise, must be supposed to be removing tumors, not from his own brain, but from his patients'. If his operation produces, as Mr. Russell's doctrine implies, a tumor in the surgeon's brain, this must be regarded as a tumor which is *not* "physical" in any practically significant sense, nor physiologically involved in the surgeon's bodily mechanism; while the tumor in the patient's brain, which is not composed of percepts, must be taken as the only "physical" tumor (in such a sense) with which the operation has to do. Similarly, the Russellian brain which, under circumstances previously mentioned, is, at the same moment, partly hard, cold, glittering and translucent and partly hot, opaque, white and fluid, must be assigned to an order of being entirely extraneous to the world of both the physiologist and the physicist.

The only terms, in short, upon which the proposition that percepts are in our brains can (if at all) be accepted imply a sort of intra-cranial dualism. There must be supposed to exist inside our heads, two utterly disparate sorts of entities, one "physical" in the usual full-blooded sense, the other "physical" only in a peculiar and shadowy sense; one physically efficacious and conforming to physical laws, the other either otiose or, if it performs any causal rôle at all in determining bodily behavior, doing so in a peculiar manner foreign to the conceptions of physical science. Now it does not appear that much, if anything, is gained by thus spatially juxtaposing entities clearly not physical in any ordinary sense with entities which are in that sense physical. If a dualism is forced upon us by the facts, it seems simpler not to crowd both orders of being into the same places in the same space; for their supposed compresence there only gives rise to new problems and new anomalies. It is not a convenient nor a useful hypothesis that when you wake from a dreamless sleep the inside of your physical head, already presumably occupied by a brain, suddenly receives further contents in the form of extended objects having all the empirical characters of bedroom furniture—and all this with no increase in your weight or perceptible enlargement of your cranium. It is not a convenient nor a useful hypothesis that the electrons in the brain which interact electromagnetically with one another are also literally juxtaposed with, or interpenetrated by, percepts of moon and stars, or images of the events of the day before yesterday, which have no such electromagnetic properties. These observations are merely a restatement of a principle which, usually tacitly, guided the physicist-philosophers of the seventeenth-century: the principle that it is to the advantage of the philosophy of nature to keep the physical order homogeneous. They felt—and, as it seems to me, for sound reasons—that the admission of a radical discontinuity *within* it was more to be avoided than the admission of a radical discontinuity between it as a whole and an essentially distinct and disparate realm of being.

Yet the vestigial shred of physicality theoretically saved for perceptual and other content by affirming their bare epiphenomenal presence in physical space, and in what are, in a sense, definite positions in that space, will, I suppose, seem to some, as it seems at times to Mr. Russell, to be a great philosophic advantage. It still remains, however, to be determined whether even this shred can legitimately be preserved, and whether, in final analysis, Mr. Russell can consistently claim to have preserved it.

This question we can best approach by now considering the most obvious apparent objection to the thesis that our percepts are in our heads. This was briefly suggested in the preceding lecture: it consists in the fact that, if "head" is used in its ordinary sense and we are assumed to have but one head apiece, the thesis seems to be contradicted by our perceptual experience. While we cannot see our own heads—or at all events our own skulls—we can touch them and pass tape-measures around them, and from mirror-images we commonly believe that we get certain indirect visual information about them; and we thus determine their positions and magnitudes, relative to other perceptual objects, in a single space which we assume to be common to sight and touch. And in this space the other perceived objects are perceptibly outside *these* heads. My visual field extends far to right and left of the region occupied by my skull; when I touch my forehead with my hand, it is the front or outside, not the inside, of my forehead that I touch. This Mr. Russell, of course, does not deny; he therefore seeks to meet the difficulty by a supplementary hypothesis. Since percepts *must* be in our heads, and since they plainly are not in the heads with which we are, or suppose ourselves to be, already familiar, another head must be postulated to provide the required lodgment for them. And since this other head is not apparent in the space in which the other perceived objects are situated (and if it were, would itself be a percept, and therefore inside some head other than itself), we must further postulate another space in which to situate it. "The statement that my percepts are in my head is only true in connection with *physical* space. There is also a space in our percepts, and of this space the statement would not be true. . . . The space of percepts, like the percepts, must be private; there are as many perceptual spaces as there are percipients." And in my perceptual space, "my percept of a table is outside my percept of my head." [36] But in physical space, which is "neutral and public," both percepts, table and head, are contained; and the statement that my percepts are in my head means that there also exists an unperceived head, which is "a physical object in physical space," [37] and somehow contains or surrounds all my percepts. Thus, in order to avoid the bifurcation of nature, we equip ourselves with two heads and two (or more) spaces.

To judge of the success of this way of meeting the difficulty, we

[36] *Philosophy*, pp. 137–8.
[37] *Ibid.*, p. 138; it will be observed that two sorts of "physical head" are implied. Perceptual heads are physical, but the imperceptible heads "in physical space" are "physical" in another and more exacting signification of the word.

must try to define more sharply the distinction between physical and perceptual space, and to this end must first ask the question which was raised in the preceding lecture concerning the distinction previously made by Mr. Russell between "private" and "perspective" spaces. Are the "perceptual" and "physical" spaces of the present hypothesis (a) merely distinct, non-overlapping regions of one continuous all-embracing space—the "perspective space" of the earlier theory; or are they (b) distinct spaces not constituting parts of any one connected spatial system—distinct in the sense either that they are different *types* of space, or that, even though of the same type, points in the one have no spatial relations with points in the other, so that, if the coördinates of a place or object P in the one system were defined, nothing would be stated or inferrible as to the position of P with respect to any axes defined in the other system? If the distinction is interpreted in sense (b) it—though introduced in the interest of a unification of the world of percepts and the world of physical objects—would seem in fact to result only in their more effectual divorce. If the private perceptual space of each percipient is not only self-contained but incapable of location in or spatial relation to physical space, or to any spatial order common to both, then my perceptual head and the objects perceived in my visual field cannot be said to be *in* my physical head. The private spaces and their contents would find no place in the physical world, and nature would be as deeply bifurcated as in any of the older forms of dualism. For since the dualists of earlier periods, as has been already remarked, must after all have known as well as anyone that visual and tactual data have *apparent* position and extension, what they must presumably have been awkwardly trying to convey when they said that sense-data are "in the mind" was that the perceived positions and extension of such data are purely "subjective," *i.e.,* private, and are not capable of spatial correlation with those of objects in the physical world. In order, then, to find in Mr. Russell's multiplication of spaces, and therewith of heads, any aid towards the desired escape from a dualism of essentially the traditional sort, it would seem necessary to assume interpretation (a): to say that there is one space or space-time—"physical space" in a more comprehensive sense—of which perceptual space and "physical space" in a narrower sense are merely regions, the one inside, the other outside, my brain.

But in fact both ways of construing the distinction may be found in Mr. Russell's recent use of it, though one of them, to misuse the language of biologists, is dominant, the other recessive, a survival of the comparatively naïve, virtually pre-relativistic conception of space characteristic of *The Analysis of Mind*. The interpretation of the distinction which alone is serviceable to Mr. Russell's purpose of overcoming psychophysical dualism is, however, the recessive one.

(a) This interpretation seems to be conveyed by the statement that the private space which "each person carries about can be located in physical space by indirect methods";[38] or, again, by the remark that "the essential assumption of what is commonly called the causal theory is, that the group of percepts" of various observers of what is called one object "can be enlarged by the addition of other events, *ranged in the same space about the same center*, and connected with each other and with the group of percepts by laws which include the laws of perspective. The essential points are (1) the arrangement about a center, (2) *the continuity between percepts and correlated events in other parts of the space derived from percepts and locomotion*."[39] The latter point is not demonstrable, but it secures "simplicity and continuity in the laws of correlation suggested by the grouping of percepts. . . . Its merits are therefore of the same kind as those of any other scientific theory"; and Mr. Russell announces that he will "henceforth assume it."

Taken in conjunction with other statements this is, certainly, confusing, not to say confused. For we are told elsewhere that each percipient "carries about with him" not one private space, but

[38] *Philosophy*, p. 140.
[39] *Analysis of Matter*, p. 217.

several, of which the most important are visual and tactual spaces; and that the spatial relations which are perceived "between objects seen simultaneously, and also between objects touched simultaneously, . . . cannot hold between a visual and a tactual percept"; between the latter only temporal and causal correlations can hold.[40] It should follow that *perceptually* visual data and touch data are never in the same perceptual space, and that the common space to which we assign them is a logical construct. But if the spaces of the several senses are thus essentially incapable of spatial correlation, it is hard to see how they all can be truly located in one physical space, even "by indirect methods." But for the moment we must ignore such seeming inconsistencies, and simply recognize that at times Mr. Russell appears plainly to be conceiving of percepts and physical objects, including physical heads, as joint-occupants of a common three-dimensional space, or at least as having spatial relations *inter se* which constitute a single, connected system of such relations.

When this is assumed, what will be the spatial relations of our physical heads to our perceptual heads and to perceptual objects in general? Can we, in the first place, assume that the "physical head"—which, it must be remembered, we cannot perceive—is a "head" at all, in the ordinary sense of the word? Mr. Russell appears to think so, for he writes that all the events of my experience "together, in *physical* space, occupy a volume smaller than my head, since it certainly does not include the hair, skull, teeth, *etc.*"; the head here in question obviously must be the head[41] which is "physical" in the sense of being extra-perceptual, since that alone is the container of my percepts. But the assumption that *it* is provided with such organs and appendages, or that it has any particular shape, is obviously irreconcilable with the interpretation of the causal theory of perception which Mr. Russell has given. We have been told that we must "maintain an attitude of complete agnosticism as regards all but the mathematical properties" of

---

[40] *Ibid.*, pp. 145–147.
[41] *Analysis of Matter*, p. 145.

the physical world extraneous to our actual percepts—that, in other words, we may assume no more about it than that one or more differences, of unknown sort, exist in it corresponding to every experienced difference in perceptual content: and "hair, skull and teeth" are presumably not "mathematical properties." That the unperceived external counterpart of what I tactually experience, or my neighbor visually experiences, as "my head" is itself, in any intelligible sense, a head, we clearly are not, upon Mr. Russell's principles, entitled to affirm.

If, however, we pass over this inconsistency also, another somewhat difficult feature of the hypothesis presents itself. We are now to assume that a "physical" head is a perfectly good head, duly furnished with skull, eyes, nose, *etc.;* and we naturally ask how big a head it will be. Since by hypothesis it contains all our perceptual objects and the whole perceptual space—*i. e.,* the region of the one general perspective space in which these are spread out—it must evidently be at least as large as that region. The reader of Mr. Russell must here be especially on his guard against confusing his heads. It is natural to hark back to the familiar perceptual head and think of the supposedly intra-cranial percepts, and perceptual space, as smaller than *that* head is, or is commonly conceived to be—in other words, to think of them as very much reduced replicas of the objects "around us" which we see and touch, and of the perceived distances between them; and Mr. Russell's language is sometimes such as to encourage the reader in this confusion. But the percepts which are said to be in your head, since they are simply what you see and touch, are precisely as large as they sensibly appear to be; and the extent of your perceptual space at any moment is precisely the perceived extent of your visual or tactual field.

Whether that field as actually given has three or only two dimensions is a long-controverted question in psychology which Mr. Russell regards as still an open one [42]—though most contemporary psychologists, I imagine, would not agree. But we need not

[42] *Philosophy,* p. 138.

attempt to deal with the question here. Two dimensions, at least, perceptual space is universally allowed to have; and thus my physical brain must stretch to right and left, and up and down, as far as my vision perceptually reaches, and my skull will lie somewhere out beyond those limits. If a physical skull fits a physical brain pretty closely, as a perceptual skull does a perceptual brain (*i. e.,* my percepts of other people's skulls and brains), and if perceptual space, *i. e.,* the region occupied by the percepts which constitute my physical brain, is two-dimensional only, what is suggested (though not with necessity) is that physical brains are long and wide but almost flat; but if three dimensions are assigned to perceptual space, this, of course, will not follow. In any case, in terms of sensible distance and magnitude, we should apparently have very large heads. But *how* large—how distant in perspective space out beyond our private spaces our *physical* "hair, skull, teeth," *etc.,* are—we should, I take it, have no means of determining, since a physical head is imperceptible. Even when two persons bump their heads, what they experience, according to this theory, must consist of two sets of visual and tactual and other events occurring wholly *inside* their respective physical heads; the external contact remains unperceived. And though it may be inferred to have taken place, where it took place must remain unknown. One place where it did *not* take place, however, is, by the hypothesis, certain; namely, where it seemed to do so, at the surfaces of the two (or more precisely the four) perceptual heads. There will really be four such heads concerned, because *each* percipient will have both the other person's visual head and his own tactual (and perhaps partly visual) head inside his own physical head, as percepts identical with parts of his own brain. These four, as parts of the physical world, will also be "physical heads," in a sense; but of course, there will also be the two "physical heads" in the stricter sense in which we have been using the expression—*i. e.,* imperceptible and qualitatively indeterminate— making a total of six physical heads involved in every bump.

Now, I will not say that these particular features of the hypothesis (when construed in the sense now under consideration) are impossible; but they do seem somewhat odd and fantastic, and it is hard to see how the conception as a whole notably simplifies our general view of nature. The imperceptible skull which at each moment walls in our whole extended perceptual field, instead of being in the midst of it, as empirical skulls appear to be, is not an addition to the sum of things which there seems sufficient reason to accept; for, be it remembered, the only reason proposed for accepting it is that we cannot otherwise find a head to put our percepts into. The possibilities that they are not in any head, or that the perceptual space in which they are is not itself a part of, or spatially correlated with, the space of the physical world, still remain available alternatives.

(b) And it is in fact, as has been intimated, in this last way that Mr. Russell himself, in the dominant and more consistent strain in his recent philosophy, interprets the distinction between the two spaces.[43] Any other view is incongruous, in the first place, with the degree of agnosticism which is fundamental in the whole theory. Modern mathematics has shown that many kinds of space, or types of quasi-spatial order, are conceivable; and with respect to the space belonging to the world of causal objects beyond our perception the same principle holds as with respect to qualities: we are entitled to assume a structural parallelism with perceptual space but nothing more. The sort of space-relations which we actually perceive, "most obviously among visual percepts, are not identical with those which physics assumes among the corresponding physical objects," but have only "a certain kind of correspondence with those relations." When, e. g., "we represent the position, for physics, of visible objects by polar coördinates, taking the percipient as origin," the relations which the physicist employs in assigning even the angular coördinates are not those which we perceive in the visual field, "but merely correspond with

---

[43] On the relation of the two conceptions of space, cf. *Analysis of Matter*, pp. 333–42.

them in a manner which preserves their logical (mathematical) properties." Thus "we need not assume that physical direction has anything in common with visual direction," except that "two objects which produce percepts which differ in perceived direction" must themselves differ in some correlative way.[44]

In so far as this is merely a deduction from Mr. Russell's semi-agnostic premise, it does not, of course, tell us that perceptual and physical space *cannot* be of the same sort, but only that we have no sufficient grounds for supposing that they are. Contemporary physics, however, offers reasons for a more positive assertion of the disparateness of the two; and these reasons Mr. Russell accepts, despite the narrow limits which he has set to our knowledge of the physical world. What we have hitherto been calling "physical space" is, of course, in the theory of relativity, space-time. But the space of perception is not space-time. The objects in a visual field are not separated by relativistic "intervals," but by perceived distances, two- or three-dimensional, with no commutability of the values of spatial and temporal dimensions. And to this fact Mr. Russell himself calls attention in a passage which I have cited in a previous lecture: "In the world of percepts, the distinction between space and time does really exist, and *space does really have certain properties which relativity denies to physical space*. Thus to this extent the correspondence between perceptual and physical space breaks down."[45] But this, surely, is a very great extent; it means that the mode of relatedness subsisting between percepts is essentially different from that subsisting between Minkowskian "events," which are the components of the external world of relativistic physics. Thus to one who takes—as does Mr. Russell—the general theory of relativity realistically, the world of perception becomes, in relational constitution as well as in its qualitative content, a realm of being radically antithetic to physical reality.

In the original and ingenious essay towards a reconstruction of fundamental scientific concepts which constitutes Part III of *The*

[44] *Analysis of Matter*, p. 252.
[45] *Analysis of Matter*, p. 338; italics mine.

Analysis of Matter this differentiation of the two spaces is carried still farther. The hypotheses there set forth are, indeed, presented as merely tentative—as ideas which "may hereafter prove fruitful and have already a certain imaginative value." [46] But they are not of course, to be regarded merely as an arbitrary flight of fancy; they are a sketch of a possible way of conceiving of the structure of the physical world "far simpler than any yet evolved" and at the same time, as Mr. Russell thinks, definitely suggested by certain recent developments in physics. And the desired simplification is sought chiefly "through giving up the attempt to make physical space resemble the space of percepts." The argument is too long and too full of technical physics to be reproduced here; but it can perhaps be presented in a highly syncopated form which will not be altogether misleading, and will at least bring out the specific contrasts between the two spaces.

(a) It is, of course, not certain, but it appears to Mr. Russell highly probable, that the discontinuity revealed by the discovery of quantum phenomena is a primary and universal structural characteristic of nature; indeed, "it seems impossible to resist the view," that Planck's constant "represents something of fundamental importance in the physical world." [47] If this is admitted, it follows that the hypothesis of a discrete space-time is also probable, since through it, and apparently through it alone, we can "imagine a theoretical physics which would make the existence of the quantum no longer seem surprising." [48] But, of course, the space of actual perception and the perspective space which is an imagined extension of it beyond the confines of actual perception are continuous; hence, once more, the world of perception appears to have a radically different constitution from that to which theory points as the constitution of the physical world.

(b) Seeking further to give definite, and also the simplest adequate, content to the notion of a discrete space-time Mr. Rus-

[46] *Analysis of Matter*, p. 271.
[47] *Ibid.*, p. 365.
[48] *Ibid.*, p. 366.

sell proposes a re-interpretation of the concept of "interval." It
seems to him—for specific reasons which I omit—that "too much
effort has been made to regard interval as analogous to distance
in conventional geometry and time in conventional kinematics." [49]
All that is, in relativistic physics, essential to the concept may be
reduced to the notion of a system, or family-tree, of events which
have the relation of causal antecedent and consequent to one another or to common causal ancestors or descendants. "There is a
causal relation whenever two events . . . are related by a law
which allows something to be inferred about the one from the
other." [50] Such a relation may obtain between events which are
not linked together by any continuous space or any continuous
process. In this theory, then, "spatial distance does not directly
represent any physical fact, but is a rather complicated way of
speaking about the possibility of a common causal ancestry or
posterity." Since there is thus in external nature no such fact as
distance, in the ordinary sense, there can also be no such phenomenon as continuous motion; that concept is no more than "a convenient symbolic device for dealing with the time-relations of
various discontinuous changes." When a light-wave is supposed
to travel from one atom to another, we are not to assume that "at
every moment of the intervening time the light-ray is at a certain
spatial distance" from the emitting atom.[51] Motion of any sort,
indeed, "cannot be one of the fundamental concepts of physics";
whether conceived as continuous or otherwise, "it is merely a convenience in stating physical laws." [52] But in perceptual space distance is a fact; it is one of the actually perceived relations
constituting what we commonly mean by the word "space." And

49 *Ibid.*, p. 369.
50 *Ibid.*, p. 367.
51 *Analysis of Matter*, p. 380. Whether time also can be derived from causality
—in which case it also would be peculiar to perception and alien to the "physical
world"—Mr. Russell leaves an open question (*ibid.*, p. 381). Even in the theory
of relativity, without these new additions, Mr. Russell observes that "it is hardly
correct to say that a particle *moves* in a geodesic; it is more correct to say that the
particle *is* a geodesic (though not all geodesics are particles)"; *ibid.*, p. 313.
52 *Ibid.*, p. 356.

motion—certainly *some* type of motion, and, as would generally be held, continuous motion—is also actually perceptible.[53]

From this second feature of his transformation of the concept of physical space, Mr. Russell draws a consequence which appears contrary to the one which I have been suggesting. The meaning of this concept has now been reduced to that of causality; and since it is admitted that "percepts can be effects or causes of physical events," it is, he concludes, plain that "we are bound to give them a position in physical space-time."[54] But I have been maintaining that Mr. Russell's own hypothesis implies that percepts cannot be in the physical space-time that he defines. There is a contradiction here; but it is, I think, Mr. Russell's. His definition of space-time had both a positive and a negative clause: events, which are its terms, were said to be in causal relations to one another and *not* to be in the relations characteristic of perceptual space. If the negative clause had been lacking, no simplification of the fundamental concepts of physics would have resulted from the definition. But when both clauses are borne in mind, it is evident that percepts, being in perceptual space, cannot be events in physical space-time. Mr. Russell has apparently reached the conclusion which—in order to avoid complete dualism—he requires, simply by forgetting a part of his definition. The actual logical outcome of his argument is that when events in the extra-perceptual physical world give rise, in some mysterious manner, to percepts, they therewith generate also a space, or a type of spatial relation, in which they themselves are not contained, or of which they are not terms. It is, of course, conceivable that the percepts, besides being related to one another in perceptual space, should also be terms in the

[53] Mr. Russell attempts to show that perceptual motion need not be regarded as continuous (*ibid.*, pp. 278–279). This, however, is in a portion of his argument in which he is attempting, not to separate the world of physics and the world of perception, but to bring them together. If, however, *no* motion, properly so-called "belongs to the world of physics," the *rapprochement* must be unsuccessful, whatever the nature of perceptual motion.

[54] *Ibid.*, p. 383. On the following page Mr. Russell surprisingly adds: "Percepts are not known to have any intrinsic character which physical events cannot have." Are not distance, continuity, motion, and in general spatial relatedness, intrinsic characters of some percepts?

same sort of relation which physical events have *inter se* to the exclusion of the spatial relations—*i.e.,* should be effects and causes of such events. This, however, still leaves the world of perceptual content a world apart in every respect *except* causal relatedness; and if—disregarding the negative side of the definition—we say that this means that both are in "physical space," the import of the latter term has now been so transformed and attenuated that the proposition is compatible with any of the historic forms of psychophysical dualism, except (oddly) the strictly parallelistic varieties of that doctrine.

Thus Mr. Russell really presents a generative theory of space, as well as of sensa; his position is, indeed, curiously reminiscent of Kant's—or, more precisely, of Kant's in those moments when he was still trying to be a sort of dualistic realist.[55] There is, for the contemporary philosopher also, a world of *Dinge-an-sich,* now called "events"; these are "outside us," but they are not in space (in the ordinary sense of the term), which is purely subjective, in other words, is a mode of relatedness holding only between the objects of perception; they have, however, (as Kant's things-in-themselves were really conceived by him to have, despite his declarations to the contrary) the relation of cause to the percepts, and the qualitative diversity of our sense-data is due to them, though they possess none of the qualities of the data. The theory of Mr. Russell differs from Kant's, however, in that "events" are supposed to be known to be multiple and discrete, and to have causal relations to one another as well as to percepts, so that they retain more of the characteristics commonly ascribed to physical objects.

Yet Mr. Russell, in many passages, draws a conclusion about the historical affinities and metaphysical consequences of his own theory which is, I suggest, precisely opposite to that which ought to be drawn. He supposes that the view that "mind and matter are quite disparate" has, historically, rested upon "a notion that we know much more about matter than we do, and *in particular*

---

[55] This similarity is partly noted by Mr. Russell himself, *philosophy*, p. 239.

upon the belief that the space of physics can be identified with the space of sensible experience"; when, therefore, "the separation of physical and sensible space is logically carried out," the "groundlessness of traditional views about mind and matter" is demonstrated, and Descartes' metaphysical aberration is corrected.[56] But it surely is clear that the more you separate physical and sensible space, the more you affirm the disparateness of matter and sensory content—which presumably is the traditional view here in question. And in its essentials, though not in detail, Mr. Russell's dualistic outcome is closely akin even to Descartes'. It is a manifestation of the same perennial tendency of theoretical physics to simplify the conception of the physical world—*i. e.*, the world as it is apart from the occurrence of perception—by purging that world of the characters belonging to the objects of sensible experience. Mr. Russell differs from Descartes (on this issue) only in that his purgation is more thorough; while Descartes still sought to construct the causal world behind the show of sense-experience out of a space similar to that with which we are acquainted in perception, though excluding from it all sensible qualities, Mr. Russell seeks to exclude from that world not only the qualities but also (in the full development of his hypothesis) space itself, in the usual sense of the word. It is unlikely, no doubt, that, in its details, Mr. Russell's new tentative theory of "the structure of the physical world" will gain acceptance among physicists, or prove permanently satisfactory to its author; but in its aim and general principles it is in harmony with the characteristic tendency of contemporary theoretical physics—which is to say that it carries the simplification and mathematization of the conception of the world behind and beyond sense-experience to a point unimaginable by any seventeenth-century philosopher. But it is hard to understand how anyone can hope to find the way out of psychophysical dualism by traveling farther than Galileo and Descartes along the road which they opened.

In view of Mr. Russell's conclusions as to the meaning of the

---

[56] *Philosophy*, p. 239; italics mine.

distinction of physical and perceptual space, what becomes of the separation of our physical from our perceptual heads? What a physical head is to be understood to be, when the "space" in which it exists has been reduced to relations of causality between nonspatial events, it is not easy to describe; but evidently it will be so different from what has ever before been meant by a "head," that it seems misleading to call it by that name at all. In any case, it obviously cannot surround our perceptual head, or be assigned any other position relatively to it, by setting up coördinates in our perceptual space. If "somewhere" means having relations of distance and direction to some perceptible object—or, indeed, to anything—then our physical head, upon the theory outlined, isn't anywhere. And the same, of course, must be true of our brains, which were said to be inside that head. And yet we are still told that percepts are "in our heads" and are part of the stuff of our physical brains. This, clearly, cannot be true in the final Russellian sense of these terms. A thing which is somewhere, namely, at a place in the space of perception, cannot be a member of a class of things none of which are in that space or anywhere else.

How little Mr. Russell himself, in his more cautious summaries of the outcome of his reasonings, professes to have reduced the content and process of experience to the terms and relations constituting the physical world may be seen, finally, in the sudden transformation which his assertion of the unity of the two undergoes, in the penultimate chapter of *The Analysis of Matter*. Here, too, it is true, the position reached is described in terms which obscure its actual outlines; but the exaggeration has now shifted to the other side. "On the question of the stuff of the world" the theory propounded, we are told, "has certain affinities with idealism." This, however, is simply an indirect way of saying that the theory propounded is dualism. For it includes an express rejection of both idealism and phenomenalism, *i. e.*, of the theses that *all* reality is "mental," or at all events cannot be affirmed not to be.[57]

[57] *Op. cit.*, pp. 215, 388; *Philosophy*, p. 290.

The "affinity" of the doctrine, with idealism consists merely in the assertion that *some* things that exist are mental. These things, it is true, are said to be in our heads; it is, in fact, now declared that "what is in our heads is the mind (with additions)." This *seems* equivalent to unsaying what has just been said; for a thing that is in the head, *i. e.,* is a part of a physical object in physical space, would not be "mental" in any usual sense of the term. But we have sufficiently seen that the only sense in which (in his main doctrine) Mr. Russell affirms that percepts are in physical space is that they have causal relations with physical objects.

It is, to be sure, added—as a further point of affinity with idealism—that in this theory "the part of the stuff of the world" that does not consist of mental events "resembles them more than it resembles the traditional billiard balls." By this is meant that in the newer physics the solid, persistent, moving atoms out of which the physical world was once supposed to be constituted have been replaced by transitory, non-moving, character-complexes, or "events," in a relativistic space-time. This seems to Mr. Russell to make matter "less material than is commonly supposed"; in the very latest developments of theoretical physics, "the last vestiges of the old solid atom have melted away, and matter has become as ghostly as anything in a spiritualist séance." In so far as recent physics conceives of the components of matter as entities having a very small finite duration, it undeniably imputes to them one attribute usually possessed also by percepts; but so far from increasing the points of likeness between the two *on the whole,* it immensely heightens—as we have seen—the contrast between them. The very "ghostliness" of the atom in the particular theories of atomic structure to which Mr. Russell here refers, is the sort of ghostliness which belongs to a mathematical formula; and there is nothing more unlike a mathematical formula than perceptual content—unless it be affective content. When the physicist's matter becomes, in this sense, more ghostly, it becomes far more dissimilar from the experienced part of the "stuff of which the world is composed" than were "the traditional billiard balls."

The old-fashioned atoms, though everlasting, were *like* some concrete objects of sensible experience, namely, billiard balls; but unperceived "events" in space-time, though short-lived, are like no concrete object of sensible experience. Between the two parts of reality there thus remains a wide and unconcealed cleavage.

The pretension to have unified the "stuff" of the world being definitely abandoned, the whole issue is abruptly—at the eleventh hour—shifted. It becomes, not a question of existential identity, or of similarity of attributes and relations, but of causal connection. The possibility of "bringing psychical events within the material of physics," proclaimed in the preamble, now implies only the existence of *one-way* causal relations between happenings in the two realms of being. The gist of the theory, in short, is reduced to an affirmation—and a rather less than half-hearted affirmation—of epiphenomenalism—which is, of course, a common form of psychophysical dualism. It is only in this point that "the position advocated has more affinity with materialism than with idealism"[58]—which, once more, is an "affinity" not incompatible with a formal rejection of the essential thesis of materialism. It is conceded that "the thoughts of Shakespeare or Bach do not come within the scope of physics." But "their thoughts are of no importance to us: their whole social efficacy depended upon certain black marks, which they made on white paper. Now there seems to be no reason to suppose that physics does not apply to the making of these marks, which was a movement of matter just as truly as the revolution of the earth in its orbit. . . . And no one can doubt that the causes of our emotions when we read Shakespeare or hear Bach are purely physical. Thus we cannot escape from the universality of physical causation."[59]

Into the question of the merits of epiphenomenalism it does not fall within the purpose of these lectures to enter; and there is the less occasion to do so because Mr. Russell at once proceeds to point out the possibility that "the minute phenomena in the brain

[58] *Analysis of Matter*, p. 388.
[59] *Ibid.*, p. 392. There seems to be here some relapse into billiard-ball physics.

which make all the difference to mental phenomena belong to the region where physical laws no longer determine definitely what must happen." [60] In other words, the universality of physical causation is admitted to be dubious. With these admissions the pretension to have "brought physics and perception together" so as to "include psychical events in the material of physics" is, surely, renounced altogether. But even if the denial of the efficacy of psychical events be maintained, the two realms still remain admittedly distinct, existentially and qualitatively, from one another.

It must, moreover, be borne in mind that it is only in a special and restricted sense that the adoption of epiphenomenalism (if it *were* adopted, as by Mr. Russell, in the end, it is not) would bring psychical events, even with respect to causal laws, within the scope of physics. From the assumption that all mental existents have physical causes it does not follow that they exemplify the laws of physics, *i.e.*, the laws supposed to hold good of the behavior of physical realities outside experience. The pink rats seen by a dipsomaniac have, as everyone agrees, physical causes; they owe their existence to some change in the brain produced by excessive ingestion of alcohol. But they do not possess physical properties, and they naturally, therefore, do not conform to physical laws. They have no mass; they do not enter into the equations of thermodynamics; you cannot predict their behavior by conceiving of *them* as constellations of electrons and protons. And if epiphenomenalism is true, their non-conformity to the causal laws of the physical world all the more clearly appears; for, upon that theory, though they are real existents, their existence and the changes occurring in them have no physical effects, whereas all physical events possess causal efficacy with respect to other such events. The same conclusions will hold for what are called veridical percepts, if percepts are what epistemological dualists (including Mr. Russell) say that they are. Physics, indeed, by employing its own methods and categories only, could never discover that *any* per-

60 *Ibid.*, p. 393.

cept will arise when a certain brain-change occurs, not to speak of discovering what particular percepts will arise. We ascertain this only, in Mr. Russell's phrase, "through the more intimate qualitative knowledge" which we possess concerning mental events. "A man who can see knows things which a blind man cannot know; but a blind man can know the whole of physics. Thus the knowledge which other men have and he has not is not part of physics." Hence "there will remain a certain sphere which will be outside physics"; [61] and this will be the entire sphere of mental events as such. Once again, then, the attempt to overcome the divorce between the world of perception and the world of physics only manifests more plainly the irremediable incompatibility between them.

The review which we have made of the course and issue of Mr. Russell's reasoning on the psychophysical problem seems to me eminently instructive. No philosopher of our time, as we have seen, has been more earnestly resolved to abolish "the distinction of physical and mental"; none, perhaps, has been better fitted to succeed in this enterprise, if success in it is possible; and none has more insistently and confidently assured us that success has been attained. And yet the universe which is depicted in his latest works consists—upon final analysis—of two mutually exclusive and wholly dissimilar classes of particular existents. To one of these belong all the sensible qualities, feelings, and thought-content; and though the entities composing this world are not in a single universal Newtonian space, certain among them, namely, those given through sight and touch, have spatial relations to one another. To the members of the other class we may not ascribe either sensible and affective qualities or, in the same sense of the term, spatial relations; in the sense in which they may be said to be in "space," they are in a different space. The members of the former world do not conform to physical laws; they are, in short, "outside physics." The first world is the world of experienced

[61] *Ibid.*, p. 389.

content; the other is the metempirical physical world behind the content and causally prior to it. A universe made up of two orders of being thus contrasted and thus related is in all essentials the familiar world of dualistic philosophy.

Thus far in our examination of Mr. Russell's later theory we have been considering chiefly its success as a logical device to enable us to conceive of the contents of perception, of memory, *etc.*, as parts of the physical world. The result has been to show that the device does not accomplish the purpose for which it was primarily designed. The experienced characters and relations of the content still prove irreconcilable with the properties of physical reality—and most plainly of all with those properties as Mr. Russell himself is disposed to define them. But we must now look at the theory that percepts and other content are "in our heads" from another aspect. Though propounded as a solution of the psychophysical problem, it obviously also has an epistemological liability: it must be such as to render the fact of knowledge intelligible, or at least conceivable. But this liability the theory does not meet. As a variety of the Hypodermic Philosophy, it is necessarily incapable of giving any account of the distinctive peculiarity of the biological phenomenon of knowing—*i.e.*, of the ability of the cognitive animal in some sense to reach outside his skin. For it implicitly denies that he does so. It places the entire material of his knowledge inside his head—or would so place it, if it were not that his head, too, disappears in the process. All that is presented in my perception, or in any cognition, being, upon this hypothesis, a bit of my brain, it is manifestly only my brain that I know—if, indeed, I can be supposed to know that. Not merely the qualities but also the relations of both perceived and inferred objects should, according to the theory, be embraced within those limits. Thus, for example, as we have seen, the space of my visual field is an intra-cranial space; and even the region of space or space-time which I think of as beyond the present momentary "event" which is my head, must itself, *as content,* be within my head.

Yet Mr. Russell himself is, on occasion, equally insistent upon the transcendence of the object of perception or of inferential knowledge. The causal theory of perception which he holds manifestly implies this. If I know that there is a somewhat—however vague qualitatively it may be—which acts upon my brain and there produces certain effects, that somewhat, at least, must be other than its effect and must be spatio-temporally exterior to my brain; and my ability to conceive of it, and to frame a (by hypothesis) true judgment about it, therefore signifies that I somehow lay hold upon something that is not within my head. Mr. Russell thus presents us with two incompatible views about the position of the visual *cognoscendum* relatively to the body of the knower. When he is preoccupied with the psychophysical problem he arrives—under the influence of his desire to unify the mental and the physical—at a conclusion on this point which contradicts the conviction to which he is led by his reflection on the problem of perceptual knowledge—the conviction which is "as certain as anything in science." His particular form of psychophysical monism, in short, is at variance with his epistemological dualism. And the significance of this lies in the fact that his form of psychophysical monism is not only one of the typical forms, but is also—as our previous analyses seem to show—the last hope, of that sort of philosophy. Finding, after many futile wanderings, no other place to go in the physical order, the percept (with all other content) sought refuge, under Mr. Russell's guidance, within the skull of the perceiver. But once shut up there, it could in no manner get out again; and it thereby lost all value for cognitive purposes. Intra-corporeal solipsism is thus the logical outcome of this last ingenious effort to give the whole content of our experience a habitation in the physical world. Now intra-corporeal solipsism is a self-contradictory doctrine; it cannot be defined without implying a space and time beyond the present bodily event within which everything that is ever apprehended is, nevertheless, declared to be contained. But even if the contradiction inherent in such a conception be passed over, this last recourse of psychophysical monism is equivalent to a denial of the possibility of a knowledge

of the external—in this case, the spatially external—world. For
the awareness of the transcendence of the object, upon which Mr.
Russell, when writing as an epistemologist, justly insists, cannot
be defined in physical terms. The bare local presence in my brain
of certain bits of quasi-material stuff, even though they are clothed
with all the sensible qualities, does not constitute an apprehension of a universe of extra-cranial realities—which nevertheless
must be apprehended, if I am even to be entitled to say that it is
in anything intelligibly describable as my brain that those "parts
of the physical world" have their being.

VIII

DUALISM AND THE PHYSICAL WORLD

Our inquiry thus far has been concerned almost wholly with a hypothetical question. It is primarily with hypothetical questions that philosophical inquiries ought, I think, to be concerned. Philosophy would proceed with a somewhat steadier gait, and agreement among philosophers would come about more rapidly, if they would oftener put the problems they discuss, and especially those they first discuss, expressly in this form: If certain things (which some philosophers or other men believe) are provisionally taken as true, what other things must be or may be true? A great part of philosophy,, in other words, should consist of attempts to determine what sets of propositions, in certain fields of investigation, properly go together. It is not natural to philosophers, as a rule, to attack their problems in this manner; for they are likely to be eagerly absorbed in the question of the truth of the protases —the prior and supposedly more fundamental propositions decision about the tenability of which the method of hypothetical inquiry postpones. But the haste of many philosophers to settle what appear to be the more fundamental issues first, and their consequent reluctance to discuss in a spirit of scientific detachment questions of the mere congruity of suppositions, has been highly detrimental to philosophy. It tends, for one thing, to bring the more controversial and less soluble problems to the fore from the start, and thus renders effective intellectual coöperation between philosophers having different convictions on fundamental and (supposedly) non-hypothetical questions difficult and unusual. The idealist, for example, is not commonly much interested in the special problems of the realist; why should he be—he is likely to ask—since those problems arise only in consequence of presuppositions which he is quite sure are false and even absurd? And the realist often more than reciprocates this attitude. If both could be persuaded to refrain for a time from raising the prior question and to collaborate in good faith in working out the implications and possibilities of both presuppositions, the moment of divergence and mutual incomprehensibility would at least be deferred, and by this less direct attack upon the fundamental issues we should, I suspect, be more likely to arrive in the end at a settlement of them. In any case it might well be that by such a method philosophy would presently come to consist chiefly of a large and well-defined body of hypothetical conclusions—concerning the consequences of certain postulates or the compatibility of various sets of theorems—about which there was an approach to general agreement among philosophers, together with a small number of ultimate categorical questions about which agreement was found to be unattainable. And it might, in that case, be plausibly conjectured that these residual disagreements were not unconnected with incorrigible diversities of temperament or mental type amongst philosophers.

To have reduced the content of philosophy even to this degree of order and conclusiveness would assuredly be a great gain. We should then be able in some fashion to answer the question which, as Professor Hocking has reminded us, the ingenuous undergraduate and the general public are always and altogether naturally putting to the philosophic teacher: "What does Philosophy say?" Our answer would then be "Philosophy, by the consensus of nearly all who have devoted methodical thought to its problems, says quite definitely a number of things; but what it thus says relates in all cases to what you necessarily must or reasonably may believe *if* you believe certain other things of a logically more fundamental sort. But for the present Philosophy, if the term implies such a consensus among philosophers, cannot say whether these logically prior things ought or ought not to be believed; and the history of man's reflective experience gives some ground for the surmise that there are congenital diversities among human minds which render generally convincing argument with respect to these latter questions impossible. On these matters, then, Philosophy remains, and perhaps must permanently remain, silent, though philosophers are, and will doubtless continue to be, voluble. On such issues, then, if you feel it needful to hold any opinion about them, you must make your own option, in accordance with the particular mental constitution with which Nature has endowed you."

I do not mean, by indicating this as an outcome to which, even at worst, such a method of procedure in philosophy might lead, to express a settled opinion that nothing more is possible. It would be hasty to assume, in the present state of the evidence and after man's very brief and very ill-conducted reflective experience, that a gradual convergence of views even upon the prior questions cannot be hoped for. But if that is a possibility, the best road even to it, I suggest, is through the discussion and clarification of the sort of hypothetical questions mentioned. For this procedure consists in systematically and comprehensively working out the implications of provisional postulates; and a postulate which to a certain type of mind may seem overwhelmingly alluring and conclusive, when considered in itself, will often, even to the same mind, appear plainly absurd or contrary to facts of experience when its total consequences are made explicit. The history of philosophy is strewn with the wrecks of supposedly self-evident truths which, when their full meaning was developed, proved to be in fact self-contradictory. The great trouble with philosophy has been that so many philosophers have been the sort of men who fall in love with an idea at first sight. Whether, then, philosophy is destined to reach generally convincing conclusions only upon its hypothetical questions, or also upon the fundamental categorical questions, in either case it would, I think, be favorable to its progress towards its attainable goal if the usual order of procedure were reversed and the hypothetical issues—the probably more manageable problems as to the logical connections and affinities of various opinions—were dealt with first.

Whatever the truth or falsity of these incidental observations about the method of philosophical inquiry, it is, at all events, this method that has been followed in these lectures. We have not, so far, been asking whether dualism of the one sort or the other is true; we have been asking only whether, when the existence of a real and at least in some measure knowable physical world is postulated, either sort of dualism can be avoided without contradiction either of the implications of realism itself or of admitted facts. Can—we have been inquiring—all or any of the content actually and indubitably given in perception or other forms of supposedly cognitive experience be believed to be identical with the independently existing realities with which, upon the realistic hypothesis, these data enable us to become to some extent acquainted; and, if the notion of a physical order is defined in certain very general terms which seem to express the essentials of the common conception of physical reality, can these data, and all the rest of the content of experience, be conceived to find a place in that order? In short, can a realistic philosophy dispense with the hypothesis of the existence of ideas—in approximately though not quite precisely the sense in which that term was commonly used by the philosophers of the seventeenth century? The hypothetical character of this question does not, of course, mean that it is artificial, arbitrary, or unimportant. It happens that the greater part of mankind, and, in particular, most men of science, are still believers in a physical world; it is therefore not superfluous to inquire upon what terms that belief may consistently be held. And if a negative answer to the question propounded is reached —if it can be shown that a non-dualistic realism is an impossible kind of realism—this is manifestly equivalent to proof of a far-reaching conclusion, transcending the scope of the hypothetical question—a proof, namely, that the proposition "ideas (in this sense) exist" is a necessary part of *nearly* every possible sort of philosophy.[1] For it is, of course, only from the standpoint of realism that that proposition is likely to be challenged, since the idealist is convinced *ab initio* that ideas, together with minds and their acts, make up the whole sum of existence. To make it evident to everybody that "ideas" are in fact indispensable in the realist's world as well as the idealist's would be to reëstablish peace over a considerable part of the troubled domain of philosophy—a part in which peace had reigned, with but one or two slight interruptions, from the beginning of modern philosophy until the present century.

Our review of the grounds, the principal vicissitudes, and the outcome of the contemporary revolt against dualism seems to me to have put us in a position to give a fairly definite and confident answer to this hypothetical question. We have been observing a species of experimental test of the logical possibility of a physical realism which shall also be an epistemological or a psychophysical monism, or both. The attempt to bring the experiment successfully to a positive issue has, we have seen, been carried on during the last thirty years with extraordinary persistency and ingenuity. The thing has been tried by many philosophers and in many different ways; there has been no lack of speculative courage or imagination or logical subtlety in the conduct of the enterprise. Regardless of the outcome, those who have taken part in the experiment have rendered a substantial service to philosophy. For, as we have already recognized, realistic epistemological monism and realistic psychophysical monism are ways of thinking about knowledge and about the nature of things which have great *prima facie* plausibility. Both hypotheses are normally and quite intel-

---

[1] If by "idea" is meant—as I here mean—a non-physical experienced particular, a philosophy which held all content to consist of universals would not, obviously, admit the existence of ideas, and would not be a psychophysical dualism. But if it were combined with a physical realism and assumed physical reals to be particulars, it would still be a form of dualism, both in the epistemological and metaphysical senses. A sceptical phenomenalist might hold that we have no means of judging whether or not the data of experience are identical with physical objects, if—which we also cannot know—there happen to exist physical objects. This would be equivalent to the proposition "experienced content may consist only of ideas, and must be treated by the philosopher and scientific theorist as if it did, though we cannot be sure that it does."

ligibly attractive to the reflective mind, or at least to certain types of reflective mind; it is natural to wish that they might prove to be legitimate combinations of beliefs. For each, if it could be shown to accord with itself and with the indications of experience and the necessary presuppositions of knowledge, would seem to promise an immense simplification and unification of our understanding of the constitution of nature as a whole and of our place and rôle in it. It is therefore a great advantage to have had a mode of thought to which the human mind will always have a natural inclination tried out so energetically, tenaciously and resourcefully as it has been in our generation.

But our examination of these efforts seems to show that the result of the experiment is negative. The logical elements which so many philosophers, since our century began, have been trying to synthetize into a coherent body of doctrine, refuse to combine. Where they are not directly at variance with one another, they are at variance with empirical facts, or with inferences from empirical facts which realistic philosophers who believe that natural science gives us some probable information about an external world, cannot consistently deny. Neither knowledge nor nature seems to be quite so simple, unitary, and transparent a thing, nor the phenomenon of knowing so much all-of-a-piece with the rest of nature, as it would, in many respects, be agreeable and convenient to believe; indeed, the very hypotheses which seemed to promise such simplification and clarification have proved, when their implications were drawn out, to give us a picture of the world more confusedly mixed, more unintelligibly heterogeneous, and less congruous with the working presuppositions of natural science, than the theories for which they were to have been substituted. The failure of the enterprise of monistic realism has been exhibited, not merely through the analyses and criticisms which have here been applied to its main arguments and to its explicit or implicit consequences, but also through the actual course of the movement, the abandonment, by those most eager to defend an ostensibly monistic philosophy, of its key-positions, and eventually of all of its essentials, so that in the end these philosophers seemed to be merely repeating a formula which had lost all distinctive and important meaning. The constructive part of the attempted revolution began with a thorough and drastic program; the literal identity of the data of perception with the object of knowledge, and of all data, "wild" and tame, with true parts of the physical world, was asserted unqualifiedly and unequivocally—though even in that phase of the movement, it must be admitted, not quite unwaveringly. But this bold program ended quite literally, as the second lecture pointed out, in chaos: the account of the make-up of the physical world which, when worked out consistently, it implied, proved unbelievable, while the account which it gave of knowledge proved inconsistent with itself, with the assumption of the possibility of perceptual or other error, and with the conclusions of physics and physiology, which this sort of realism was committed to accepting, as to the manner in which percepts are conditioned. Though this program still finds some faithful adherents, most of the later champions of an ostensibly monistic realism have abandoned it, tacitly or explicitly, and have admitted, or strongly insisted upon, "the relativity of experienced data to percipient events." This seemed on its face to be, not a repudiation of dualism, but a confession of faith in it; and though the equivocality of the terms employed, and the introduction of ingenious if obscure supplementary hypotheses, seem to have enabled a number of contemporary philosophers who accept this or similar formulas to suppose that it is neither a dualistic nor an idealistic creed that they are uttering, when the actual logical content of their conclusions is examined the supposition appears ill-founded.

The probative force of such a survey of the results of these attempts of representative realistic philosophers to escape dualism depends, it is true, upon whether the actual attempts may fairly be supposed to exhaust the logically possible ways of going about the business. But with respect to the main point it is clear, I think, that our review has covered·the typical possibilities. For evidently there are only two general ways of conceiving of the relation of the constitution of the physical world to the characters of the content of perception. What are called physical entities or events may either be supposed to possess the same kinds of characters as percepts and images and to be in the same spatial and temporal order with them (or in the same type of spatial and temporal order), or they may be supposed not to do so. Both alternatives have been considered, since both have been represented among the types of realism current and influential in the past quarter of a century. Pan-objectivism was an attempt to carry out thoroughly and consistently the former supposition. It postulated from the outset, not only that there are existents not conditioned by percipient or cognitive events and that in perception we are apprehending such existents, but also that all the attributes of the percept as experienced, and all its relations except that of being experienced, independently characterize such objects. That the attempt was unsuccessful, that it proved impossible to avoid either sort of dualism, even with premises thus fashioned for the purpose, has been shown. The only other possible supposition, with regard to the same question, is that some or all perceptual and quasi-perceptual data differ, in greater or less degree, from the entities composing the physical world; that they have qualities which physical entities do not have, or are characterized by certain modes of relatedness (other than their relation to a percipient) which no physical entity possesses, or lack certain modes of relatedness which all physical entities possess. That *some* view of the second general type must be adopted has—as the first lecture pointed out—seemed evident to most men from a very early stage in the history of reflection. It seemed evident because the object of perceptual knowledge was assumed to be independent and common, *i.e.,* not variant with the diversities of its relations to various percipients, and to be operative in a uniform causal order; while the simplest experiences of perspective and other illusions showed that at least a great part of visual, auditory, and other content is not independent and common, and that many of the characters thus diversely experienced cannot be supposed to be effective factors in a uniform causal order.

Broadly speaking—and excluding, in particular, the recent episode of neo-realism—the entire subsequent history of reflection on the question has been marked by a deepening of this cleavage between the two kinds of existents, and by the exclusion from the physical world of an ever-increasing number of the experienced characters and relations of the data of sense-perception. This tendency, initiated through the pressure of the considerations just mentioned, has been intensified in modern thought through the influence of a theoretical motive potent in seventeenth-century science—the desire to conceive of a physical universe susceptible of purely mathematical treatment. In recent natural philosophy the same tendency has been driven to still greater lengths through certain specific developments in theoretical physics resulting, or supposed to result, from definite experimental discoveries—i. e., through the theory of relativity and the quantum theory. The second possible supposition, in short, naturally resolves itself into an identification of the postulated "real physical objects" with "scientific objects"; and scientific objects are now more unlike perceived objects than they have ever before been in the history of science. They have not only been divested of almost all qualities of the kind given in sense-experience, but have also been translated into a world of which nearly all the distinctive and constitutive relations are not those which perceptual data are experienced as possessing. If current physics is taken as a description of the objective physical order—as earlier physics was commonly taken by realistic philosophers and men of science—then the disparateness of the two realms of being is greater than had ever before been supposed, and the impossibility of believing in their identity is so much the more evident. It is one of the major ironies of the history of philosophy that the beginning of the revolt of many realistic philosophers against dualism almost precisely corresponded in time with the discoveries, and the resultant introduction of new theories, in physics which tended to make dualism (of both sorts) seem more than ever unavoidable. Nevertheless, a valiant and ingenious effort to show that the acceptance of the most extreme of these most recent developments in physics is compatible with a realistic psychophysical monism has been made, in the later doctrine of Russell. This, too, we have examined; and if our reasoning was correct, this effort also has failed to achieve its object—and failed for reasons inherent in the nature of the enterprise. It is, of course, evident—the point is worth repeating —that even a view of the second type which stops short of these extremes is psychophysically dualistic in principle; if *any* class of data is admitted to have characters foreign to the physical world, or to fail to conform to physical laws, nature is *eo ipso* bifurcated. And when *some* content is recognized as non-physical, there are, we have seen, evident reasons for including (at the least) all visual sense-data and all images in the non-physical class, and therefore for denying their identity with any parts of the external world about which we may be supposed to receive by means of them most of our information. In every direction, then, escape from either dualism seems to be blocked for the realistic philosopher.

In arriving, by means of this review, at a reasoned conclusion with respect to these questions, we have reached the principal objective proposed at the beginning of these lectures. The revolt— within the realistic provinces of philosophical opinion—against dualism, both psychophysical and epistemological, has failed. The content of our actual experience does not consist wholly, and it is unprovable and improbable that any part of it consists, of entities which, upon *any* plausible theory of the constitution of the physical world, can be supposed to be members of that world; it consists of particulars which arise through the functioning of percipient organisms, are present only within the private fields of awareness of such organisms, are destitute of certain of the essential properties and relations implied either by the historic concept of the "physical" or by the contemporary physicist's concept of it, and possess properties which physical things lack. They *are*, in short, essentially of the nature of "ideas," as Descartes and Locke (for the most part) used that term. And it is through these entities that any knowledge which we may attain of the concrete characters of the physical world, and of any other realities extraneous to our several private fields of awareness, must be mediated; so that we are brought back to Locke's conclusion, despite the heroic efforts of so many philosophers of our age to escape from it: "it is evident that the mind knows not things immediately, but by the intervention of the ideas it has of them." If the word "nature" is used—though I think it is unhappily so used—to mean exclusively the world as it is, or may conceivably be, apart from all experience, *i. e.,* apart from the processes of conscious perception and thought and phantasy and feeling, then between "nature" and experience there is a radical discontinuity; for the occurrence of those processes adds to the sum of reality not only particular existents, but kinds of existents, which "nature"—if so defined—though it engenders them, cannot plausibly be supposed to contain.

It may, however, seem that the triumph of dualism has been all too complete, that these arguments explode the foundations of all realism. Especially may the developments in recent physics to which I have referred appear to some to have this effect. The question that now presses for consideration, it may be said, is no longer whether (as the pan-objectivist happily and innocently supposed) everything we perceptually experience is "objective" and "physical," but whether *anything* we experience is (even in the epistemological sense) objective and revelatory of the nature of the physical world. The theory of relativity is generally conceived to have rendered dubious and equivocal, if not to have disproved, the spatiality of physical objects in their macroscopic aspect; and the latest hypotheses concerning the minute components of "matter" and their relation to energy-quanta to have, so to say, disembodied matter itself. And what is left is a set of mathematical formulas useful for predicting the sequences of perceptions, but which many physicists find it impossible to construe as descriptions of physical reality. Thus Jeans, speaking of intra-atomic processes and of radiation, writes: "It is difficult to form even the remotest conception of the realities underlying all these phenomena. . . . Indeed, it may be doubted whether we shall ever properly understand the realities involved; they may well be so fundamental as to be beyond the grasp of the human mind." [2] Similarly Eddington concludes his recent summary of the philosophical implications — and non-implications — of contemporary science by assuring us that all that physics has to report about external nature is that "something unknown is doing we don't know what"; that when, for example, we see an elephant sliding down a hill, the impression of the "bulkiness" of the elephant which we experience "presumably has some direct counterpart in the external world," but that this "counterpart must be of a nature beyond our apprehension," and that "science can make nothing of it." Or, as Eddington alternatively suggests, it is possible that "our final conclusion as to the world of physics will resemble Kronecker's view of pure mathematics: 'God made the integers; all else is the work of man.'" [3]

This new agnosticism among the physicists, then, manifestly verges upon phenomenalism, and it thus seems to threaten the position of the psychophysical dualist from another side. So little seems to be left of the physical world of the older realism that the residuum may appear hardly worth salvaging. Thus the result, not merely of the present discussion, but of recent reflection in general, will doubtless be regarded by idealists as tending to vindicate *their* type of monism. It will appear to them that if it can be shown from realistic premises that the only internally possible kind of realism is a dualistic realism, then it is by so much the more evident that no kind of realism is tenable. What has been exhibited in the foregoing lectures, they will be likely to say, is the pleasing and instructive spectacle of the armies of realistic philosophy marching up the hill and then marching down again,

[2] *The Universe Around Us*, p. 128.
[3] *The Nature of the Physical World*, pp. 291, 253, 246.

to pretty much the position which had been reached at the beginning of the eighteenth century—a position which at that time had already been shown to be incapable of defense against the idealist's attack. If it is admitted that, as Locke declared, "the mind, in all its thoughts and reasonings, hath no immediate object but its own ideas," then the consequences which Locke's successors drew from this proposition must, we shall be told, again be drawn. And if the new physics—also setting out from realistic preconceptions—reduces the so-called physical universe to a bare x, of which we can say, at most, only that there must be in it *some* difference corresponding to every difference in our perceptual content, then the term "physical," as applied to it, ceases to have any distinctive meaning.

In this situation it seems worth while to consider afresh what reasons—other than "instincts," to which some realists seem to me to appeal too simply—can be given for believing that there is a world of existing particulars which are nobody's "ideas"—which, in other words, are independent of awareness—and to ask how much, or what sort, of knowledge of that world it is permissible to suppose that we can attain. But before entering upon these questions, I must again emphasize the fact that they lie beyond the main argument of these lectures. Whatever our conclusion with respect to them, the answer to our original hypothetical question remains unaffected. If no good grounds for believing in a physical world can be offered, that will be no reason for reconsidering that answer. A philosopher can but follow where the argument leads; the considerations upon which our conclusions were based were not such that they would be invalidated by the discovery that they entail a further unintended and undesired consequence.

The case for physical realism should not, I think, be made to rest primarily or wholly—as it is by Russell in his later period—upon the assumed necessity of postulating external causal objects to account for our percepts—objects about which we can infer no more than that there are differences of some kind in them, corresponding numerically, but not necessarily or probably in their qualities, to the differences between percepts. It is true that if there *are* external objects, and if they cannot be identical with our data, we must be able to infer so much, at least, about them, if we are to base any judgments whatever concerning them upon perception. And it is also true that our disposition to assume that our experiences have causes is somewhat too disparagingly described when it is called mere "animal faith." It is a faith, indeed; but—in the form represented in the phase of Mr. Russell's philosophy to which I have referred—it is a highly critical and extremely attenuated faith. And it is a part of the general faith that reality has a greater degree of orderliness, of interconnection of parts, and therefore of intelligibility, than is manifested in the confused phantasmagoria of unsupplemented sensation. But it is not the primary form of that faith; it is derivative from something more fundamental. For there is no obvious gain in the coherency and intelligibility of the world if you merely take an isolated momentary bit of perceptual content and assert concerning it: This must have had a cause external in some sense to itself.

The more fundamental postulate to which I refer—and the better reason for accepting realism—will begin to appear if we consider what the "independence" which might be ascribed to physical reals, and would constitute the first essential of their physicality, would be. It would have to do primarily with the *time* of their existence. Consciousness in general, and the consciousness of this or that sensible object in particular, is fluctuating and intermittent. For you an object now exists and now does not exist; when you are in deep sleep or a swoon the whole world is non-existent. The primary function of "real objects," the way in which the belief in them helps us to regard the universe as more coherent than sense-experience, consists (as was implied in our definition of the notion of a "physical world") in their filling the temporal gaps between actual perceptions. The "independence" of a thing means, concretely, its continued existence, or the continuance of a connected series of events of which it is a member, at times when it is not being attended to by me, nor necessarily by any one like me. The starting-point of the argument for physical realism, I suggest, is the plain man's normal and reasonable belief that the processes of nature do not stop when he stops noticing them. It is not the "outerness" of the object perceived, *when* it is perceived, but the *persistence of something which is in some manner connected with what is perceived, during the interperceptual intervals,* that is the primary natural postulate out of which the belief in an external world, in objects which exist though they are not given in experience, arises. How irrepressible this belief is may be judged from the emphatic affirmation of it even by phenomenalists who ostensibly refuse to admit any metempirical realities. Thus Petzoldt, after declaring that "there is no scientific meaning in the assumption that there exists behind experience something-or-other as its bearer or generator," forthwith proceeds to castigate those who will not believe in "a perdurance of objects which is independent of us"—who fail to regard the fact that "things always turn up again quite independently of whether I have had my eyes open or not, at the place they previously had, or at some place wholly independent of my thought."[4] Petzoldt, in short, apparently finds it superfluous to suppose that there are any common and independent realities behind our experiences, but impossible to conceive that there are none between our experiences.

It will be observed, incidentally, that a realism which takes this as its starting point is of necessity epistemologically dualistic. The "independence" thus ascribed to real existents is primarily the status of not-being-now-present-to-consciousness; but it must nevertheless be now apprehended, we must be able to mean something by it—if dualistic or any other realism is even thinkable; and therefore it must be apprehended indirectly. Any so-called "independence" which an object might be said to possess *while* being perceived or thought-of would be merely a potential inde-

4 *Das Weltproblem vom positivistischen Standpunkte aus,* p. 138.

pendence—a capacity to go on being when unperceived or un-thought-of.

The belief in the continuance of things or processes between perceptions is not a blank act of faith, as would be the postulation of an external causal object for a single momentary percept; it may be said to be—not, indeed, rigorously verified—but strength-ened by one of the most familiar of empirical facts—namely, that the same uniform causal sequences of natural events which may be observed within experience appear to go on in the same man-ner when not experienced. You build a fire in your grate of a certain quantity of coal, of a certain chemical composition. When-ever you remain in the room there occurs a typical succession of sensible phenomena according to an approximately regular sched-ule of clock-time; in, say, a half-hour the coal is half consumed; at the end of the hour the grate contains only ashes. If you build a fire of the same quantity of the same material under the same conditions, leave the room, and return after any given time has elapsed, you get approximately the same sense-experiences as you would have had at the corresponding moment if you had remained in the room. You infer, therefore, that the fire has been burning as usual during your absence, and that being perceived is not a condition necessary for the occurrence of the process. But a con-sistent idealist or phenomenalist cannot say this. He is committed to the proposition either that the fire has not been or, at all events, cannot legitimately be assumed to have been, burning when no one was perceiving it; his doctrine amounts to a gratuitous as-sumption of the universal jumpiness or temporal discontinuity of causal sequences. The most that he can admit—and he cannot admit less—is that fires and other natural processes behave *as if* they went on when unobserved; if he desires to make this seem more intelligible, he may invoke some pre-established harmony, or resort to species of occasionalism—assuming that when you return to the room after an hour God (as Descartes would have said) deceives you by putting into your mind a percept of a grate full of ashes, though *these* ashes are not the effects of any fire.

But such "explanations" of the facts are plainly arbitrary and far-fetched; they multiply types of causal agency beyond necessity. And to be content with a mere *Philosophie des Als-Ob* in such a case—to say that, although nothing at all that was like a fire or would have caused you to perceive a fire, if you had remained in the room, was really happening while you were absent, nevertheless all goes on as though the fire had been burning during that interval—this, surely, is a singularly strained and artificial notion, wholly foreign to the normal propensities of our intelligence.

Naïve realism, however, infers more from this type of fact than is warranted; it supposes that while you were not in the room *exactly the same* phenomena were going on as you would have experienced had you been there—the play of color in the flames, the qualities experienced by you in thermal sensation, and so on. To suppose this is to assume that certain of the factors in the case —namely, your presence in the room and your psychophysical constitution—make no difference in the content of your experience. This positive assumption of the complete irrelevance of certain actual antecedents or concomitants of a given effect is not only gratuitous and improbable, but is in conflict with familiar empirical evidences of the concomitant variation of sense-data with differences in the perceptible natures or states of percipients. What is reasonably inferrible is that some process capable of causing an organism constituted as you are, to have the perceptual experience of a burning fire, has been continuously going on while you were not in such relations to it as actually to perceive any fire. The causal theory of perception is thus derivative from, not logically prior to, the postulate of the continuance of the orderly sequences of nature during interperceptual intervals. The world of external causal entities or events is the world that you are obliged to assume when you accept the evidence for such continuance, while recognizing the probability that your own makeup, as a body or a mind or both, plays some part in determining the qualitative character of your percepts. The specific qualities characteristic of the potentially unperceived, that is, interperceptual, process, remain, so far as these considerations go, undetermined; you cannot, thus far, tell how much of what you experience is due to external events, how much to the nature of "that which is acted upon" by these events. But this does not weaken the reasons for believing that there *are* such temporally persistent and therefore independent events. Matter, or the physical order, still remains, not only as, in Mill's phrase, " a permanent possibility of sensation," but as a continuing existent capable of causing sensations under certain circumstances.

Before inquiring further whether we can plausibly ascribe any physical attributes more definite than these to the persistent causal background of our intermittent and confused sense-experience, it will be well to examine the contention, already mentioned, that, *if* we cannot do so, we ought to ascribe "mental" attributes to it —in other words, that the entities and events, really composing the fire, after *our* psychic additions to it are subtracted, are of the nature of "mind stuff." The burden of proof, of course, rests upon those who assert this. I shall here consider only the most recent attempt to sustain this burden.

The principal argument for the proposition that the external world consists of mind-stuff, as presented by Eddington, seems to be as follows: "The physical atom, like everything else in physics, is a schedule of pointer readings." Pointer readings are, of course, simply a certain class of actual or potential sense-data in which physicists happen to be especially interested. Now "the schedule," *i. e.,* this class of data (as well as others), "is, we agree, attached to some unknown background." But in one case the background is not unknown. "For the pointer readings of my own brain I have an insight which is not limited to the evidence of the pointer readings. That insight shows that they are attached to a background of consciousness." Hence, "if we must embed our schedule of indicator readings in some kind of background, at least let us accept the only hint we have received as to the significance of the background—namely, that it has a nature capable of manifesting itself as mental activity." Let us, in other words, attach the background "to something of a spiritual nature of which the prominent characteristic is *thought*."[5]

Now there is in this, in the first place, an ambiguity. What is meant by "the pointer readings of my own brain"? Does it mean any actual, *i. e.*, sensible pointer readings of which I am aware by means (as it would be ordinarily expressed) of the functioning of my brain, or does it mean solely the pointer readings which I get when I am observing the processes supposed to take place *in* a brain not my own? If the former meaning is intended, it is not, in fact, true that the *background* of the percepts is known to be "consciousness." When the physicist is observing a pointer reading, *i. e.*, experiencing a percept so describable, the "background" of this percept presumably is *not* his act or state of being conscious of it. His consciousness is, no doubt, concomitant with, and a condition of, its presence in his experience. But when we speak of a "background" we mean something which is, so to say, on the other side of the percept; we presuppose three factors in the situation, *viz.*, the physicist's consciousness, the given perceptual content, and a *tertium quid* which underlies the content, is the cause or condition of the presentation of that particular bit of content to his consciousness, and is the member of this trinity which would remain if *his* consciousness, and therewith its immediate content, were eliminated. And we have no evidence at all that the third factor is of the same nature as the first. If it were initially postulated that the observer's consciousness is the sole and sufficient condition of the existence of the percept, that all that is involved in the situation is his consciousness *plus* the percept, the supposition of a "background" would be excluded. If it is not excluded, if there is assumed to be an entity which presents itself for his awareness under the guise of the percept, why should this also be a consciousness? Why should the percept have consciousness on *both* sides of it? No reason for thinking that it need do so seems to be offered.

The alternative possible interpretation of the argument is that

---

[5] *The Nature of the Physical World*, pp. 259, 260.

it relates to percepts *of* brains.[6]   Of "my own brain" I do not, of course, have any direct perception; but other persons, such as brain-physiologists, might conceivably have percepts of it, and in so far as these are percepts of metrical properties of it, they may be called indicator readings. In this case, the situation would be that certain of *their* percepts are supposed to be evidence of the occurrence of the phenomenon of consciousness in me; that they are such, the physiologists could learn only by my telling them so, or through inferences—based upon generalizations from previous experience, all of which ultimately rest upon such verbal reports —from my behavior. If this is the argument intended, it manifestly leaves much to be desired as an inductive proof.   It consists in inferring, from the fact that one small class of percepts are associated with consciousness, the conclusion that *all* percepts of any percipient *are* consciousnesses, and that consciousness is thus the universal character of the background of our percepts. The inference is hardly coercive, nor does it appear to have any assignable degree of probability.

It is, however, supported by a consideration drawn from the presumption of continuity. "It seems," observes Eddington, "rather silly to prefer to attach to the background something of a so-called 'concrete' nature, and then to wonder where the thought comes from." But unfortunately the mind-stuff theory leaves us still wondering where the "thought"—of the kind that we experience—comes from; it affords no real escape from the recognition of discontinuities. For mind-stuff is not supposed to be the same kind of thing as either data or the awareness of them; it is not assumed to have "the more specialized attributes of consciousness"; it is below even "subconsciousness"; "only here and there," we are told, "does it rise to the level of consciousness"; and it is not, according to Eddington, "spread in space and time,"[7]

[6] That this is more probably the view which Eddington intends to express is indicated by his approving citation (p. 278) of a famous thesis of W. K. Clifford's: "The succession of feelings which constitutes a man's consciousness is the reality which produces in our minds the perception of his brain."
[7] *Ibid.*, pp. 260, 280, 277.

whereas our consciousness assuredly is spread in time and our visual and tactual sensa in space. It is very difficult, therefore, to understand what can be meant by the assertions that it "is of a nature continuous with that revealed to me" in a case of visual or other perception, and that we can "more or less successfully construct the rest of the external world" in terms of mind-stuff from our acquaintance with "our own ends of the fibres of it which run into our consciousness."[8] Such a reconstruction would certainly not lead us to conceive it as composed of mind-stuff. For it would be very odd that it should manifest itself to us, *not* in our consciousness, but in our content, *i. e.*, that it should be the "background" of our sense-data. There is nothing more unlike consciousness than a sense-datum. The emergence in experience of such perceptual objects as a pointer reading, a brain, or a motor-car, remains at least as mysterious from the standpoint of the hypothesis that the reality behind these, that which "produces" such percepts "in our minds," consists of non-spatial and non-temporal consciousnesses or "feelings," as from any other standpoint. Such a theory obviously offers us no hypothetical explanation, of a scientifically serviceable sort, of the actual characters, diversities, and laws of connection, of our perceptual content. It seems better to leave the background of the perceptible world indeterminate, if we must, rather than to adopt a hypothesis concerning it which rests upon an inductive inference so peculiar, and renders the relation of the external world to the data of experience less rather than more intelligible. Neither, then, the arguments examined, nor, I think, any others which have ever been propounded, present convincing reasons for holding that the perduring independent background of our sensory content consists either of other such content of wholly unknown percipients, or of other consciousnesses, which by some unknown sort of action upon us cause our sense-data. In the absence of such reasons, we do well either to proceed upon the hypothesis that the cosmical back-

[8] *Ibid.*, p. 278.

ground is of a non-mental sort or to admit our ignorance as to its nature.

Are we, then, driven to this latter admission? Are we, in other words, left in that state of near-agnosticism about the external world which is exemplified by the utterances of certain physicists which have been quoted and by the later theory of Mr. Bertrand Russell? Is it the case that either (a) we have no reasons for believing that the background has *any* of the attributes and modes of relatedness characteristic of perceptible objects, *e. g.*, of our visual or tactual data, with the possible exception of causality and discrete multiplicity, or (b) that we have decisive reasons for believing that it has not any such attributes or modes of relatedness —so that it would be inadmissible even to accept such a belief as a provisional postulate? The usual position of the dualistic realist in the past—and until a very recent time—has, of course, been that there are some reasons for ascribing to the physical world a few of the more fundamental characteristics of the world of perception, and that, even if these reasons are not rigorously probative, the belief in question is a natural assumption which no one can prove to be false. He has held that physical things must, indeed, be denied all the characters which vary with percipients— which are manifestly functions of standpoints; and that there is no good reason for supposing that such characters as color, sensible temperature, odor, and the like, exist apart from sensation; but that there is a residuum of properties—extension, shape, relative position, temporal succession, motion—which may plausibly be regarded as characterizing the components of independent physical reality. And the reason—other than "instinct" or "animal faith"—given for crediting the physical world with these characteristics has been that, by doing so, we could apparently frame a coherent, simple, unifying, scientifically serviceable set of hypotheses as to the nature of the relatively few causal processes which determine our manifold individual sense-data and explain both their diversities and their uniformities—the sort of hypotheses exemplified by the ordinary optical theory of perspective, refraction, *etc.* This position is represented, so lately as 1925, by Broad's *The Mind and its Place in Nature.* Mr. Broad in that work argues that if we "study carefully and in detail," the nature of our sensa and their correlations, we find reason to conceive the physical world "as a spatial whole on the analogy of the visual field." "The hypothesis that what appears to us as external objects and what appears to us as our own bodies are extended and stand in spatial relations . . . accounts for the correlations between . . . constituents of perceptual situations and for their variations as we move about. And it is difficult to see that any alternative hypothesis which does not logically reduce to this one will logically account for such facts"—though "about the minuter details of the physical spatio-temporal order there is room for much diversity of opinion and for much future modification and refinement, as the facts adduced by the Theory of Relativity show." Hence it is "practically certain that the nature and relations of the persistent and neutral conditions of sensa *must* be interpreted by analogy with visual sensa and their relations in the visual sense-field." [9]

Can such a position, or any approximation to it, any longer be held? It is perhaps worth remarking—though not too much weight should be given to the fact—that men of science still seem usually to think in terms of such analogies, though with important changes in detail. They are radically agnostic about the physical world only intermittently, or when the wind is in a certain quarter. Thus physicists and astronomers are accustomed to debate, from the standpoint of the relativity theory, whether the universe is finite or infinite in extent, and, if it can be shown to be finite, of just what shape it is, and how many million years would be required for a ray of light to complete "the journey round the whole of space" and return to its starting-point. And, as Jeans tells us, "it has been quite seriously suggested that two faint nebulae," previously supposed to be extremely remote from us, "may actually be our two nearest neighbors in the sky, M 33 and M 31, seen the long way round space"—*i. e.,* that "we see the fronts of two

[9] *Op. cit.,* pp. 203–4.

objects when we look at M 33 and M 31 and the backs of the same two objects when we point our telescopes in exactly the opposite directions." This, Jeans remarks, is perhaps "only a conjecture"; but "many more startling conjectures in astronomy have . . . proved to be true."[10] The raising of such questions and conjectures seems superfluous, not to say meaningless, unless it is assumed that there is a physical world which has extension and in which it is possible for light to travel, *i. e.,* to reach successively different positions. The habitual fashion of speech of our astronomers and physicists plainly betrays the fact that they conceive themselves to be concerned with the problem of ascertaining the probable nature of relatively persistent physical realities behind, and causally related to, the diversities of our transitory perceptual data.

But it will, no doubt, be said that this is merely a careless or syncopated way of expressing themselves which men of science have fallen into—or, if seriously meant by them, that it is at all events of no philosophical moment. None of these hypotheses and discussions really relate to a "background"—to the characters of realities either actually or potentially outside sense-experience. There are no such existent particulars in the universe as M 33 and M 31, no "long way" and "short way round space," no "shape," either spherical or cylindrical, ascribable to the physical whole of things; there is just "something, we don't know what." All such terms express merely a conceptual frame-work devised for theoretical purposes, a series of scientific fictions. Our perceptual experience takes place as if such entities existed and such events occurred; it is therefore useful to employ the notions of them; but the only factual elements in the scheme consist of private sense-data of individual physicists, *plus,* perhaps, certain unknown quantities of which merely the number may be supposed to be correspondent with the number of differences in the percepts.

From this conception of the character of the business in which the physicist is engaged one consequence not always noted seems

[10] *The Universe Around Us.,* pp. 81, 80.

to follow. If all specific hypotheses relating to things other than perceptual data are to be regarded as fictions, certain classes of hypotheses frequently advanced and discussed must be illegitimate. For though it may be useful to interpolate in thought fictitious processes *between* actual perceptions, it can hardly be useful to extrapolate them beyond the region of any possible perception. Yet astronomers are accustomed to advance hypotheses concerning, for example, the sources of solar energy, from which they draw inferences as to the past and future duration of organic life upon the earth, and the state of this planet and of the solar system long before man's appearance and long after his disappearance. They describe for us the birth of the earth through the tidal action of some other celestial body which (fortunately for us) approached near to the sun probably some 2000 million years ago. They usually affirm the almost certain truth of the second law of thermodynamics, and therefore predict the eventual, though unimaginably remote, "heat-death" of the physical world. Now the events described by these propositions in astronomy and physics are presumably neither actual nor possible experiences of any mortal; nor can the propositions be considered fictions which somehow enable us to infer past or predict future actual experiences. If, then, the sole legitimate subject-matter of science consists of percepts and their inter-connections, together with the number of correlated differences in an otherwise entirely undefined background, no propositions concerning the origin and early history of our system, or the ultimate distribution of energy, would be admissible in science. The temporal range of the discourse of the astronomer would be limited to the history of our species, or at most of percipient organisms. All else would be gratuitous, if not meaningless, fairy-tales—neither true nor useful. If, on the other hand, cosmogonies, histories of the solar system, accounts of what took place in early geological time, and the like, are to be regarded as legitimate and significant parts of the province of science, it can only be upon the condition that these hypotheses are propounded as descriptions of events that actually happened without observation. The descriptions must in any case, of course, be admitted to be highly incomplete and abstract; but they do not, if of any scientific consequence, reduce to the vague proposition that "something, we don't know what," happened before, and will happen after, the presence of human or other percipients upon the cosmic scene.

But even these considerations are less than conclusive with respect to the question with which we are now concerned: whether any intelligible and consistent theory, in terms of particular existences or events, which would accord with, coördinate, and account for the uniformities and differences of our sense-experiences, can be formulated. For the dualist may (I should maintain) legitimately adopt the rule of procedure implied in the passage of Broad's last cited—*viz.,* that *if* a theory, and only one theory, of this kind appears attainable, the fact constitutes a positive reason for regarding that theory as a probable (though doubtless exceedingly inadequate) account of the constitution of the independent causal background of experience. If everything in perception—when we "study it carefully and in detail"—takes place as if certain extra-perceptual events were occurring, in accordance with certain laws, as the common determinants of the otherwise inexplicable similarities and diversities of the data of different percipients, and if through such a theory we are led to the discovery of perceptible facts previously unknown, it is simpler and more in harmony with the normal assumptions of our reason to suppose that those events do occur, rather than that they do not. Though the universe *may* be a systematic and elaborate deception, in which everything in our experience intricately conspires with everything else to suggest to us beliefs which are not true, it does not seem necessary or rational to start with the supposition that this is the case. If this is admitted, the issue immediately before us reduces to two questions: has theoretical physics thus far succeeded in formulating a unique, coherent, non-self-contradictory theory of the kind indicated: and even if it has not succeeded in doing so, must this failure be regarded as sufficient reason for assuming that the external causal order is probably not analogous to our sense-fields in any respect except that it contains numerically distinct elements?

Upon the first of these questions—in view of the present difficult and confused situation in physics—philosophers ought perhaps to refrain from expressing or having any opinions whatever; certainly the duty of such abstention is now often pointed out to them by physicists who meanwhile make haste to deduce large epistemological and metaphysical conclusions from the latest of the rapidly shifting hypotheses of their science. Complete silence on these matters is certainly the dictate of prudence for one who is neither physicist nor mathematician. Nevertheless, the questions lie before us; our inquiry has brought us face to face with them, as any discussion of the present logical position of philosophical realism must do; and it is scarcely possible for any reader of recent writings in natural philosophy to remain wholly devoid of provisional impressions as to the probable answers to these questions. It is perhaps better to be imprudent than to be evasive; and I shall therefore venture to state my own impressions, and even to offer some reasons for them—while fully realizing the antecedent probability that the impressions, and still more the reasonings, of a layman on these subjects will fall into error. Even errors or misunderstandings, if definitely expressed, are not incapable of contributing to a better understanding of a logical situation. There are four aspects of current physics which are chiefly pertinent to the question whether that science can be taken as offering any measure of probable knowledge concerning physical realities underlying our perceptual experience; upon each of these, then, I hazard a few observations.

(1) That the theory of relativity, by itself, establishes the impossibility of a characterization of physical reality in terms more specific than a bare numerical correspondence of differences in that reality with differences in observable indicator readings, does not seem evident. The special theory initially presupposes the occurrence of the relative motion of bodies and the motion of

light. Now relative motion can mean nothing except the temporally successive occupancy of different positions in a specified coördinate system or with respect to a designated reference-body. And from a hypothesis which tells us that such motion has certain previously unsuspected effects, the conclusion that there is no such things as motion in external nature hardly follows. It will, however, be said that the theory by its implications, though not by its initial postulates, transfers space, time and motion from the physical to the mental world, and by doing so excludes the supposition that the physical world may "be interpreted by analogy with visual sensa and their relations in our visual fields." The theory is supposed to achieve this result by showing that the positions, velocities and shapes of perceived objects, and the dates of perceived events or the durations of processes, are "relative to the standpoints of observers." On this, three brief remarks may be made. (a) In the first place, even if the theory has this consequence, it still does not leave us wholly in the dark about the background of our sensa. It assumes that there are certain entities, namely, "events," which are present in that background and correspond to, if they are not existentially identical with, the successive data which make up the content of our experience; and though it places the former in a scheme of geometrical relations which are not those of the data of sense-experience, it permits—and, as ordinarily held by physicists, requires—us to conceive of the "events" *in* the new scheme of relations as constituting an objective order which is definitely correlated with our sense-data. Thus we have already seen even Eddington, after explaining that the shortening of moving rods in relative motion is "true, but not really true," adding that, thanks to Minkowski, physics has discovered "a way of keeping the accounts of space" which *is* "really true," namely, the conception of the four-dimensional continuum of space-time, which "exhibits realities (absolute things)." [11] Such a world of "realities" is manifestly not one of which we are supposed to be in complete ignorance; and it seems to perform the functions of

11 *The Nature of the Physical World*, p. 34.

a "background" at least more satisfactorily than does mind stuff. (b) The "standpoints," moreover, to which the diverse peculiarities of our perceptual data are said to be relative are supposed to be physical, not mental, standpoints. They, and their consequences, would—so far as the special theory as a physical hypothesis is concerned—be found in a world in which there were no conscious subjects or percipient events. The "standpoints," in short, are still merely states of unaccelerated relative motion; and if there *are* no states of relative motion, there are no standpoints, in the sense pertinent to the theory, and therefore no consequences of differences of standpoint. It is as impossible to remain in the world of relativity as it is to enter it without making use of the concept of motion. (c) Finally, the general theory appears permeated with the ideas of space (of a sort) and motion, of differences between regions occupied by "matter" and regions not so occupied, of the effect of velocity upon mass, of absolute accelerations, and of "the totality of the stars" as a sort of absolute or cosmical reference-system by means of which the occurrence of such accelerations is made intelligible. If phenomenalism is adopted on *other* grounds it is, of course, possible to interpret the theorems of relativity-physics in conformity with that philosophical preconception—in other words, to treat them as fictions; but there is nothing in the theory itself which imposes this interpretation and nothing which implies a radical agnosticism about the objective nature of things.[12]

(2) A much more serious difficulty in the formulation of a concrete explanatory hypothesis about the nature of the common physical world underlying our sense-data appears to be found in that portion of physics which deals with the minute constitution of "scientific objects" and with the phenomena of radiation presumably attributable to the action of these ultra-microscopic entities and processes. It has been, ironically enough, in the course

---

12 If space permitted I should wish to present a much more extensive examination of certain of the philosophical inferences usually drawn from the relativity theory; some of them, especially those concerning simultaneity and duration, seem to me to abound in confusions and inconsistencies.

of the attempt to furnish us with precisely such a hypothesis that physicists have been led into their present state of either dubiety or dogmatic agnosticism. They began innocently, with, as a rule, no sceptical or phenomenalistic bias, to take bits of sensible matter to pieces theoretically. Here was a visible and tangible table, a piece of bread, a rusting metal, a crystal, water, a gas: of what were they made? So far as any one of them presented different appearances or manifested different qualities to separate percipients, it must, no doubt, be held not to have in itself, or in the limited region which it actually occupied, these discrepant characters. But it was not through a progressive extension of the notion of the perspectivity of the properties of things that the present difficulty arose; it would doubtless have arisen even if all men had always perceived the table as having the same color and the same shape. What happened was that, even when corrections were made for such obvious diversities of the sensible appearances of gross material objects, it was found that they still behaved in ways which suggested that they were made up of smaller parts which had characteristics and modes of action other than those macroscopically observable; and that when it was assumed that they *were* so constituted, great masses of otherwise unintelligible facts concerning the macroscopic objects could be regarded as consequences of a relatively small number of properties and laws of behavior of the minute parts, and previously unobserved facts at the macroscopic level could be predicted. Thus, quite apart from that translation of the sensible characters of objects from the status of "realities" to that of "appearances" which results from (in the broader sense of the term) relativistic considerations, there took place a further process of the same kind resulting from the reduction of perceptible gross matter into components more and more unlike that which they composed—the resolution of the apparently continuous substances of every-day experience into discrete and moving molecules, of these into compounds of a small number of chemical elements, of these into atomic units, and of these into electrons and protons. In the second case as in the first, for the characters which were discarded from physical nature the "mind" had to take over the responsibility—an ever-increasing burden of responsibility; the entities or characters which were removed from the category of matter were transferred to the category of sensa. But while this heightened the contrast between perceptual content and the external world, and thus strengthened the position of psychophysical dualism, it had no necessarily subjectivistic implications; and while, by stripping the entities in the external world of quasi-sensible and therefore imaginable qualities, it left their qualitative nature undefinable, it did not render them essentially incomprehensible, so long as the theory of the minute constitution of matter still took the form of consistent mechanical models. When, early in the present century, atoms were resolved into groups of units of electrical charge—itself qualitatively undefined—the dequalification of matter (if I may so call it) seemed to reach completion; but electrons continued to be conceived as somethings which had position, magnitude and weight, which formed definite spatial patterns within the atom, and which moved—even though it were in a somewhat paradoxical manner and in accordance with laws quite different from those which served for describing the perceptible motions of macroscopic bodies. And so long as these conceptions prevailed among physicists, the dualistic realist in philosophy could still derive from physics a fairly concrete and definite, though admittedly very fragmentary, account of the nature of the physical world and of what was going on therein.

The real crisis in this branch of physics—from the point of view of philosophical realism—came only when, very recently, and under the pressure of definite experimental facts, the physicists began to experience wholly unprecedented difficulty in the attempt to provide definite and consistent mechanical models, in terms of relative position, magnitude and motion, of the minute constituents of matter. The principal source of this difficulty is now, doubtless, generally familiar, since it has of late been set forth by a number of qualified specialists in such a way as to be somewhat intelligible even to the layman. It arose through the discoveries

leading to the introduction of the quantum theory and the resultant conflict between the considerations which seem to require an
undulatory conception of light and other fundamental entities of
physical theory, and those which seem to require a corpuscular
conception. The hypotheses previously devised to explain certain
experimental data seem to contradict those which best serve to
explain certain other experimental data. If you deal exclusively
with one set of empirical facts (such as interference-phenomena)
you can work out a satisfactory theory about them, but it does not
accord with the theory to which you seem to be forced when you
try to give an account of what lies behind other, apparently
equally well-established, facts, such as quantum phenomena.
There would be no harm in this if the two sets of phenomena in
question were separate and unconnected; the trouble is that it appears to the physicist necessary to regard them as different aspects
of the *same* events, namely, radiation and the behavior of the electron or proton within the atom when affected by radiation or when
emitting it. Physicists thus find themselves confronted with the
apparent necessity of conceiving of (*e. g.*) light as both undulatory and corpuscular; yet the two notions imply mutually exclusive properties and effects. This, in the words of a distinguished
physicist, "constitutes one of the most formidable problems which
physical science has ever encountered." [13]

It appears, on the face of it, not only formidable but insoluble,
if strictly identical entities—photons or electrons or protons—are
assumed to be literally and exclusively undulations and also literally and exclusively corpuscles; resourceful as theoretical physics
is, it commands no expedient for rendering a *contradictio in ad-
jectis* thinkable. Consequently the ingenious hypotheses which
have been proposed for dealing with the difficulty do not—if I
understand them—combine both concepts literally in a single coherent model. In the theory which appears to prove most serviceable and therefore to have received the widest provisional acceptance among physicists, the wave-mechanics of de Broglie and

[13] W. Wilson in *Enc. Britannica*, 14th edition, vol. 18, p. 818a.

Schrödinger, we still, it is true, find such terms employed as "form," "oscillation," "frequency," "dispersion," "impact," and the like, which suggest familiar and picturable types of spatial attributes and motions. Even wave-mechanics thus has the air of a mechanical model. But it is a delusive air, for the terms seem no longer to have their ordinary meanings. What is to be conceived as "oscillating," we are told, is an entity called ψ which, if defined at all in a manner analogous to the concepts of classical physics, can only be interpreted as a probability—the probability that an electron is somewhere within a certain area. There is thus "no definite localization" of the electron or particle, "though some places are more probable than others." [14] Now, though it is possible to conceive of the oscillation of an electron or proton, or of the undulation of a continuous "sub-ether," it does not seem possible to attach any meaning to the "oscillation" or "undulation" of a pure probability, nor to the localization of a particle in a place which is no place in particular.[15] Thus the conceptions in which the analyses of theoretical physics up to the present terminate have no real analogy with visual or tactual sensa and their perceptible relations in our sense-fields; and, as most physicists now appear to agree, "the de Broglie-Schrödinger undulations become merely a mathematical implement for computing probabilities and cannot be regarded as physical entities in the ordinary sense of the term." [16]

Such, in brief, has been the course of the modern physicist's analysis of matter and of the processes of radiation. I venture to think—with the diffidence becoming a non-physicist—that its outcome is not necessarily quite so devastating to the physical world as it is often represented as being. For the final step, in which it abandons the description of relative positions and motions and turns to a mathematical "dodge" (to use Eddington's word), need not be, and by the physicist is not, taken as annulling the previous

---

[14] Eddington, *op. cit.*, p. 216.
[15] *Cf.* the remarks on this of H. W. B. Joseph in *Hibbert Journal*, April, 1929, pp. 421–2.
[16] Wilson, *op. cit.*, p. 827a.

stages of the analysis in terms of positions, motions, *etc.* We have a series of inferences in which bigger moving things are treated as actually composed of progressively smaller moving things with different properties and modes of motion; but the last stage does *not* consist in similarly resolving electrons or protons into probabilities or algebraic symbols. If it did, the macroscopic objects certainly could not be composed of them. The physicists manifestly continue to think of molecules, atoms, electrons, as "darting hither and thither, colliding, rebounding," and the like. Such conceptions are absolutely indispensable to them in their actual work; and certain of the experiments which have led to these theories all but display charged particles doing these things before our eyes. While the particles themselves are imperceptible, what are taken to be the tracks produced by their motions through, *e. g.,* water-vapor, and the points at which some of these tracks deviate from the straight lines where the particles collide with atoms, may be seen, and photographs of them are available in current manuals and popular expositions of recent physics.[17] These events plainly are not conceived by the physicists as collisions of one logical probability with another probability; they are conceived as collisions of small space-occupying and resistant units with larger units at definite places—*viz.,* at the places where the paths of the two intersect. Alpha-particles, in fact, are supposed to behave much after the manner of billiard-balls. It is partly because such things as the tracks are observable that it is inferred that there exist quasi-corpuscular moving entities; and the inference is either valid or it is not. True, there is the other sort of phenomena, illustrated by the experiments of Davisson and Germer and G. P. Thompson on electrons and by Dempster's recent experiment in projecting hydrogen protons through calcite crystals, which exhibit these entities as producing on photographic plates certain definite diffraction-patterns, *i. e.,* evidences of interference, which lead to the inference that both electrons and protons have wave-like properties. But here again the experimenter assumes that he

[17] *Cf., e. g.,* Jeans, *The Universe Around Us,* pp. 106–111.

is (for example) shooting hydrogen protons through a crystal in a vacuum, *i. e.*, producing motions of finite extended things of which the shape or structure can be judged from the fact that they cause a particular type of patterns on the camera-plates; and if he is not doing this, the inference that there are protons which have wavelike properties does not follow. It is, indeed, impossible to conceive that the *same* individual entities have both sorts of properties at once—nor do they ever exhibit both sorts of effects at once in the same observable datum in the same experiment. But it seems at least hasty to infer from effects pointing to the occurrence of *both* undulatory and corpuscular insensible processes in nature, the conclusion that neither undulatory nor corpuscular processes, nor motion of any kind, occur.

What the mere logician would be likely to suggest in such a situation is that the theoretical analysis is incomplete or over-simplified, and that both kinds of properties ought not to be attributed to the same individual entities under the same conditions. A theory which seems to imply that the imperceptible entities or events inferred to account for perceptible events are self-contradictory is obviously unsatisfactory; it stands in need of some sort of supplementation or modification to remove the contradiction. But the conceptions of wave-mechanics, however serviceable as mathematical implements for computing probabilities, are not likely to satisfy the philosopher, nor, in the long run, the physicist, because, if taken as descriptions of actual events, they do not remove the contradictions but only substitute new contradictions— those of moving probabilities and of particles which are somewhere in a spatial field but nowhere in particular in it. The notion of probability here can legitimately express only our inability to determine with precision, under certain conditions, where in the assumed field the particle is; this indeterminateness of our knowledge cannot properly be treated as a property of the particle —unless it is to be made a rule of physical reasoning (as it seems by some physicists to be) that our limitations are to be converted into positive attributes of the objects with which physics deals.

The progress of modern chemistry and physics, their most brilliant successes in unification and prediction, have depended, for the greater part, upon the sort of inference exemplified in all but the last stage of the process above outlined—and even exemplified to some degree in that—namely, upon assuming, behind the qualitative diversities and the patterns and motions of sensible objects, a series of entities which, however destitute of sensible qualities, are still conceived as also forming patterns, performing motions, and under certain conditions offering resistance to, or in some way modifying, one another's motions. That the permanent abandonment of this procedure—*i. e.*, of the use of all quasi-mechanical concepts—would be productive of equal progress in the future, does not, in the light of past experience, seem probable; and what is certain is that it has not at present been consistently abandoned in the actual practice of the investigator.

Nevertheless, that the theoretical physicists—whose affair it undeniably is—have not yet been able to devise new hypotheses which wholly remove the antinomy into which certain experimental results, interpreted in the light of certain hitherto current hypotheses, have led them, seems to be true; and we must therefore answer one of the questions earlier propounded by saying that physics does not at present offer us a coherent and intelligible description of the minute constitution of the material world and processes occurring therein. It offers us two thus far unreconciled descriptions of what are assumed to be the same processes, *plus* new provisional mathematical devices for computing the probabilities of certain events. But that physical theory has reached the limit of its resources in this matter, that it will in the end leave its present chief paradox unresolved, or that it will eventually content itself with the proposition that behind our percepts something unknown is doing something, we don't know what, is neither certain nor likely. And, lest all this seem merely the expression of the prejudices of a philosopher, I quote a recent remark of the eminent author of the quantum theory: "In the face of this peculiarly difficult situation in which theoretical physics at present finds itself, it is certainly not possible to dismiss summarily a feeling of doubt whether the current theory, with its radical novelties, is really upon the right road. The decision of this fateful question depends wholly upon whether, in the further continuously advancing effort at the construction of the picture of the physical world, the indispensable contact with the world of the senses continues to be sufficiently maintained."[18] While an avoidance of confident conclusions on any of these matters behooves the philosopher at the present juncture, it is equally evident that at a moment when physics is in a state of unprecedented instability, with new fundamental hypotheses making their appearance at intervals of a few months, it is not less fitting that the physicist should be slow in drawing philosophical consequences from the imperfectly synthetized results of his investigations and from tentative conceptions which are still in process of verification and reconstruction.[19]

(3) There is another development in contemporary physics, not resultant merely from the apparent antinomy of the wavelike and corpuscular properties of light, electrons, *etc.*, which has been widely hailed as having even more momentous results for epistemology and metaphysics. According to Heisenberg's principle of indeterminacy it is impossible to determine with a high degree of precision both the position and the velocity of an electron— though either its position alone or its velocity alone could theoretically be so determined. What is inferred from this by Eddington is that "the description of the position and velocity of an electron beyond a limited number of places of decimals is an attempt to describe"—not something which lies beyond the reach of exact scientific determination—but *"something which does not exist."* The fact that "an association of exact position with exact momentum can never be discovered by us" must, it is suggested, be explained by the assumption that "there is no such thing in nature."

18 Planck, *Das Weltbild der neuen Physik,* 1929.
19 It is worth noting that to Wilson it still "seems possible to retain the notion of elementary particles, electrons, photons, *etc.,* located in space and time—or more probably in a five-dimensional continuum" (*op. cit.,* p. 827).

When an electron is not interacting with a light-quantum and is therefore unobservable, it "virtually disappears from the physical world, having no interaction with it." [20]   In the same doctrine of the new theoretical physics Professor Dewey has seen even more significant and far-reaching implications for "the underlying philosophy and logic of science." The principle of indeterminacy seems to him a decisive vindication of a species of relativism. Heisenberg, it is suggested, has taken "the final steps in the dislodgment of the old spectator-theory of knowledge." "What is known is seen to be a product in which the act of observation plays a necessary rôle. Knowing is seen to be a participant in what is finally known." And this in turn is construed as a vindication of the conception of knowing as always, and by its very essence, instrumental in intent and function; the principle of indeterminacy, in short, shows that "knowing is a case of specially directed activity instead of something isolated from practice," a "search for security by means of active control of the changing course of events." [21]

No metaphysical consequences, however, can be deduced from the physical principle of indeterminacy except with the aid of a purely metaphysical assumption; and since the issue here, too, is pertinent to the fundamental logic of philosophical realism, it is worth dwelling upon a little. The assumption in question, in the argument of Eddington, is: Whatever is not experimentally observable does not exist. And this is construed as meaning that a thing which *does* exist, or a process which *does* go on, during a certain time—even though unobserved—ceases to exist, or to go on, at times during which physical conditions arise which would, even if it did exist, prevent it from being *theoretically observable with a high degree of precision*. The assumption, be it noted, is not the radically subjectivistic one that what is not actually observed does not exist. It is not, as Eddington remarks, to be confused with the "doctrine well-known to philosophers that the

[20] *Op. cit.*, pp. 222–228; italics mine.
[21] *The Quest for Certainty*, pp. 201–204.

moon ceases to exist when no one is looking at it." Though professing to have "not the least idea what is the meaning of the word existence when used in this connection," Eddington nevertheless declares that "in the scientific world there *is* a moon which appeared upon the scene before the astronomer, reflects sunlight when no one sees it, . . . and will eclipse the sun in 1999 even if the human race has succeeded in killing itself off before that date," *etc.* "The moon—the scientific moon—has to play the part of a continuous causal element in a world conceived to be all causally interlocked." (This seems hard to distinguish from the supposedly mysterious proposition that "the moon exists when no one is looking at it," and may more briefly be expressed, as it is presently by Eddington himself, in the latter form.) But though, under the special circumstances mentioned, the moon is unobservable by any actual spectator, it is not unobservable by imaginary spectators; there would be nothing, in other words, in the case supposed, to prevent a spectator from witnessing the eclipse of 1999—except the causes which prevented there being any actual spectator to witness it. But the case of the electron, it is explained, is quite different from that of the moon. For not even imaginary observers could determine with a high degree of accuracy both the position and velocity of a single electron at a given moment. The reason for this is that in order to be observable the electron must "be illuminated and scatter light to reach the eye"; but "in scattering this it receives from the light a kick," *i. e.,* its momentum is altered by the process used in observing it. Now we cannot determine experimentally what its momentum was or what it would have been if it had not been acted upon by the light-quantum; nor can we predict precisely the amount of the kick. However, by giving the electron only a very little kick— *i. e.,* by using a quantum of small energy—we can reduce this uncertainty to a minimum; the littler the kick, the less the velocity during the observation need be supposed to differ from the velocity before the kick was received. The particular difficulty here is not the fact that an uncertainty in the determination of momentum

cannot be wholly eliminated, but that the (hypothetical) experimental means which could be taken for reducing *this* uncertainty would at the same time diminish the accuracy of the
observation of the electron's position. For to give it only a very
little kick from the light means using light of longer wave-length;
this results in larger diffraction images; this "reduces the accuracy of our microscope"; and thus neither we nor an imaginary
observer would—when the kick given the electron was slight—
be able, at least with any sort of microscope now known, to see
precisely where, within the atom, the electron was while we were
observing it. If, on the other hand, we increase the kick, *i. e.,*
diminish the wave-length of the light, in order to make our microscopic observation more exact, we should obviously also increase
the difference between the momentum of the electron after its illumination and that which it had when unilluminated.[22]   Thus,
while "it does not hurt the moon to look at it"—while "there is
no inconsistency in supposing *it* to be under the surveillance of
relays of watchers while we were asleep"—"it is otherwise with
an electron." Even though we armed our (imaginary) observers
with (imaginary) flashlamps to keep a more continuous watch on
the doings of the electron than we can keep, this would still leave
us—or them—in ignorance as to what it was, or would be, "doing in the dark," since "under the flashlight it will not go on doing what it was doing in the dark." It is on these grounds, then,
that the conclusion is based that—unlike the moon—the electron
"*between whiles* virtually disappears from the physical world,"
and that "the locality of the electron within the atom does not
exist."[23]

[22] *Op. cit.,* pp. 224–5; italics mine. There is, of course (as has been previously
indicated) implied by the Schrödinger theory an indeterminateness of the position of
the electron in the wave with which it is associated; but this is not the point here
in question. The former indeterminacy Eddington conceives to be derivative from
Heisenberg's principle: "I would not regard the principle of indeterminacy as a
result to be deduced from Schrödinger's theory; it is the other way about" (p. 225).
[23] *Ibid.;* what is intended to be conveyed by the qualification "virtually" I am
unable to determine. According to the reasoning elsewhere employed by Eddington
the moon, as well as the electron, should consist of mind stuff not "spread out in
space and time." This would make the nature of unperceived solar eclipses rather
difficult to understand.

Now this reasoning is somewhat hard to follow. We are apparently permitted and, indeed, required, to assume at first that the electron—like the moon—does exist when unobserved (*i. e.,* "in the dark"), and is then doing something within the atom, though we cannot tell precisely what. Its metaphysical troubles begin only when we set about observing it. In order to do this we must turn both our (ideal) microscopes and our flashlights upon it; and if the light is fine enough to give us accurate images in our microscopes, its quantum will be so "rough" as to "knock the electron out of the atom."[24] And this last expression apparently is forthwith taken (at times) as equivalent to "knocking the electron out of existence." But this strikes one as a paradoxical potency for light-quanta to possess. For (a) a "kick" is just an alteration of the momentum of what is kicked; and the terms "to have momentum altered" and "to cease to exist" are not obviously synonymous. And (b) the evidence that light has this sinister power of destroying that with which it interacts seems to be lacking. It interacts, for example, with the moon whenever that satellite is being observed by us. And the observable moon is supposed to consist of illuminated electrons and protons. Are we to infer that the moon cannot exist when we are observing it, or not, at any rate, when or in so far as light-quanta of any considerable energy are acting upon it, though it may exist at other times? In that case, how can "the scientific moon play the part of a *continuous* causal element in a world conceived to be causally interlocked"? (c) Turning the light on the electron, however, was supposed to be the means of observing it. But it would surely be surprising if a physical process acting upon a physical entity had simultaneously the dual effect of rendering it observable and robbing it of its existence. (d) And inasmuch as it is (in the argument outlined) assumed that the electron would be observable after the illumination, by means of ideal microscopes, the argument cannot really be that, because what is not observable cannot exist, the electron cannot exist *after* the illumination and the

[24] *The Nature of the Physical World,* p. 225.

resultant kick. For since it is then that it *is* observable (even though unobserved), it is then that it may (by the hypothesis) be supposed to exist. (e) But herewith the entire argument changes its character. The difficulty now relates to the status of the electron *before* the kick. Because we can observe it only under illumination, we now conclude that it is to the unkicked electron that the reasoning applies. Thus it is the electron when our flashlights are *not* directed upon it that is non-existent, while the illumination of it, *i. e.,* the physical procedure prerequisite to observation, so far from knocking it out of existence, knocks it into existence. (f) But this conclusion is contrary to the initial postulate that the electron existed and was doing something in the dark. It is, furthermore, contrary to the assumption that there was something there for the light-quantum to act upon. A real quantum does not give a real kick to a non-existent electron. (g) On the other hand, if the major premise, "what is not observable does not exist," is assumed, the prior non-existence of the electron follows immediately, quite apart from the special physical considerations from which the principle of the alternative indeterminacy of either position or velocity is deduced. For when unilluminated the electron is by hypothesis not observable at all; and consequently "there is no such thing in nature." The only possible relevance of the indeterminacy-principle to the question of the *prior* state of the electron would appear to lie in the fact that the greater the accuracy of the microscopic image, the less precisely would the ideal physicist be able to infer back from an observed velocity after the kick to the unobserved velocity before it. But if there previously was no electron, the problem of determining its prior velocity does not arise. In short, the Heisenberg principle either has nothing to do with the case, or else it presupposes that the electron as truly exists before its illumination (*i. e.,* when it is not observable) as after it. But if the latter horn of the dilemma is accepted, it implies the falsity of the premise that whatever is not observable is non-existent. It excludes, in other words, the supposition that in the time-intervals in which the physical instruments of observation are not, or for definite physical reasons cannot be, brought to bear with precision upon a given region, there are no physical entities present in that region, upon which entities, at other times or under different physical conditions, such instruments may be brought to bear.

Often, it is true, what seems to be implied (*e. g.*, by Eddington) is that the effect of illumination is, not to knock electrons out of existence, but merely to deprive them of the privilege of enjoying both definite position and definite velocity at the same instant. Now it may, of course, be questioned whether a thing can be said to have *any* velocity at an instant: there is a logical puzzle here as ancient as Zeno of Elea and as modern as Bergson, which I shall not now discuss. At all events, the precise determination of velocity, if conceivable at all, would seem to presuppose the precise determination of position at two or more instants. It is hard to see how—if we assume that some meaning can be attached to "instants" and that the electron exists—it can objectively have definite velocity (in a specified frame of reference) *between* two instants without having equally definite positions *at* those instants. Suppose this conceivable, however: why should we believe it to be a fact? Because—we are told—it is known that the experimental conditions which would permit relatively precise observation of the one attribute would preclude precise observation of the other. But what is supposed to be known with respect to determinability of *position* is inferred from an assumed effect of one of these conditions upon images in our microscopes, not from its effect upon the electron. Why, then, should we transfer this effect to the electron? We know that if a moving-picture reel of a horse-race is run off very slowly, the picture will not represent the original speed of the horses; and that if the reel is run off at a rate which represents this, the details of the horses' action will not be perceptible to us. We do not infer from this that the features of the horses' motion which we can thus observe only separately, and under differing conditions, were not jointly characteristic of that motion when it occurred—that known peculiarities of the instruments used (including our optical apparatus), whereby we are prevented from observing two characters of an object at once, also prevent that object from having both of these characters at once. On the contrary, we ordinarily attempt to distinguish the effect of the peculiarities of our instruments from the characters of the objects observed. Yet in the present case our physicist reasons in precisely the opposite manner. He assumes that he knows the nature and the locus of incidence of the modifying factor, namely, that it consists in the length of the light-wave and the resultant diffuseness of the microscopic image; he nevertheless insists upon imputing this effect produced at the *terminus ad quem* to the *terminus a quo*. In any case, the notion of an electron upon which light from a flashlamp is acting and of which the position, if not the velocity, is then approximately determinable, is not equivalent to the notion of "something, we don't know what."

A somewhat different philosophical inference, exemplified by the remarks of Dewey already cited, is sometimes drawn from the principle of indeterminacy. This does not rest upon the simple metaphysical assumption that what is at certain times not sensibly observable or theoretically determinable with precision does not exist at those times, but upon the consideration that the principle illustrates the dependence of the characters of what is observed upon the physical procedure prerequisite to observation. We can observe the electron only under illumination; but this affects its momentum; this is taken as establishing the general truth that *what* a thing is when we observe it is always modified by the operation whereby we observe it; and this is construed as meaning that it is somehow relative to us, the observers.[25] It is chiefly for this reason that we are often told of late that "the principle of indeterminacy is epistemological"; and it is on this ground that the principle is said to show that "knowing is a participant in what is

---

[25] This argument is not in fact, it will be observed, deduced from the principle of indeterminacy in general, nor from the special principle of the alternative indeterminacy of the position or velocity of an electron. It is based merely upon one of the premises of the latter, namely, that a light-quantum when directed upon or emitted by an electron would give the electron a kick.

finally known." That the percipient event is a condition necessary for the existence of the perceptual content, and that there are
numerous conditions, both physical and mental, which determine
in part the character of what is finally perceived, dualistic philosophers have, of course, always held. If this is all that is meant
by the proposition quoted, it did not await recent physical theory
for its formulation or its vindication. It is, so interpreted, in
essence the same as the venerable doctrine of the subjectivity of
the secondary qualities and of the perspective visual appearances
of things. Mankind, in short, has known, almost from the beginning of reflection on these matters, that the physical instruments
of observation, *e. g.* eyes, may affect the character of what is observed. But it would seem that something more than this is intended to be conveyed by the proposition. It is not the nature of
the content of perception, but of *any object of possible knowledge,*
that is apparently declared to be determined by "knowing." This,
however, clearly does not follow from the physical considerations
from which it is deduced. It is not "knowing" that, for the
physicist, affects the momentum or the position of the electron,
or even the precise determinability of these; it is the action of a
certain physical process or instrument upon a certain physical
entity. Even if we should accept Eddington's reasoning—or rather,
one of the three discrepant forms of it—and say that what happens to the electron is that it is by such action knocked out of existence, it is not knowing but a light-quantum that accomplishes
the feat. And to assert (what is apparently all that the physicist
has reason for asserting) that we know that the wave-length
which least alters the electron's momentum is the one which most
impairs the precision of our hypothetical observation of position,
is to imply precisely the "old spectator-theory of knowledge."
The *cognoscendum,* or object of reference, is in this case the electron as it exists under the specified experimental physical conditions, *i. e.,* when illuminated. If I can be said truly to "know"
this physical object of reference, or any fact concerning it, I know
it as it would have been if my cognitive act had not occurred.

To maintain that I cannot so know either it or anything else, is to deny the possibility of any objective knowledge—as has been sufficiently pointed out in the fourth lecture.

It may, of course, once more be argued on other grounds that we do *not* know that electrons, or other entities belonging to the physicist's universe of discourse, exist except in so far as we perceive or conceive them; but these other grounds—the traditional arguments of phenomenalism—are in no degree strengthened by the fact that physicists find that certain means which must be employed to bring certain objects under exact observation must at the same time modify in some degree certain attributes of those objects. The means either exist physically (*i. e.,* potentially apart from perception) or they do not; the objects either exist physically or they do not; and the modification is either known to be produced or it is not. That neither the means nor the objects *can* so exist or be known does not follow from the proposition that the former interact with the latter and in doing so produce changes in them which render them thereupon observable. On the contrary, if the interaction is supposed to be an actual interaction, both factors in it must physically exist. And even if it were supposed (as by the authors quoted it apparently is not supposed) to be merely a scientific fiction, the character imputed to it must still be independent of the circumstance of my thinking of it—if it is a *scientific* fiction at all. It must, that is, be the particular *kind* of fictitious interaction which best serves theoretically to explain the empirical events (assuming that fictitious causes are capable of explaining empirical events); and what I am in this case supposed to "know" is that it is that kind of fiction, and would be, whether I happened to bethink myself of it or not. There is, after all, an important difference even between scientific fictions and private hallucinations.

I am therefore unable to see that the principle of indeterminacy, or the experimental evidence which has led to its formulation, has the decisive and revolutionary consequences for epistemology which recent writers have attributed to it. It leaves the issues upon which it is supposed to bear in the same logical position as before. The statement of it, and the argument for it, are usually expressed in terms of which the implications are transparently realistic. Nevertheless if you approach it with subjectivistic or phenomenalistic preconceptions, it is not impossible—by a suitable change of phraseology—to express it in a way consistent with such preconceptions. Whether these are necessary or probable preconceptions must still be determined by considerations extraneous to the principle itself.

(4) A more radical argument against the possibility of obtaining from the physicist any information about the underlying realities of nature rests upon general logical considerations; it is not primarily due to recent advances in physics, but was many years ago set forth by Henri Poincaré. The issue with which we are now concerned, let me recall, is whether one, *and only one,* concrete theory of the constitution of the physical world, explanatory of certain uniformities and diversities of our percepts, is attainable. And the decisive obstacle to an affirmative answer to this question lies, it is suggested, not in the fact that no such theory is possible, but in the fact that, on the contrary, "any aggregation of phenomena, however complicated, is always susceptible of an infinite number of purely mechanical explanations." The moment the physicist passes beyond the limits of the actually perceived, to interpolate hypothetical entities and processes between one datum of perception and another, there is no theoretical limit to the number of hypotheses, accordant with the empirically known facts to be explained, which might be set up. Of these possible hypotheses some are, indeed, scientifically preferable to others, because they are simpler, or more convenient for mathematical handling; but since these grounds of preference are purely subjective, they are not reasons for supposing the hypotheses adopted by the scientific theorist to be truer descriptions of the imperceptible or unperceived realities. And this general consideration, it

is pointed out, is illustrated and confirmed by the contemporary position in physical theory; in Bridgman's words: "However much one might have been inclined fifty years ago to see some warrant for ascribing physical reality to the internal processes of a theory because of its success in meeting the observed situation, certainly no one of the present generation will be capable of so naïve an attitude after our illuminating experience of the physical equivalence of the matrix calculus and the wave mechanics." [26]

Now if it be true that there are no considerations, other than those of convenience, which set any probable limits to the range of diversity of equally good explanatory hypotheses, we must unquestionably conclude at once that no physical theory whatever concerning imperceptible "scientific objects" can have any probable validity as a description of realities. We should be, in the nature of the case, forever debarred from claiming any knowledge of natural existences other than our percepts or smaller than the *minima sensibilia*. And it is, of course, true that there is no limit to the number of *conceivable* hypotheses; if we choose to give our imaginations free play, we are not even confined to mechanical or to mathematically formulable explanations. It is not demonstrably impossible, for example, that what exist inside the atom are colonies of very small but very malicious fairies, who make a special point of playing perplexing tricks upon physicists; and such a hypothesis would quite simply and adequately explain much in contemporary physics. Nevertheless, I suggest that certain generic characters of the perceptible phenomena which the physicist is investigating indicate certain probable generic characters of the events underlying these phenomena. The physicist does not leap into the world of the imperceptible all at once. He begins with the observation of certain properties and movements of perceptible and measurable extended things; and in the earlier history of modern science he (mainly) was occupied with determining the laws of the relative motions of these things. By means

[26] *Science*, Jan. 10, 1930, p. 21.

of these laws he made inferences to the existence of things which had never been perceived; but the things inferred were of the same general kind as the things from the behavior of which they were inferred. When certain unaccountable perturbations of the motion of Uranus were noted, astronomers did not forthwith devise radically novel hypotheses nor revise the laws of motion; Adams and Leverrier simply determined the orbit and mass of a hitherto unperceived planet, which was thereupon telescopically observed. And when the physicist turns from his macroscopic problems to the attempt to determine the minute structure of matter, he begins in the same way. His logically primary and crucial departure from the ordinary sensible appearances of things is not, in fact, a step into the imperceptible, but only into the microscopic. To the naked eye, fluids at rest, like other material substances, appear continuous and devoid of internal motion; and particles dropped into them appear merely to move slowly downwards under gravitational force. But if a particle so small that it is just possible to see it with a high-power microscope is dropped into a fluid, it behaves in a way quite different from that which naked-eye observation seems to show; it performs the sort of irregular dance known as the Brownian movement. The physicist's next step carries him clean over into the world of the imperceptible; yet it is a very little step indeed. He merely infers that, as the particle in the water which is just big enough for him to see is in irregular motion, so other adjacent particles not big enough to see are in similar motion, and that the movements of the visible particle are due to collisions between it and the others. He assumes, in other words, so long as the assumption works, that the things he can't quite see are of the same general nature as those he can see—i. e., are extended and capable of motion— and that the motion observed need not be assigned to a different type of cause from that which would be inferred if the particles surrounding it were of a perceptible order of magnitude. And by means of this assumption he is enabled, with the help of further observational data, to work out the entire kinetic theory of fluid pressure, and in turn to find its implications exemplified in further specific features of the visible Brownian movement.[27]

The procedure illustrated in these elementary instances—that of assuming, so far as possible, that the broad structural characters of the perceptible are also the structural characters of the inferred-unperceived or imperceptible—is not logically coercive; but on the other hand, it is not arbitrary nor dictated solely by considerations of subjective convenience, except in the sense in which all inference may be said to be so dictated. The initial transition in the reasoning from the Brownian movement to the hypothesis of the molecular constitution of fluids and gases is almost irresistible; it consists merely in continuing to make the same sort of inference which you always have successfully made in the case of macroscopic entities and phenomena. There is no antecedent reason for supposing that the powers of our eyes or lenses define the lower limits of magnitude for all possible discrete existents; and none for supposing that the things beyond this accidental and variable threshold of perceptibility are not entities to which the more general categories applicable to the perceptible apply. The rule of employing the type of hypothesis which permits continuity of inferential procedure or explanatory method, of construing the unobserved by analogy with the observed, is the only one which is *not* arbitrary. It rests upon the working assumption that the persistent world with which in sense-perception we are in some sort of contact has, with all its diversity, some uniformity of constitution at all levels of analysis. Since this assumption conceivably may be false, the acceptance of it involves an element of faith; but it is the kind of faith which makes a science possible, which permits us to proceed upon the supposition that we may know something of things which we do not actually see and of events which we have not actually experienced. When this rule of procedure at any point breaks down, by leading to inferences

---

[27] This is, of course, not intended as an account of the history of the kinetic theory, but only as a simplified statement of the natural order of the steps which might logically lead to it.

concerning the observable which do not accord with the facts, it must, of course, at that point be abandoned, and our ignorance there be admitted. But it need not and should not be abandoned hastily or beyond necessity. And what I am suggesting is that its general break-down is not yet conclusively demonstrated; that the complexities and perplexities of modern physics do not forbid us to believe in a not wholly unknowable physical world, not perceived by us directly nor without "psychic additions," to which world, nevertheless, the concepts, not only of number and causality, but also of space, time, change and motion are applicable.

And in this belief I am, once more, encouraged by the behavior of the physicists. For example, the distinguished investigator from whom I last quoted a seemingly radical denial of the possibility of "ascribing physical reality to the internal processes of a theory," proceeds upon the next page to summarize two recently acquired "points of view" (already mentioned in this lecture) which seem to him "sufficient, in connection with other physical knowledge which we already have, to determine the nature of the elementary processes and entities which analysis of our physical experience discloses to us"—"the qualitative nature of the underlying elemental processes and entities." And, laying it down as a "cardinal principle that the properties of a thing have no meaning which is not contained in some describable [but not necessarily by us attainable] experience," he concludes that, given the points of view already established, "our intuitions should be able to tell us what to expect in various experimental situations involving elementary things"—that "our intuitive grasp of an elementary situation may be tested by our ability to describe what to expect in terms of conceptual experiments." [28] This seems to imply that we have some reason to believe that at "the frontiers of physical exploration" we actually come upon "underlying elemental processes and entities," and that, different as they are from the entities of perceptual experience, they are still of an intuitable nature, that is to say, not wholly without analogy to our sensa and their

[28] Bridgman in *Science*, 1930, p. 22.

relations in our perceptual fields. If they are not assumed to be of such a nature, the useful method of conceptual experiment could hardly be applied to them. Hypothetical experiences are describable only in terms derived from some characters of perceptual experience.

Contemporary physics, then, does not seem as yet to have given the death-blow to man's natural belief that he lives in a physical world which is, in its general structure and the modes of relatedness of its components, somewhat like the world which he perceptually experiences. That it conclusively vindicates this belief I am not maintaining, though I think it still lends some support to it. But the belief in question is at worst a natural and almost universal prejudice of mankind; and I can not but think that the burden of proof rests upon those who demand that we abandon a prejudice of this sort. What is certain is that, unless or until full and clear evidence of its falsity is offered, the prejudice will not disappear from men's minds—just as it manifestly has not really disappeared from the minds of physicists.

I speak of this belief as a prejudice; yet it is at least not a blind nor wholly inexplicable prejudice. It is born of, or at all events is nourished by, certain specific experiences at the macroscopic level and of perceptual objects. Let us, then, return to the world of perception to note what those particular aspects of it are which chiefly sustain such a belief, and to ask whether these are not such as to suggest its legitimacy. And in doing so, let us hold fast to the results reached in our inquiry before we entered upon the consideration of the bearing upon this belief of modern physical theories. We shall, that is to say, take three conclusions as already established: (a) there is an order of existences or events which persists when unperceived; (b) this is causally related to our sensa; (c) the particulars belonging to it cannot be identical with our sensa. Our problem, then, is whether, given these premises and the common facts of every-day experience, we can reach any further probable propositions concerning the extra-perceptual, neutral, causal order. One such proposition, manifestly, is that we have power to act upon this order. Processes which apparently go on unperceived can be initiated by percipient beings. And the unobserved interperceptual causal processes will vary (as their subsequently observed effects will show) with variations in the specific characters of our sense-data while we are initiating those processes; e. g., if I build my fire of wood instead of coal, the time required for it to burn out will be shorter and the ashes which I find on returning to the room will be of a different quality. It is equally a fact of everyday experience that certain percepts or images do not initiate (or are not correlated with) processes capable of continuing during interperceptual intervals and producing observable terminal effects identical with those observable when the entire sequence of intermediate stages has been attended to. If I merely imagine or dream of a fire in the grate, I do not—after ceasing so to dream or imagine—experience the visual and tactual content called ashes. Purely visual content is not found by us to be sufficient to start fires (or to give sensible evidence of the physical equivalent of a fire having started in the extra-perceptual world), or to be correlated with the initiation by us of any physical process. The same fact is illustrated by the comparative sterility of pink rats. If I am able to initiate a physical process, my action (if experienced at all by myself) is experienced in the form of tactual and kinaesthetic as well as (in some cases) visual sense-data; it is, in short, one of the primary discoveries of experience that tactual and kinaesthetic sensations have a different and more constant relation to the physical causal order than do visual percepts or images. The former are the phases of our experience in which we as percipients appear to have causal contact with that order. And it is reasonable to suppose that this fact throws some light upon the nature of the external causal world.

Furthermore, if, like everyone else, we assume that there are many percipients, and that they can through language convey some information to one another about the characteristics of their respective sense-data, we find that each of them is able to act upon the other percipients, that is, to determine in some degree what experiences they shall have; and that this action upon them is usually, and probably always, conditioned upon initiating (in the sense and in the manner already indicated) physical processes. If I light a fire, other men as well as myself will feel the heat; they may, in consequence of my action, observe a sensible fire continuously while I do not; while if I imagine or dream of a fire, their experience remains unaffected. One of the two principal reasons why we do not regard dream-fires as indications of the occurrence of events (at least the kind of events ordinarily connected with sensible fires) in the persistent and therefore independent world is that they do not cause others to have sensations of warmth or to find perceptible ashes in their perceptible grates. Purely private percepts are called illusory, not merely because they happen to be private, but because they do not causally interact directly, or in the manner in which other qualitatively similar percepts do, with the world which is the medium of communication and interaction between us.

Now what observably happens when I thus act upon the external world and through it affect other men's experiences and my own subsequent experiences, is usually that with my perceptible body I push and pull other perceptible objects about in my perceptual space. And with the movements which I thus determine as data of my own perception there may be—under conditions empirically definable—correlated perceptions of movement in the experience of others. They report to me that they see what they call my body moving, and other objects moving in ways uniformly connected with my bodily movements. That their percepts of what they call my body are not my body itself is true—if the arguments on this matter previously set forth are correct; and it is also true that the perceptual objects which they see moving in consequence of my bodily movements are not existentially nor qualitatively identical with those which I see, nor yet with any entity in the neutral causal order. The question may nevertheless be asked: Are the causal processes in the external world which are initiated by motions (*i. e.,* by those which I perceive) and which terminate in motions (*i. e.,* those which other men perceive) also of the nature of motions? The idealist answers definitely in the negative; the phenomenalist and the all-but agnostic physicist answer that we have, at any rate, no reason whatever for thinking so. But there are, I think, certain considerations which, though not demonstrative, make an affirmative answer to the question the more plausible.

(a) In the first place, it is at least not *impossible* that the processes which cause and link together the percepts of different times and different persons are of the same general sort as the causal sequences which empirically occur within our perceptual experience. No fact of experience, obviously, can prove the contrary.

(b) It is a simpler assumption about the unperceived causal processes that they are of the same sort as those perceived, rather than of some wholly different sort. In making such an assumption we still follow the rule of continuity in our conjectures about that which we cannot directly experience. We do not postulate differences in the nature of things beyond necessity. If I suppose that, when I have the experience of moving my body and pushing and pulling something about, thereby producing effects in the neutral causal order, I *am* pushing or pulling something about, and that this *is* a way in which effects in that order are produced, I am enabled to conceive of the external world with which I am in relation in action as fundamentally homogeneous with the perceptual world; and though it may not be so, it appears to me more sensible to proceed upon the hypothesis that it is, so long as there is no good evidence to the contrary.

(c) The spaces in which our perceptible effective bodily movements take place, whether or not they are literally parts of a single Space, are at all events congruent; they fit together in a remarkable way. For example, a hundred men from as many different places are summoned to attend an international conference in Geneva. They thereupon consult maps, time-tables, Baedekers, to find the routes to take in order to reach that city. These useful works were prepared by yet other men. They do not, however, purport to be descriptions of the arrangement of things in private perceptual spaces of their authors; they profess to represent a set of spatial relations which will hold good in the perceptual experience of any inhabitant of the earth. The routes which they describe are not routes to a hundred private Genevas, but to a single Geneva conceived to have a determinate position in some common or public spatial order. And by a series of movements of their own legs, assisted by motions of trains and steamships, which follow spatial directions symbolized in the maps and guidebooks, the delegates to the conference presently find themselves having similar (though not identical) visual and tactual percepts, for example, percepts of the Quai Mont Blanc, and in a position in which they can sit down in the same room and talk to one another. The result may be that the construction of battleships in certain other places will be discontinued. The idealistic or phenomenalistic account of this affair is that there is no common space such as is represented by the maps, and that no motion of what could strictly be called the body of any delegate took place. What happened was merely that their minds—which were throughout in no place at all—after first having private percepts of maps and then having visual and other sensations, of motion, resulting, perhaps, in sensations of sea-sickness, subsequently experienced certain resemblant sense-percepts which they mistakenly called by the single name "Geneva," and others which they called the bodies and voices of their fellow delegates. In reality, therefore, the delegates never met. Their private sequences of sense-data, for no known or conjecturable reason, happened eventually to coincide in part; at approximately the time when one of them had the kinaesthetic sensations of opening his mouth and using his vocal organs, the others had correspondent visual sensations and also certain sound-sensations of (more or less) intelligible words; but they were no nearer one another when this occurred than at the beginning. Now this is, no doubt, conceivable, in the sense that it is not formally self-contradictory; but it seems to me incredibly far-fetched, and I cannot avoid the suspicion that the human species (including physicists and even idealistic philosophers) is constitutionally incapable of really believing it—of thinking in this fashion of this type of experience. Men have always believed, and will, doubtless, continue to believe, that the way to arrive at a place is to go there; and they will always be recalcitrant to a view which requires them to hold, or to regard it as probable, that (for example) the ill-fated passengers of the *Titanic* were not really in the same ship or even in the same space. So long as the experienced bodily movements of a number of separate percipients thus fit into a single spatial pattern; so long as, in consequence of motions in convergent directions in that pattern (and not otherwise), the percipients find themselves face to face; so long as (to vary the illustration) through such bodily movements (and not otherwise) they are enabled not only to destroy the bodies of other men but also to bring all *their* perceiving to an end, by firing bullets in the direction in which the other men's bodies are perceived—so long men will naturally conceive of the processes in the common world through which their respective sense-data are caused as occurring in a single common spatial or spatio-temporal order and as consisting of motions therein. That this conceived common space is literally identical with their perceived spaces they may find reason to doubt; that the bodies which effectively move in it have all the properties of the bodies sensibly perceived, or are particulars existentially identical with them, they will find good reasons for denying. But the fact that their apprehension of bodies must be recognized by them to be mediate or representational and to contain "psychic additions" and distortions need not, and pretty certainly will not, prevent them from thinking that they have bodies—unique bodies, that is, each of which belongs to one percipient, and is not merely the multitudinous aggregate of the percepts of it—bodies which are therefore assignable to the public spatial system, which have positions relative to other bodies, which can change these positions, and in doing so cause changes in other bodies and modify thereby the sense-content, or even bring to an end the existence, of other percipient beings.

In all this, it may be said, I am forgetting the theory of relativity, which shows that there is no general frame of nature, no common space or time for different percipients. But I have never observed relativistic physicists hesitating to assume that the imaginary voyagers whom they describe as roving about the heavens at enormous speeds can send light-signals to one another, whatever their relative velocities or the length of their journeys; and I find such physicists always assuming that these signals will take time in passing from one "system" to another, and that their course will be deflected if they happen to pass through the gravitational fields to be found in the neighborhood of material bodies. That relativity physics dispenses, and shows the plain man how to dispense, with the notions of a general spatial order (whatever its novel geometrical properties) or of moving entities therein, consequently still seems to me difficult to make out; and I surmise, therefore, that the plain man's prejudice in favor of the belief that he has a body which moves in a public space, and that, in general, the causal processes in the persistent neutral world consist (at least in part) of the motions of bodies, will not by this doctrine be corrected, but rather confirmed.

Such, then, is a brief and incomplete indication of the normal genesis of this prejudice. It gains further strength from a hundred other characteristics of ordinary perceptual experience, which there is no time to recall.[29] It is, I venture to suggest, a prejudice to which the plain man and even the philosopher may continue

[29] Cf., e. g., certain considerations mentioned by Mr. Russell (somewhat inconsistently with his own general doctrine) and cited above, p. 276.

to yield without the fear of imminent confutation—and one which even the physicist will find it useful to take (as he usually does) as the starting-point of his further analyses and of his extension of our understanding of the world we live in. He does not extend that understanding by informing us that there is taking place in the world "something, we don't know what"; and if his analyses lead him to conclude that there is no common spatio-temporal order through which we act upon one another, the conclusion is less probable than the proposition which it denies—and at the same time presupposes.

IX

THE NATURE OF KNOWING AS A
NATURAL EVENT

The hypothetical conclusion which we reached at the beginning
of the preceding lecture was a conclusion pertinent only to the
case of the physical realist. If you are to believe in a real physical
world, then—so the argument ran—you must necessarily be a
dualist in both senses of the term: you must hold (a) that there
are given in experience particular existents which are not parts of
that world, and you must hold (b) that whatever knowledge of
real objects you have is indirect or representative, that the datum
whereby you know any such object is not identical with the object
known. Resuming our inquiry at this point—after some divaga-
tion into a collateral issue—we proceed to consider two further
questions, relating exclusively to the second of these propositions.
The first question is whether that proposition is valid not exclusively from the standpoint of the realist, but from any standpoint
—in other words, whether epistemological dualism must be accepted by anyone, be he realist or idealist or phenomenalist or
pragmatist, who believes that the phenomenon called knowing
ever does actually occur. The second question is whether, in final
analysis, epistemological dualism itself is tenable—whether the
notion of the apprehension of an existent (whatever be its metaphysical nature) by means of the immediate presence in experience of *something other than itself* is psychologically intelligible,
or even conceivable without self-contradiction. Our two questions, then, more briefly stated, are: (1) Is the mediate character
of knowledge implied by idealism (or kindred doctrines) as well

as by physical realism? (2) Is mediate knowledge possible—and if so, how?

The comment will, of course, naturally suggest itself here that the second question ought to come first, and that, indeed, it should have been dealt with at the very beginning of our whole inquiry. But this order of procedure would, I think, be a mistaken one, in spite of its air of logicality. It is, for reasons which I have already suggested, better to begin with hypothetical questions, to make explicit the necessary but frequently overlooked implications, with respect to a given problem, of the various types of opinion which have been held by philosophers, or by common sense, instead of attacking directly the seemingly fundamental and decisive issues. And the advantages of this procedure are well illustrated in the case of the questions now before us. One of the principal and most plausible grounds for accepting idealism, as a metaphysical doctrine, has at all times consisted in the assumption that epistemological dualism is a gratuitously complicated, or even an intrinsically absurd, account of what occurs when anything is known, and that idealism is a way, and the only way, of escaping from this supposed absurdity. But if it is the fact—as I think we shall find it to be—that the idealist as well as the realist is irretrievably committed to the theory of indirect or representative knowledge, then both of them are likely to come with more open minds to the question whether that theory is really so gratuitous or so absurd as had been supposed. They are, indeed, under such circumstances, likely to come to it with a rational presumption in its favor. For—unless one is prepared to admit in advance that there is an absurdity inherent in the very idea of knowledge—it would appear antecedently improbable that a conclusion which is equally inevitable from the standpoint of either of the two possible general types of metaphysical doctrine is itself impossible. When this improbability is realized, a less hasty and prejudiced examination into the supposed difficulties of that conclusion should result.

(1) We turn, then, to our first question. The answer to it is

to be found in some very simple considerations already intimated. The idealist does, of course, avoid an admission of epistemological dualism with respect to the knowledge of the physical world, inasmuch as he denies that there is—in the sense in which we have been using the term—any physical world to be known. He is content (in this matter) with his private world of perceptual content. His sense-data have an indubitable, if transitory, existence; each of them is precisely what it is immediately experienced as being; and he seeks for nothing possessing similar generic characters beyond or behind them. The being of sensible things is simply their being sensed; and their true characters are therefore their sensed characters. And it is because he has, in dealing with the special problem of perception, thus contrived very easily and summarily to rid himself of the difficulty of understanding how things can be known indirectly, that the idealist has often supposed that he has avoided that difficulty altogether. But this is an illusion, and a very naïve and transparent one, arising chiefly from an excessive preoccupation of epistemologists in the past with the problem of perception.

For the type of cognitive—or putatively cognitive—experience with which a systematic epistemological inquiry ought to begin is not perception but retrospection, or, more specifically, remembrance. This is the primary mode of knowing, which must be presupposed, tacitly or explicitly, in any reflection upon the implications of what is sensibly given; and it is the kind of knowledge about the reality of which there is least disagreement. It is the one which involves the smallest transcendence of absolute scepticism, and from which it is improbable that the most resolutely subjectivistic of philosophers really dissents. Its thin end is of an exceeding thinness; it amounts to no more than the assumption that one was not born at this moment, that one has had experiences of which one now knows, though they are not the experiences which one is now having. If Descartes had been as critical and methodical in rebuilding his world as he was in shattering it, he would have seen that the existential proposition which, in his reconstruction, should have immediately followed the *cogito ergo sum* was *memini ergo fui*. He could not, indeed, have formally deduced this from the *cogito;* he could not, strictly speaking, have justified it by reasoning; but he could, by simply keeping his attention fixed upon his own consciousness, have, so to say, seen *cogito* transforming itself into *memini* before his eyes. Small as this step might have seemed, it would have altered the direction of Descartes' subsequent course of reasoning; and if he had taken it, the history of modern philosophy might well have been widely different from what it has been, and less involved in confusion.

For any belief in the possibility of true remembrance is not only a step out of subjectivism; it is also a step into epistemological dualism. Why this is true was briefly indicated in the first of these lectures; but it is perhaps advisable to recapitulate and complete the argument here. In memory and other retrospection there is a conscious and intrinsic reference to a reality other than the content given. The perceptual datum, as Berkeleian idealists and neo-realists both like to remind us, is not presented in unreflective experience as standing for an existent not itself; *merely* to perceive is not to be explicitly aware of a contrast between datum and *cognoscendum*. But merely to remember *is* to be aware of a contrast between the image presented and the event recalled. No man doubts that, when he recollects today the acts he performed yesterday, those acts are not occurring today and yet that something which somehow exhibits their character is an item in his experience today; or that when, for example, he brings to mind the look of a dog he owned when a boy, there is something of a canine sort immediately present to and therefore compresent with his consciousness, but that it is quite certainly not that dog in the flesh. Retrospection is thus a case in which the duality of the datum and the thing known is immediately manifest, so that to deny the duality is to deny that the kind of knowing which retrospection purports to be is possible at all; whereas in the case of perceptual knowledge the duality becomes evident only through an analysis in which certain postulates about the external world are necessary. The direct evidence for epistemological dualism from the nature of the memory-experience is, then, as plain for an idealist as for a realist, if the idealist admits that he had a past and is not wholly unacquainted with it. Everyone who ever says "I remember," and uses the word in its natural and familiar sense, is bearing witness to the possibility of mediate or representative knowledge.

It is, of course, true that some philosophers and psychologists profess to reject this account of what occurs when a man remembers. Two opposite objections to it have been raised. (a) With the first I have already dealt: it consists in the assertion that the thing remembered has *not* ceased to exist, and may therefore now be directly contemplated. This, if literally meant, is a paradox, begotten of a theoretical prejudice, which I find it impossible to take seriously; and if it is not literally meant, it is irrelevant. From the standpoint of physical realism its absurdity is doubly evident; for what is remembered is not only, by the assumption inherent in memory itself, something past, but it is often also, by the assumption of the realist, something not present in the physical world. The dog remembered was once flesh and blood; it is now dust; but it is a dog and not dust that is the object of the remembrance. But from any standpoint, again, the absurdity is patent. To remember is *eo ipso* to assign to the object a date in a temporal sequence which is not the date of the act of retrospection nor of the givenness of the image. Even if what is called the same individual thing still exists, it is to a by-gone phase of its existence that memory refers; to apprehend a present state of anything is not to remember. And, of course, if memory consisted in the actual presence in consciousness of the object to be known, it would necessarily be infallible. (b) The other way of attempting to escape from the dualistic implication of the fact of memory is by denying the existence of memory-images. When a man says "I remember," there no doubt is, it is granted, something of a peculiar sort given in his experience, or, at all events, taking place in his body; but this, whatever it be (about which theories may differ), is neither an actual past event nor a simulacrum referred to a prior date. It is merely some distinctive present form of sensory content or physiological behavior. About this only two brief remarks need, I think, be made. In the first place, it is simply a dogmatic denial of the occurrence of a type of experience which most persons are quite as certain of having had as they are certain of anything. It is true, indeed, that memory-content is often of a highly abstract and symbolic or verbal sort; what is now introspectably present may be rather the name than the likeness of a vanished object or a by-gone happening. Yet it is also true that the content is often of a more or less vividly imaginal character; the testimony to this is far too definite and abundant to be summarily set aside. Empirical science is presumably science which is based upon human experience; and a psychological theory which tells us that there are no such things as images experienced when people are remembering rejects *a priori* a voluminous mass of empirical evidence which does not happen to accord with the theorist's preconceptions. And, in the second place, be the memory-content as non-imaginal and abstractly symbolic as it may, it is still symbolic *of* something, and that something is apprehended as past; this is the distinctive *quale* of the retrospective experience. Even if we should attempt to give a purely behavioristic account of what is *present* in memory, should describe it as a particular kind of muscular "set," or as a movement of molecules in the larynx or some other anatomical region, unless this were in some fashion conceived as corresponding with or referring to some antedated event, at least to some earlier behavior, it would not be to anything of the nature of memory that our description would be pertinent.[1]

These attempts to conceive of retrospection in general, and of memory in particular, in a non-dualistic way are, then, unsuccessful; when not equivalent to denying that we ever remember at all,

_____

[1] A third conceivable way of seeking an alternative to the admission of the duality of datum and *cognoscendum* in memory would be through the theory that data—in this case as in perception—are "mere essences." Concerning this theory enough has, I think, been said in the second and fourth lectures.

they are equivalent to admitting that memory is a mode of representative knowledge. In short, there is either no such phenomenon as retrospection, or else in it, at least, the relation of the immediate content to the fact or object known is of that loose, indirect, mediate sort which the epistemological dualist supposes to be characteristic of knowing in general. And all that we call empirical knowledge consists primarily of memories, taken as true portrayals of past events as they were when they happened. A good deal of the contemporary philosophy which purports to be a generalization of the methods of scientific inquiry is obsessed with a single phase of it, with what may be called the moment of experimentation; it tends to demand that all that can be called "known" shall be immediately exhibited in the way in which the sensible result of an experiment is exhibited at the instant at which the experiment is completed. But even the assumption of the relevance of the result to the antecedent inquiry is itself a piece of retrospection; and the result itself becomes available for use only when it becomes memory-content, a record of a by-gone sequence of natural events, which is, by faith, translated into a picture of probable future sequences. We somewhat misleadingly say that science is based upon experience—misleadingly, because the noun has no tense. Some current misconceptions would perhaps have been avoided if we had made a practice of saying that science is based upon the experienced, that is to say, upon the remembered. We should then have clearly realized that it always consists in beliefs about objects which are not now present to us, and remain, indeed, in their own individual being, forever inaccessible.

There is a familiar type of idealistic metaphysics in which these facts are recognized, so far as human knowing is concerned, but an attempt is made to escape their implications by invoking an Absolute Mind whose knowing is not subject to our infirmities. To the Absolute, we are told, all reality is present at once with just that immediacy with which small private fragments of it may be present to any one of us in a single moment of consciousness.

Past, present and future, though distinguished, are not only simultaneously apprehended but simultaneously and univocally real in the eternal and all-comprehending Moment which is the Absolute Experience; and the parts which compose this Experience—it is sometimes added—constitute a system of mutually determining elements, so that nothing is independent of anything else, and the events of today may constitute, in part, the cause or *ratio essendi* of the events of yesterday. While this conception seems to me a flat self-contradiction, I do not wish to discuss it here; for it has no pertinency to the question before us, nor to any epistemological issue. The knowing with which we are concerned is the knowing of finite beings whose yesterdays are never compresent with today and in whom remembrance attains no immediate and completely indubitable hold upon its object. Any other kind of knowing is an affair of the Absolute alone, which throws no light upon the situation in the temporal world, nor upon the manner in which we temporal creatures contrive to do what, upon that hypothesis, is beyond the Absolute's power—namely, to know portions of reality which are not directly present to the knower, nor within the existential limits of the knowing.

Of the other form of intertemporal cognition, actual or supposed—that is, foreknowledge or expectation—the dualistic implications are, if possible, even more manifest; and thus those pragmatic philosophers who curiously tend to conceive of the future as the sole region upon which our interest and our intellection are directed must, not less certainly than the idealist, admit that the *cognoscendum* is not apprehended through actual possession. For such pragmatists knowledge is pre-presentative if not representative. Future events not only are not now being experienced, but they have never entered into experience nor into existence, *as* events; and upon them no sane mortal can suppose his cognitive grasp to be direct and assured. Yet unless we can truly be said in some sense to be capable of referring to and foreknowing some future events, all our other knowing is, not, indeed, spurious, but—as the pragmatist rightly enough insists—barren, and irrelevant to the occasions which chiefly make knowledge needful to the expectant, purposive, and plan-devising creatures that we are.

Both retrospection and forecast, then, are crucial and undeniable examples of the fact that knowing—if there *is* any such phenomenon—may, and at least in certain cases must, consist in the apprehension of a particular existent through the presence in a given experience of some existent other than itself. To deny this is to deny not only that we can have any knowledge of an external world, but also that we can have, or even conceive the possibility of having, any knowledge of any experience beyond the immediate and certain content of a single specious present of a single knower. Here, at least, the object is present vicariously or not at all. If there were in this mode of knowing no recognized contrast between what is given and what is meant, it would not do for us what, in the perpetual flux of consciousness, and in our urgent need to escape from the limitations of that flux, we want knowing to do; and, on the other hand, it would permit no doubts about the truth or adequacy of our apprehension of the object upon which our cognitive act is directed, and demand no venture of faith when we go about our business tentatively taking that which now appears to us as evidence of that which truly has been and is to be.

(2) We pass now to our second question. It concerns the truth of the thesis—frequently maintained by philosophers who are themselves, as we have just seen, epistemological dualists—that any theory of indirect or representative knowledge is redundant and, in the last analysis, self-contradictory. This general type of criticism takes two forms, according as the point of difficulty in the dualistic view is conceived to be (a) the assertion that the object is not *directly* known or (b) that it nevertheless *is* known. (a) Those who fix upon the first point declare that to say that a thing is not known directly—is not itself "before the mind" at the time of the cognitive event—is equivalent to saying that it is *not* at that time known and that verification of a judg-

ment concerning it at any time is impossible. Any correspondence-theory of knowledge, it has been endlessly reiterated, is tantamount to a denial of the possibility of knowledge. If the realities about which we judge, in our perceptual or other judgments, are forever beyond our grasp, it is mere irony to speak of our "apprehending" them. The two supposedly correspondent existences, idea and object, can never be brought together for actual comparison; and the truth of the judgment can therefore never be established. (b) And, on the other hand, it is argued, the dualist, in distinguishing between the datum which he apprehends directly and the "real object" which he professes to apprehend indirectly, implies that he *has* the latter as well as the former present to his consciousness—and present with precisely the status of "objectivity" or "realness" whereby it is supposed to be differentiated from the mere datum. But if so, it is not only superfluous but inconsistent to maintain that it is through a substitute which is not in the same sense "real" that the object is known. In short, an object is at any moment "before the mind" or it is not. If it is not, it obviously is not at that moment being known. If it is, then it is *that* object, and not some other entity, that is before the mind. Epistemological dualism is thus a self-refuting thesis; it cannot be stated without being in that statement implicitly denied. The dualist may, it is true, introduce a verbal distinction between data which are "merely present" for awareness and those which are "present-as-absent"; but the distinction is unintelligible. There are not two ways of being present for awareness, but only one.

These arguments, and especially the latter, as was noted in the second lecture, were among the more serious and plausible of the considerations which originally gave rise to the revolt against dualism. They are arguments against the possibility of mediate knowledge as such, and are therefore pressed by both the realistic and idealistic critics of dualism. That they cannot legitimately be used by the former has already been shown on two quite different grounds—first, because realism proves unable, in any of its forms, to assign to the datum the characters and spatio-temporal situations and modes of action which it ascribes to the real physical object; and second, because the monistic realist's position is liable to the same type of objection which he here brings against the dualist. His doctrine implies what he reproaches the dualist for plainly asserting. For it implies that he and other men can be aware of things which are not, as existents, immediately present for awareness. If he does not admit this, he denies the knowable reality of things independent of awareness. He, too, is by the inherent logic of his doctrine committed, though against his own intention, to affirming that content may be within the circle of actual experience as if extraneous to it. The present objection to dualism is thus at bottom an objection to all realism, including that residuum of realism which inevitably remains even in the doctrine of the idealist. But to show that the vicarious presence of objects, at least in intertemporal cognition, is implied by everybody who believes such cognition to be possible, is not to eliminate the apparent paradox of vicarious presence. It is, therefore, as we have recognized from the outset, incumbent upon the dualistic philosopher to attempt to make clear finally, not only (to use an apposite distinction of Bradley's) *that* the doctrine of the mediate character of knowledge *is* true, but also *how* it *may* be true —to "explain how consciousness can be of an absent object."

To do this, however, the dualistic philosopher need only invite men to observe yet more carefully what they are doing when they are, or conceive themselves to be, knowing the past or the future. In the case of retrospection or anticipation, as in other cases, knowing manifestly does not consist in blankly glaring at isolated and unrelated bits of content. The content is permeated with relational categories; its parts are given as having diverse situations in one or another schema of relations, of which the temporal distinctions of relative date—before-and-after, past-present-and-future—are one type. We can know yesterday today, and know it *as* yesterday, without either actually going back to it or bringing it again into present existence, simply because what is before the mind today is a pattern of dated events. The pattern is given, and has its psychological existence, today, but it *includes the relative date of its own existence as one of its terms* or components; and in this pattern its own date or locus of existence is recognized as identical with that of our awareness, and as not identical with that of the particular event, within the pattern, upon which our cognitive attention is specifically directed. To experience at a given moment a pattern of temporal succession is not the same as passing through a succession of experiences. In a historical chart the relations both of simultaneity and of succession of certain happenings are alike simultaneously spread out in a spatial arrangement which you may take in at a glance. Nevertheless, if you are acquainted with the plan upon which the chart was drawn up, you perfectly clearly distinguish between the spatial pattern which you see and the temporal relations which it symbolizes; and you do not, because the names or descriptions of the historical events in question are before your eyes all at once, have any difficulty in understanding that what the historian intended to convey was not that these events occurred all at once. It is, then, this power which we obviously have—one without which there could be no historians, inasmuch as historical propositions could have no meaning—of thinking relations of succession without thereby experiencing them, that makes retrospection possible, and defines the sense in which remembered events are present-as-absent. It is their symbols only, the images or the words which represent them, that are literally and indubitably present. But the remembered events, though not in this sense present, are presented. For the given characters of the symbols are referred to a situation in the conceptual schema which is external to that which the symbols are recognized as having therein. The symbols, in short, have a date of givenness and a date of reference, which are clearly distinguished. The practical function of knowledge, upon which it is the current fashion to lay so great emphasis, is secondary to this function of intertemporal transcendent reference, and derivative from it. Knowledge is, no doubt, among other things, an instrument of control and a means of adaptation to the predetermined conditions and limitations of purposive action. But its distinctive efficacy for this end lies in its power to bring past and future within the scope of present consciousness; and its uncertainty and fallibility lie in the fact that it does not bring the *actual* past and future within the confines of time or place that bound the existence of present consciousness and of its data.

The solution, then, of the supposed difficulty in the conception of knowing as mediate is evident. To claim knowledge of what is not temporally coexistent with the knowing, is *not* to have the intended object of knowledge *in propria persona* "before the mind"; and the epistemological dualist in expressing his thesis does not fall into the contradiction of asserting that he has that object before his mind and at the same time asserting that he knows it only through the presentation in his experience of something which is not that object. What his thesis means, or should mean, is that at the moment when any man believes himself to be, *e.g.*, remembering, there is before him both a particular concrete datum—usually an image—and the conception of a mode of relatedness in which mutually external existences, including this datum, may stand to one another; and that the character of the datum either is ascribed to a locus (in that relational order) conceived as other than that in which it is actually given (other, namely, than the here-and-now locus), or is at least regarded as capable of presence in that other locus. This ascription of the character to some locus of the not-present and not-given is not equivalent to, and is in knowledge—when, at least, it is at all reflective—not confused with, its veritable presence in such a locus; for it is as an externality in *existence* that the mutual externality of the loci is conceived. The notion of existence, which is so often treated as mysterious and incomprehensible, appears to be so only because it is fundamental in our thinking and irreducible; intelligence cannot take a single step without employing it. Those who think they have dispensed with it are transparently deceiving themselves. We are empirically acquainted with its meaning by ourselves being—and by the being, at any moment, of our present data. But we can, and must, and persistently do, extend it to objects and events to which we impute positions not our own in that order of temporal relations which we conceive as including and transcending our own position and that of our data. And when we do this we mean something more than the fact of our so extending it—more, that is, than the fact that those objects are now presented to us as so situated in that now presented frame. We mean, precisely, that that to which we extend it had, or will have, existence in its own position as truly as we and our data (including our concept of the temporal order of relations) now have existence; but in that order, the only part of which we are now *experiencing* the existence, and of which we can assert the present existence, is the part within which we and our data are situated. Thus it is that we can, at a given moment, contrast the reality of a not-present event with the givenness of the datum (whether percept or image) by which we apprehend it, and even with the givenness of the conceptual schema by means of which we are enabled to frame the distinction between the present and the not-present, the datum and the *cognoscendum*.

The "how" of mediate knowing being thus made intelligible primarily by a scrutiny of intertemporal knowledge, of which the mediate character is certain, the purely epistemological paradox supposed to inhere in any dualistic theory of perception disappears. There is nothing more paradoxical in the conception of a knowledge of physical objects by means of sensa not identical with those objects than there is in the conception of a knowledge of past events by means of memory-images not identical with those events. The two phenomena are, indeed, for the dualistic physical realist, not merely analogous but in one respect identical. Any true judgment ascribing any character of a present sensum to a physical object must always, he has come to realize, be a retrospective judgment, since none of the processes which he supposes to intervene between the object and the occurrence of the percipient event take place instantaneously. The *modus operandi* of the transcendent reference in memory and in perception is thus far, then, precisely the same; though everybody makes that reference in the case of memory, while only those who assume a physical world, and accept certain propositions of physicists and physiologists as pertinent to that world, do so explicitly in the case of perception. But there is, of course, a further difference, arising from the fact that the parts of the field of visual perception have extension and relative spatial positions. The instructed dualist not only antedates the characters of his sensa when and in so far as he ascribes them to physical things, but he also refers some characters to spatial positions other than those in which they are perceived. If he adheres to the theory of a single space in which physical objects and also all the visual data of all percipients are situated, he nevertheless judges the actual rails or the real star to be situated in that spatial frame in positions less or more widely distant from those occupied by their sensible appearances. And if he finds this theory untenable and believes sensa to have position only in a multiplicity of private perceptual spaces, he still (unless his physical realism is of a quite evanescent sort) *conceives* of a public space or space-time, to some conceived locus in which he assigns some attribute found in his sensum. But upon neither theory does he suppose that the actual rail or star is itself the content given. The something "before his mind" by means of which he conceptually distinguishes the real object from his sense-datum, is an idea of a character (actually and certainly possessed by the datum) as existing in a place which—in one or the other of the two senses just distinguished—is not the perceptible position of that datum in his visual field. The distinction of the locus of the real object from that of the datum is sometimes purely negative—the distinction between "here" and "somewhere else." But some distinctions of this general type we all constantly make; and, just as in the case of the contrast between the date of the givenness of the memory image and that of the occurrence of 'the remembered event, so in this spatial transcendent reference to a place external to a perceived place, we think the object as an existent there without assuming that its existence is, by virtue of our so thinking, empirically given, as the existence of the datum indubitably is given.

The fundamental fact here too, in short, is that we can and incessantly do apply the existential predicate to regions beyond our present or actual experience, and that we also constantly recognize that this predication of existence is not identical with what is predicated. The concept of a beyond is not the beyond; nevertheless it is *of* a beyond that it is a concept. That we possess concepts of one and another sort of beyond—of times not now, of spatial objects not perceived, of experiences no longer, or not yet, or not by us, enjoyed—and that such conceived beyonds are, in our cognitive activity, the matters with which we are, or mean to be, concerned, is one of the things we know best about ourselves as thinkers and would-be knowers of other beings. Though, when put in general and therefore abstract terms, this may seem to have an air of mystery about it, nothing is in fact more familiar to us; for we are knowers by constitution and habit, and it is in this act of transcendent reference that knowing as a psychological phenomenon—in so far as it is more than bare sensation without meaning—consists. To deny that items of content may be actually experienced as signifying things not themselves, because not occupying the same places as these items in one or another of those frames of relations by which reality is conceived by us as sundered into mutually external parts, is to deny the primary empirical fact concerning the nature and function of knowing as a natural event.

We have been considering the knowing of particular existences from, so to say, the inside; we have been observing what it appears as to the knower. Accepting the results thus reached, we may now define the distinctive character and the rôle of knowledge in the economy of nature. Essentially, knowing is a phenomenon by which the simple location of things is circumvented without being annulled.   Upon any metaphysical theory deserving of serious consideration reality is an aggregate of *partes extra partes*.[2]   Every particular is in its own time, or its own place, or its own point-instant in space-time; or (for the idealist) it is an act of consciousness, or a subject of consciousness, or a presentation in the experience of some supposedly "windowless monad," each of these being numerically distinct from other entities of the same type.   Existents, in short, whether they are physical or mental or both, are many; they are bounded, and the bounds of their being mean mutual exclusion.   This is not equivalent to asserting that they are without relations, or that they do not causally interact, or even that they may not be mutually implicatory.   But it is mere confusion of thought to suppose that any of these interconnections between particulars amount to a transcendence of the separateness and identity of the particulars.   If things are said to be related, it is so much the more evident that they do not (with respect to any determinate mode of relation) escape from their reciprocal exclusiveness; for it is only where there are distinct terms that there can be said to be real relations. But though things exist in their own places and not elsewhere, they may get-reported elsewhere; and the being-known of a thing is its getting-reported where it does not exist—and its getting-reported there *as* existing at the locus or region in which it does exist.   Any theory of knowledge which does not recognize both these distinctive peculiarities of the cognitive phenomenon, fails to provide either for actual knowledge or for possible error.

According to the contention of these lectures (with respect to the epistemological issue) this two-fold requirement for a thing's getting-reported is fulfilled, and can be fulfilled, only in one way —in the way, namely, of partial or symbolic reproduction in the awareness of a cognitive organism which is at the same time capable of thinking of some general scheme or order in which existences have separate and mutually exclusive situations, and of

---

[2] Among theories deserving of such consideration I should not include any Eleatic or Vedantic monism, or its modern counterparts.

referring attributes of the data (*i.e.,* sensa or images) of which it is directly aware to external situations in that order. These situations may be "external" in one or both of at least two respects: (a) They *must* be external to the situation of the event by which the representation is proximately generated, or by which the awareness of it is conditioned. Thus, if it is admitted that there is a spatial order containing real bodies, including those of cognizing organisms, the event in question occurs somewhere within the region defined by the organism's body, and probably within its brain. If any character of any object or event whatever, other than a single brain-event, at any time gets reported—even the vague character of being something-or-other outside the brain and causally related to the datum—this first sort of externality is obviously implied. But it is also implied by any non-solipsistic form of idealism. The existent known is at least external to the cognitive mental event assumed to take place "in" an individual mind— namely, it is either "in" some other mind, or has a different temporal locus in the series of events constituting the history of the same mind. (b) Some data, *e.g.,* visual sensa, are directly presented as spatially external to the locus of the event which is (at least by the realist) assumed to generate them or to condition the awareness of them; they are, that is, perceived as having spatial positions outside the perceived body. It is partly this fact which has led to the belief of the naïve realist that "external" objects can get reported directly. But there are empirical reasons—set forth in the earlier lectures of this course—why the sorts of existences which the realist believes himself to know through perception cannot be identical in their spatial or temporal situations with such visual data; and there therefore may—and by the realist must—be recognized a second sort of externality, namely, spatial or temporal externality to the loci in which the sense-data appear. Thus—with the very debatable exception of pure self-awareness —the existents which get-reported must (irrespective of the difference between realists and idealists) always be admitted to be in fact external to the situations of the knower, of the cognitive event, and of the data without which, nevertheless, those existents would remain unknown.

Since it is admitted—again upon any theory—that the data by which external existences get-reported are conditioned by particular cognitive events (either physical or mental), and since there are familiar empirical reasons for supposing that the peculiarity of any such event (or of the organism or mind in which it occurs), as well as other circumstances external to the locus of the original existent in question, affect the character of the datum, there arises from the standpoint of the knower a characteristic difficulty inherent in the nature of the cognitive phenomenon— that of discriminating, if possible, those features of the datum which can be taken as reporting characters possessed by the external existent at the locus of reference, and those which are to be taken as additions or modifications due to the cognitive event, or to other extraneous circumstances, and therefore as existing only at the locus of givenness. There is no summary and purely logical way of complete escape from this embarrassment; for the two opposite assumptions which might seem to eliminate it are both manifestly impossible. If we could show, or even legitimately postulate, that the percipient or other cognitive event is always purely "instrumental"—that what is presented in awareness can never differ, by addition or alteration or dislocation, from the *cognoscendum*—we should escape the difficulty. But when thus generalized, the instrumental theory is equivalent to the assertion of human infallibility; and if not generalized, it leaves the situation unaffected. At the other extreme is what I have termed the theory of the perspectivity of the characters of data. This too, if generalized, would, in a sense, eliminate the difficulty; but also, if generalized, it would be equivalent to the denial of the possibility of any knowledge whatever. No existent at one place could ever get itself in any degree truly reported at another place to another existent. Since we can admit neither man's complete inerrancy nor his continuous and complete ignorance of aught but his momentary, private, self-generated content, the line must be drawn somewhere between these extremes—and is by every man, when actually functioning as a cognitive animal, always tacitly or explicitly drawn somewhere between them. Upon the question where it is to be drawn, certain considerations have already been suggested; but with this question we are not at this point concerned. For so long as it is admitted that *some* knowing of external existences occurs, that there are realities not now, not here, and not ourselves, which get reported to us here and now, the existence of differences of opinion as to the precise extent of what is thus known cannot affect the validity of the conclusion which we have reached as to the *generic* nature and natural function of knowing. And it is highly important in philosophical procedure to keep this general question distinct from and unconfused by ulterior questions of detail.

This account of knowing both accepts and qualifies, it will be seen, certain epistemological theses characteristic of idealism, of monistic realism, and of (in one sense of that ambiguous designation) pragmatism. Even the most subjective idealist is right in saying that, in a sense, we never in knowing "step outside the circle of our own ideas" or "transcend experience." For it is never the true *cognoscendum* as an existent that is present to us as an actual experienced datum. But the monistic realist is also right in saying that—in so far as we know at all—we always, in another sense, step outside the circle of our own ideas. For that which we apprehend through any particular idea must always be assigned in thought to a locus in some conceived order (temporal or other) which transcends the locus at which the idea as an existent is in fact situated. And the type of pragmatist who insists upon the necessity of postulation, of belief which outruns empirical evidence, is also, in an important sense, right. For since the externality of the *cognoscendum* to the idea of it is, in so far as it is now actually apprehended, externality within a scheme of relations which is, at any moment of cognition, also a present datum, a piece of schematic imagery now before me, the acceptance of it as valid and as trustworthy as a clue for action is an act of belief which goes beyond purely experiential proof. No judgment concerning a particular existent—other than the immediate and transient private datum, about which no act of judgment is necessary—can conceivably attain experiential verification in any literal sense; for the existent complex of ideas which is the content of the judgment can never, by any finite and temporal knower, be brought into the same locus with the existent to which it refers. Since our knowing is characteristically concerned with beyonds, we know by faith. But not all beyonds of which we can frame ideas are the objects of faiths for which we have motives equally persuasive, urgent, or irrepressible, equally deeply rooted in our cognitive constitution, and equally reconcilable with one another and with what—through our primary faiths in the reality of remembrance and in the existence of other knowers—we believe to have been the constant and common course of experience.

Upon realistic premises, the getting-reported of an existent at a locus not its own is, of course, dependent upon certain physical processes. In sense-perception there is, first, a series of causally-linked events, conforming to ordinary physical laws, temporally and spatially intervenient between the object and the peripheral nerve-terminus, and another series of such events within the nervous system; and there is, further, the wholly unique phenomenon of the production, as an effect of these neuro-cerebral processes, of certain non-physical entities and events, *viz.,* sensa and the awareness of them. There are, in short, changes in certain physical structures which generate existents that are not physical in the sense in which those structures are; and these non-physical particulars are indispensable means to any knowledge of physical realities. Repellent as this conception still is to many scientific men, there is no conclusion of empirical science about the physical world—supposing that there in any sense *is* a physical world—which is better established; the proof of this is set forth in the first seven of these lectures. The getting-reported of a past experience of an organism in the subsequent experience of the same organism is likewise physically conditioned, first by certain purely physiological phenomena, and then by the cerebral events which generate images. But neither the processes which transmit certain physical effects of the action of the external object, or of the past event, nor even those which produce sensa and images, are equivalent to the getting-reported of that object or event. For that, there must arise—presumably at a late stage of organic evolution—as physically conditioned non-physical effects, at least two further functions: (a) a power to conceive of some realm or order of inter related existents which includes but extends beyond the organism itself and the sensa and images which are immediately present to it; and (b) a propensity of the organism to think some of the characters of the immediately given as actually or potentially belonging to external situations in that order. This propensity is spontaneous, and in that sense instinctive, in the cognitive species of organism; but it is capable of extensive modification and control through experience and reflection. It could not be destroyed without destruction of the cognitive function itself.

There is the best of precedents for concluding a long and abstract discussion of difficult philosophical matters with a myth; and I shall therefore bring to an end this attempt to describe the distinctive nature of knowing among natural phenomena by suggesting the way in which Plato might have told the story in the *Timaeus,* if he had been enough of an evolutionist to conceive of the production of living creatures as proceeding from lower to higher, and if he had been more definitely mindful of the problem of the character and genesis of natural knowledge.

The Demiurgus, after he had fashioned Time as the moving image of Eternity and Space which provides a home for all created things, and had made the elements and the lower orders of living beings, found something still wanting in the universe. These creatures, he said, confined within the narrow bounds of their separate being, are wholly strangers to one another. Each of them fills only its own little span of time and place; and the things they suffer and the deeds they do endure but for an instant and are then lost in the non-being of the Past. No report of that which befalls at one moment reaches those which have their being in other moments; and what exists in one place, though it may act upon things which are in distant places, does not thereby cause its own nature or its own being to be revealed there. That the existence of mortal things should be thus confined within strict limits is necessary; what is then cannot be now, what is there cannot at the same time be here. This law of their being not even I can alter; and it is therefore not in my power to remedy the externality of things to one another, nor to overcome their transiency, by causing any one of them to be present both in its own place or time and in that allotted to another. Yet a world in which all that comes into being not only perishes but leaves no rumor of itself behind, and in which every part of the Whole is blind to all the other parts, is surely more imperfect than even a world of mortal creatures need be; nor does it have in it every kind of animal which a complete world ought to have. Let me, then, consider how I may remove this imperfection, so far as the nature of things allows. It is clear that I must, first of all, arrange that the Form or nature or quality which is embodied in a thing existing in one region of being, and causes it to be the kind of thing that it is, shall also be present in another region and shall be embodied in another thing. Yet it is also clear that this will not be enough. All that this alone would bring about would be that the second thing would resemble the first, that two parts of the Whole would have like natures; and this is already accomplished in the world of blind and mutually external parts which I have thus far made. Nor will it even be enough to provide that there shall at some times and places be creatures that, besides having natures of their own, natures which for the most part they possess without perceiving them, shall also have the power to behold present simulacra of things existing formerly or afterwards or elsewhere. For merely to behold what is in fact a simulacrum is not to obtain through it an acquaintance with that of which it is a simulacrum. What is needful is that the nature which belongs to one region of being shall be not only reproduced in another, nor merely, when so reproduced, be beheld by a creature having its existence in that other region, but that it shall be reproduced and beheld as if present in the region in which it first existed, and as belonging to a thing which had or has its being there; only so can any creature see another as being another, and the mutual blindness of the parts be in a certain measure overcome.

To make this possible I must create a new kind of animal, of which the chief peculiarity will be that it will have the power and the habit of looking upon some of the natures which it perceives, not merely as states of itself existing in the place where it is, nor merely as qualities of things existing at the time and place at which it beholds them, but as states and qualities of other beings in other times and places. In order that it may do this, the new animal must be enabled to frame some general image of the Whole—not, indeed, of all the things which are parts of the Whole, for that is not a gift possible to mortals—but of the nature of a Whole having many parts, of which the animal itself, with the time and place in which it exists and perceives any qualities, is seen by it as but one part and that a small one, having fixed bounds, beyond which lie the other parts. By means of such an image this animal will be able to ascribe qualities which it at any time beholds to regions of the Whole lying outside the bounds within which, when beheld, they exist; it will have the power of imputing otherness and beyondness to what it perceives, and thus need not be blind to the rest of the universe. So considering, the Demiurgus proceeded to add the gift of knowledge to the many other less excellent gifts which he had already distributed amongst the various grades of living things; and he created the animal man to receive and have the custody of this gift.

INDEX

Abro, A. de, 163, 177, 181, 182.
Agnosticism. *See* External world, near-agnosticism concerning.
Alexander, Samuel, 8, 86–90, 236.
Anatomists and physiologists, misapprehension among, 288, 293, 295.
Anima mundi, Neoplatonic, 206.

Bacon, Francis, 23–24.
Bacon, Roger, 23.
Bergson, Henri, 4, 96, 177, 206, 361.
Berkeley, George, 61–62, 65, 67, 250, 288, 381.
Bifurcation of nature, 4, 35, 97, 102, 110, 118, 156, 230, 233, 299, 328; denied by Whitehead, 188, 193–195, 197, 225, 231–232, 237, 278, 280.
Birkhoff, 199.
Born, Max, 180, 181.
Bradley, 388.
Brains, physical features of, in Russell's first theory, 261–264, 274; in his later theories, 288–297, 311.
Bridgman, P. W., 6, 366, 369.
Broad, C. D., 22, 61, 119, 128, 132, 145, 172, 174, 198, 201, 259–261, 264, 275, 281, 285, 288, 341, 344.
Broglie, M. de, 350–351.
Brown, H. C., 211.
Burtt, Edwin A., 2, 153–154.

Cartesian dualism. *See* Descartes.
Causal theory of perception: in Russell's first theory, 250, 256; in his later theories, 276–278; remarks on, 331–332.
Cave-man, a non-bifurcationist, 35.
Clifford, W. K., 338.
Cognoscenda, defined, 15; conceived as apprehended by others, 18.
Corpuscular properties of light, etc., difficulties arising from, 347–352.
Cusanus. *See* Nicholas of Cues.

Davisson, C. J., 352.
Democritus, 56.

Dempster, A. J., 352.
Descartes, 1–6, 7, 20, 30, 32, 46, 65, 127, 188, 231, 235, 237, 310, 329, 334, 380, 381.
Dewey, John, 13, 26, 49–54, 102–105, 212, 356, 362–363.
Drake, Durant, 134, 139.
Dreams, hallucinations, etc., 6, 34, 40, 85–93.
Dualism, epistemological: two senses of, 18–19; natural roots of, 12, 21–30; not avoided by James, 58; nor by neorealists, 71–73; nor by objective relativists, 147, 185; nor by Kemp Smith, 187–188; escape from, 135; grounds of, in Whitehead's philosophy, 221–223; accepted by Russell, 235, 236, 314, 316–317; implied by idealism, 379–380, 384; redundant or self-contradictory, 386–392. *See also* Memory as evidence for; Physico-physiological argument for; *and* Relations in.
Dualism, psychophysical: two senses of, 10, 36; natural genesis of, 13, 33–34; fused with epistemological dualism in theory of representative ideas, 39–40; motives of revolt against, 43; not avoided by James, 58; nor by neorealists, 73–74; nor by Laird, 91–92; nor by objective relativists, 132–133, 185; nor by Kemp Smith, 187–188; nor by Whitehead, 225–235; nor by Russell, 273, 280, 304–316; review of grounds against, 323–328. *See also* Epiphenomenalism.
Dunlap, Knight, 62–64.

Eddington, A. S., 5, 180, 330, 336–339, 346, 351, 355, 356–363.
Einstein, Albert, 4–6, 34, 82, 100, 145, 162, 176, 179, 181, 200. *See also* Relativity, physical theory of.
Eleatic monism, 394. *See also* Zeno of Elea.
Epiphenomenalism, 313–314.